D1593113

# POLITICAL SURVIVORS

# POLITICAL SURVIVORS

The Resistance, the Cold War,
and the Fight against Concentration
Camps after 1945

**Emma Kuby**

**CORNELL UNIVERSITY PRESS**    **ITHACA AND LONDON**

First published 2019 by Cornell University Press

Printed in the United States of America

Library of Congress Cataloging-in-Publication Data

Names: Kuby, Emma, 1981– author.
Title: Political survivors : the resistance, the Cold War, and the fight against
    concentration camps after 1945 / Emma Kuby.
Description: Ithaca : Cornell University Press, 2019. | Includes bibliographical
    references and index.
Identifiers: LCCN 2018029856 (print) | LCCN 2018032294 (ebook) |
    ISBN 9781501732805 (pdf) | ISBN 9781501732812 (epub/mobi) |
    ISBN 9781501732799 (cloth : alk. paper)
Subjects: LCSH: Commission internationale contre le régime
    concentrationnaire—History. | Concentration camps—History—20th century. |
    Holocaust survivors—Political activity. | Human rights workers—Europe—
    History—20th century. | Holocaust, Jewish (1939–1945)—Influence. |
    Cold War—History.
Classification: LCC HV8963 (ebook) | LCC HV8963. K83 2019 (print) | DDC
    365/.4509409045—dc23
LC record available at https://lccn.loc.gov/2018029856

# Contents

# Acknowledgments

It is a great joy to thank the people who helped me write this book.

I owe my longest-standing intellectual debts to the professors I encountered as an undergraduate at Brown University, chief among them Carolyn J. Dean. I am tremendously fortunate that she has remained a mentor and interlocutor over these many years. Great thanks are due as well to the scholars who trained me in graduate school at Cornell University. I first came upon the topic for this book in a terrific seminar led by Peter Holquist, to whom I remain grateful. Natalie Melas helped me to become a better reader, offering insight at every turn. Steven L. Kaplan taught me much of what I know about both French history and intellectual rigor. And Dominick LaCapra made everything possible through his faith in my abilities and his scholarly generosity. I also wish to thank the extraordinary fellow students who converged in Ithaca during my years there, including Franz Hofer, Kate Horning, Taran Kang, Gregg Lightfoot, Julian Lim, Michelle Moyd, Marie Muschalek, Ryan Plumley, Guillaume Ratel, Camille Robcis, Sarah Senk, Heidi Voskuhl, and Emma Willoughby. Peter Staudenmaier deserves special thanks: he supported this project from beginning to end. Thanks, as well, to other members of the Cornell faculty who helped and encouraged me, especially Vicki Caron, Holly Case, Duane Corpis, Isabel V. Hull, and Michael P. Steinberg, and to Christophe Prochasson and Gisèle Sapiro for their valuable assistance in Paris.

Since leaving Cornell I have remained surrounded by remarkably supportive colleagues. At Northern Illinois University, I am especially indebted to Sean Farrell, Heide Fehrenbach, Beatrix Hoffman, Brian Sandberg, and above all Jim Schmidt. It is impossible to enumerate the ways that my dear friend and long-haul carpool companion, Andy Bruno, helped bring this project to fruition; for all of them, I am grateful. NIU also provided institutional support through its Research and Artistry Grant program. At Princeton University, where I was fortunate to spend the fall of 2015 at the Shelby Cullom Davis Center for Historical Studies, conversation with Phil Nord improved the book immeasurably. I also profited from the wisdom of other historians at Princeton and in its environs, including Ed Baring, Eleanor Davey, Anson Rabinbach, and my wonderful "fellow Fellows": Susan L. Carruthers, Pierre Fuller, Marie Kelleher, and Arnaud Orain. Warm thanks, too, to the incomparable Jennifer Goldman.

Other scholars, near and far, have helped me at every step along the way. Most importantly, I wish to thank Sam Moyn and Sandrine Sanos for their astute and elucidating comments on the manuscript. Both of them have been staggeringly generous to me. Other friends and colleagues over the years, including Judy Coffin, Elizabeth Everton, Patricia Lorcin, Mark Meyers, Terry Peterson, and Todd Shepard, helped improve individual chapters. Jennifer Foray smoothed the way for me at many points in my journey and commented on key passages as I revised. Jonathan Judaken, Steve Kantrowitz, Ethan Katz, and Hugh Wilford made illuminating suggestions on particular problems, while Ben Brower and Judith Surkis provided invaluable support for the project as a whole. Mary Louise Roberts offered much-needed counsel at more than one critical moment.

This project would have been impossible without the aid of archivists and librarians throughout Europe and the United States. I am especially indebted to Laurence Le Bras at France's Bibliothèque Nationale, who facilitated my access to Germaine Tillion's uncataloged papers, and to the staff of the Bibliothèque de Documentation Internationale Contemporaine, whose knowledge and good cheer made multiple visits over the years a pleasure. My gratitude is also due to Louis Martin-Chauffier's family for permission to view his papers at L'Institut Mémoires de l'Édition Contemporaine. At the other end of the long process that went into making the book, it has been a delight to work with Cornell University Press. I owe my magnificent editor, Emily Andrew, a great deal for bringing the manuscript there. Many thanks to Cambridge University Press for permission to reprint portions of my article "In the Shadow of the Concentration Camp: David Rousset and the Limits of Apoliticism in Postwar French Thought," *Modern Intellectual History* 11, no. 1 (April 2014): 147–173. Thanks as well to University of Nebraska Press for permission to reprint portions of my chapter, "From Auschwitz to Algeria: The Mediterranean Limits of the French Anti-Concentration Camp Movement, 1952–1959," in *French Mediterraneans: Transnational and Imperial Histories*, edited by Patricia M. E. Lorcin and Todd Shepard, 347–371 (Lincoln: University of Nebraska Press, 2016).

Finally, I wish to thank my friends and family. I could never have finished drafting *Political Survivors* during my son Theodore's infancy without the support of a beloved community in Madison, Wisconsin, including Amaya Atucha, Courtney Berner, Andy Bruno, Drew Ciancia, Kathryn Ciancia, Sarah Frohardt-Lane, MJ Hecox, Caitlin Henning, Dan Kaplan, James Levy, Nate Maddux, Lucy McLellan, Guillaume Ratel, Carly Stingl, and their families, as well as Patrick Downey at the Victory. Special thanks are due to Courtney and MJ, who more or less literally cheer-led me across the finish line. Talking shop with my brother, Will Kuby, has been a lifeline at many points; I count myself inordinately lucky to have such a gifted fellow historian for a sibling. My dear parents, Pamela Goldberg Kuby and

Mark Kuby, were a source of unwavering love and support while I wrote. Teddy brought me joy at every turn. And my husband, Brian Bockelman, has lived with this work for longer than anyone. I thank him for his patience and humor over the years, for his countless intellectual contributions to the project, and for the sustaining love he has given me as I have endeavored to tell a difficult story about men and women who bore witness to great suffering.

I am not myself a witness to the events related in this book. Yet I do feel a profound connection to the postwar European moment. Posted as a US Army doctor in Le Mans, France, in 1945, my maternal grandfather, Morris Goldberg, tried frantically to learn what had become of his mother, brother, sisters, and other relatives in Kobryn, a largely Jewish town that had been part of Poland before the war. As it transpired, all had been murdered except one small niece, rescued by gentile neighbors. In his plea for emergency permission to escort this orphaned child to his Ohio home and "erase from her memory" the traumas of the past, Morris wrote movingly of his desperation to leave Europe, "this continent which has brought so much grief to the world and to itself." I did not know my grandfather. But I have often wondered what he would have thought of his granddaughter's decision to turn her gaze upon the continent he wished never to see again, and of her efforts to comprehend what could and could not be erased from memory in the wake of its great catastrophe. I hope that he would have understood. *Political Survivors* is for my family, the living and the dead.

# Acronyms and Abbreviations

| | |
|---|---|
| ADIR | Association Nationale des Anciennes Déportées et Internées de la Résistance (France) |
| AFL | American Federation of Labor |
| AIADIJ | Association Indépendante des Anciens Déportés et Internés Juifs (France) |
| AJC | American Jewish Committee |
| CDJC | Centre de Documentation Juive Contemporaine (France) |
| CIA | Central Intelligence Agency (United States) |
| CNPPA | Confédération Nationale des Prisonniers Politiques et Ayants Droit (Belgium) |
| ECOSOC | Economic and Social Council of the United Nations |
| ExPoGe | Nederlandse Vereniging van Ex-Politieke Gevangenen (Netherlands) |
| FEDIP | Federación Española de Deportados e Internados Políticos (Spain/France) |
| FLN | Front de Libération Nationale (Algeria) |
| FNDIR | Fédération Nationale des Déportés et Internés de la Résistance (France) |
| FNDIRP | Fédération Nationale des Déportés et Internés Résistants et Patriotes (France) |
| FTUC | Free Trade Union Committee (United States, affiliated with the AFL) |
| GIP | Groupe d'Information sur les Prisons (France) |
| ICFTU | International Confederation of Free Trade Unions |
| ICRC | International Committee of the Red Cross |
| ILO | International Labor Organization |
| IMT | International Military Tribunal |
| IRD | Information Research Department of the Foreign Office (Britain) |
| NMT | Nuremberg Military Trials |
| OPC | Office of Policy Coordination (United States) |
| PCF | Parti Communiste Français (France) |
| PCI | Parti Communiste Internationaliste (France) |
| POUM | Partido Obrero de Unificación Marxista (Spain) |
| RDR | Rassemblement Démocratique Révolutionnaire (France) |

SFIO      Section Française de l'Internationale Ouvrière (France)
UDHR      Universal Declaration of Human Rights
UGTT      Union Générale Tunisienne du Travail (Tunisia)
UNADIF    Union Nationale des Associations de Déportés, Internés, et Familles
          de Disparus (France)

# POLITICAL SURVIVORS

# INTRODUCTION

In late 1949, with tensions running high in Cold War France, former Nazi concentration camp inmate David Rousset issued a manifesto on the front page of the weekly cultural review *Le Figaro littéraire* calling on his fellow survivors to denounce the Soviet gulag. Stalin's prisoners, he charged, were suffering a "hallucinatory repetition" of the German camp experience, similar in every respect.[1] Rousset made this "Appeal"—at once an indictment and a call to arms—from a position of hard-won authority: his renowned postwar testimonies on Buchenwald and Neuengamme had earned him widespread recognition as France's "witness among witnesses."[2] Now he ignited the most significant public debate on Soviet repression that would take place in the country before the 1970s. Controversy over his appeal swept up everyone from Jean-Paul Sartre, Maurice Merleau-Ponty, and Albert Camus to members of the National Assembly, peaking in a 1950–1951 libel trial in Paris that pitted Rousset against another camp survivor, Communist Party intellectual Pierre Daix. The case generated an international media frenzy and ended with a judgment that Rousset had not, as Daix charged, fabricated his evidence about the gulag's horrors. Most observers interpreted the outcome as a public relations blow against Stalinism; American philosopher and intelligence liaison James Burnham rejoiced at "the best anti-Communist job he had yet seen."[3]

The "David Rousset Affair" is often invoked as a set piece in accounts of Cold War French history, since it dramatically illustrates the extent to which intellectual life in this era was dominated by controversy over communism.[4] But Rousset's publication did not only produce a momentary blaze of scandal. It also gave

1

birth to an international collective of Nazi camp survivors who made it their mission to fight against the continued existence of "concentration camps" in the post-1945 world. Over the course of a decade, this organization, the International Commission against the Concentration Camp Regime (Commission Internationale contre le Régime Concentrationnaire, or CICRC), targeted not only the gulag but also political internment systems around the globe, from Francoist Spain to the People's Republic of China to Greece, French Tunisia, and even, in 1957, war-torn French Algeria. Claiming to speak on behalf of more than one hundred thousand former camp inmates from seven different Western European countries, the CICRC's core delegates conducted heavily publicized mock trials and pioneering on-site inquiries. They responded to petitions from all over the world for international oversight of prison conditions, published a constant stream of literature on political incarceration and forced labor, gained coverage in Le Monde, Le Figaro, the New York Times, and the Times of London, and testified at the United Nations. In an era of toothless enforcement for the principles articulated in the 1948 Universal Declaration of Human Rights, and in the absence of any hope for a permanent peacetime successor to the International Military Tribunal at Nuremberg, the commission improvised novel and creative mechanisms by which to take governments to task for political violence against their own subjects. No contemporaneous European entity so visibly promoted the principle that states on both sides of the Iron Curtain should be held internationally accountable for criminalizing dissent.

The CICRC's influence flowed in large part from the intellectual and political prominence of its leading participants. Since publishing a prizewinning 1946 analysis of life and death in the Nazi camps, Rousset had moved in lofty circles: he was a friend to Sartre, an "indispensable" guide to Hannah Arendt, and a constant presence in Paris lecture halls and at activist rallies.[5] Many of the French survivors who answered his call were likewise authors of landmark works of testimonial literature, and nearly all were esteemed public figures. They included ethnographer and Ravensbrück survivor Germaine Tillion, who was an authority on kinship in Algeria, and Catholic writer and editor Louis Martin-Chauffier, a former inmate of Neuengamme and Bergen-Belsen with a long history in antifascist politics. Central to the group as well were Pasteur Institute entomologist Alfred-Serge Balachowsky (Buchenwald), Gaullist politician Edmond Michelet (Dachau), lawyers Paul Arrighi and Léon Mazeaud (Mauthausen, Buchenwald), Le Monde journalist Rémy Roure (Buchenwald and Auschwitz), medical researcher Charles Richet (Buchenwald), and Catherine Goetschel (Ravensbrück), a heroine of the Resistance struggle in Normandy. They were joined by international counterparts such as José Ester Borrás, an anarcho-syndicalist militant who fled Spain in 1939 and eventually landed in Mauthausen; Father Damien (Henri) Reumont, a key figure in the Belgian worker-priest movement following his imprisonment in Esterwegen; and Lise Børsum, a dynamic Oslo-based journalist and Ravensbrück memoirist. According to Tzvetan Todorov, one of the rare scholars to have recognized the commission's historical significance, "The political, religious, and philosophical convictions of [these men and women] could not have been more varied. The only things that united them were the shared experience of having been imprisoned in the Nazi camps and the shared conviction that, in the world they inhabited, the greatest urgency was to make other camps disappear."[6]

Rousset and his followers certainly presented their work as the embodiment of a universalizing ethos born of great suffering, undertaken in the service of a global humanity under continued threat. They claimed to speak for "those who are what we were yesterday," enacting an affirmation of mankind's essential solidarity that transcended politics and erased borders.[7] In reality, though, such expansive ideals papered over the group's more particularist identities and agendas. These render its deployment of memory on behalf of new victims more complex and troubling than Todorov imagined—but also far more interesting. For one thing, despite the eventual geographic scope of its investigations, the CICRC remained true to its origins in Rousset's 1949 "Appeal"—it was above all opposed to Stalin's camps. The project therefore became enmeshed in the era's cultural Cold War pitting pro-American actors against pro-Soviet ones in a contest for the hearts and minds of the world's peoples. In 1951, the CICRC began receiving monetary backing from the US Central Intelligence Agency (CIA). The survivors' organization was not the creation or the puppet of its financial supporters; Rousset, though a willing and witting party to the relationship, reacted with scorn on the few occasions when his beneficent "friends" offered counsel. Most other CICRC members, oblivious to the source of their organization's funding, proceeded without fretting over American opinion at all. Nevertheless, their self-styled identity as independent voices of conscience representing only the victims of state violence, not states, was based on a falsehood.

The commission's claims to cosmopolitan universalism were also belied by its exclusionary membership policies. Jewish Holocaust survivors were not permitted to join as such; only men and women who had been deported to the Nazi camps for acts of wartime resistance could do so. This policy was not a consequence of antisemitism in any straightforward sense—Jews who had been imprisoned as resisters were welcome, and other Jews were involved in the CICRC in all manner of ways. The group's legal counselor Théo Bernard was a former Drancy inmate, its American supporters were mainly Jewish, and—astonishingly—its secretary was Léon Poliakov, perhaps the most important Holocaust historian of his generation. But in a postwar France where deported resisters were venerated as patriotic, republican heroes, while Jewish "racial" survivors were, generally speaking, still only the objects of hazy pity, restricting formal membership to those in the former category permitted Rousset to legitimize his endeavor in culturally potent terms.[8] The prohibition also helped sustain the CICRC's mobilization of the recent past for a struggle against ongoing persecution of dissidents, resisters, and rebels, a project that depended on viewing Hitler's camps, first and foremost, as institutions of political repression. For CICRC members, World War II's paradigmatic victims were those, like themselves, who "became slaves of the SS uniquely because of their convictions and their commitment to them."[9] This understanding of Nazi atrocity raised few eyebrows in the Western Europe of the early 1950s, where "the Holocaust" did not yet register as a conceptual category. Nevertheless, the CICRC could not afford to admit voices that might contest its interpretation of the camps. The group's project depended upon drawing historical parallels, and, as Rousset quietly acknowledged, "Birkenau remains beyond comparison."[10]

The CICRC, then, was not simply a mobilization of "memory," as such, on behalf of "humanity," writ large. It was an effort to leverage a specific way of remembering the violence of the Second World War for specific ends, in an intellectual and political context of high-stakes conflict unique to the postwar era in Western Europe—especially France. This book explores why a movement of non-Jewish, noncommunist Nazi camp survivors dedicated to bearing "expert witness" against political repression and incarceration was so successful in demanding the world's attention in the 1950s, thereby advancing norms of international obligation toward states' internal victims. But it also considers why this remarkable organization disintegrated before the decade was out, riven by conflict over many issues—including Jewish membership—but definitively destroyed by its confrontation with decolonization. Ultimately, the CICRC's attempt to address the dynamics of internment, terror, and torture during France's Algerian War (1954–1962) shattered members' fragile antitotalitarian consensus about the meaning of Hitler's camps. This book explains why. In so doing, it offers a new account of how the memory of Nazi atrocity both spurred and distorted Europeans' efforts to make sense of the persistent violence of the post-1945 world.

## Witnesses to the "Concentrationary Universe"

Rousset and his followers came together at a moment when human rights had yet to crystallize as a singularly privileged international discourse for stigmatizing state violence.[11] Instead of drawing upon a language of rights, therefore, CICRC participants put forward a framework for activism grounded in visceral, bodily invocations of World War II's atrocities.[12] It was reliant on two concepts. The first was captured by the phrase "the concentrationary universe," Rousset's own celebrated coinage and the title of his slim, searing 1946 meditation on the Nazi camps. *L'Univers concentrationnaire* proposed that Buchenwald, Sachsenhausen, Ravensbrück, Neuengamme, and their counterparts formed a singular, coherent, and fully articulated sphere of suffering that was "closed off" from the planet inhabited by "normal men."[13] Taken as a whole, this "universe" of absolute degradation possessed no meaningful parallels with other institutions in human history: Rousset understood "the concentration camp" as a monster born in National Socialist Germany circa 1933 and did not seek out precedents in turn-of-the-century European imperial practices, in World War I–era detention facilities, or in Joseph Stalin's interwar USSR.[14] The Nazis, he wrote, had "introduce[d] into modern history a new procedure of dehumanization."[15] But this did not mean that he viewed their project as inimitable, a singular anomaly. On the contrary, he insisted that it constituted a "warning"—a reproducible archetype of radical evil. "Other peoples" might undertake an "analogous experiment" at any point if humanity was not vigilant.[16] Rousset's transformation of *concentration* into an adjective, *concentrationnaire*, was intended to signal this perpetual menace. (Despite French readers' embrace of the term, no English equivalent developed; telling the CICRC's story demands making do with "concentrationary.")

From Rousset's assertion that mankind's concentrationary age was ongoing arose a second conceptual pillar: the figure of the Nazi camp survivor as an expert witness.[17] According to Rousset, as the only men and women alive who knew in their "muscles" what Hitler's camps had been, former deportees were "the professionals, the specialists" in recognizing the mechanisms of human abjection.[18] "Others," he wrote, "those who were never *concentrationnaires*, can plead poverty of imagination, incompetence. . . . But us—*we lived this tragedy*."[19] Their experience allowed them—and them alone—to comprehend the danger that the camps posed to the human condition. Thus when Rousset issued his 1949 appeal to fellow survivors, he stressed that "I am not asking you to request an inquiry" into the gulag, "but to take it in hand yourselves."[20] No one else was "technically and morally qualified" to do so.[21] This would become the CICRC's defining tenet. In truth—as evidenced by the exclusion of Holocaust victims—the organization's claim to "specialist" authority was not anchored in traumatic experience alone. It also relied on members' status as former resisters and, implicitly, on their professional credentials. Nevertheless, as the commission entered a well-populated postwar field of international NGOs claiming expertise in various human problems, it stood apart in its members' embrace of a collective identity as "witnesses before other men."[22]

Thanks to the immediate postwar labors of the individuals who would form the CICRC, the "concentrationary universe" and the experientially expert witness were already widely embraced concepts by the time the anti–concentration camp movement came into being. Rousset's own publications, including not only *L'Univers concentrationnaire* but also a sprawling 1947 novel, *Les Jours de notre mort*, were particularly important in this regard.[23] "Sadly neglected" by scholars today, in his own time the ex-Trotskyist Rousset was, as Samuel Moyn argues, "the single most important interpreter of the camps" for readers on both sides of the Atlantic.[24] His acts of literary testimony shaped the moral imagination of his era, providing contemporaries with a descriptive and normative vocabulary for voicing comment on otherwise unspeakable sites. What is more, until it was displaced by memory of the Jewish genocide in later decades, the *univers concentrationnaire* functioned for many Western Europeans as, in Moyn's terms, a "powerful synecdoche" for all Nazi evil.[25] Shoah survivors themselves were among those who embraced the concept in the late 1940s—as were admirers of the USSR, since Rousset's language of potential reproducibility was not originally intended as a crude means of equating Nazi and Soviet "totalitarianism" but as an effort to recuperate meaning from an otherwise senseless experience of agony. Thus, as writer François Bondy observed in 1952, the *univers concentrationnaire* quickly became "a keyword of our conscience, and even that of the Communists."[26] The "universe" it referenced appeared genuinely universal.

As a result, Rousset joined other members of the Resistance deportation in assuming an exalted status in postwar France as prophetic envoys with an urgent message to convey to "normal men." Such recognition was not yet available to Jewish Holocaust victims; as Annette Wieviorka has argued, although genocide survivors offered copious testimony from the start, widespread acknowledgment of their status as "witnesses" arrived only years later.[27] But the situation of Resistance deportees in the immediate postwar moment was different. In a battered France shamed by military defeat, foreign occupation, and the Vichy government's collaboration with the Third Reich, their suffering in the camps was honored as the highest possible expression of courageous, redemptive national self-sacrifice. Hence their words of testimony to that suffering were greeted with respect bordering on reverence. They were "the only elect that He has marked with his stigmata / The only priests that the Dove has visited," wrote Catholic poet Pierre Emmanuel in a 1945 "Hymn of the Witnesses" dedicated to future CICRC member Louis Martin-Chauffier. "We call down upon these martyrs the gift of tongues: / May they prophesy into the empty hearts."[28]

Four years later, David Rousset drew on this legacy of prestige and pathos in founding the CICRC. Disenchanted with revolutionary politics following a short-lived attempt to launch a new leftist party with Sartre, Rousset cast his

1949 proposal to investigate the Soviet gulag as a solemn enactment of survivors' duty to bear witness rather than a calculating act of Cold War combat. As communists now discovered, to their dismay, France's most celebrated author on the Nazi camps occupied a commanding position from which to condemn the Soviet ones. The idiom of the *univers concentrationnaire*, moreover, was readily transformed into a weapon for that purpose. Though in reality most gulag inmates (like most Nazi camp internees) had not actually been arrested for individual political offenses, Rousset's indictment of the Soviet forced labor system as an apparatus for punishing resistance proved galvanizing in France and other recently occupied countries.[29] Meanwhile, because his famous 1946 and 1947 acts of testimony had depicted the Nazis as "inventing" concentration camps, Rousset could now position the gulag, whose existence had long been known, as a new problem for Europeans, an alarming repetition of Hitler's unprecedented crimes.[30] Still more useful for anti-Soviet purposes was the fact that his discourse of concentrationary suffering operated in binary terms. For Rousset, "true concentration camps" existed in dichotomous opposition to all other detention facilities and sites of unfree labor, however foreboding, from Vichy France's internment centers to postwar European camps for displaced persons to the penal work gangs of the Jim Crow American South.[31] There was "no relation" between concentrationary and non-concentrationary carceral institutions, he averred, no gray zone connecting them.[32] To condemn the USSR by means of this black-and-white vision was to declare the capitalist West the moral champion in the Cold War regardless of any other human rights violations on its part. It was, as the eminent Catholic writer and resister François Mauriac marveled, a "brilliant shortcut."[33]

Brilliant it may have been, but had Rousset and his followers done nothing more than draw an embarrassing connection between German and Soviet sites of captivity, their story would be a footnote in the history of Cold War antitotalitarianism.[34] The real significance of the campaign emerged out of members' efforts to frame their activism as a means of mobilizing memory of the Nazi camps to articulate universal norms for responding to state violence. These efforts infuriated leftist critics, who insisted that ends-oriented political judgment had to trump affective processes of memory and identification. "The truth is that even the experience of an absolute like the concentrationary horror cannot determine a political position," Rousset's former friends Sartre and Merleau-Ponty admonished him.[35] They electrified anticommunists, however, and thereby set in motion a dynamic by which the commission—not *despite* its Cold War partisanship but *because* of it—succeeded in furthering acceptance of what might now be called human rights ideals.[36] For instance, the commission's heavily publicized 1951 restaging of Nuremberg as a trial of the USSR led multiple commentators to endorse the still-controversial idea that a government could commit "crimes against humanity" in peacetime, against its own subjects, and ought to be held accountable by international actors for doing so. Rousset and his followers also helped to establish a point left undecided by the International Military Tribunal: that the concentration camp was, as the *Economist* put it, "in itself a crime against humanity."[37] It was only the third time that the magazine had used the term since Nuremberg—and the first to describe a state's violence toward its own citizens.

The CICRC's investigations in the West were even more important than its anti-Soviet actions in giving substance to the principle that, after the catastrophes of recent history, repression of domestic dissent and colonial rebellion demanded supranational oversight. Conducting inquiries in Spain, Greece, and French North Africa may originally have been a way for the commission to vaunt its evenhandedness. But members—many of whom had identified as antifascists since the Spanish Civil War, and some of whom were anti-imperialist militants as well—took up the work with gusto. The results were impressive. In an era of intense anxiety over sovereignty, Western governments nevertheless authorized the commission to conduct unprecedented on-the-ground prison inspections because they did not wish to join the USSR in refusing—or to snub a group of heroic Resistance deportees. In 1952, Rousset's group became the only international nongovernmental organization ever to access the interior of Francisco Franco's carceral system, interviewing detainees and openly publishing its critical findings on Spanish wrongdoing. Five years later, it accomplished a similar feat in the wartime internment centers of French Algeria. In such efforts, and in a 1956 off-site investigation of Chinese labor camps, members offered a deliberate enactment of the internationalist values of what Rousset once called the *univers solidaire*, a utopic counter to the *univers concentrationnaire*.[38]

The CICRC expressed its commitment to human solidarity by demanding that the world community heed the voices of sufferers, wherever they were. In fact it oriented its entire activist program, East and West, around the dissemination of victim testimony. A reliance on first-person accounts of anguish to "name and shame" purveyors of atrocity was, in itself, nothing new in the 1950s: victim narratives had been tools of nineteenth-century abolitionist campaigns, interwar efforts to condemn mass violence, and so on.[39] The CICRC, though, was able to invest testimony with heightened evidentiary significance for post-1945 audiences as a result of members' own stature as patriotic heroes and expert witnesses. By performatively transferring their personal moral authority to fellow victims, participants insisted that Europeans pay as much heed to imprisoned Chinese peasants, say, or persecuted Algerian nationalists, as to the martyrs of Dachau and Buchenwald. In a sharp break from Nuremberg's precedent of "trial by document," the group also offered a new vision of international justice centered on a universal "duty" to provide victims of state violence with "a chance to speak about their lives and their misfortune." Its 1951 mock trial of the USSR, for example, constituted a procession of gulag survivors relating "what they have suffered . . . in accordance with the truth of their experience" before a court composed exclusively of former Nazi camp inmates, who ultimately offered their own verdict as yet another act of testimony.[40]

Despite such bravura performances, however, over time the CICRC's claims regarding the universal import of concentrationary memory came under increasing strain. As a project premised on a rigid equation between past and present—as members had conceived of both circa 1949—the commission was ill-prepared to respond to new forms of violence, or to absorb gradual changes in the ways that other Europeans remembered Nazi atrocities. For example, while many antitotalitarian commentators responded to a 1952–1953 wave of antisemitic persecution in the Eastern bloc by placing fresh commemorative emphasis on Hitler's Jewish genocide, CICRC members were compelled to remain silent: invoking Treblinka and Sobibór would have imperiled their non-racialized construction of the meaning of the Nazi camp system. As the decade progressed and the Soviet gulag contracted, Rousset and his followers also found themselves employing increasingly tortuous logic in order to maintain that "the concentrationary universe" was an appropriate way to describe the current global landscape of repression. The conceit of expertise born from experience broke down, too, as the organization addressed camps in parts of the world about which participants possessed little knowledge, such as China. And in the wake of the 1956 Hungarian Revolution, crushed by Soviet-backed forces as the West looked on, some CICRC participants—including Rousset—began to question whether "bearing witness" was an adequate response to the agony of distant victims or merely voyeurism masquerading as action.

Ultimately, however, it was not in Hungary but in Algeria that Rousset's commission met its end, largely because the fraught politics of decolonization scrambled the Cold War alliances upon which the group was built. The CICRC's internal unity was shattered by its leaders' differing positions on France's terrible struggle to retain its Algerian territory, giving the lie to their earlier claims that experience, not ideology, naturally determined survivors' responses to post-1945 acts of state violence. At the same time, the transatlantic partnership with the CIA broke down as the commission focused increasing energy on Western imperial abuses; the group's funding was cut off after Rousset defiantly insisted on investigating French Algerian prison camps in 1957. The consequences were devastating. But an even more important cause of the CICRC's demise than its loss of funds was a "loss of interest" in "these concentrationary questions" among French members consumed by the tragedy unfolding across the Mediterranean.[41]

As Germaine Tillion explained to fellow Ravensbrück survivor Lise Børsum in 1960, the commission's backward-glancing activist framework, designed for continental purposes, now revealed itself as an impediment rather than an aid to clear-eyed confrontation with the historically specific violence of a declining colonial power.

The CICRC's failure to pass through the Algerian crucible suggests a need to rethink existing models of past sufferers' potential to engage in acts of "moral witnessing" or "exemplary memory" through drawing general lessons from their experiences.[42] According to literary scholar Michael Rothberg's influential theory of multidirectional memory, for instance, remembrance of Nazi atrocity during the Algerian War set in motion a "productive, intercultural dynamic" of identification among victim groups that "served to catalyze" deeper French awareness of the Holocaust while also stimulating demands for justice on behalf of Algerians.[43] In defending the notion that "solidarity, in other words, is a frequent—if not guaranteed—outcome of the remembrance of suffering," Rothberg highlights the case of camp survivors, who, he argues, "immediately experienced" French torture and internment practices in Algeria "as unwelcome echoes of the past."[44] The CICRC's story unfortunately does not bear out this assertion. On the contrary, the principle that ethical action should arise through processes of identification constrained commission members from expressing solidarity with Muslim Algerians. This was in part a result of cultural distance, but it was also because France's abusive practices in the Algerian War—which had their own genealogy in the *longue durée* of colonial repressive policy and their own political logic in a brutal decolonizing struggle—failed to map neatly onto those once employed in the Nazi SS camps. The comparative framework that the commission had long championed thus permitted pro-colonialist participants to dismiss French acts of colonial violence as "sentimental children's stories" compared to the horrors of Dachau and Buchenwald.[45] Meanwhile, it led the group's anticolonialists to conclude that a meaningful response to the crisis in North Africa could not derive from remembrance of earlier German crimes at all.

The CICRC's story, then, suggests that the relationship between memory and morality is never fixed but, rather, exists as a question that must continually be answered in historical terms. More specifically, it illuminates both the power and limits of remembrance deployed for putatively universalist ends in the aftermath of the Second World War. Despite the absence of Holocaust consciousness and the frailty of human rights discourse in the 1950s, this was a period rich in efforts to draw lessons from the recent past to bear witness for a still-suffering humanity. But those particular lessons were contingent, politicized Cold War constructions that broke down in the encounter with the fresh atrocities that accompanied the collapse of European empires. "Never again!"—however powerful a rallying cry after the world war's catastrophic violence—proved a problematic dictate for the era of decolonization. Beyond assuming a fixed and partial understanding of what, exactly, the recent catastrophe had entailed, it also demanded a static reading of the present as a site of potentially endless traumatic repetition. History, however, does not actually repeat itself—a fact CICRC members came to realize, painfully, in the course of the Algerian War. Of course, some forms of knowledge are indeed gained through experience, and the process of drawing analogies, comparisons, and correspondences between past and present forms of injustice is often both enlightening and motivating. But the history of the CICRC's final years suggests that as a basis for human solidarity, memory of modernity's worst atrocities is not as robust, productive, or "universal" as we might wish.

## From French Intellectual History to Global Politics and Back Again

I first encountered the untold story of the anti–concentration camp movement as a French intellectual historian interested in David Rousset's 1949–1950 conflict with Sartre over memory, political judgment, and morality. When I began to wonder whether his "Appeal" had generated consequences beyond the rarefied pages of *Les Temps modernes*, I discovered a history that was institutional in nature, international in scope, and entangled with the ambitions and endeavors of multiple state actors. The CICRC's rise and fall could not be traced by examining French sources alone, nor could I restrict myself to the kinds of materials that intellectual historians traditionally study. Ultimately, my effort to do justice to the organization's complicated story led me into archives across continental Western Europe, Britain, and the United States. Although, regrettably, nearly all CIA files relevant to the story told here remain closed, documents in other American archives proved indispensable in reconstructing, to the extent possible, the web of external support that helped sustain the commission.[46]

Despite this "grubbing in the archives," however, ideas retain primacy in the account that follows—not, certainly, as free-floating causal forces but as constituents of the postwar social imaginary that cannot be reduced to Cold War "positions" or stratagems.[47] For the CICRC's survivor-members, concepts such as "the concentrationary universe" and "the witness" were not simply rhetorical hammers with which to bludgeon Stalin. They were structuring components of their world and identity—and I insist that it is possible to analyze them as such without minimizing the calculated political uses to which they were put. The book is thus not only a history of the activities, agendas, and alliances of an organization that, as it happened, was largely populated by intellectuals. It is also an intellectual history.

French history, too, remains at the heart of the study despite the European and transatlantic dimensions my research has assumed. There are three reasons for this. First, most of the CICRC's leaders were French men and women. Second, though the commission functioned as an international collective for the majority of its existence, both its birth and death were predominantly French affairs. Indeed, they are inexplicable outside the contexts of France's confrontation with the Second World War and later the Algerian War. Third, the CICRC's practice of internationalism was francocentric. Of course, to write about a European-run, American-funded, world-oriented entity demands practicing transnational history. But this is different from uncritically reproducing past actors' claims to have transcended the bounds of the nation-state—and, for the purposes of this book, I have found it more illuminating to treat international nongovernmental organizing as a rhetoric and vehicle for people still deeply invested in intra-national disputes than to consider it evidence of expanding "global community."[48] Indeed, I have sought to highlight directly the unquestioned assumptions about (imperial) national sovereignty and identity that both animated and undermined CICRC leaders' efforts to enact a universalist ethics.

To tell the commission's story as a French intellectual history is, in part, to restore its founder to his forgotten place in the postwar intellectual landscape. Sartre, Merleau-Ponty, Camus, Simone de Beauvoir, Pierre Naville, Edgar Morin, Jean-Marie Domenach, fellow survivors Jean Cayrol and Robert Antelme, and many other thinkers in this period approached Nazi evil, Soviet violence, and global human suffering in explicit or implicit dialogue with the author of *L'Univers concentrationnaire*. Bringing to light Rousset's half of the conversation—which, crucially, was expressed not only in his writing but in his activist performance of "witnessing" through the CICRC—helps reveal the true nature and stakes of their arguments. Specifically, it shows the limitations of the still-influential post–Cold War interpretive paradigm that characterizes disputes among leading Fourth Republic French intellectuals as contests between reckless defenders of communist revolutionary terror and lonely, brave bearers of what Tony Judt called "the burden of responsibility."[49] My goal is not to reverse familiar binaries of enlightenment versus blindness, purity versus partisanship, and ethics versus politics by "unmasking" one of Stalin's fiercest detractors as a tainted beneficiary of CIA largesse. It is, rather, to suggest that key aspects of postwar French intellectual history cannot be captured in such terms at all. That Rousset's anti-gulag intervention was reliant on the erasure of Birkenau's crematoria, for example, and that Sartre and communist critics pointed this out at the time, obviously does not mean that the latter were "right" to dismiss or downplay Soviet crimes.

Instead, it suggests that historians must resist the reductive logic of the morality play if we are to grapple with intellectual complexity in the past—and especially during the Cold War. Thus, rather than "looking for heroes in postwar France," this book aims to understand the operative categories of analysis and judgment that were available to the era's writers as they responded to ongoing terror and injustice, from Kolyma to Algiers, and to demonstrate how thoroughly their debates were shadowed by the dark legacies of World War II.[50]

This approach yields a picture of the period between 1945 and 1962 that looks different from that painted by many scholars of postwar French intellectual life and collective memory. Historians interested in the seismic shifts that followed the 1961 Adolf Eichmann trial in Jerusalem, the events of May 1968, and the rise of US-Soviet détente have tended to treat the decades immediately following the Second World War as the "before" to a later explosion of popular and intellectual interest in ethics, testimony, remembrance, victimhood, empathy, and suffering. By analytically decoupling the rise of witnessing, as such, from the emergence of the Jewish Holocaust victim as a paradigmatic voice of memory, this book demonstrates that French intellectuals' self-conscious turn to an ethics of testimony (*témoignage*) had roots in the early Cold War. In effect, through offering up the mediating figure of the (prominent, non-Jewish, noncommunist) Nazi camp survivor as a stand-in for humanity writ large, Rousset and his fellow CICRC members insisted decades ahead of the so-called "era of the witness" that *témoignage* was the correct response of Western subjects to both their own past suffering and the current pain of distant others.[51] Their influential adoption of this position did not only predate the emergence of Holocaust consciousness in France but was predicated on its absence, since it relied directly upon the cultural authority of the Resistance deportation. Through "concentrationary" discourses of remembrance, these political survivors–turned–Cold War activists fostered norms of secular testimony that were only later naturalized as constituting a post-Holocaust, apolitical defense of universal human dignity.

Of course, the CICRC was distinct from later projects of *témoignage*. David Rousset's self-proclaimed vocation as a "spokesman . . . interpret[ing] the speech of the victims" may have anticipated what anthropologist Didier Fassin calls a "new configuration of testimony" in the humanitarian world beginning in the 1970s, as aid workers became "spokespeople for the oppressed," but he and other commission participants had a relationship to victim testimony different from that of activists who joined post-1968 NGOs.[52] This is because they explicitly understood themselves as fellow victims of the "same" atrocities. The survivor-witnesses of the CICRC were not compassionate, professionally competent outsiders offering relief, nor were they "moral spectators" moved to pity in the sense Luc Boltanski has described.[53] Rather, they were haunted past sufferers who now claimed to recognize, with horror, that there remained "in my block, in my box, on my plank, with the same vermin and the same dread, a man, a brother."[54] Rousset's group, then, cannot be conceived of as a clear-cut forerunner to later organizations devoted to third-party witnessing. It can, however, be viewed as a heretofore overlooked element in the intricate, highly contingent genealogy of postwar global moral sentiment, a genealogy from which the 1950s has too often been excluded. Thus I approach the CICRC's rise and fall not as a story of hidden origins but as a lens onto the role and meaning of "witnessing" in the organization's own troubled and violent historical moment.

The book begins with the end of the Second World War in Europe. Its first chapter tells the story of how the commission's future leaders made their way home to France after the Nazi camps were liberated and took up the lifelong work of testimony. The chapter explores the process by which, years before the CICRC formed, figures such as Rousset, Tillion, and Martin-Chauffier established their public identities as expert witnesses by laying claim to an exclusive form of knowledge born of suffering. Chapter 2 relates how Rousset drew on this identity in crafting his bombshell 1949 "Appeal." By analyzing the evocative language of his open letter as well as the astonishing wave of responses that the text provoked in France, I demonstrate that the uproar was fueled not merely by Cold War side-taking but also by deep disagreement over how the country's wartime suffering should be remembered—and what bearing such memories ought to have on present-day political choices.

From the story of the "Appeal," I move beyond French borders to chart what was ultimately the key consequence of its publication: the creation of a European survivors' movement to combat the *univers concentrationnaire*. Chapter 3 recounts the internal debates that accompanied the organization's founding, one over what counted as a "concentration camp," and the other, closely related, over which wartime experiences made individuals eligible for membership. Along the way, new characters appear. The first of these are the Belgian, "Spanish republican," Dutch, West German, Norwegian, and Danish survivors who now joined Rousset's endeavor through a complex process of adapting his vision to non-French national modes of memorializing the Nazi camps. The second are a set of American labor leaders and intellectuals whose enthusiasm for the anti-concentrationary project eventually helped Rousset receive CIA funding. Finally, the chapter introduces Poliakov and Bernard, using their insider-outsider status in the CICRC to explicate the group's troubled relationship to Jewish suffering. The figure of the Holocaust victim, I argue, cannot be viewed as simply absent from an initiative that, behind the scenes, was largely run by a historian and a survivor of the Final Solution. Rather, it constituted a haunting "other" against which the organization defined itself.

The following two chapters serve as a paired examination of what the CICRC's work looked like in practice. Chapter 4 is centered on the commission's 1951 mock trial of the USSR; it treats the event not only as a creative attempt to mobilize Nuremberg's legacy for Cold War ends but as an effort to advance and expand that legacy through placing victim testimony at the heart of its symbolic enactment of international justice. By considering the group's 1952 investigation in Spain, chapter 5 illuminates how the anti-concentrationary model functioned when survivors targeted a right-wing dictatorship with historic ties to Nazi Germany, rather than a communist state. The inquiry, crowned with dramatic testimony before the Ad Hoc Committee on Forced Labor at the United Nations, was a milestone of international "witnessing" in the name of Spanish political prisoners. But, as the chapter demonstrates, it also exposed the inflexible nature of the commission's memory-based criteria for evaluating detention regimes and the fragility of Nazi camp survivors' claims to authority derived from experience.

Chapter 6 moves forward in time to span the commission's busiest years, from a 1953 inquiry in French Tunisia to large-scale protests against the Soviet repression in Hungary in 1956. It first highlights internal debates over members' cultural competence to investigate in Africa and China, which hinged on whether the Nazi camps could really be understood as universal archetypes of inhumanity. It then explores how the commission struggled to continue asserting the "concentrationary" nature of the Soviet repressive apparatus as the gulag shrank and, at the same time, as genocide slowly became less marginal to Western European conceptions of the Nazi camps. Finally, it considers the commission's engagement with the Hungarian Revolution—including its failed lobbying efforts through the United Nations—and explains why the episode left some members disillusioned with the politics of witnessing. Chapter 7 explores how all these tensions came to a head during the CICRC's 1957 Algerian investigation. While stressing Rousset's accomplishment in shedding light on France's shadowy prison camp regime, the chapter focuses primarily on how the project destroyed his organization—not only by severing its funding relationship with the Central Intelligence Agency but also by compelling members to conclude, regretfully, that the violence of decolonization could not be addressed through direct comparison to World War II's atrocities.

Before launching readers back to the spring of 1945, one further prefatory comment is necessary. I admire the commitment of the individuals who took part in the Commission Internationale contre le Régime Concentrationnaire, and I have tried to write about their ideas and experiences with empathy and respect. As French president François Hollande noted on the 2015 occasion of Germaine Tillion's symbolic reburial in the Panthéon, the courage of Resistance deportees was profound—and was not confined to their wartime acts. But respecting the commission's members is a different matter from limiting critical inquiry into their ideals and allegiances, their priorities and exclusions. The historian, for better or for worse, cannot join Hollande in accepting at face value the moral authority that Rousset and his followers assigned themselves—and, in turn, denied to others—as witnesses for a suffering humanity. To the contrary, the task of illuminating the movement's meaning and significance in its own time demands a reckoning with the limits of its universalism. My goal has thus been to treat my protagonists, despite all of their losses, as flesh-and-blood, fallible human beings who continued to make new choices after 1945. I hope that, in its own way, this approach pays tribute to CICRC members' passage through catastrophe. By taking seriously their fierce determination to fight on—publicly, politically, and polemically—I aim to do justice to their own understanding of what it meant to survive.

# SURVIVORS AS WITNESSES IN POSTWAR FRANCE

It was the day after the day that would never come. As Allied troops liberated Nazi Germany's concentration camps in the winter and spring of 1945, French men and women who had managed to live through the murderous final months of captivity began to trickle homeward. These camp survivors constituted only a rivulet within the floodwaters of displaced humanity on the move in Europe in 1945; indeed, they were a small minority even among those returning to France, far outnumbered by prisoners of war and various types of laborers.[1] Most of those deported to Hitler's concentration camps from France during the war were now dead. Of the more than 75,000 people deported as Jews ("racial" deportees), only some 2,500 (3 percent) survived; the majority had been killed upon arrival at Auschwitz or another extermination center.[2] A much higher proportion of France's nonracial deportees lived out the war: of the roughly 65,000 men and women deported from the principal territories of occupied France to Nazi concentration camps or prisons for political reasons, as punishment, or for Resistance activity, over 31,500—that is, more than 48 percent—returned to France.[3] Among them were the future leaders of the CICRC.

This chapter traces the trajectory of these survivors from the liberation of the camps through the initial years following their return, exploring their efforts to make meaning—for themselves and for others—out of their experience in the "concentrationary universe." This immediate postwar history constitutes a necessary prologue to the 1949 creation of Rousset's commission. Its eventual members were not yet scanning the horizon for fellow sufferers who "are what we were yesterday," but they were hard at work articulating the collective memory on which such equations would eventually depend. Though the CICRC was an international venture, its intellectual origins lay in French conversations about how to attribute retrospective meaning to *la déportation*. Before any project of denouncing the continued existence of "concentration camps" in the name of Hitler's victims could come into being, the group's French leaders already had to possess a shared narrative about what kind of institutions the Nazi camps had been and what the fact of their existence signified about human nature. Still more importantly, they needed to inhabit a distinct, self-conscious, and widely respected position as witnesses—expert witnesses—whose personal knowledge of the potential depths of human abasement positioned them not only to testify about the past but to intervene decisively in the present.

Though the CICRC's eventual leaders faced many of the same challenges as other returnees trailing home from the German camps in 1945, Jewish and non-Jewish, they were not ordinary survivors. First and foremost, all had been deported as resisters. In a newly liberated France that retroactively accorded to the Resistance an enormous measure of prestige and authority, seeking a legitimizing counternarrative to the story of ignominious military defeat, misery, and collaboration that appeared to define the Vichy years, this fact was essential. Even within the select category of "Resistance deportees," moreover, the future leaders of the CICRC stood out: most had achieved prewar distinction in their fields—law, journalism, government, literature, science, religion—and several had been active in France's rough-and-tumble party politics of the 1930s. After their return to France, they continued these pursuits. However, they also took on new public tasks, from a new position: the concentration camp survivor. For the CICRC's founders, thanks to their elite status, this identity was resoundingly affirmed by society. Consider one admiring 1947 description of David Rousset: "Stocky, powerful, a black patch on his left eye, his teeth ravaged but without it affecting his pronunciation, he speaks with authority—and what authority! That of a survivor."[4] It was also deeply felt on a subjective level. "We are no longer exactly living men [*vivants*] like the others," declared Louis Martin-Chauffier. "We are survivors [*survivants*]."[5]

What did it mean to be a *survivant*? Though the CICRC's founders offered different answers to the question, in the end they agreed that to be a survivor was to be a witness, a *témoin*.[6] In a postwar France awash with popular and intellectual interest in *témoins* (a vocabulary applied to all manner of authors writing from "experience"), these men and women grappled with their losses by engaging in a set of tasks that today we might call "primary witnessing": speech acts relating one's own past bodily and psychic sufferings.[7] Thus, between 1945 and 1948, a striking number of them offered public testimony about what Rousset labeled the *univers concentrationnaire*, constructing themselves as conveyers of a terrible, quasi-sacred knowledge about the machinery of abjection and the limits of human endurance.

David Rousset, Germaine Tillion, Louis Martin-Chauffier, Alfred-Serge Balachowsky, Rémy Roure, and other eventual participants in the CICRC testified in a variety of modes, from experimental works of literary fiction to matter-of-fact first-person reportage, from speeches and sermons to scholarly articles and even legal testimony from the witness stand. Some understood "witnessing" as a spiritual act, others as a secular form of political praxis. But all shared two convictions, each grounded in a seeming paradox. First, they believed their testimony mattered because the Nazi camps, though unprecedented in human history, nevertheless possessed universal significance and generalizable import—"lessons," even—for mankind's future. Second, they insisted that since bearing witness was both imperative, as the fulfillment of a limitless obligation for the fact of having survived, and at the same time impossible, since the essence of the camps could never be conveyed in language, it constituted a never-ending task, a project to occupy the rest of their lives. Thus, by the late 1940s, in different ways, these survivors had come to understand "the witness" as a permanent and activist identity, one imbued with epistemological authority and oriented toward the needs of the present.[8]

The testimony on the Nazi camps that the CICRC's future leaders produced can be jarring to read today, because it belonged to a postwar moment when "the Holocaust," as such, was not the primary frame through which the French (nor, indeed, the West) interpreted Nazi atrocity. Rousset, Tillion, Martin-Chauffier, and the others were well aware that Hitler had engaged in mass murder on a racial basis; Rousset, in particular, was quite vocal about this fact. But none of them conceptualized genocide (a newly coined word that was still barely used in France) as the "*crime majeur*" of Nazism and the central tragedy of the deportation, nor did they promote the notion of a categorical difference between their own wanderings in the "camp universe" and the fate of Europe's Jews—that is, between Buchenwald and Birkenau. Their postwar writings certainly helped solidify a "concentrationary" rather than an "exterminationist" paradigm for understanding Nazi criminality.[9] But it is important to stress that these texts emerged in a France where public discussion of the deportation was already heavily oriented toward the experience of resisters rather than Jews, for many reasons: their higher survival rate and hence disproportionate presence among "the returned"; the ready availability in 1945 of photographic images of concentration camps but not extermination facilities; the French Provisional Government's campaign (begun before the war ended) to assimilate all France's *absents* into patriotic symbols of unified national martyrdom; Jewish survivors' own understandable reluctance to highlight their differences from much-celebrated

Resistance deportees; and gentile commentators' parallel unwillingness to stress Jewish particularity—a product of Dreyfusard republicanism now heightened by revulsion at Nazi racism.

It was within these broader demographic and discursive contexts that the future leaders of the CICRC crafted their universalizing accounts of camp "society" and positioned themselves as figures of newfound authority on the basis of their sacrificial hardships. Such self-constructions served both to advance ideological agendas (for example, through Marxist interpretations of Nazi depravity) and to anchor claims for recognition (for example, in campaigns for recompense from the French state). However, they must not be viewed exclusively in instrumental terms, and should certainly not be treated as presciently instrumental Cold War maneuverings. Although the CICRC did eventually deploy the twin concepts of the "concentrationary universe" and the "expert witness" for anti-Soviet ends, these ideas served elemental needs rather than strategic ones as they emerged between 1945 and 1947. They permitted survivors to link the "before" and "after" of their lives into a coherent narrative, and to build an affirmative identity for themselves on the very ground of their past victimization. Thereby, they provided a fragile language to retrieve value from a devastating experience of loss and pain.

## Surviving the Survival

The CICRC's story began with the fact of survival—of living, against the odds, to see the liberation of the camps. Survival, miracle that it was, did not mean an easy salvation. The starving, sick French men and women who met the liberators of Buchenwald, Ravensbrück, Dachau, Mauthausen, and other camps greeted the event with joy, certainly—if they were well enough to register what was taking place. But they quickly faced new tribulations. While survival in the short term did not present the same challenges for Resistance deportees as it did for Jewish Holocaust survivors, their post-liberation ordeals were real, and in many cases enormous.

Foremost among them was regaining France. The repatriation process from the Nazi camps to French soil varied immensely; scholars have justly commented that there were nearly as many trajectories of "return" as there were individual returnees.[10] In some cases it took days; in others, weeks or months. Most traveled by plane, train, military truck, boat, or a combination of these; a few—particularly those who had escaped from death marches or evacuations as Hitler's empire disintegrated—rode on more primitive conveyances or even walked great distances.[11] Although it is easiest to generalize about the repatriation of men and women liberated by American soldiers from the large western camps, here too fates diverged sharply. For instance, while every French survivor present at Buchenwald on April 11 was evacuated from the camp by April 27—that is, sixteen days after the arrival of US forces—the French "return" from Flossenbürg and Dachau required a tortuous process stretched out over weeks. The small number of French survivors who found themselves in Soviet-controlled territory at war's end had to wait still longer: most did not come back until late July or August. At Bergen-Belsen in the northwest, meanwhile, where typhus and dysentery raged and quarantine was imposed, roughly fourteen thousand additional prisoners, including Frenchmen, died in the weeks after the April 15 arrival of the British; few were permitted to return home until May.

A case in point is Louis Martin-Chauffier, an important future member of the CICRC. Well established at fifty as a major Catholic writer and editor, Martin-Chauffier had taken part during the war in high-level activities in Emmanuel d'Astier de la Vigerie's Libération-Sud resistance network; in addition to serving as editor-in-chief of the important clandestine newspaper *Libération*, he had also been a leading member of the underground National Committee of Writers and founder of the National Committee of Journalists. He was arrested by the Gestapo in April 1944. Following his deportation, Martin-Chauffier spent nearly his whole captivity in Neuengamme but was shipped to Bergen-Belsen in the war's final weeks, a stroke of fate that terrified him at the time but spared him the murderous April 1945 evacuation of Neuengamme and likely saved his life. However, he was so enfeebled by hunger and disease by the time the British liberators appeared that he penned a farewell letter to his family and, with the help of some comrades, dressed himself to be buried. Only weeks later did he emerge, haltingly, from the fever-dreams of typhus. Olga Wormser-Migot, dispatched to the liberated camp by the French government, remembered catching sight of his gaunt, ghostly figure as he wandered the grounds clutching his "most precious possession," a box of condensed milk.[12] On May 27, French priests managed to smuggle him home with forged *laissez-passer* papers that stretched the truth considerably to proclaim him well enough to travel.

Other eventual leaders and supporters of the CICRC underwent "the return" very differently. Ethnographer Germaine Tillion, an exceptionally early resister who was arrested in 1942 for her activities with the Musée de l'Homme network, convalesced for weeks in Sweden along with other Frenchwomen rescued from Ravensbrück by the Swedish Red Cross on April 23, 1945.[13] She did not arrive back in France until July. The future historian Hélène Maspero repatriated even later: she was evacuated from Ravensbrück to Königsberg and passed three full months in Poland after that sub-camp was finally liberated by the Red Army on May 2. Meanwhile, Catholic politician Edmond Michelet remained in place by choice until mid-June, directing French affairs in what he called "the autonomous Republic of Dachau under the American protectorate."[14] Lawyer Léon Mazeaud came home much earlier, from Buchenwald. Nevertheless, he remembered the wait as unbearable: "The days crawl by as we wait to return, heavy and monotonous for exhausted bodies. The camp has no more water; we lack soup; the toilets without sewage disposal are revolting. We do not feel free."[15] David Rousset, who ended the war in the chaotic, cadaver-choked hell of Wöbbelin, was liberated on May 2 and repatriated on May 18—first by car (driven by a drunken GI), then military plane and train. In the interim, he was received by American general James Gavin along with fellow deportee Albert Rohmer, an eminent Strasbourgeois *résistant* and doctor. Rohmer returned to France on June 1, on which date he was received with great pomp as part of a celebration orchestrated by Henri Frenay's Ministry of Prisoners, Deportees, and Refugees to mark the return of France's "millionth prisoner," a POW named Jules Garron.[16]

As the staging of this patriotic commemorative ceremony symbolically linking Rohmer with Garron suggests, Charles de Gaulle's provisional government of 1945 was committed to the notion that, for the sake of unity, no distinctions should be drawn among the different categories of those who had been "absent" from national territory during the war. Indeed, as historian Pieter Lagrou argues, in a France where the language of deportation remained labile, Frenay—himself a Resistance hero—sowed "deliberate confusion" to blur the lines between political prisoners, POWs, labor conscripts, "racial" deportees, and so on, portraying them as a single bloc of martyrs for a cohesive France.[17] "They Are United, Do Not Divide Them!" was the slogan of the National Movement of Prisoners of War and Deportees, an organization created by his ministry. One of its posters bore the words, "Germany: A Concentration Camp."[18] But confronted with the far more desperate bodily condition of actual camp survivors, Frenay and his subordinates realized that, pragmatically speaking, they would require additional help.[19] "We were all skeletons," Tillion remembered, "all haggard creatures."[20] Horrified journalists described them in similar terms: "caricatures of human beings," "dead men whose skeletons show," "ghosts," "walking dead."[21] Most were suffering from severe malnutrition and many from assorted ailments that would become known as "pathologies of the deportation."[22] Survivors themselves—including Buchenwald deportee, prickly Gaullist patriot, and future CICRC member Dr. Charles Richet (*fils*)—pioneered the study of these illnesses, which dogged many returnees for the rest of their lives.

In the immediate term, these survivors needed basic care to recover from the brink of physical calamity. Some went from the famous volunteer-staffed intake center at the Hôtel Lutetia or a different regional point of entry directly to the hospital.[23] Others convalesced in rest homes or under the care of family. The process was often lengthy. Consider Rousset, who had weighed over two hundred pounds upon his arrest in 1943. When he returned to France, he had lost more than half of that—which, his wife Sue wryly noted, still made him appear the picture of good health among his cadaverous comrades.[24] He nevertheless spent weeks at the Hôpital Pasteur in Paris recovering from typhus and a lung infection. His teeth were ruined, his muscles weak. He experienced frightening amnesia. His friend Maurice Nadeau hardly recognized the "dying man" in the hospital bed before him: "How did he become this old wrinkled child, this little bag of bones?"[25] Released to Sue's care, Rousset retreated to Saint-Jean-de-Monts in the Vendée, where he slowly regained passable health.

While physical care for former deportees' "physiological misery"[26] was usually forthcoming, their psychological pain was not fully acknowledged in a postwar society that wished to view them as robust heroes whose suffering had been the consequence of "willing sacrifices" for France.[27] Overall, there was little public discussion of survivors' emotional health. Exploration of psychic disorders remained minimal, even within the medical literature on "pathologies of the deportation," until years later.[28] The French state's long-awaited May 16, 1953, decree providing guidelines for classification and evaluation of "disabilities resulting from infirmities or sicknesses contracted during the internment or the deportation" did recognize two psychological diagnoses, "asthenia" and "emotional hypermnesia." Tellingly, though, it included a lengthy discussion of how to distinguish their actual victims from survivors engaging in "dramatics," "egocentrism," or "obsessive or hypochondriac ideas."[29] Such marginalization and outright suspicion of psychological debility endured over the years despite the fact that for many, the physical discomfort of convalescence was decidedly secondary to the lingering effects of horror, fear, despair, grief, and desolation. To be clear: non-Jewish deportees such as those who would later join the CICRC had usually not lost their entire families; their homes and possessions awaited them more or less intact, as did their prewar professional, social, and religious networks. Nevertheless, many of them were traumatized: technically "liberated," they remained "imprisoned in memories and repetitions" of their experiences.[30]

Consider Tillion, who is often justly celebrated for her astonishing psychological resilience—she authored a five-act comic opera for her comrades while in Ravensbrück—but who nevertheless traversed the "return" through a fog of pain. Her mother Émilie, deported alongside her, had been gassed in the camp's final weeks, and news of this loss, brought to a desperately ill Tillion while she herself hovered between life and death, left her in a state of "total indifference" about her destiny. She returned home to learn that her grandmother had also died during the war. "I had no one anymore," she remembered. "Ravensbrück had eaten my life." Tillion was physically "totally devastated," "exhausted," and "at the end of my strength." She recalled sitting down in the middle of the sidewalk in Paris on occasions when she found she could walk no further. She suffered for a time from nightmares as well. "I was in a very deep blackness, in an extreme blackness—I repeat it to you, in a very deep blackness. . . . I was in a black hole. . . . Let's say that it was very, very, very black." This worst period passed, but Tillion continued to feel that she survived the immediate postwar years "without doing it on purpose, if one can say that."[31]

Tillion was not alone among future CICRC participants in having lost at least one family member in the camps or in Resistance combat. For many, recovered bodily autonomy provided first of all what Joanne Reilly has called the "freedom to mourn."[32] Rémy Roure, former political editor at *Le Temps*, learned upon liberation from Buchenwald that his wife had died in Ravensbrück—and that his son, a young lieutenant, had been killed by a German grenade. The lawyer and northern zone Combat militant Elisabeth Dussauze (later Ingrand), deported in 1942, discovered that her brother had been beheaded by the Gestapo. While Catherine (Agnès) Goetschel languished in Ravensbrück, arrested in 1943 as a leader of the Normandy "Cohors-Asturies" resistance network, her Jewish husband died in Auschwitz.[33] When lawyer Paul Arrighi returned from Mauthausen, he had to inform his wife that their beloved son Pierre had perished in the camp in August 1944. Life back in France, Arrighi bitterly concluded, constituted an extension of the "absolute solitude" of man's existence in the concentrationary universe.[34] Maspero expressed similar feelings. Arrested in the summer of 1944 with her husband Henri, a prominent sinologist, she came home to find that he had died in Buchenwald just weeks before its liberation. Her elder son Jean, meanwhile, had been killed fighting the Wehrmacht. "Much later," a friend remembered, "when people inopportunely asked her what was hardest to bear about her deportation, she responded without fail, 'The return.'"[35]

This is not to suggest that the aftermath of liberation brought no joy. Indeed, some of the men and women who would later form the CICRC recorded breathless happiness at regaining their homeland, reuniting with family, and returning to "civilian" life. Small acts of autonomy could produce immense satisfaction: Rousset exulted to an interviewer in 1946 about "the simple fact of walking on a sidewalk, in a crowd, freely. . . . The return of the deportee is a kind of childhood renewed, in full consciousness—a relearning of life, in which each mechanism is savored!"[36] Others, too, referred to liberation in the language of rebirth: Michelet, for instance, wrote movingly of "our second coming into the world of the living, our *re-naissance*."[37] But some preferred to be discreet in their delight at being alive when so many had died. Abruptly drawing a curtain over the scene of his homecoming in the final lines of his 1947 testimonial *L'Homme et la bête*, Martin-Chauffier (whose deported son had also survived, in

Buchenwald) claimed that "What follows is no one's business. Happiness has no need of confidants and does not bear witness."[38] In this sentiment he was typical: most survivor testimonials written between 1945 and 1948 concluded at the instant the narrator again touched French soil.[39] The "return," whether joyful like Martin-Chauffier's or troubled like so many others, was the end of the story.

But the return to France was not, in fact, simply an end—it was also a beginning. Those who came back from the camps were men and women, not saints or ghosts. In most cases, they could now reasonably expect their hearts to go on beating for decades. This was not necessarily a welcome realization. And yet, even unwilled, life continued. After they had restored their bodies from the worst ravages of disease, maltreatment, and hunger—and in some cases, well before they had managed to do so—survivors had new choices to make. To acknowledge this fact is not to disregard their ongoing trauma, or to deny the hold that memory exerted over their postwar existence. Their passage through the "camp universe" may have constituted the overwhelmingly central event of their lives—Martin-Chauffier would later call it "the only authentic experience that I ever completely had"—but this did not mean they now lived on merely as sanctified vessels of remembrance.[40] The dichotomy sketched out by Tzvetan Todorov between those melancholic survivors obsessively dedicated to "remembering, reiterating, harping on about, and keeping alive" the past and those "able to accept living in the present," as if the two constituted distinct groups of people, is misleading: *all* survivors, by definition, lived day to day in relation to both the terrible past and the difficult present.[41] The postwar lives of those who would join the CICRC largely revolved around attempts to articulate what, precisely, connected the two.

## From Survivor to Witness

The "return" to France required a difficult reintegration into hearth and home, but for many deportees it was not a moment of retreat into the private sphere. On the contrary, even very frail survivors took up a remarkable array of political, civic, and social tasks; their activities ranged from sitting in the Provisional Consultative Assembly or even the cabinet to sending lesson plans about Nazism to French primary school teachers.[42] They were especially preoccupied with the problem of justice in France's purge of wartime collaborators, the *épuration*, and some took to protesting outside the courtrooms of judges perceived as overly lenient. In a country not famed for its associational life, they also organized themselves quickly and thoroughly—a feat accomplished by drawing on networks of solidarity established in the camps. The roughly fifty *fédérations*, *associations*, and camp-specific *amicales* that former deportees created by July 1945 were primarily geared toward mutual aid, but some also functioned as loci of lobbying and activism.[43] The future leaders of the CICRC were nearly all serious participants in such associations: Michelet, for instance, was president of the Dachau Amicale, Martin-Chauffier vice president of the Neuengamme group. Tillion and Dussauze sat on the governing council of the Association Nationale des Anciennes Déportées et Internées de la Résistance (ADIR), a women's organization that included most French Ravensbrück survivors, and Father Michel Riquet was a leader of the country's largest "umbrella" survivors' association, the Communist-dominated Fédération Nationale des Déportés et Internés Résistants et Patriotes (FNDIRP). Mazeaud, meanwhile, led its rival, the Fédération Nationale des Déportés et Internés de la Résistance (FNDIR), an elitist Gaullist organization that averred it was "proud to count among its members only *résistants*, deported for acts of resistance."[44]

As the future French members of the CICRC reentered the French public sphere through associational endeavors, they also engaged in individual and collective projects of testimony. These were long-dreamt-of acts. In Neuengamme, Martin-Chauffier remembered later, "I was not afraid of death, and rarely, against my will, I wished for it as an end to my sorrows. But I wanted to live, in order to testify."[45] He was not alone in this sentiment: for many French deportees—political and "racial"—the desire to bear witness motivated endurance in the camps, and one of the earliest actions undertaken by those who managed to survive was often to produce a statement about their experience of deportation. David Rousset began dictating his grimly hallucinatory portrait of the *univers concentrationnaire* to Sue while he convalesced, pouring out the entire manuscript over the course of three weeks. Within days of his return to Paris, a prematurely aged Rémy Roure arrived in the offices of *Le Monde* to lecture his colleagues about Buchenwald and Auschwitz. In the Swedish sanatorium where she recuperated, Tillion began collecting detailed depositions from fellow Ravensbrück survivors for use in a planned work on the camp; she started drafting it long before she had regained her health.

Over the subsequent decade, the men and women who would go on to join the CICRC offered testimony about the Nazi camps in a variety of genres and forums, overtly positioning themselves as witnesses whether they were speaking in court, addressing a classroom of students, or crafting a book. Annette Wieviorka has distinguished between postwar *témoignage* that was documentary in nature and "essentially directed toward producing knowledge" versus more complex, enduring works that went "beyond the testimonial" to "pose the problem of the meaning of the deportation."[46] This distinction is too sharply drawn for the products of future CICRC members: even their most ambitious, sweeping analyses of the Nazi camp system were intended as testimony, and even their most resolutely minimalist narratives of individual experience gestured toward larger questions of meaning and interpretation. Approaches did vary, however. Some penned impressionistic, first-person articles offering fragmentary glimpses into life and death in a particular camp; these appeared in venues ranging from the front page of *Le Monde* to obscure bound collections of regional deportee voices.[47] Others participated in the government-directed Commission on the History of the Deportation and the Internment, a collective effort on the part of selected deportees to "bear witness against the Hitler regime and the Vichy regime."[48] Maspero spoke to school groups; Father Riquet, meanwhile, delivered a testimonial to man's endurance in the camps as the closing homily of the July 1945 Mass for Deportees and Prisoners at the Palais de Chaillot in Paris, attended by 150,000 people.[49] Russian-born Pasteur Institute entomologist and Buchenwald survivor Alfred-Serge Balachowsky, meanwhile, was among the handful of *anciens déportés* to take the stand at Nuremberg before being dispatched on a government-sponsored speaking tour of the United States. He also authored, "for the enlightenment of the civilized world to which I have returned," a brief pamphlet on Nazi depravity that was translated into English and distributed under the title *"Lest We Forget": Camps of Death in Germany.*[50]

Despite these wide-ranging activities, the most visible acts of testimony undertaken by future CICRC members were book-length published works. Charles Richet's *Trois bagnes*, coauthored with his son and niece in 1945, was the earliest of these; David Rousset's terse, masterly 1946 *L'Univers concentrationnaire* was the most famous. Eschewing individual narrative, this Renaudot prize–winning work offered a structural and—loosely speaking—Marxist study of what Rousset insisted was a new sort of human institution: "the concentration camp." A year later Rousset published a long companion volume, *Les Jours de notre mort*; composed as a polyphonic "novel" in a mix of first- and third-person prose, the book aimed to convey the horrors of Buchenwald and its satellites through a kaleidoscopic panorama of scenes and set-pieces. Tillion, meanwhile, wrote a steely eighty-eight-page text for *Ravensbrück*, a collective volume produced in 1946 by French survivors of the women's camp. Louis Martin-Chauffier's 1947 *L'Homme et la bête*, in contrast, was a deeply personal, narratively structured work of Catholic witnessing—a testament to man's faith and endurance in the face of unfathomable suffering. So, too—though with different political overtones—were Léon Mazeaud's contribution to *Visages dans la tourmente* (coauthored with his brothers in 1946) and Edmond Michelet's *Rue de la liberté*, which he did not publish until 1955.

It is important to stress that the CICRC's future members were not unique in their production of testimonial literature. As Wieviorka first established, the period from 1945 to 1948 saw a veritable outpouring of "*témoignages*" from French survivors, including many Jews.[51] But those who would go on to lead the CICRC (along with a handful of other survivors including Robert Antelme and Jean Cayrol) were unusually well positioned to influence perceptions of the deportation through their testimony. This was true for multiple reasons. First, these men and women were already intellectual or political elites and, in some cases, established literary figures. They possessed a fluid command of language—and, moreover, had existing relationships with leading editors and publishers. Thus, for example, Rousset's *L'Univers concentrationnaire* was originally written as a set of articles for Maurice Nadeau's newly founded *Revue internationale*; subsequently, *Les Jours de notre mort* was previewed in Jean-Paul Sartre's *Les Temps modernes*. Martin-Chauffier put out *L'Homme et la bête* through the prestigious Éditions Gallimard, with which he had previously published. *Ravensbrück* was solicited by editor Albert Béguin for his Swiss "Cahiers du Rhône" series, a lauded collection originally conceived as an outlet for exiled luminaries during France's dark years. Such venues were unavailable to ordinary deportees, Jewish or not.

Of course, prewar prominence was not the only or even the primary reason that future CICRC members were granted access to conspicuous tribunals. These survivors also possessed clear-cut and impressive pre-deportation Resistance credentials, which for a time served as the single most significant markers of political and intellectual legitimacy in postwar France.[52] This point demands some explication, because the public tended initially to view *all* concentration camp returnees as combatants for the nation, "Resistance heroes who deserved the highest honours."[53] This was thanks to the obfuscating efforts of the Frenay ministry, to obdurate official silence about the deportation of common-law criminals during the war, to an emphasis on the plight of absent comrades in the Resistance-dominated press of 1944–1945, and to the tiny number and social invisibility of surviving "racial" deportees, many of whom were not French citizens. It was also facilitated by *anciens déportés'* own insistent portrayal of the camps as arenas for continued patriotic or antifascist battle, both armed (as, for example, in *Le Patriote résistant*'s 1946 "Buchenwald, Cursed Penal Colony but Glorious Page in the French Resistance") and spiritual (as in Louise Alcan's description of fellow Jews in Auschwitz as "combatants without weapons" against the SS).[54]

Advocates of survivor unity—including the leadership of the FNDIRP—mobilized such representations to insist that all deportees had "paid for the Resistance" and should be considered *résistants*.[55] But despite their efforts, hierarchies in which future CICRC members occupied the top rung quickly emerged.[56] Victims who had originally been targeted on the basis of immutable characteristics might be the objects of pity and even aid, but only those whose suffering in the camps could be incorporated in a voluntarist, patriotic narrative of martyrdom could be recognized as "giants of sacrifice and saintliness," who, having undergone their ordeal on behalf of a national collective, now possessed newfound political and moral authority within that collective.[57] Writer Albert Camus, for example, repeatedly affirmed that he was referring exclusively to "political deportees" when he wrote in May 1945, "Everyone must know that a single hair of one of these men holds more importance for France, and for the entire universe, than twenty politicians. . . . They and they alone are the guardians of honor and the witnesses to courage. . . . [Theirs are] the most precious French lives." Unsettlingly, Camus's article *did* allude to deported Jews—by explaining that one of the many tribulations faced by as-yet unrepatriated resisters in Dachau was the "terrible odor of death" that drifted their way from the Jewish sector of the camp.[58]

The distinction between resisters and other survivors was not simply a matter of reputation. Rather, it was so fundamental to postwar French understandings that it was eventually enshrined in law. In 1948, deportees who could provide formal proof of Resistance activities (defined in narrowly militaristic Gaullist terms that disadvantaged communist claimants and worked to the benefit of those who would eventually join the CICRC) were awarded a distinct status, guaranteeing them not only the prestigious appellation of *Déportés et internés résistants* but also a "*carte du combattant*" conferring indemnities and benefits analogous to those of Great War veterans.[59] Jewish "racial" victims and others who had been deported for reasons other than Resistance acts were subsequently granted only lesser, nonmilitary benefits.

Future CICRC members found themselves on both sides of the survivor community's epic internal struggle over the 1948 legislation. In fact, the original Assembly bill was introduced by one of them, Dachau survivor Émile-Louis Lambert. "Without undervaluing . . . the sympathy deserved by the miserable victims who were affected by Nazi barbarity in one way or another," he lectured, "it is nonetheless incontestable that the martyrs of the Resistance have to occupy the top position in the hierarchy of urgencies." Other future CICRC members—Riquet, for example—fiercely opposed Lambert.[60] But whether or not they endorsed the distinction between *résistants* and other survivors, the men and women who would later join the commission all unquestionably fell into the former category themselves. And all benefited from that widely affirmed identity as "voluntary combatants in the harshest of wars" in locating publics before whom they could bear witness to their experience.[61] Indeed, speaking as representatives of "the Resistance" at the height of its postwar mystique, these figures summoned enormous authority. Justifiably proud of the activities that had resulted in their original arrest, many of them laid claim to this authority through inscribing their testimony under the sign of Resistance combat.

Martin-Chauffier's *L'Homme et la bête*, for instance, was dedicated in part to "My Resistance comrades," and tracked his calvary in Neuengamme by a calendar of "*maquis*" victories at home in France.[62] *Ravensbrück* included Tillion's clandestine nom de guerre in her brief biographical sketch. Richet dedicated *Trois bagnes* to Charles de Gaulle, "who gave us faith," and recounted in the book's preface his own pre-deportation acts of resistance; a decade later, Michelet's *Rue de la liberté* began with an endorsement by de Gaulle.[63] Testifying on behalf of a community of fallen comrades-in-arms "who gave their life in the camp . . . for the honor of humanity" and for "country, freedom, civilization"—a community postwar France was eager to consecrate—these authors offered moving homage to the dead as soldiers for a greater cause.[64] In so doing, they also granted increased resonance to their own voices.

Intellectual or political elite status, an active role in deportee organizational life, and unassailable Resistance credentials, then, were distinguishing characteristics that set future CICRC members apart from other authors of testimony in the immediate postwar years. But, crucially, these men and women shared more than a checklist of sociological similarities. They also had ideas in common. Though their postwar outpouring of written and spoken testimony was diverse in form, genre, tone, and content, nevertheless, considered as a body, it was undergirded by a discernible set of common assumptions about the Nazi camp experience and the task of bearing witness.

First, the eventual leaders of the CICRC shared a conviction that the Nazi regime had carried out an "absolutely new collective crime, [an] unprecedented attack against man," heretofore "unthinkable and impossible" in human history.[65] To their immediate postwar eyes, this crime was not genocide but rather the invention of "the concentration camp universe," a realm "without points of reference, without security, without justice, without hope, where everything was unpredictable, where evil became virtue and good became undefinable."[66] Second, they infused their passage through this dark world with meaning by insisting that although the camp was indeed "another planet," it nevertheless offered "positive lessons" that were "transposable to our [postwar] universe."[67] These lessons—about the mechanisms of dehumanization and the possibilities for resisting it—were particularly urgent because the newness of Nazism's assault on man was no guarantee against its replication: "under a new guise, similar effects could reappear tomorrow."[68] Third, therefore, the CICRC's founders believed that bearing witness to life inside the camps was a "*devoir*," a duty. To speak about what one had seen was sometimes framed as a debt owed to God for having survived where so many others had died, or as an obligation to the dead themselves. But, primarily, witnessing was understood as a moral imperative directed toward the living: "normal men" had to be warned.[69] Fourth, however, paradoxically, these survivors agreed that full communication regarding the realities of Buchenwald, Mauthausen, and Dora was impossible: what they had experienced was fundamentally "intransmissible" in language, existing outside the limits of representation. Any effort to "re-create" the camps for others, "no matter [its] accuracy," was doomed to failure in the end.[70]

The tension between this fourth conviction and the previous three was very painful for those who would go on to form the CICRC. However, it also developed in them a permanent sense of mission: bearing witness became a continuing, open-ended project precisely *because* no individual instance of testimony could succeed. And for these non-Jewish survivors, the grim certainty that, in the end, "only the deportees can understand the concentration camp regime," while terribly isolating, was also affirming.[71] In conjunction with their other views about the novelty, significance, and universally relevant "lessons" of the camp experience, it meant that they now stood as sacred guardians to a "secret garden" of knowledge permanently inaccessible to others.[72] Survivors—and survivors alone—possessed a unique expertise concerning humanity's heart of darkness. This formulation recast humiliating agony as an exclusive education, thereby salvaging purpose for the future from the abyss of the camps.[73] Thus between 1945 and 1947, individuals with different conceptions of what was involved in "testimony" nevertheless all came to see themselves as filling a special moral and political role in the postwar world—not simply as *anciens déportés*, nor even as *anciens déportés de la Résistance*, but as expert witnesses. The cases of Rousset, Tillion, and Martin-Chauffier—worthy of consideration for their own sake, for these were the most enduringly influential testimonial voices among the CICRC's eventual leaders—are illustrative of the process by which this identity formation took place.

## Voices of Witness

Nothing in David Rousset's prewar biography foreshadowed his postwar emergence as France's "witness among witnesses." He was born in 1912 to a family of modest means in Roanne. His parents were observant Darbyist Protestants. When his father's bicycle business failed, the family moved to Paris and his father took a job as a metalworker at Citroën; the young adult David found that he preferred Gide to his parents' Bible and eventually took courses in philosophy and literature at the Sorbonne.[74] As a student in the tumultuous early 1930s, he quickly became politically engaged, joining the tiny Trotskyist movement populated by men such as Pierre Naville, Yvan Craipeau, and Gérard Rosenthal. Rousset pieced together a living during this period as a correspondent for various

American publications, but struck no one as a great literary talent or a likely leader of men. The journalist Jean Rabaud remembered him in the 1930s as a "fat, stocky boy, full-faced, with rebellious hair, a cordial laugh, a beautiful deep voice, organizing revolutionary groups and giving speeches at meetings. He was, moreover, a maniac for theories, a pontiff in the club."[75] His friends viewed him affectionately but found him difficult to take seriously. A tennis accident at age fourteen had left him with a glass eye, which further undermined his gravity. (It would have the opposite effect after the war, when observers assumed he had lost the eye in Buchenwald.)

Rousset and his friends obeyed Trotsky's 1934 "*entriste*" dictate that French followers should militate from within the Socialist Party, but they were expelled in July 1935 as Socialist leaders cleared the way for an electoral alliance with the Communists. Upon the 1936 founding of an independent Trotskyist party, Rousset joined its Political Bureau and was assigned to work on colonial questions, a task that put him in contact with North African nationalist Messali Hadj and cemented his lifelong anticolonialism. Rousset was a cosmopolitan: he traveled incessantly—to Germany, Czechoslovakia, Spain, Morocco—and married an Englishwoman, Sue Elliott, whom he met at the Bibliothèque Nationale. He also participated in the 1938 founding of the Trotskyist Fourth International. When France fell, he entered into clandestine resistance along with his comrades, attempting to foment dissent and desertion among German occupying forces. He was arrested by the Gestapo on October 12, 1943, and held in Fresnes prison near Paris until January 1944. He later described Fresnes as a "paradise" next to the German camps, a comparative evaluation that helped inform the unyielding distinction he would later draw between concentrationary and non-concentrationary forms of detention.[76] Rousset then passed fifteen months in Nazi concentration camps and satellite camps, first Buchenwald, later Porta Westfalica, Helmstedt, Neuengamme, and Wöbbelin. In *L'Univers concentrationnaire* and *Les Jours de notre mort*, he depicted such places as constituting a "separate universe, totally closed off," that followed its own internal logic and customs. The various planets in this "universe"—Buchenwald, Dachau, Sachsenhausen—were "not all identical or equivalent," of course, but they could be spoken of within a framework of shared characteristics, essentially as a single imagined site.[77] Rousset depicted this space as an obscene, Ubu-esque kingdom where bodily suffering, unending physical exhaustion, and deliberate degradation stripped away men's dignity, leaving them "naked" and, in the end, producing "the total dissolution of the individual." The reduction of life to bare biological processes and the utter debasement of the human being as such—not merely physical death—was the purpose of the system, Rousset insisted: after all, there were simpler ways to produce corpses.[78] In the camps, he wrote, "death fades. Torture triumphs, always alive and active, spread out like an arch over the shattered world of men." This multiform torture was intended to "castrate free minds" and exact from prisoners a recognition that "they are cursed."[79] Thus the camp universe was best understood as "an amazing and complex machine of expiation," intended to call into being a particular kind of subject: *l'homme concentrationnaire*, a wretch who would perish persuaded that he was "fundamentally bad . . . a waste product of humanity."[80]

But prisoners appeared as an undifferentiated mass of *hommes concentrationnaires* in Rousset's account only at first glance. He also insisted that each of their "city-states" be understood as a fully articulated "society," and therefore a space of struggle and moral choice. Both his books, especially the expansive *Jours*, laid emphasis on the life-and-death internal hierarchies of this social sphere, with its "aristocrats" and "plebes," its competing national groups, and its ongoing warfare between "politicals" and common-law criminals. Rousset devoted much attention to describing how prisoners with advantaged status not only possessed a greater chance of surviving but also became implicated in the camps' infernal machinery. "Except for the roll calls," he underlined, "it was very rare to see an S.S. officer in the camp": detainees themselves policed fellow inmates, often through terror.[81] Even those in the privileged class who resisted corruption and sadism—in Buchenwald, many of them German communists—were nevertheless compelled to enter a gray zone of collusion by selecting other detainees either for brutal work commandos or for temporary shelter in the infirmary, thereby determining who lived and died. Rousset presented such choices as driven by a calculus about whose lives would best help preserve communist detainees' hard-won dominion over the hated criminals, under whose savage rule the early years at Buchenwald had been "incomparably more appalling" than even the hell that followed.[82] He allowed the multitudinous cast of *Les Jours de notre mort* to debate the moral repercussions of these decisions at length, but his own sympathies (like those of other future French CICRC members, including even fierce anticommunists such as Balachowsky) were clear: in an impossible context, actions taken to preserve certain lives in the name of their utility to the collective had been necessary and defensible.[83] Rousset underlined the point by dedicating *Jours* to the German communist *kapo* Emil Künder.

In both his emphasis on the production of *hommes concentrationnaires* rather than corpses and his treatment of the "camp universe" as a "society" populated primarily by political prisoners and criminals, Rousset—like most French people in the late 1940s, survivors or not—took Buchenwald, not Birkenau (and certainly not Einsatzgruppen mass shooting sites) as his template for Nazi evil. He was well aware of Hitler's slaughter of Europe's Jews, and the genocide was not absent from his testimony.[84] In fact, "racial" deportees figure prominently in the cast of *Les Jours de notre mort*; a depiction of Jewish women and children being gassed constitutes one of the book's first set-pieces. ("Why the gas chamber?" one Jewish character dares to ask; his interlocutor—a non-Jewish fellow detainee—responds, "Why were you born?")[85] In 1948, Rousset assembled *Le Pitre ne rit pas*, a documentary volume on Nazi antisemitism; in a different publication that same year, he claimed that "the Jew was the first victim sacrificed in the concentration camp world," the canary in the mineshaft of Hitler's Europe.[86] Nevertheless, he insisted that the crimes committed in extermination camps be understood within the overarching, unitary framework of "the concentrationary": Birkenau may have been Nazi Germany's "greatest city-state of death," Rousset asserted, but between it and "the 'normal' camps," there was "no difference in nature, only in degree."[87] Both were geared toward the destruction of human beings. And, for Rousset, the representative victim of this diabolical system was not the Jew annihilated immediately upon arrival at a killing center but the political prisoner forced into a deliberately interminable progression toward death. He would maintain this position throughout his life, writing in 1984 that "however horrible the massacres were, they were only massacres. . . . The *crime majeur* of Nazism was not to have killed on a grand scale. It was to have organized a society—the concentrationary society—*where one could live* within the obliteration of human values."[88]

Rousset made this particular comment in the context of rebutting Holocaust denier Robert Faurisson's notorious attempt to defend Hitler by questioning the existence of gas chambers. Forty years earlier, his aim in offering similar observations was quite different. In the 1940s, portraying the camp universe as a single, all-encompassing system—and as a space in which struggle continued rather than a murder factory—facilitated Rousset's effort to locate universalizable "lessons" in his own experience. These were not ingenuous, inspirational homilies: *L'Univers concentrationnaire* and *Les Jours de notre mort*, which drew their literary inspiration from Alfred Jarry and Franz Kafka, often appeared to resist the attribution of any meaning whatsoever to the camps, treating the whole affair simply as a "tragic farce."[89] In the end, however, Rousset—a Marxist, an amateur sociologist, and a survivor intent on making a new life in the wreckage of catastrophe—could not settle for this. Instead, he insisted that the miseries he and fellow detainees had undergone possessed import; their suffering had been meaningful and might even produce "positive results" for mankind as a whole.[90] Refusing to interpret the camps as evidence of inherent German depravity or (to borrow a felicitous phrase from his friend and fellow survivor Robert Antelme) to place his wartime experiences "between parentheses," Rousset insisted that Buchenwald, Neuengamme, Dachau, and Ravensbrück stood as a "warning" of what other societies, too, might be capable of doing.[91]

This universalizing lens was implicit in the very term *concentrationnaire*, which, while not precisely a new coinage, was obscure enough to be greeted as such by Rousset's contemporaries: *Minerve* called it a "neologism," while *Franc-Tireur* claimed that Rousset had "created" this "extraordinary word" entirely "from scratch, out of necessity."[92] In transforming "concentration" into an adjective, Rousset sought to suggest that the Nazi camps provided a template or archetype that could be replicated—or, indeed, as a reviewer for *Carrefour* fearfully suggested, "become the rule, proliferate."[93] This was because there was nothing uniquely "Nazi" about them. "It would be easy to show that the most characteristic traits of both the S.S. mentality and [prewar German] social conditions can be found in many other sectors of global society," Rousset wrote. Therefore, "it would be a dishonest act—and a criminal one—to claim that it is impossible for other peoples to try an analogous experiment." In other words, the German camps may have constituted a heretofore unimaginable assault on the human being, but it did not follow from this that the project would *remain* unique following Hitler's defeat. To the contrary, the "concentrationary universe" now lived on in the postwar world as a permanent possibility and a constant threat, against which there was "a very specific battle to be waged."[94]

It was directly from this universalizing, present-oriented interpretation of the camps that Rousset's valorization of the act of testimony and the figure of the survivor-as-witness emerged. Because the *univers concentrationnaire* was potentially replicable, he wrote, to speak about one's own ordeal in it was not primarily a commemorative act. Rather, testimony constituted a prophetic attempt to alert "normal men," who "do not know that everything is possible."[95] As deportees, Rousset instructed his fellow survivors, "we lived through the most complete alienation. In so doing, we learned its laws. By virtue of this experience, we are certainly more capable than others of recognizing its early warning signs. Therefore, our highest mission consists of transmitting this experience to others."[96] This redemptive, purposeful formulation positioned survivors as the keepers of otherwise inaccessible knowledge for humanity. Their suffering had been painful but in the end productive, according to Rousset, because it had granted them this precious expertise, this "marvelous arsenal of war" for the struggles that lay ahead.[97]

Even as he urged other survivors to "transmit" their experience, however, Rousset admitted that this aspiration could never truly be realized: the essence of the camps was "impossible to transmit" in mere language.[98] Regardless of how many "*témoignages*" they read, those who had not dwelt in Buchenwald, Auschwitz, or Dachau would remain ignorant: their "intellects" might admit the truth, but "their muscles do not believe."[99] As such phrasing suggests, Rousset's reimagining of the Nazi camp world as a kind of perverse pedagogical institution hinged on an insistence that survivors' expertise arose from bodily experiences unique to them: they had "known the humiliation of blows, the weakness of the body under the whip . . . the ravages of hunger." As a result, they were forever "set apart from others."[100] It was a gap that could not be bridged with words, however artfully marshaled.

Rather than bemoaning this fact, Rousset deployed it to make the case that survivors *themselves*, as a self-conscious category of subjects, had to participate in post-1945 French political life. It was "inadmissible, impossible, that we would purely and simply return to being the men that we were before," lectured Rousset, who originally planned to complete his oeuvre on the Nazi camps with a third volume, *Lazare ressuscité*, devoted to the choices confronted by returnees. Rather, "our role today . . . is to fight as representatives, as witnesses, against the alienation of man in all its facets." Deportees alone, cast by Rousset the lapsed Protestant as an elect, were equipped to lead this fight. "Although there are only a handful of you," he told an FNDIR audience in 1947, "you can be very powerful. In an extremely serious period not only for our own history but, more generally, for the history of our entire civilization, you can be the decisive agents who tip the balance of power in the direction of a struggle for the complete liberation of man, precisely because you have been, in the full sense of the term, slaves."[101] This political activity—not a recounting of past hardship for its own sake or a "working through" of individual trauma—was the real meaning of testimony. "It matters little that we have suffered," he wrote a year later. "It matters little that we say it. It matters infinitely that we explain the foundations of these sufferings and cry out as loudly as possible that they remain intact—and that there can be salvation for no one without their destruction."[102]

David Rousset's portrait of the camp "universe" and his conception of survivors as witnesses to a reproducible human disaster were exceptionally influential in postwar France, and beyond. Though the "massive, bulky, full-bodied" Rousset, with his "big round head," his "fleshy mouth," and his glass eye that "dragged upward," was no one's vision of a dashing clandestine militant, his postwar interventions marked him out nonetheless as a figurehead for the entire Resistance deportation.[103] His two landmark works of testimony captured the imagination of writers and intellectuals across the political spectrum, from Thierry Maulnier to Albert Béguin, Georges Bataille, Hannah Arendt, and Jean-Paul Sartre and Maurice Merleau-Ponty, who recognized Rousset's engagement with existential themes of choice and freedom and sought him out as a contributor for *Les Temps modernes*.[104] Rousset's work also became a touchstone in the literature of fellow survivors.[105] But if the author of *L'Univers concentrationnaire* was viewed as having produced "the fundamental document" on the camps, his was not the only means of framing survivors as experts whose voices were vital in the postwar public sphere.[106] From different intellectual and political starting points, other future CICRC members also arrived at this conclusion. Perhaps the most significant case is that of Germaine Tillion. Her emphasis on data contrasted with Rousset's more impressionistic, experimental attempts to capture the essence of the *univers concentrationnaire,* and she viewed testimony as reportage geared toward comprehension and justice rather than an act of prophecy or political combat. Ultimately, however, like Rousset, Tillion endorsed the notion that survivors possessed an expertise that others—what one deportee-reviewer of *Ravensbrück* called *"les profanes"*—could never acquire.[107] They therefore had a role to fill in the post-1945 world.

Tillion was already an accomplished ethnologist when she was deported in 1943 at age thirty-six, and her understanding of the role of "the witness" was mediated by her academic training in anthropology under Louis Massignon and Marcel Mauss as well as her fieldwork in Algeria in the 1930s.[108] She conceived of herself as a witness not only *after* Ravensbrück but *in* the camp—a professional witness, dedicated to recording (in hidden notes when possible, by memory when necessary) every detail of daily life, from guards' names to the workings of the infirmary to the number dead in each block. Tillion later claimed that this systematic fact-finding response on her part "took place automatically": to document the camp's horrors and its rulers' misdeeds was "instinctive" given her training, and moreover, in a situation of grotesque helplessness, "it was also a way of dominating! I look at you, I judge you, I weigh you, and you are, what are you? You're a minuscule flea that I study under the microscope."[109] To Tillion, knowledge painstakingly assembled, secretly logged, and conscientiously shared with fellow prisoners was power. Its preservation, moreover, enacted a duty toward a larger collective and an imagined future world: "It seemed certain to me, unfortunately, that very few of us would survive—but I conjectured that we would not all die, and I wanted to give Truth every possible chance to emerge from this well of desolation and crimes."[110]

As these comments suggest, Tillion, unlike Rousset, conceived of witnessing as a documentary practice, oriented toward the provision of information. This is not because she subscribed to a mindless empiricism: she actively defended the need for an "individual note" in camp testimony, "which in itself is of interest and perhaps must be respected."[111] However, Tillion believed that a comprehensive historical and moral understanding of Ravensbrück's significance, and of Nazi crime more broadly, could emerge only through methodical amassing of evidence. For her, data and details were tools with which she might make sense of the suffering she had endured—and, perhaps, seek justice for it. They also served a legitimating purpose: a hysterical victim's tale of woe might be disbelieved, but who could dispute the sterile authority of a mortality table? Thus, back in France in 1945, Tillion threw herself into the hunt for further "verified facts" about German crimes through the Commission on the History of the Deportation and the Internment and began writing her contribution to *Ravensbrück*, tellingly titled "À la recherche de la vérité" (In search of the truth).[112]

This essay—while not impersonal, and indeed quite moving in its outrage—essentially constituted a scholar's study of "the camp" as an institution. It overflowed with names and numbers (within a "margin of error"); with dates; with budgets and calculations; with charts and chronologies; with fastidiously cross-checked lists.[113] Like Rousset, Tillion was interested in the internal hierarchies of camp "society," and much of "À la recherche" was devoted to intricate discussion of the pecking orders (and death rates) of different national groups in Ravensbrück. She had a great deal to say, as well, about distinctions between common-law criminals, racial deportees, and political prisoners (this latter group disaggregated into "authentic Resisters" and "dead weight").[114] But in contrast to *L'Univers concentrationnaire* and *Les Jours de notre mort*, "À la recherche" did not ride into battle under the absurdist banner of Jarry's King Ubu: Tillion deployed her figures and tables to insist that the system possessed a *rational* meaning, one that had little to do with expiation and everything to do with money.

It is striking that among the future leaders of the CICRC, it was the Gaullist patriot, not the Marxist antifascist, who insisted that the camps be interpreted as economic institutions. Rousset, like other French leftists, diagnosed the rise of Nazism as the result of a crisis of capitalism and emphasized forced labor as a standard, global feature of the camps. He maintained, however, that inmates' work was "intended as a means of punishment. Using *concentrationnaires* as a labor force is of secondary interest; it is a preoccupation that is foreign to the true nature of the concentrationary universe."[115] Tillion's account was different. According to *Ravensbrück*, the "originality" of Nazi atrocity lay not in the fact of mass killing but in "organizing this extermination in such a way that, instead of being costly to the exterminators, on the contrary it brought them considerable profits."[116] Sadism, she conceded, "also had its place in all this," but it was only "thrown into the bargain."[117] More essential was that "the Ravensbrück business remain prosperous."[118] Tillion, who distinguished clearly between "work camps" and "extermination camps" and who understood that the latter had primarily targeted Jews, nevertheless maintained that all "were built on the same principle": the gassing operations at Auschwitz-Birkenau, in her estimation, constituted "a commercial business that was not in the red."[119] Her insistence that a calculating heart of instrumental reason beat within the Nazi beast allowed her to grant intelligible import to what she had endured in the camps, and to fashion her testimony into a chilly indictment of cold-blooded crime rather than a wail of anguish.

This prosecutorial orientation toward witnessing governed "À la recherche," which—unlike most survivor memoirs—dwelt extensively on SS officialdom and especially on Heinrich Himmler's personal responsibility for (and profit from) the camps. It came through still more clearly in the reports Tillion dispatched to ADIR's newsletter *Voix et Visages* from the 1946–1947 Ravensbrück war crimes trial in Hamburg, conducted by a British military tribunal. These texts operated within multiple logics of "testimony": first, Tillion understood her own unflinching presence in the courtroom, while her former tormentors were tried, as an act of bearing witness; second, the reports themselves were crafted as "eyewitness" statements on the proceedings, as Tillion attempted to provide her comrades with a minutely faithful account; third, after the verdicts were handed down—eleven death sentences, but also four prison terms—Tillion offered an impassioned argument about the importance of the survivor-as-witness for the execution of justice.[120]

This last point was not an obvious one to make in 1947. Victim testimony played a strikingly minor role in post–World War II war crimes proceedings; Nuremberg and the subsequent trials were simply not conceived as a forum for camp survivors to tell others about their suffering. Indeed, prosecutors feared that their "strong bias against the Hitler regime" could taint the entire undertaking.[121] At the International Military Tribunal, the French and the Soviets did call a few primarily non-Jewish returned deportees—including Balachowsky—to testify to specific acts of Nazi criminality; the British and the Americans, however, pursuing a strategy of "trial by document," did not. Survivor statements were a more prominent feature of subsidiary trials focused on the personnel of camps such Ravensbrück, since they were relevant to assessing the actions of individual defendants; thus a handful of former inmates, including Frenchwoman Irène Ottelard, served as witnesses for the prosecution in Hamburg. But their voices enjoyed no privileged status, and, indeed, they were often treated with suspicion.

Tillion placed this fact at the center of her indignant summing-up of the trial. The single most important defect of the Hamburg proceeding, she wrote, was that "against many of the accused, *there was not a single prosecution witness.*" She did not suggest that survivors should have been given a greater role as an outlet for their pain; rather, she insisted that they alone possessed the *knowledge* that could have allowed the judges to reach appropriate verdicts. Warden Margarete Mewes, for example, was sentenced to only ten years because she appeared innocent of direct participation in murder; survivors' July 1945 depositions against her to France's Service de Recherche des Crimes de Guerre Ennemis, accusing her of personally administering poison to eleven inmates, were somehow absent from the prosecution's dossier. This was, Tillion wrote, an "incredible act of negligence, but one that nevertheless could have been repaired, for if I had been able to see the dossier upon my arrival in Hamburg . . . I would have immediately noticed the absence of the Mewes document, which I had a copy of in my luggage," and the appropriate victim-witnesses could have been called to the stand.[122]

Survivors also possessed other, less concrete forms of knowledge that the prosecutors and judges, according to Tillion, could not access. They alone understood the inadequacy of ordinary conceptions of justice in the face of the enormity of Nazi crimes; they alone glimpsed that the putatively "representative" sample of atrocity that could be discussed within the constraints of time and space governing a courtroom was not really representative at all: "It is false," she insisted, "that through ten crimes, one can understand a hundred thousand."[123] In 1947, this realization led Tillion—already in her "very deep blackness"—to near-despair. In an article that, devastatingly, appeared in *Voix et Visages* next to her mother's obituary, she railed at the unbridgeable chasm that separated the court's officers from the women of Ravensbrück. Listening to a defense attorney challenging Ottelard's veracity as an eyewitness (particularly excruciating because Ottelard was now physically blind as a result of medical negligence in the camp), "one feels alone, and one has a heavy heart. . . . We ought to have died, and we are alive. What are we complaining about?"[124]

In the end, however, the disappointment of formal international legal processes did not leave Tillion with a sense of helplessness. Instead, it imbued her with the conviction that she and her fellow survivors "alone in the world" possessed the ability to carry out a genuine "confrontation . . . between the crime and its reparation, between the violation of justice and its reestablishment."[125] Others, even acting in good faith, were not capable of this. After all, before being deported, she herself had been unable to comprehend the true depths of Nazi depravity from written reports: "I had to see with my own eyes," she wrote in *Ravensbrück*, "how far the cruelty of some and the cowardice of others could go to understand their reality definitively."[126] Now, once again, she employed an idiom of ocular witnessing and bodily experience as a privileged path to truth: only those who had "seen with our eyes" and "weighed and measured with our suffering" the camp's "monstrosities" could fully grasp what justice required.[127] We will see later how this conviction informed the CICRC's entire project, and in particular the eventual decision to rely almost entirely on victim testimony in the 1951 "trial" of the Soviet gulag. In 1947, that work was still far off; Tillion remained single-mindedly focused on the continued task of bearing witness to Nazi crimes. Despite the shortcomings of Hamburg, she vowed, "All that can be done for truth, for justice, we will do it." This would entail difficulties, frustrations, and failures. But in the final words of a public letter to her ADIR comrades,

Tillion shrugged: "*eh bien*, that's the ransom for life. We are alive, too bad for us."[128]

While Tillion was reporting from Hamburg, Louis Martin-Chauffier was dividing his time between Paris and the remote Île aux Moines, located in the Gulf of Morbihan in his beloved Brittany. The frail writer's range of activities in 1945, 1946, and 1947 would have been astonishing even for a man in perfect health: he sat in the Provisional Consultative Assembly in the summer of 1945; joined the Commission on the History of the Deportation and the Internment that fall; became president of the National Committee of Writers in 1946; wrote regularly for the major national papers *Le Figaro* and *Libération* in addition to contributing articles to journals such as *Les Lettres françaises* and *Le Patriote résistant*; co-authored the 1947 book *L'Heure de la choix* on France and the emerging Cold War; and spoke widely to domestic and international audiences about the Nazi camps. His major work of postwar testimony, however, was the 1947 memoir *L'Homme et la bête*. This book shared Tillion's insistence that the "*crime majeur* of Hitlerism" was the concentration camp as such, not genocidal extermination (the sole identifiably Jewish figure in its pages, appearing in a single sentence, is a political deportee).[129] In other respects, however, a more different work from Tillion's "À la recherche" can scarcely be imagined. Where her conception of witnessing was infused with anthropological influences, Martin-Chauffier approached the task of "testifying" as a Christian. Where Tillion produced facts and figures that might establish the contours of Nazi atrocity and thus function as a *j'accuse* against its perpetrators, Martin-Chauffier bore witness to the experiential texture of human suffering in the camps—and to the mysterious forces by which, he estimated, roughly "one man in twenty was successful in holding on to his humanity."[130]

*L'Homme et la bête* was structured as a narrative of Martin-Chauffier's procession through the Stations of the Cross—or, rather, his precipitous descent into hell. From Montluc prison and the Compiègne internment camp in "Book I" to Neuengamme in "Book II" and finally Bergen-Belsen in a brief, nightmarish "Book III," Martin-Chauffier spoke to readers in the intimate, first-person singular voice of an individual man—weak in body, little inclined to love his fellow man, wavering in faith—trapped in desperate circumstances. (One exception comes when Martin-Chauffier marks the arrival at Neuengamme, where "we were nothing anymore except anonymous heads of cattle," by temporarily adopting choral narration.)[131] The book chiefly testified to its author's own calvary of relentless bodily and psychic suffering and his concomitant spiritual journey as a Catholic—it functioned as a martyrology, bearing witness not to the particulars of Nazi atrocity but to the power of God's grace. Remarkably, given this premise, Martin-Chauffier managed to sidestep sentimentality or smugness. This is because he depicted his own dry, "detached" character in clear-eyed and unflattering prose; *L'Homme et la bête* never hinted that Martin-Chauffier's own unlikely survival had somehow been merited by saintly behavior, nor that faith in God had permitted him to adore his fellow man even in the pits of hell.[132] He flatly rejected any Christian claim for "pity" or love toward his tormentors. As he remarked while demanding death sentences for the Nuremberg defendants in 1946, "Charity does its work after justice has established the natural distinctions. It is permissible to pray for them, but not to demand that they be pardoned."[133]

*L'Homme et la bête* also avoided offering a pat religious interpretation of Neuengamme because Martin-Chauffier insisted throughout that members of *two* groups had possessed the psychic resources to resist dehumanization: the Catholics and their most godless counterparts, the communists. Adherents to these two creeds had in common a sense of solidarity "that the Communists called collectivism, the Christians communion of the living"; moreover, they all possessed some variety of faith and thus "were protected against the temptations of despondency by the feeling of a time beyond themselves, which would perpetuate them."[134] *L'Homme et la bête* was published in late 1947, as the Cold War intensified. Thus, in a France where Communist Party members had been expelled from the government, had directed massive (and massively repressed) strike waves that threatened to halt industrial recovery, and stood accused by many political leaders, including Christian democrats, of attempting to foment civil war, Martin-Chauffier wrote pointedly about the ways in which Catholics and communists had helped one another in Neuengamme. He noted that he, personally, survived only thanks to intercessions on the part of Communist Party inmates: "As for me, I owed my life . . . to the initiative of my communist friend, Professor [Marcel] Prenant, who, seeing me waste away in the cellar where the weaving Kommando had been cooped up for the winter, managed—thanks to another communist, André—. . . to get me named a kitchen maid for the SS."[135] Through such statements, *L'Homme et la bête* also "bore witness" in an explicitly political vein, affirming—in the face of growing evidence to the contrary—the possibility for postwar "dialogue" among French people of varying political persuasions.[136]

As this discussion suggests, Martin-Chauffier's depiction of the Nazi camps—like all testimony—was not a pure, unmediated distillation of experience but rather an account shaped by ongoing events. Stories like *L'Homme et la bête* about what had happened to Frenchmen in the camps were molded by the fact that they were told *in*, *to*, and *for* postwar France. Martin-Chauffier did not directly acknowledge this: he had nothing to say about the lability of memory, the subjective nature of "truth," or the irresolvable tensions inherent in the project of testimony. Nor did his authorial voice situate him in a specific postwar moment. (*L'Homme et la bête* makes no explicit reference to any occurrence after May 1945.) Indirectly, however, the relationship between the traumatic past and the fraught, uncertain present was the real subject of the book. Still more insistently than his secular counterparts, Martin-Chauffier suggested that his suffering in the *univers concentrationnaire* had been meaningful because it had imparted lessons of abiding value: camp survivors "had seen what man is capable of," for better and for worse.[137] This knowledge was the "fruit of . . . experience" and hence inaccessible to others: "How," he asked, "would one bear witness when one had not suffered?"[138] Therefore, even as he languished close to death in the Neuengamme infirmary, "I thought about the return, about the tasks that awaited me . . . [and] about the means by which to prove equal to them. It mattered little that this return remained highly uncertain. If it took place, I had to be ready."[139]

This passage, written in 1947, is best read not as a faithful transcription of Martin-Chauffier's actual internal monologue in the sick bay two and a half years earlier, but rather as a postwar articulation of a distinctive political and ethical identity for the survivor-as-witness. The idiom in which the Catholic author laid claim to this identity was that of duty; a "deliberate entry into service" for Christ was required in exchange for "this surplus of life that [was] miraculously granted to us," he wrote.[140] A debt was owed to the camp's dead, as well: in a speech to fellow Bergen-Belsen deportees in April 1947, Martin-Chauffier suggested that those who had survived now stood as permanent envoys—"*chargés de mission*"— for their fallen brethren.[141] But behind his humble language of "solemn obliga- tions" and "fatal vocation" also lurked an exalted sense of purpose.[142] For those who had lived to be liberated, wrote Martin-Chauffier, there could now be "no question of peacefully pursuing a private career," nor of "moving along toward a calm old age." Like it or not, survivors had a role to play as *engagés* in post- war political struggles.[143] They alone, having withstood history's most concerted effort to destroy it, could best defend "the dignity of man."[144]

It was this insistence on an ongoing, public identity for survivors as combat- ants on behalf of universal values that would eventually draw Martin-Chauffier to the CICRC. His mystical understanding of the "lessons" of the camps cer- tainly differed from that of his secular counterparts (particularly Rousset, who was reproached by Catholic reviewers for the "lack of spirituality" in his testi- mony).[145] So, too, did Martin-Chauffier's approach to "witnessing" as a spiritual act, closely tied to martyrdom.[146] But, in the end, he shared with Rousset and Til- lion the fundamental belief that traumatic experience had set a handful of men and women apart from all others. The only question now was what, in concrete terms, these Lazarus-like figures ought to do with their terrible knowledge of the *univers concentrationnaire*.

The CICRC did not come into being until 1950. By late 1947, though, the base- line intellectual conditions for its emergence were already in place among future members: first, a conception of Nazi atrocity centered on "the concentrationary universe" (not the death camp or the mass grave) and the extreme abasement of man as such (not genocide); second, an understanding of survivors as witnesses to a potentially replicable form of human suffering. These convictions would eventually allow the CICRC to launch its crusade against the gulag, and to make the case that, from a victim's perspective, the Nazi and Soviet camp systems were indistinguishable. This chapter has dwelt on the immediate postwar moment—the era of "the return"—in order to make clear that future CICRC members did not instrumentally craft their narratives about Nazi violence and survivorship in anticipation of this eventuality. Their attempts to fashion a postwar identity imbued with the authority of experience had more to do with recuperating meaning from otherwise senseless agony than with presciently positioning themselves to later pursue an antitotalitarian political agenda. And their insistence that Hitler's *crime majeur* was "the camps" rather than the Shoah was certainly not a calculating bid to pick the "right atrocity" with which to better equate German and Soviet evil.[147] Though their postwar testimony was often geared toward political ends, those ends were rarely anticommunist; in fact, as in Martin-Chauffier's insistence on "dialogue" or Rousset's defense of *kommando* selection procedures in Buchenwald, they are usually better described in the opposite terms.

This point is driven home by a glance at the acclaim that greeted future CICRC members' immediate postwar publications on the far left. The clearest and also the most significant case in point is Rousset's 1946 *L'Univers concentrationnaire*, which communist and *communisant* readers embraced despite their distaste for his Trotskyism (or, rather, as we will see in the following chapter, his very recent ex-Trotskyism). The president of the FNDIRP, a fellow-traveler and Buchenwald survivor named Henri Manhès who would later accuse Rousset of unspeakable crimes, wrote to him in 1946 with congratulations for having produced "the only book up to now, among all those published, that understood how to provide the atmosphere of the Camps."[148] This was "an essential book," Louis Parrot asserted in the party-controlled intellectual journal *Les Lettres françaises*.[149] Reviewer Pierre Fauchery wrote in the communist weekly *Action* that "No other testimony gives us a comparable impression of understanding this inconceivable universe." Fauchery, like others, specifically celebrated Rousset's assertions regarding the potential imitability of the Nazi project: "Let us never forget," he wrote, "that this universe was nearly ours, and its possibilities still circle insidiously near to us."[150] Neither he nor other left-wing reviewers were concerned in 1946 that the concept of the concentrationary realm could later be weaponized against the USSR. Nor, it is worth underlining, did Jewish readers (or anyone else) accuse Rousset of strategically minimizing the suffering of "racial" deportees in order to present "the camp" as a universalizable phenomenon. On the contrary, what little Jewish criticism of Rousset's work did emerge by the end of 1947 charged that it *overplayed* racial persecution and insufficiently highlighted Jews' involvement in Resistance activities.[151] Most Jewish authors greeted his books with praise, and unhesitatingly adopted his language. "For us, many of whom wandered in the *univers concentrationnaire*," explained Bernard Lecache, ". . . M. David Rousset has relieved us of a great weight" by unveiling the camp system in all its "atrocious authenticity."[152]

Interestingly, one reviewer in 1946 did already recognize the potential of "David Rousset's word" to serve as the conceptual basis for an attack on the USSR. This was the Catholic writer Pierre-Henri Simon, who wrote in *L'Aube* in July that "the concentrationary age has not passed with the cyanide pill or the slipknot for the Nazi assassins: it goes on, it promises us other spectacles." Simon—later an important opponent of torture in Algeria—did refer to the abuse of prisoners "even in our own country" as evidence for his claim. But his primary concern was for "these Balts, these Ukrainians, these Poles absorbed in the shadowy immensities of the East." "I wish I could be certain," he wrote, "that at the hour I write there are not hundreds of thousands of human beings—men, women, and children mixed together—who reach out their bowls for vile soup, subjected to the labor of slaves. . . . Alas! I have too many reasons to believe the contrary!"[153] Rousset kept a clipping of Simon's article, as he did of many reviews of his books, but there is no evidence it left any particular impression on him. His own articulation of "the concentrationary" as an anti-Soviet tool was still years away.[154] When it arrived, it would be exponentially more explosive than Simon's 1946 version. This was not only because global Cold War hostilities and domestic French tensions over communism would heighten so dramatically between 1946 and 1949. It was also because Rousset would be able to speak with the established authority of the camp survivor, the "witness before other men."

# DAVID ROUSSET'S COLD WAR CALL TO ARMS

On November 12, 1949, David Rousset issued his "Appeal" to fellow deportees demanding that they investigate the USSR's "concentrationary universe." Even among survivors, he was hardly the first to propose similarities between Hitler's and Stalin's camps. But then, the outsize effects of certain texts—their transcendent status as "events" in modern history—is not a simple function of original position taking: Émile Zola's 1898 "*J'accuse!*"—to give the most evident example—was far from the first piece of writing to insist on Alfred Dreyfus's innocence. The landmark status of Rousset's "Appeal," much like that of Zola's broadside a half century earlier, arose from the intellectual and political environment in which it appeared, the identity of its author, the chain of reactions and consequences it unleashed, and—most of all—the authoritative idiom in which it was crafted.

First off, the "Appeal" ignited a firestorm because it landed in a tinderbox: France by late 1949 was crackling with Cold War tensions. Debates about Stalin's aims and policies were not new among French intellectuals and political elites, but the pre-1939 Parti Communiste Français (PCF) had been a marginal force compared to the "party of 75,000 executed" that, thanks in part to its impressive overrepresentation in the Resistance and the Resistance deportation, emerged from World War II commanding the country's single largest share of votes. Still more importantly, US-Soviet tensions polarized the French political landscape after 1947. As the Cold War's early milestone events unfolded—the creation of Cominform, the Prague coup, the Berlin blockade, the founding of NATO, Germany's partition—the question of how France could choose or maneuver between the two blocs loomed large. In addressing it, the country underwent a series of spectacular controversies concerning Stalinist state violence.

The "Rousset Affair" proved the most spectacular of them all, in part because of the reputation of the man who launched it. Rousset issued his "Appeal" not only as France's most prominent voice of literary witness to the deportation, but also as an intellectual who moved in formidable leftist company. After a break with the Trotskyist party in 1946, occasioned—as we will see—by his desire for closer cooperation with the "Stalinists," he collaborated on various projects with prominent left-wing intellectuals, activists, and journals, entered into talks with the communist-supported Cooperative Générale du Cinéma Français for a film version of *Les Jours de notre mort* (Louis Daquin was to direct, but the project never came to fruition), and drew closer to *Les Temps modernes* editors Maurice Merleau-Ponty and Jean-Paul Sartre. In 1948, he, Sartre, and several other non-communist leftists founded the Rassemblement Démocratique Révolutionnaire (RDR), an "assembly of free men for revolutionary democracy" that attempted to reject "capitalist barbarism" while also resisting alignment with the Soviet Union.[1] The RDR had collapsed by the time the "Appeal" came about, but Rousset's reputation was still that of a Marxist militant—France's "principal Marxist witness" to fascist atrocity—and his name remained tied to Sartre's.[2] US and British Cold War propagandists, having so far identified mostly "right-wing deadbeats, Catholics, Gaullists, and smalltimers" to spread their message in France, could scarcely believe their good fortune when they saw Rousset's byline.[3]

Their satisfaction only grew over the following months as the "Appeal" set off a French polemic about the USSR's *univers concentrationnaire*. The text was shouted about on Parisian street corners and on the floor of the National Assembly; it was the subject of diatribes in neighborhood circulars, full-page cartoons in mass-circulation dailies, and intellectual treatises in highbrow journals. Sartre wrote about the "Appeal" on no fewer than four occasions between 1950 and 1961. Rousset also compelled the most visible representatives of France's deportee community to weigh in. One result was a schism in the Fédération Nationale des Déportés et Internés Résistants et Patriotes, as noncommunists resigned en masse. Another was a flurry of individual responses from a virtual who's who of survivor writers and intellectuals. Most notably, Pierre Daix, a communist Resistance hero and Mauthausen deportee, denounced Rousset's project as "a new ideological basis for the mobilization of peoples to continue Hitler's war" and asserted that the evidence in the "Appeal" was fabricated.[4] This contention gave Rousset a pretext to continue his public relations battle against the PCF: he sued Daix and his editor for defamation, triggering a media extravaganza.

The resonance of the "Appeal"—positive and negative—did not result only from Rousset's fame and the tense Cold War climate in France. It was also a product of the rhetorical force of the text, which has gone unanalyzed even by those who have most strenuously applauded it as a testament to its author's intellectual responsibility. The document was fashioned as a manifesto on the dictates of memory. In excruciatingly sensory language—the feeling of feet slowly freezing, the "stink of men dying in their own excrement"—it made the case that other victims were now experiencing a "hallucinatory repetition" of the same suffering that Nazi camp inmates had undergone.[5] Rousset deployed the singular figure of the *homme concentrationnaire* to argue that the gulag was not merely similar to the German "camp universe" but an extension of it. From this premise, he articulated a gut-wrenching call for former deportees to bear witness, insisting that traumatic memory could serve as the guide to politico-ethical judgment in the present—that, indeed, it provided the only reliable compass with which to navigate the bewildering Cold War world. The "Appeal" not only played heavily on survivors' guilt-laden sense of duty; it also exalted their status as purveyors of prophetic testimony, "specialists" who possessed knowledge that other men lacked. The contention that camp returnees were now expert in the mechanisms of dehumanization had been central to Rousset's writings since 1945; the "Appeal" gained its power by marrying this nebulous notion to a concrete project, a clear-cut crusade.

Implicitly—and this was what so perturbed Sartre—the "Appeal" used the figure of the survivor-witness to model a new, postrevolutionary vision of mankind's responsibility in the face of distant suffering. Sartre and Merleau-Ponty approached the text as an anti-Soviet screed, to be sure, but they also understood it—correctly—as a manifesto on the changed conditions of possibility for political action in a world haunted by the camps. As 1949 dawned, Theodor Adorno penned his now-famous statement that "to write poetry after Auschwitz is barbaric."[6] Months later, Rousset seemed to be insisting that to practice revolutionary politics after Buchenwald was impossible. Hence the urgency with which even non-survivors felt moved to embrace or denounce his plea.

Rousset's explicit message, however, was unmistakably addressed to members of the actual survivor community, and in the long run its most important sequel was the formation within that community of the Commission Internationale contre le Régime Concentrationnaire. What is more, the internal tensions that colored Rousset's manifesto—which was, at once, both a moving act of testimony on behalf of sufferers and a shrewd political intervention—presaged those that would beset the CICRC throughout its existence. This chapter therefore takes the "Appeal" as its subject, situating the call to arms first within Rousset's own intellectual biography, and second within the debates over memory and judgment, ethics and politics, survival and responsibility, to which its publication gave rise.

# Free Men for Revolutionary Democracy

Rousset's path to the "Appeal" was a winding one. When the text appeared, many of the communists who denounced it emphasized the author's Trotskyist affiliations, asserting that it was a predictably vile attack on Stalin from a follower of his erstwhile foe. In fact, however, Rousset's political evolution in the four years following his early 1946 departure from the postwar French section of the Trotskyist Fourth International, the Parti Communiste Internationaliste (PCI), better explains his decision to attack the Soviet "concentrationary universe" than do his earlier ideological commitments.[7] The "Appeal" was not a crypto-Trotskyist document but rather the fruit of its author's disillusionment with radical politics in the Cold War era, as once-heralded avenues of utopian possibility were closed off one by one.

Rousset broke with the small, fractious PCI when a late-1945 document he drafted, "Propositions for a New Appreciation of the International Situation," was unanimously rejected by his comrades. The "Propositions" advocated a "revision" of the Trotskyists' hostile stance toward the USSR, arguing that the radical break in history marked by World War II made clear the need to "silence some of our disagreements with Stalinism, and to do so deliberately and fundamentally." Influenced by his admiration for German communists in Neuengamme, and believing that the invention of concentrationary means of dehumanization signaled the need to rethink prewar political categories, Rousset proposed that "the Stalinist bureaucracy, with all its flaws, with its conservative and reactionary mentality, nevertheless represents one of the decisive bastions of socialist revolution in the world today."[8] For his espousal of this "criminal and dangerous position," the PCI's Central Committee demanded Rousset be excluded from the party; he left in early 1946 "in the face of general reprobation and very pronounced hostility."[9]

After his break with the PCI, Rousset continued to advocate for revolutionary socialism. Capitalism, he asserted, "is decomposing and rotting."[10] However, he never returned to the pro-Soviet stance of the "Propositions." Rather, as the Cold War hardened, he grew adamant that Europe had to locate a path forward that rejected alignment with either bloc. Rousset was insistent that, in France, this path could not be forged by any existing political formation—not the Socialist Party ("the incarnation of impotency") and certainly not the Gaullists, whom he viewed as authoritarian.[11] Hence, as literary success propelled him into elevated circles, the author of *L'Univers concentrationnaire* and *Les Jours de notre mort* oriented his exchanges with new interlocutors, especially Sartre, around the quest to inaugurate a new revolutionary politics.

The result was the RDR, launched in February 1948. Its founding statement, signed by Rousset, Sartre, and other assorted noncommunist intellectuals of the left, averred that "between the putrefactions of capitalist democracy, the weaknesses and flaws of a certain social democracy, and the limitations of communism in its Stalinist form, we think that an assembly of free men for revolutionary democracy is capable of lending new life to the principles of freedom and human dignity by tying them to the struggle for social revolution."[12] The "assembly" was not a party, its leaders stressed; communists, socialists, and Trotskyists could join without abandoning their current affiliations. Nevertheless, it possessed a "Program" (written by Rousset), a fortnightly paper (*La Gauche*), central offices, an enthusiastic corps of militants, and even an anthem.[13] The RDR's early meetings were well-attended; for a time, Rousset's exuberant demand for fifty thousand members by the summer of 1948 appeared realistic. He threw himself into the endeavor of attracting them, understanding that his presence was key to the group's cachet. At one early meeting, reported *Le Monde*, Sartre "was applauded, but much less than M. David Rousset."[14]

The body of political exegesis that Rousset produced in the service of the RDR over the course of 1948—including two lengthy conversations he held with Sartre and ex-Trotskyist lawyer Gérard Rosenthal, transcribed and published by Gallimard as *Entretiens sur la politique*—constituted an attempt to give content to the organization's "revolutionary" politics. Rousset insisted that "capitalism no longer has a future" in Europe, and his positions on domestic social conflict as well as colonialism were uncompromisingly leftist—and indistinct from Sartre's. He supported the massive 1948 French miners' strike "without reserve" despite the PCF's leadership, for instance, and called for "granting the peoples of [France's] overseas territories the right to independence."[15] However, Rousset also condemned the USSR and French "Stalinists," particularly as it became evident that the PCF would never permit its members to join the Rassemblement. His attacks on Soviet communism were made in the name of socialism and couched in a Trotskyist rhetoric focused on the USSR's tentacular bureaucracy: the country, Rousset wrote, was home to "forms of exploitation often more ferocious than those of capitalism," oppressing ordinary workers for the benefit of a privileged ruling class.[16] He would not engage in "imbecilic anti-Soviet demagoguery," he told Sartre, but neither did he believe that such a system "could enable—even in the very distant future, even very indirectly—the preparation of a future liberation" of mankind from its chains.[17]

Rousset's critical analysis of the USSR was at this juncture voiced from the position of a leftist intellectual, not a Buchenwald survivor; an uninformed reader of *Entretiens sur la politique* would have been incapable of guessing which participant had once been a camp inmate. Meanwhile, his contributions to *La*

*Gauche* positioned him more consistently as a former resister than as a former deportee. Nevertheless, as the months passed, Rousset did begin to suggest—at first without reference to his own experience—that the Soviet Union was economically reliant on unfree "forced labor." By August 1948, he used a more explosive term: Stalin, he suggested, was employing "concentration camps."[18]

This accusation was not novel in the France of the late 1940s. Historians have long underlined the French left's attraction to Stalinism, portraying a postwar intellectual arena dominated by figures who were willfully blind to Soviet crimes.[19] While this evaluation does have some basis in reality—hence Rousset's genuine daring in publishing his "Appeal"—it has created the misleading impression of a decades-long French reign of silence about the Soviet camps broken only with the 1974 publication of Aleksandr Solzhenitsyn's *Gulag Archipelago*.[20] In fact, discussion of forced labor in the USSR was commonplace in France from the 1930s on, and information about Stalinist internment practices abounded. By the time Rousset invoked the problem, he joined a cacophony of voices: Albert Camus insisted on the existence of Soviet "concentration camps" and the "utilization of political deportees as laborers" in multiple venues (including *La Gauche*) in 1948; Michel Riquet regularly editorialized in a Christian vein against the USSR's "concentrationary regime"; and the topic had even been broached in the pages of *Les Temps modernes*.[21] Perhaps most importantly, 1947 saw the French-language publication of Soviet defector Victor Kravchenko's *I Chose Freedom* (*J'ai choisi la liberté*), a damning "insider" account of the Stalinist system of governance. The book attested to a variety of horrors, among them "the pervasive presence of prisoners, concentration camps, and forced labor colonies."[22] Its sensational claims and commanding first-person voice transfixed French readers, including Simone de Beauvoir, who urged Sartre to print excerpts.[23]

*I Chose Freedom* was, in truth, ghostwritten by American journalist Eugene Lyons and shepherded into print as part of a concerted US propaganda effort. The book's emphasis on Soviet "slavery," in particular, dovetailed with a campaign launched in March 1947 by the American Federation of Labor's semi-autonomous foreign policy group, the Free Trade Union Committee (FTUC).[24] Founded in 1944, the FTUC was chaired by Jay Lovestone, an "inveterate schemer" whose missionary anti-Stalinism after quitting the Communist Party offers a textbook example of convert's zeal.[25] Under his leadership, the FTUC decided upon a crusade against "slave labor" in the Soviet Union, conceptualized as a violation of workers' "basic human rights."[26] The project started with a March 1947 "Manifesto against Slave Labor" in the *International Free Trade Union News*; the following year the AFL and its member unions began lobbying for the United Nations Economic and Social Council to investigate "forced labor" systems around the world. Both US and British government agents eventually jumped in on the act, with the British Foreign Office's new propaganda arm, the Information Research Department (IRD), proving particularly energetic. IRD representatives, for example, hit upon the idea of introducing damning passages from the USSR's own Labor Codex into evidence at the UN.[27]

American and British campaigners against Soviet "forced labor" employed a more flexible rhetoric than that in which Rousset's "Appeal" would eventually be voiced. Their belief that forced labor was "the most effective anti-Communist publicity theme" was based not on a conviction that tales of interned, under-fed work crews would directly resonate with memories of Nazi atrocity but on a general sense that they would "disturb organised labour and all progressive and humanitarian opinion."[28] Thus although these cold warriors did some-times invoke Nazi camps, this was hardly their singular point of reference. At the United Nations and elsewhere, American speakers favored unflattering com-parisons to chattel slavery in the antebellum US over parallels to recent German practices.[29] For its part, the IRD drew associations with "Pharaonic times when slave labor was used in the building of the great pyramids and other construc-tional operations."[30] Former Mensheviks in the US such as David Dallin and Boris Nicolaevsky, meanwhile, situated Soviet "slavery" in relation to myriad practices that "appeared at different junctures of history, at various stages of civi-lization, under the most diverse political and economic systems," from ancient Athens onward. Their 1947 *Forced Labor in Soviet Russia* (translated into French in 1949) did identify Nazi Germany as one purveyor of the "slave system," but because Dallin and Nicolaevsky viewed Hitler's great crime as genocide—their synecdoche for Nazi evil was "the ovens of Maidenek," not the work battalions of Buchenwald—the point was incidental to their overall historical argument.[31]

Comparison between Hitler's and Stalin's internment facilities also func-tioned as only a minor element in the most important indictment of Soviet state violence to take place on French soil before Rousset's "Appeal": a 1949 libel suit brought by Victor Kravchenko against the communist literary review *Les Lettres françaises*. The trial came about when PCF supporter André Ulmann (writing in the journal under a pseudonym) charged that *I Chose Liberty* was a fabrica-tion of American Secret Service agents. Although the accusation was, as Irwin M. Wall puts it, "at least a half-truth," Kravchenko sued *Les Lettres françaises*.[32] The ensuing court case was an epic circus of political pageantry, involving over a hundred witnesses—some Soviet subjects, some prominent French communists and fellow-travelers—and was exploited for propaganda by both the party and its foes.[33] As the proceedings stretched from January into March, participants evoked a plethora of Soviet sins: the terror with which agricultural collectiviza-tion had been imposed and the famine it had subsequently produced, the tor-tures employed by the secret police, the ignominy of the Molotov-Ribbentrop

Pact, the penury of ordinary workers, the persecution of Christians, and so on. Kravchenko's own favored vocabulary for discussing his homeland was generic: he peppered his speeches in court with references to "tyranny," "oppression," "dictatorship," and also "barbary," but not with parallels to Hitlerian violence.[34]

The Kravchenko case was not, in other words, a trial firmly centered on the problem of "concentration camps," much less on comparison between the Nazi and Soviet versions of such institutions. But David Rousset cannot have failed to notice that it was in the rare moments when such comparisons *were* invoked that French public opinion was most moved by the proceedings. Most important by far in this regard was the testimony of Margarete Buber-Neumann, a communist who fled Nazi Germany for the USSR in 1933 and subsequently survived imprisonment first in Karaganda and then, after Stalin's handover of German communists to Hitler, in Ravensbrück. One month into the trial, she insisted to the court that a camp archipelago just like Hitler's blighted the Soviet landscape. As Albert Béguin wrote, her words cut through the "judicial buffoonery" of the event as a whole. Like many left-leaning intellectuals, Béguin was contemptuous of Kravchenko as an individual: trailed by a whiff of treason and possessed of a sordid personal life, he was easy to dismiss as a charlatan. But Buber-Neumann was not. When she spoke, Béguin wrote, "the comedy was interrupted. . . . The tone of truth imposed itself. And a testimony that obeyed no propaganda was suddenly welcomed in the silence of an instant, shielded from the racket and the antagonistic impostures."[35]

As multiple observers then and since have noted, Buber-Neumann's "testimony that obeyed no propaganda" constituted the most effective propaganda of the entire Kravchenko trial.[36] Rousset, for one, declared himself inspired by its "extraordinary impact."[37] And by the spring of 1949, he was ripe for such inspiration. His political orientation was evolving toward outright anticommunism, animated by a growing conviction that the Soviet Union contained a vast system of "concentration camps." Ian Birchall dates Rousset's "clear shift" toward Cold War alignment against the USSR to a January 1949 trip to the US, but in fact it was already evident in his writings earlier. By late 1948, he had begun not only to attack the Soviet gulag but to do so in the voice of a former Nazi camp deportee.[38] "I turn toward many of my friends who are still in the Communist party and were deported with me," he wrote that December. "I say to them: How can you accept . . . the existence of concentration camps in the Soviet Union?"[39]

By this point, as Cold War tensions continued to build, the RDR's guiding premise of siding with "neither Washington nor Moscow" was becoming untenable. Indeed, weakened by the hostility of the parties, the organization was dying. Its last hurrah, for all intents and purposes, was an April 30, 1949, "International Day of Resistance to Dictatorship and War" in Paris. American intelligence services covertly funded the participation of American, German, and Italian delegations, believing the mass gathering would serve as a powerful counter to the May Day rallies of the Communist "peace movement." To their disappointment, it was instead—according to Irving Brown, Lovestone's point man in Western Europe—"as near to a fiasco as possible."[40] Sartre, wary of Rousset's increasingly evident anticommunism, declined to participate in person; this produced a domino effect as other intellectuals followed suit.[41] "I have the disagreeable impression that I am being used," a frosty Albert Camus wrote to Rousset as the latter tried frantically to lure him back into the fold.[42] The result of the defections was a chaotic program, discredited in the eyes of French leftists by American speakers' praise for the North Atlantic Alliance. The Rassemblement was revealed, wrote Rousset's onetime Trotskyist comrade Pierre Naville, as "flatly (even ferociously) reactionary."[43] To American anticommunists, meanwhile, French participants' efforts to equate US and Soviet imperialism appeared farcically unfair. "If those who attended were actually representative of the [French] non-Communist left," philosopher Sidney Hook claimed, "it is testimony of the devastating effect of the war and Nazi occupation on its political education."[44] In the wake of this disaster, the RDR unraveled into factionalism and backbiting before disappearing for good less than two years after its founding.

The movement's death left Rousset politically homeless and stripped of allies by the summer of 1949. The "assembly of free men" may have been a quixotic venture, but it was also a real attempt to resist the antagonistic logic of the Cold War, criticize both capitalism and Stalinism in the name of universal values, and champion an independent vision of revolutionary, democratic socialism. In hindsight, it is perhaps evident that such a project—spearheaded by intellectuals more interested in debating fine points of Marxist philosophy than conducting grassroots organizing—could never have succeeded. The effort was further doomed by the global and domestic circumstances in which it unfolded: a policy of alignment with neither "bloc" proved an impossible tightrope to walk in the era of the Berlin blockade, and especially in the midst of violent 1949 debates over France's ratification of NATO. Nevertheless, the Rassemblement had offered a certain hope—and as it disintegrated, its individual leaders found themselves at a crossroads. Disheartened and divided, they were confronted with binary choices they had tried hard to avoid.

Rousset's "Appeal," an unthinkable endeavor for him in 1945 or even 1948, was a product of this moment—not because damning new information about the gulag suddenly came to light, but because, with the death of the RDR, no possibilities really remained open to a politically passionate French intellectual besides pro- or anticommunism, pro- or anti-Americanism. Some, like Sartre, continued to agonize for months or years before choosing sides. But for Rousset, by now persuaded that millions of *concentrationnaires* languished in the USSR, the decision was not difficult. And after Buber-Neumann's testimony in the Kravchenko case, he saw his path forward in sharp detail. In late summer 1949, he penned a brief missive revealing his plan for the "Appeal." This letter was not addressed to any of his habitual interlocutors but rather to an American Embassy secretary (and, unbeknownst to Rousset, a covert intelligence agent) named Norris Chipman. It constituted a simple request for bibliographic materials on the Soviet camps; Rousset did not at this point ask for financial help or seek to involve US officials in his plan, which he described as individually motivated and fully formed.[45] Nonetheless, the letter to Chipman makes clear that in publishing the "Appeal," whatever he later protested to the contrary, Rousset understood that he was not offering an apolitical protest against human suffering. Rather, he was stepping into the pitiless arena of Cold War combat, with his identity as France's "witness among witnesses" as his weapon. Alone and disenchanted, he was ready.

## Witnesses before Other Men

Rousset's "Appeal" appeared across the front page of the November 12, 1949, edition of *Le Figaro littéraire*, a conservative weekly literary and cultural review affiliated with editor Pierre Brisson's daily *Le Figaro*. The choice of venue, in itself, signaled the crossing of a Rubicon: to publish in *Le Figaro littéraire* was to eschew once and for all any stance of Cold War neutralism or anti-anticommunism.[46] The article's massive headline read, "Help the Deportees in the Soviet Camps: An Appeal from David Rousset to the Former Deportees of the Nazi Camps." The essay that followed, spilling over onto multiple pages, was crafted as an intimate, first-person plea to an esteemed community of fellow survivors. Indeed, its first words delineated its intended recipients: "I address this appeal to all former political deportees," Rousset announced (thus excluding racial deportees from his opening sentence), to "the two great deportee organizations in France," the FNDIR and the FNDIRP, to "foreign former deportees and their organizations," and to "all those who, having survived the concentrationary universe, bore witness to it."[47] He also called on select members of this last group by name: Claude Bourdet, Louis Martin-Chauffier, Jean Cayrol, Agnès Humbert, Robert Antelme, Rémy Roure, and Eugen Kogon, the renowned German author of *Der SS-Staat*.[48]

Rousset's message to all these men and women was simple: "an extraordinary concentrationary landscape" had emerged in the USSR, analogous to that of Nazi Germany. In a "ceaselessly expanding" array of forced labor sites across the desolate northern reaches of the Soviet empire, millions of individuals—a "vast, heterogeneous group of politicals," a smaller contingent of "asocials," and a despised aristocracy of common-law criminals—toiled beyond the limits of human endurance. Reprising the sociological analysis of his seminal *L'Univers concentrationnaire*, Rousset devoted the bulk of the "Appeal" to sketching out the internal organization of "*le GOULAG*" as a self-contained "society": its economic logic and physical configuration, its pitiless hierarchies and petty humiliations. Along the way, he sought to make three linked points: first, incontrovertible evidence testified to the existence of this foreboding "universe" of camps; second, from the perspective of its inmates, no meaningful differences set it apart from Hitler's concentrationary world; and third, as a consequence, Nazi camp survivors possessed a moral responsibility toward these new victims. The Soviet *univers concentrationnaire*, Rousset wrote, "concerns all free men, and they ought to respond to it." But survivors' obligation was different: "*we lived this tragedy.*"[49]

Building on this last theme, in the closing portion of the "Appeal" Rousset revealed his plan of action. It was understandable, he wrote, if some felt there was insufficient information to declare that "the concentrationary universe exists in Russia." All he asked was "to open the dossier." He therefore proposed the formation of "a commission of inquiry . . . composed exclusively of proven former political deportees" from across the political spectrum. This group, "once united, [would] officially ask the Soviet government for the right to conduct an on-site investigation in the camps, within Russia itself." They would then—and this was the crucial point—carry it out themselves. He was not asking Nazi camp survivors "to demand an inquiry" into Soviet crimes on the part of some neutral body, Rousset stressed, "but to take it in hand and conduct it." They were the only ones qualified to do so. "The others," he wrote, "those who were never *concentrationnaires*, can plead poverty of imagination, incompetence. Us, we are the professionals, the specialists." The possession of such expertise was a "difficult privilege," Rousset acknowledged, and the work of the commission he was proposing would be arduous. But it was "the price we must pay for the surplus of life that has been granted to us."[50]

Though the "Appeal" marked a sharp break for Rousset in political terms, conceptually speaking it drew on ideas already familiar to readers of his celebrated works of testimony. First, the text hinged on his long-defended claim that "the concentration camp" was a universal institution that operated according to internally consistent "laws" to produce identical suffering "anywhere on the planet that it emerge[d]."[51] Second, it defined such camps on the basis of their bodily and psychic effects on inmates, basing the charge that the USSR's installations qualified for the label on the similarity between their victims' lived experience and its author's memories. Employing a visceral language of smells, sights, and sounds that repeatedly featured the word "same," Rousset insisted that gulag inmates "are what we were yesterday." The Soviet *"homme concentrationnaire,"* he wrote,

> is hungry. All of the illnesses brought on by physiological misery work on his body. He is frightened. He lives in the same wooden barracks as we did, or under a tent, or in earthen houses that are dark as caves. His destiny is enclosed by the same barbed wire, the same watchtowers. He toils until well beyond the endurance of his muscles under the menace of dogs and guns. Like us, he wears squalid rags, like us he has neither the means nor the time to wash. He wakes up—he, too—before daybreak, and in the evening, upon the exhausted return of the work brigade, he gets in line, an endless line, at the entrance of a hospital without any medicine. . . . I tell you that I am summing up literally hundreds of reports, and that there exist thousands of them.[52]

As this reference to "reports" suggests, a final contention carried through from Rousset's immediate postwar writings to the 1949 "Appeal": the notion that victim testimony was a privileged form of evidence. It was thanks to gulag survivors' first-person statements, he wrote, that it could be established that the USSR's crimes were indistinguishable from those of Hitler's Germany. Victims' words were not, certainly, the only form of proof in the "Appeal": the essay was illustrated with an AFL map of Soviet "slave labor" sites, drew on American government research about the gulag administration, and quoted heavily from the Soviet Labor Codex. Rousset granted the most weight, though, to "damning testimonies" from former Soviet camp inmates. In fact, he gave over much of the front-page space he had been allotted to verbatim reproductions of such texts. "You know very well that this accumulation of testimonies stalks you," he wrote to his fellow deportees. Those who had told an unbelieving world about the depredations of the Nazi camps in 1945 could not in 1949 "plug our ears" to the sound of Soviet subjects testifying to similar agonies.[53]

Rousset prodded survivors toward recognition of their obligation toward gulag victims by compelling them to remember—even relive—their own difficult past. The "Appeal" was saturated with references to "memory," "remembering," "forgetting," and "going back" in time, all designed to highlight parallels between past and present. "You remember the dogs?" he asked readers. Identical ones now "rush the Soviet deportee to the work call." And "doubtless you remember the dull malaise that Buchenwald's stone buildings awakened." Today, "the same sentiment seizes you upon examining the Russian dossier." At one juncture Rousset spoke for himself, commenting that testimony on Soviet forced labor "evokes singularly precise memories for me." At another, he urged his readers toward acts of recall in the imperative voice: "Let us remember our *misères*," he demanded, and thereby recognize that an "identical" "abandoned crowd, which can prepare nothing to defend itself . . . haunts the Soviet camps." In the essay's most unsettling passage, he wrote, "I would like each one of us to take himself back: imagine that we are, again, reunited on the large plaza of Buchenwald, under the lights and under the snow, to hear the orchestra and wait to be counted." How would his readers have responded, he wondered, if they knew that fellow inmates had been liberated but, back in the world of free men, "only knew how to speak of their own sufferings, and never spared a word to proclaim that we still lived in death?" Because the concentrationary universe was a bloc, its German and Soviet instantiations no more than variations on a theme, this was what their own current discretion amounted to. Rousset drew a stark conclusion: further "silence" was "forbidden to us. Otherwise, we no longer have the right to exist."[54]

With such passages, Rousset insisted on the moral necessity of what some scholars today call "secondary witnessing"—that is, testimony to the suffering of others.[55] Bearing witness had to mean more than solipsistic commemoration, Rousset declared: *anciens déportés* "repeat tirelessly, as we drown submerged by the indifference of life, that we must not forget. . . . [But], after all, what does it matter that we were the victorious vanquished of Mauthausen, of Buchenwald, or of Auschwitz? Life is right to rush on toward other tasks. The season of statues is that of dead men." Memory only took on significance as a call to conscience. "We know," he wrote, "that the gift that has been given to us, this authorization to live (when logic would have had us in the mass grave) can only be fulfilled through one meaning: we are the witnesses before other men to that warning about man and his society that the Nazi concentration camps constituted."[56] But survivors could not alert the world to the dire implications of the Nazi project if they denied the reality of its sequel. Because the concentrationary world lived on, to serve as its witnesses demanded forthright speech about Stalin's camps as well.

Through the universalizing logic of *le concentrationnaire*, then, Rousset offered a vision of transnational moral obligation and a stirring defense of mankind's basic dignity—yet did so without reference to human rights. "Rights talk" was common currency in anticommunist venues in the late 1940s; it featured heavily in AFL, IRD, US government, and French liberal and conservative attacks on the Soviet Union.[57] Rousset's failure to employ it thus cannot be considered accidental. It is possible that the vocabulary was tainted for him, as a leftist and an atheist, by its associations with Christian conservative politics.[58] More likely, however, Rousset sought to draw a categorical distinction between mere violations of rights—which he was happy to concede occurred worldwide—and the radical evil of the *univers concentrationnaire*. Concentration camps were not comparable to such garden-variety injustices as "the Negro problem in the United States," he wrote, and could not be discussed in the same terms. Their inmates' laments were not just another chord in the "ancient moan of the world's peoples."[59] The idiom of transgressed "rights" trivialized the horrors of Dachau, Dora, and Neuengamme; it also lent itself to arguments that the US and the USSR were similarly immoral actors rather than singling Stalin out as a lone offender.

What is more, in comparison to Rousset's own unyielding equation between self and other, "human rights" was woefully abstract in its construction of both the distant sufferer and the ethical subject called to witness. Why should the average Frenchman care if a faceless Ukrainian's "right" to "just and favourable conditions of work" as outlined in Article 23 of the Universal Declaration of Human Rights (UDHR) was being abrogated thousands of miles away?[60] But if new Buchenwalds were springing nightmarishly to life, it was perfectly clear why those who had survived the original Buchenwald had to respond. Thus, though Rousset continually referred to "man" in the "Appeal," he declined to construe this figure as a rights-bearing entity, only as one capable of great anguish. He willingly indicted the Soviets for "crimes against humanity"—a term as yet unlinked to human rights discourse, and which dovetailed with his understanding of concentration camps as instruments of assault on the human being as such.[61] But he conceived of his readers' obligation to Stalin's prisoners in absolute terms foreign to the vague exhortations on the "human family" that characterized the UDHR.[62] Gulag inmates, he declared, did not simply deserve their fellow man's nebulous concern—they demanded former Nazi camp inmates' unqualified identification. It was this group's remembered experience of trauma, not a rational appeal to a circumscribed inventory of rights, that produced the imperative to bear witness.

Before going further, it is worth underlining that Rousset's dark depiction of the Soviet "concentrationary universe" was in many respects accurate. By the time he authored the "Appeal," the prisoner population inhabiting the USSR's vast network of camps and penal colonies was near its 1950 peak of over 2.5 million men and women.[63] Although generalizations about the Soviet Union's sprawling, porous, and ever-evolving forced labor system are perilous, it is clear that throughout the postwar gulag—and especially in the "living hell" of the special camps, created in 1948 expressly for political prisoners—atrocious conditions prevailed, starvation loomed, physical exploitation was unrelenting, and life counted cheap.[64] Mortality figures are contested, but at least 1.6 million men and women died in the Soviet camps between 1921 and 1953, and historian Golfo Alexopoulos has recently suggested that this figure should be adjusted dramatically upward.[65] As Steven Barnes writes, moreover, whatever the gulag's precise death toll, "even those who survived had their lives destroyed."[66] Rousset was not wrong to describe this sphere of suffering and toil as an abomination, a "cancer" on the postwar world.[67]

Nevertheless, to use memory of the Nazi camps as a basis for condemning the Soviet ones, Rousset was compelled to flatten certain distinctions between the two systems, notably by downplaying the significance of Hitler's structured program of extermination targeting European Jewry and Roma populations.[68] The "Appeal" did contain a fleeting claim that Stalin's *univers concentrationnaire*, like Hitler's, contained at least some "Jews who are simply Jews."[69] But because Rousset's representative Nazi victim had always been the political prisoner targeted for his "convictions" rather than his identity, he did not need to argue that the USSR was engaged in systematized racial violence or genocide in order to equate its carceral project with that of the Third Reich. True, the "Appeal" conceded, there were no gas chambers in Siberia. But gas chambers were merely "extreme illustrations of the concentrationary accomplishment," not its essence—Buchenwald, for one, did not possess them, "yet no one has denied its concentrationary nature." Rousset thus maintained that the distinction failed to signify. "For [gulag] inmates," he wrote, "this difference is empty [*vaine*], because the same living conditions drive them unavoidably to that particular death which was ours, the dirty and despairing death."[70] The "ours" here referred to Resistance deportees, whose mortality in the camps had largely been the product of disease, overwork, exposure, and starvation rather than Zyklon B. Jewish Holocaust victims' noninclusion in the imagined "we" of the deportee community thus facilitated Rousset's new project from the beginning.

It would have been possible in the late 1940s to frame a comparison of Nazi and Soviet mass violence that *did* take account of the Holocaust. Indeed, in "The Concentration Camps" (1948) and *The Origins of Totalitarianism* (1951), Hannah Arendt undertook just such an endeavor. Arendt was heavily influenced by Rousset—a quotation from him provides the epigraph to "The Concentration Camps"—but it is edifying to stress what set her project apart from his.[71] On the one hand, Arendt found it simpler than Rousset to maintain a parallel between the two "totalitarian" regimes in question because she conceived of Hitler's *and* Stalin's chief victims as "the totally innocent": Jews in the first case, hapless random subjects in the latter. On the other hand, Arendt was more willing than Rousset to admit to differences of degree between the two systems: if Stalin's camps represented "Purgatory" for her, "Hell in the most literal sense was embodied by those types of camps perfected by the Nazis." In particular, she underlined the existence of SS-run "corpse factories"—Majdanek, Treblinka, Birkenau—with no parallels in the USSR.[72] This was not disruptive of her analysis because her goal was to elaborate a theory of totalitarianism, with the USSR and National Socialist Germany functioning as two similar but nonidentical case studies. Rousset's "Appeal," though, did not seek to make any conceptual or structural argument about totalitarianism—it did not even employ the word. Its comparative orientation was entirely driven by the aim of condemning the gulag. Thus it offered no explanation whatsoever for the appearance of concentration camps in both historical contexts; indeed, Rousset was purposefully vague about whether Stalin's gulag predated the Nazi *Lager* or followed their example. What mattered for him was a timeless quality of sameness in the lived experience of victims, and the ethical implications of that sameness for Nazi camp survivors.

Of course, Rousset's framing of the "Appeal" as a letter addressed only to such readers was a device. The piece did not appear in a survivors' federation newsletter, after all, but in a general-readership periodical. Its political effectiveness arose from this rhetorical sleight-of-hand, for addressing fellow deportees permitted Rousset to offer a narrative of recent history in which the Nazi camps (and not, say, the battle of Stalingrad or the triumphs of the Free French) constituted the central event of the war years, the one from which "lessons" for the future could be gleaned. By positioning his readers as survivors rather than abstract liberal subjects, Rousset was also able to articulate a vision of ethical obligation vis-à-vis distant Soviet sufferers in culturally potent terms. Affecting to speak only to those who shared his own terrible experience allowed him to sweep aside libraries' worth of French debates about the revolutionary potential of the Soviet state: so long as one accepted that gulag inmates' agony was identical to that of the former prisoners of Buchenwald and Mauthausen, Rousset argued, no complicated ethico-political calculus, tortuous consideration of Marxist principles, or weighing of show trials against Jim Crow laws was necessary to adjudicate the Cold War. The choice was clear.

In the end, evidently, Rousset's treatment of former deportees as a lonely moral elect, held to higher standards than others, functioned as an invitation to "normal men" to assent to the same perspective. That is, the "Appeal" tacitly proposed the figure of the survivor-witness as a model for Western humanity in general, and for Rousset's fellow intellectuals in particular. Against the dominant, Sartrean vision of the revolutionary *engagé*, Rousset here sketched out an alternative idea of the intellectual's calling: to offer testimony in solidarity with victims.[73] What is more, he provided a performative enactment of this in the very authoring of the "Appeal": the text was an act of *témoignage*. It was also a clear renunciation of Rousset's earlier utopian projects. "I believe," he wrote in early 1950, "that I remain Marxist in the essential."[74] But the dreams for humanity's future that animated the "Appeal" were exceedingly modest compared to those that had inspired his "Program" for the RDR two years previously. If his campaign succeeded, Rousset proclaimed, "it will be established that in our society the only impassable frontier is this extreme limit, the refusal to allow the world of the camps."[75] Minimal as this was, it would have to be enough.

## Fracturing the Survivor Community

Among French survivors, the key short-term institutional consequence of the "Appeal" was to break apart organizations in which communists and their foes had maintained an uneasy coexistence since the liberation. While the small, elitist, and uniformly noncommunist FNDIR signed on to Rousset's initiative immediately, his text produced a historic schism in the larger FNDIRP, which up to this point had remained partially PCF-controlled but nonetheless politically heterogeneous.[76] Survivors fell out along partisan battle lines, but their polemics over the "Appeal" amounted to more than another skirmish in an endless conflict over Soviet communism: at stake for participants was the very meaning of their own ordeal in the Nazi camps. Two distinctive memory regimes clashed in the struggle, each with its own implications for how former deportees ought to confront the Cold War.

Noncommunist survivors of the Resistance deportation—socialists, Christian democrats, Gaullists, disaffected fellow-travelers, and unaligned leftists—overwhelmingly endorsed Rousset's demand, and did so in ways that echoed his assumptions about the import of the recent past. They first of all assented that the baseline moral imperative in a post-1945 world was to prevent the recurrence of the "concentrationary universe." If there were "still Buchenwalds anywhere in the world," wrote Christian democratic politician and Buchenwald survivor Henri Teitgen, "mankind is implicated."[77] Robert Maddalena, a Neuengamme deportee, adopted similar language in the progressive Catholic journal *Témoignage chrétien*: "Never again that! Never again Auschwitz, never again Buchenwald, never again Neuengamme!"[78] From this starting point, some respondents jumped directly to a guilty verdict against the USSR. In an article titled "Somewhere in Europe or in Asia, Mauthausen Continues," Father Riquet deemed it "very probable" that "new Buchenwalds, new Mauthausens, new Auschwitzes reproduce elsewhere the barbary of the first ones." Later in the piece he stripped away the conditional, flatly asserting: "All that which we experienced is happening again."[79]

Beyond embracing Rousset's narrative of repetition and replication, noncommunist deportees also seized upon his claim that they themselves possessed a unique responsibility to combat Soviet state violence. In a suggestive turn of phrase, the violin virtuoso and Buchenwald survivor Maurice Hewitt approved of the "Appeal" as an awakening of *"conscience concentrationnaire,"* implying that this was an entity distinct from—and superior to—the conscience of ordinary men.[80] Like Rousset, he and other sympathetic respondents grounded "concentrationary conscience" in total, retraumatizing identification with current victims. FNDIR president Léon Mazeaud, for instance, addressing an imagined gulag inmate, insisted that "while the camps remain, gray and teeming abattoirs, we are still in the camps. . . . No one knows your suffering better than I do, my replacement. . . . Your suffering [is] my suffering which continues, an intolerable prolongation." He rejoiced, therefore, that the "Appeal" might disrupt the "quietude" and "egoism" that had descended on deportee organizations preoccupied with mere commemoration.[81] If "no deportee has the right to forget," Rémy Roure agreed in *Le Monde*, ". . . it is not enough to not forget. To retain a memory of the nightmare is nothing if one knows that this nightmare has not vanished." What, Roure mused, "could possibly be the value, the raison d'être, of associations and federations of deportees if they tolerate the idea that the concentrationary universe might still exist?"[82]

This question was aimed at the communist leadership of the FNDIRP and intended as a provocation. But Roure joined Rousset in professing a high-minded disinterest in "politics": for deportees, he wrote, the moral exigency of combating the "camp universe" transcended the squalid struggles dividing Cold War–era France. The "Appeal" was situated "*uniquement*" upon "the human plane," not "the political plane." In a similar vein, ADIR member Irène (Maryka) Delmas made the case that the nonpartisan women's organization could support Rousset's project since it "has no political character and remains within the limits of pure humanity."[83] Aging Socialist Party figurehead Léon Blum, meanwhile, who had been imprisoned in Buchenwald, wrote that "at the origin of David Rousset's initiative, there is not and there never has been any political machination. There is simply the revolt of those who were the victims, the sufferers, the witnesses of the Hitlerian abomination, who cannot tolerate the idea that it could go on in other places, or under other names."[84] Christian democratic politicians in the deportee community took the same line: in the National Assembly, Émile-Louis Lambert defended Rousset's motives from communist attack by declaiming that "it would be criminal to use these memories for political ends."[85] The Catholic poet Jean Cayrol, a Gusen survivor, was meanwhile willing to acknowledge the political implications of the "Appeal." But he insisted that they were immaterial: "Anticommunism ought to have nothing to do with this tragedy, for it surpasses human understanding: it is the supreme attempt to *abattre l'homme*. . . . No cause justifies the concentration camp."[86]

Meanwhile, it was precisely Rousset's claim to apoliticism that most enraged communist and *communisant* survivors. The "Appeal" was only intelligible to these deportees as "a crime against peace," an insidious effort to "appease the resistance of French people toward Germany" and smooth the way for a nuclear onslaught against Stalin.[87] The celebrated literary camp memoirist Robert Antelme, a PCF member, wrote to his friend Rousset "with black rancor . . . terrible rancor" to complain that the "Appeal" was "pitiful, truly sinister," and "before all else a particularly grievous manifestation of anticommunism."[88] To true believers and even to wavering party disciples (as Antelme was by this date), Rousset's disavowal of Cold War motives was laughable. His call to arms was a hackneyed anti-Soviet provocation, rendered all the more infuriating by the fact that he claimed loftier intentions. What this dangerous reactionary actually wanted, warned famed *résistante* and Auschwitz survivor Marie-Claude Vaillant-Couturier, was "for the victims of Hitler to unite with the Pétainists and collaborators against their saviors."[89]

Communist Party members were confident in leveling such charges because, for them, the presence of concentration camps in the USSR was an impossibility: the Nazi camps had been fascist institutions, products of a degenerate capitalist regime. They had also been—as Auschwitz-Birkenau "racial" deportee Julien Unger pointed out on behalf of the FNDIRP leadership—sites of industrialized mass murder where Jews had been "exterminated as a race and not as political adversaries."[90] It was "a monstrosity," wrote FNDIRP cofounder Marcel Paul, to confuse these abattoirs with the USSR's "corrective labor camps, which are the honor and pride of the Soviet government and people."[91] It is perhaps salutary to admit that if Paul's contention now appears pernicious, Unger's does not—and to acknowledge that French communist collective memory of the camps, despite its heavy emphasis on political martyrdom, could nevertheless partially accommodate the Jewish Holocaust in a way that Rousset's own "universalizing" approach to the past failed to do. What is more, communist-led groups like the FNDIRP could welcome individual "racial" survivors like Unger, as the organization now envisioned by Rousset could not. Though some Shoah victims endorsed the "Appeal," they did so while overlooking the fact that its author had excluded them from his proposed community of witnesses.[92]

Normative judgments aside, a larger analytical point emerges from this discussion: French communists agreed with Rousset that memory of the camps ought to dictate postwar choices. For them, though, the experience held different lessons: the ongoing necessity of antifascist, anticapitalist revolutionary struggle; gratitude to the USSR, "which sacrificed 17 million of its children to rescue [deportees] from slow death, from gas chambers, and from the crematoria"; disdain toward French conservatives as "kollaborationist trash"; and fear regarding the looming prospect of West German rearmament.[93] Within their schema of remembrance, associating Stalin with Hitler "betrayed the memory of all those who suffered or who died, victims of the most atrocious barbarism."[94] Rousset had suggested that failure to heed the "Appeal" would be an unforgivable act of forgetfulness; communist readers insisted that by aligning with the forces of imperialist aggression, Rousset revealed that he was the one with a "short memory."[95] The "Appeal" invited amnesia, charged Pierre Daix: it was a bid to "make us forget Hitlerism in favor of the abstraction 'concentrationary.'" With this mystificatory term, "Monsieur Rousset has 'depoliticized' the Nazi camps. He has turned them into an entity for which Man with a capital M was responsible" rather than German fascists.[96] Daix made these claims in a *Lettres françaises* article titled "Pierre Daix, Identification Number 59,807 at Mauthausen, Responds to David Rousset." The piece was reprinted on two hundred thousand leaflets, which FNDIRP members in striped pajamas sold at Parisian *métro* entrances for eight francs.[97] Such political performance art drove home the message: this was a bare-knuckles battle about the uses and abuses of the concentrationary past for the Cold War present.

As Communist Party members and their surrogates struggled to retain control of camp remembrance, they also launched a series of smears against Rousset's comportment in Neuengamme and Buchenwald, intended to undermine his authority to represent the survivor community. The engineer of the "Appeal," wrote Marcel Prenant, was "ill-founded to pose as a bringer of justice, given the memories that he left among his comrades at Neuengamme."[98] Colonel Manhès, president of the FNDIRP, who had once hailed Rousset as an unparalleled evocator of the "camp universe," leveled similar charges: given Rousset's failures in the realm of "mutual aid and solidarity" in Block 48 at Buchenwald, Manhès informed him, "you do not have the right to speak 'in the name of the survivors of the death camps.'"[99] He followed this statement with an oblique swipe at Rousset's corpulence, suggesting it marked a betrayal of the skeletal victims of Dachau and Auschwitz. Communist cartoons made the same point in visual language; one striking image, titled "To an American Tune," showed a portly Rousset in striped garb fiddling away on a violin as SS officers pushed a gaunt fellow inmate, a woman labeled "Peace," toward a scaffold.[100]

In the end, such maneuvers could not save the FNDIRP coalition. Noncommunists (including Riquet, a vice president) began to resign from leadership posts after a majority of the executive bureau condemned the "Appeal." In the wake of a stormy January 14–15, 1950, National Committee meeting, whole departmental associations followed suit, along with prominent individuals including Roger Heim, Paul Arrighi, and General Pierre Dejussieu-Pontcarral. The defectors formed a new group, the Union Nationale des Associations de Déportés, Internés, et Familles de Disparus (UNADIF), which aligned itself fraternally with the FNDIR while maintaining FNDIRP-esque membership policies welcoming to "racial" deportees. The communist survivors who were left behind oscillated between denying that a significant defection had taken place and denouncing the "dividers" and "secessionists" who "had no right to break the front of deportees."[101] As UNADIF's new members celebrated their "APOLITICAL association,"[102] communist André Leroy (a Buchenwald survivor) scoffed: "The 'apoliticals' . . . are a race that has never seen the light of day on this earth. . . . [They] want to make us carry out *their* politics."[103] They would not succeed, he vowed.

Leroy was, of course, correct that Rousset's splintering of the FNDIRP had been a thoroughly "political" maneuver. However much the author of the "Appeal" publicly insisted that "I despise politics in this matter," he privately rejoiced over the FNDIRP schism: at last, thanks to him, "the Communists are completely isolated on deportee terrain."[104] Rousset was still more pleased that PCF members' reaction to his initiative opened up the possibility of high-profile litigation. As in the Kravchenko case, it was *Les Lettres françaises* that proved willing to sling calumnies that could support a libel complaint: Daix's article, in addition to its other charges, had insisted that the evidence deployed in the "Appeal" was fake, constituting "vulgar transpositions" of Nazi deportees' testimony.[105] This was precisely the sort of injurious response Rousset had hoped for, and he immediately filed suit against Daix and his editor Claude Morgan. The court case that would ensue, he predicted, "will be an infinitely more important trial than the Kravchenko trial," for "our trial will be the trial of the Russian concentration camps."[106]

## The Intellectual Left and the "Appeal"

The *Lettres françaises* case did not open until a year after the publication of the "Appeal." In the meantime, Rousset had other battles to fight. These were with a set of noncommunist leftist writers who, unlike his enemies in the PCF, declined to dispute the existence of the gulag and therefore offered not panegyrics to the humanistic glories of Soviet "reeducation camps" but critiques of the incomplete universalism of his proposal. The first such rejoinder came from Buchenwald deportee Claude Bourdet, editor of the left-leaning paper *Combat* and one of the figures named in the "Appeal." Rousset knew Bourdet well and had high hopes regarding his response. These were quickly dashed. In a November 14 editorial, Bourdet condemned him for "only directing his blows toward the USSR." In the current political climate, such a "one-directional crusade" was unacceptable: it would "lead to the mobilization of the whole world" against the Soviet Union. Rejecting Rousset's binary between concentrationary and non-concentrationary offenses, Bourdet proposed that a spectrum of worldwide abuses were worth combating. "The number of victims and the genre of repressive methods," he wrote, "do not constitute a sufficient argument for opening one category and closing another." Accordingly, he asked Rousset, "How can you speak of the USSR without mentioning Tsaldaris's Greece" or "Franco's Spain, with its hit list of quasi-industrial terror"? A committed anticolonialist, Bourdet was particularly caustic toward his fellow survivor for his silence concerning imperial violence. "We are French," he stressed, "and first of all responsible, it seems to me, for what our country does. 'Political' prisons, police detentions—don't we have some of those ourselves right now, in Madagascar and Indochina, without even considering what is going on in North Africa?" Frenchmen would do best to "sweep in front of our own door" before pointing fingers.[107]

Bourdet's widely read article changed the terms of debate about the "Appeal," though Rousset initially attempted to brush the challenge aside. Scale mattered, he insisted, and the Soviet enterprise of repression dwarfed that of Greece. Moreover, as a Marxist he reserved the right to challenge the USSR "in the name of socialism."[108] Bourdet responded with scorn to both points, especially the latter: had not the "Appeal" called for "solidarity among *concentrationnaires* of all opinions," not only leftists? And who ever heard of a crusade "in the name of socialism" being launched in the quintessentially bourgeois *Le Figaro littéraire*?[109] Rousset realized he was beaten within the week, as even supportive respondents to the "Appeal" now hastened to specify that they endorsed the project only if it targeted "all countries where the concentrationary experience continues."[110] Cayrol, for one, echoed Bourdet directly: "We cannot let the USSR support the weight of an ignominy of which we are *all* capable," he wrote, and since "all the nations are in a pre-concentrationary situation" at best, Rousset's proposed commission would have to investigate everywhere.[111]

If Bourdet intended his criticism of the "Appeal" as a refusal to participate, Cayrol, by contrast, genuinely sought to reshape Rousset's project. So, too—and more fatefully—did his fellow Catholic, Louis Martin-Chauffier, who responded affirmatively to Rousset's plea but wrote that "the Commission cannot, without ceasing to be objective and becoming partisan, limit its inquiry to the Soviet Union alone." It should cast its gaze more widely, toward the "fascist" countries and also "the capitalist democracies—without forgetting our own." He was "with you, therefore," but only if Rousset consented to push his universalizing logic of solidarity with sufferers "all the way."[112] Martin-Chauffier, a leading PCF sympathizer following his experience in Neuengamme, had testified on the communist side at the Kravchenko trial. His approbation for Tito and discomfiture with the 1949 Rajk show trial in Hungary had since then distanced him from the party, but he remained well known as its "house Christian."[113] His conditional support was thus a coup for Rousset, to be preserved at all costs. In a December 1 letter, Rousset therefore conceded the point, writing that "the Commission should affirm the principle of an inquiry on the camps in all countries where the problem is susceptible to arise, regardless of the political or social label of the governments under consideration."[114] This was to have momentous consequences: without Martin-Chauffier's intercession, Rousset may well have founded the

CICRC as a body strictly concerned with Soviet wrongdoing rather than global conditions of imprisonment, or simply let the endeavor play out as a short-lived propaganda stunt.

These were certainly the only outcomes that Sartre and Merleau-Ponty envisioned when they first responded to the "Appeal" in early 1950, offering the single most substantive rebuttal to Rousset's project from intellectuals outside the community of former deportees. Their jointly written editorial in *Les Temps modernes* condemned the text that had appeared in *Le Figaro littéraire* "absolutely" and "definitively terminated" their association with its author.[115] This was despite the fact that they accepted the veracity of Rousset's accusations against the USSR, even acquiescing to his considerable overestimation of the imprisoned population at ten or fifteen million people. The presence of this vast number of detainees "puts entirely back into question the significance of the Russian system," Sartre and Merleau-Ponty admitted. "What we say is, there is no socialism when one citizen out of twenty is in a camp."[116] But in an echo of both Bourdet's piece and the argument Merleau-Ponty himself had made in his 1947 book *Humanisme et terreur*, they asserted that focusing exclusively on the Soviet camps amounted to "absolution" for "the capitalist world," rendering its crimes invisible.[117] Rousset, they charged, had "chosen his deportees," privileging gulag inmates' suffering over that of Spanish, Greek, Indochinese, and Malagasy prisoners.

Sartre and Merleau-Ponty argued more fully than Bourdet that any censure of Stalin unaccompanied by equal condemnation of Western state violence amounted to an attack on socialism. Though one could, they explained, criticize the USSR, "one cannot in any circumstances form a pact with its enemies," the capitalists, imperialists, and fascists who were also the enemies of oppressed peoples in the West.[118] Whatever pious language he had used, this was what Rousset had done—and in a polarized world, such an initiative was unforgivable. "Whatever the nature of present-day Soviet society," argued Sartre and Merleau-Ponty, "the USSR finds itself situated within the equilibrium of forces, *grosso modo*, on the side of those who fight against the forms of exploitation known to us." In their eyes, the struggle to replace such exploitation with socialist "recognition of man by man" remained the sole viable underlying basis for political engagement. They were particularly displeased with Rousset's argument that Soviet and Nazi camps were equivalent because they produced the same kinds of bodies-in-pain. This was ideologically fraudulent, since "we have nothing in common with a Nazi and we have the same values as a communist."[119] Ends and not only means, in other words, mattered.

In rejecting Rousset's thesis of identity between the two camp systems, Sartre and Merleau-Ponty, like communist commentators, repudiated his reading of the meaning of the recent past. For them, the chief lesson of Nazism was not the imperative to oppose state violence for the suffering that it produced but, rather, the need for revolutionary struggle to create an egalitarian world in which the recrudescence of Hitler's atrocities would become impossible. They also joined communist critics in challenging Rousset's interpretation of Nazi criminality: against the author of *L'Univers concentrationnaire*, their editorial obliquely suggested that racialized mass murder rather than "the concentrationary universe" was the Third Reich's *crime majeur*. "Before the gas chambers" were built, the two authors asserted, the German camps "imitated [*ont été calqués sur*]" extant Russian forced labor centers. But "from the moment the gas chambers were established," no comparison between the two regimes remained valid. Though they stopped short of making the point as clearly as Unger had done, Sartre and Merleau-Ponty here came closer than any other contemporary commentators to articulating how the universalizing rhetoric of "the concentrationary" elided the Jewish genocide.[120]

Still more fundamentally, Sartre and Merleau-Ponty could not accept Rousset's premise that survivors' memory of their passage through hell provided meaningful insights to guide subsequent political and ethical judgment. Rousset's supporters, they wrote, "will say that the concentration camp experience, absolute of horror, compels the man who has survived it to look first to the country that prolongs it." But "the truth is that even the experience of an absolute like the concentrationary horror cannot determine a political position. The days of life are not the days of death [*Les jours de la vie ne sont pas les jours de la mort*]." Rousset, author of *Les Jours de notre mort*, had not been transformed by his suffering in a way that gave him claim to more profound solidarities than other men possessed. Nor had other deportees. Their memory of the Nazi concentrationary world, however powerfully felt, did not provide them with an intuitive ability to adjudge the legitimacy of future violent acts. "When one comes back to life," Sartre and Merleau-Ponty wrote in a crucial passage, "for better or for worse, one begins again to reason, one chooses one's loyalties. . . . One always forgets death when one lives." Thus neither Rousset nor his opponent Daix had any right to "invoke their loyalty as former deportees" to justify their current actions: these were freely chosen and fundamentally political.[121] This was a flat rejection of memory as a grounding for ethics, and of identification with victims as a meaningful alternative to rational, radical, and ends-oriented engagement. It was the heart of their critique of Rousset; to underline the fact, they titled their editorial "Les jours de notre vie."

In the eyes of Rousset's supporters, Sartre and Merleau-Ponty overstepped by offering any comment at all on the proper "loyalties" of camp survivors. Other non-deportee writers so thoroughly embraced Rousset's logic regarding the experiential distance that separated former *concentrationnaires* from "normal men" that they hesitated even to endorse the "Appeal," fearing to tread on holy ground. Camus, for instance, wrote the following in his personal notebook upon its publication: "Rousset. What makes me stay quiet is that I was not deported, but I know what cry I am stifling in saying this."[122] He eventually found a way to cheer the initiative from the sidelines by co-signing a "Manifesto of Solidarity."[123] Pierre Emmanuel employed similarly respectful language. "You know, Rousset," he wrote, "there are men who did not experience the camps but feel enough solidarity with you to never forget, to never accept the euphemisms of untruth, and to know, instructed by your comrades and you, that the camps are in the process of becoming a society with its own organic laws."[124] While Jean-Marie Domenach at the progressive Catholic journal *Esprit* was critical of Rousset, he admitted that the Buchenwald survivor "has all rights to speak" and devoted much of his commentary on the "Appeal" to quoting responses by survivors like Bourdet, tacitly acceding to their designation as privileged mediums of conscience.[125] Sartre and Merleau-Ponty, by contrast, because they rejected the premise that traumatic experience transmitted knowledge capable of altering the ethical subject, unapologetically suggested that they knew better than Rousset what duties confronted a survivor.

The *Les Temps modernes* editors also took this position because they understood that Rousset was actually holding up the figure of the survivor-witness as a general model. This they could not accept. Bearing witness to suffering, Sartre and Merleau-Ponty insisted, was not a sufficient project for the postwar left—engagement had to aim toward more radically transformative ends. Indeed, as Merleau-Ponty had argued in *Humanisme et terreur*, pursuing those ends might demand that one tolerate or even endorse methods that produced bodies-in-pain.[126] Six months later, he and Sartre made this point more explicitly in a second editorial aimed at the "Appeal." Here they insisted that one could not condemn a given form of state violence on moral grounds simply by pointing to the traumatic experience of its victims. Responding to the charge that they should have written about the Soviet camps sooner—before Rousset forced their hand—they responded that they had not been aware of the *extent* of the Soviet forced labor system. "It is certainly cruel," they wrote,

> to tolerate the camps so long as they're *not too populated*. But ultimately, all of the regimes that history has shown to us, or now shows us, tolerate or admit horrors. . . . [Trotsky] knew, from having governed, and from having made the revolution in 1917, that Revolution brings horrors with it, that political judgment is a statistical judgment, and finally that the political question is to know what, of the horror and of the worthwhile, tends to predominate in a system, and what the *direction* [*sens*] of the system is.[127]

Thus, against Rousset, Sartre and Merleau-Ponty continued to assert a divide between experience and judgment and a distinction between morality and politics.

Merleau-Ponty abandoned this position in the early 1950s. Sartre, though, continued to carry on the argument with Rousset over the next decade, as one might worry an aching tooth. Notably, his famous 1952 open letter ending his friendship with Camus dwelt extensively on the "Rousset Affair." By this point a PCF fellow-traveler, Sartre now ridiculed the notion that Rousset and his supporters actually experienced an identificatory response to gulag inmates. Indeed, invoking French racism, he questioned the premise that people could address suffering across national borders at all. "It is difficult for a Frenchman to put himself in the place of a Turkestani" imprisoned in a Soviet camp, he wrote, and—here joining Rousset in seeing little possibility for empathy outside of total identification—concluded that it was therefore unlikely that such a Frenchman could "experience sympathy for this abstract being which is a Turkestani seen from here."[128] Thus, Sartre suggested, less noble sentiments must inspire Rousset's followers. "I have seen the anticommunists rejoice in the existence of these prisons," he wrote. "Be serious, Camus, and tell me if you please what emotion the 'revelations' of Rousset could have evoked in the heart of the anticommunist. Despair? Affliction? The shame of being a man? Go on, go on!" To respond meaningfully to suffering, Sartre again claimed, demanded not concern for victims nor attentiveness to their testimony but revolutionary action to eliminate exploitative human relations. "It seems to me," he wrote, "that the only way of coming to the aid of the enslaved over there is to take the side of those who are here." For Camus, who refused to "take sides," "I see only one solution: the Galapagos Islands." There was no meaningful space "outside" of political contestation and ideological conflict from which to bear universal witness. "Apolitical" solidarity with or among victims was a false option.[129]

Sartre's various rejoinders to the "Appeal" did not directly influence the formation of the CICRC in the same way that the reactions of Bourdet, Cayrol, and Martin-Chauffier did. But the disapproval of his former friend and colleague affected Rousset deeply, giving the impetus to many of his decisions over the coming decade. As it happened, the commission came to function as an ideal vehicle for his performative opposition to the Sartrean model of the engaged intellectual. While Sartre as a fellow-traveler abandoned "the authentic and honorable role of the *clerc*, which is to contest the State's absolute power over human beings," Rousset charged, he and other survivors visibly kept faith with the individual.[130] Over the course of the 1950s, as the commission publicized its inquiries on political detention in Spain, Greece, Tunisia, and Algeria, Rousset never missed a chance to remind reporters that he was not "choosing his deportees." Nor did he cease to protest against Sartre and Merleau-Ponty's claim that "the concentrationary horror cannot determine a political position," asserting to the contrary that "it signifies much more. In today's world—so far have we been dragged along by the debacle—it denounces that which cannot be accepted; that which tolerates no pact, no compromise, under pain of death." Survivors, who "were introduced to dehumanization not by discourse but by life," did indeed possess a political and ethical consciousness surpassing Sartre's own, he insisted.[131] In many respects, the CICRC constituted a sustained effort to prove the point.

## To an American Tune?

Rousset's claim to represent the noble lineage of the *clerc* could be viable only if his crusade was perceived as an act of conscience outside the thrall of power, independent of state interference. As he sought to foster such a perception, he was compelled to conceal a great deal. While there is no reason to doubt his insistence that he made the decision to pen the "Appeal" "absolutely alone," its litigious fall-out prompted him to seek whatever help he could find in winning his case.[132] In effect, though communist critics were wrong that Rousset's entanglements with Anglo-American backers *caused* him to write the text, they might plausibly have argued that he entered into alliance with US and British government agents as a *consequence* of its publication. The next chapter traces the full sweep of Rousset's efforts to secure Anglo-American support for the CICRC. Here, it is illuminating simply to note the assistance he received in preparing for his looming court battle with *Les Lettres françaises*.

Rousset reached out to Britain's Information Research Department on the same day he filed suit against the communist journal. IRD officials cared little about his ethics of concentrationary experience, offhandedly labeling it a "rather original line," but they were elated that their investment in propagating the Soviet Labor Codex in France had finally paid dividends.[133] "We thus suddenly found our chickens coming home to roost," the organization's year-end report noted happily.[134] Rousset was lunching with IRD's Paris officers within the week and traveling to London to peruse Foreign Office resources within the month. One agent reported that he and his lawyers, old Trotskyist and RDR friends Gérard Rosenthal and Théo Bernard, were "grateful and amazed" for British help in amassing evidence and locating witnesses.[135] Simultaneously, Rousset also sought support from US government officials as well as Jay Lovestone of the AFL, who was now secretly working in tandem with American intelligence. As Lovestone bitterly noted, Americans could do little to secure trial witnesses for Rousset thanks to the "idiotic and criminally dangerous" 1950 Internal Security Act, a

McCarthyist measure that made it difficult for former Soviet subjects living in America to travel outside the country.[136] But they provided other forms of backing. Rousset obtained documentation on "the extension of [Soviet] forced labor in all its forms" from US Embassy officials; from Lovestone himself, he received financing for the stateside services of a research assistant.[137]

US and British anticommunist crusaders greeted Rousset's initiative with outstretched hands because they glimpsed its potential to disrupt Communist Party influence over the French intellectual scene—widely viewed as the most Stalinist in Western Europe—as well as France's Resistance and deportee communities. Some expressed hyperbolic hopes: David K. E. Bruce, American ambassador to France, opined following the FNDIRP schism that Rousset "seems to have set in motion [a] chain reaction" that might well produce "the breakup or withering away" of every Communist front organization in the country.[138] Despite such enthusiasm on the part of professional cold warriors, however, the "Appeal" failed to register with the American *public*. For one thing, Rousset's own celebrity did not extend outside continental Europe. As Lovestone admitted to Chipman two months after the *Figaro littéraire* publication, "We still haven't yet hit upon some way of publicizing his name in the United States." More generally, memory of Nazi concentration camps did not possess anything like the same emotional resonance in the US as it did in the French context. The notion of the Resistance deportee as hero, prophet, or witness was foreign to American (and, for the most part, British) audiences.[139]

Nevertheless, US supporters did make every effort to translate the "Appeal" not just into English but into a generic idiom that might echo across the Atlantic. The most noteworthy instance of this was an "adaptation" of the article by the Iron Curtain Refugee Campaign, first published as a full-page advertisement in the *New York Times* (along with signatures of support from Allen Dulles, Thornton Wilder, John Dewey, John Dos Passos, Tyrone Power, Gary Cooper, and many others) and subsequently in the *New Leader*. This text stripped away all Rousset's references to an audience of Nazi camp survivors—his "us"—and repackaged the manifesto as an "Appeal to the Conscience of the World," addressed to "all free men." Rather than demanding former deportees' agonized identification with distant suffering, it called upon the "compassion" of "safe, comfortable, intelligent citizens of the West." The endeavor fell flat: transposed into the abstract register of "Humanity," the "Appeal" lost its idiosyncratic force.[140] Eventually, American anticommunists were compelled to concede that Rousset's *cri de coeur* was a valuable propaganda tool only in Western Europe: distinctive collective memories of World War II governed the possible languages with which the Cold War could be waged in different places. Of course, Rousset was implicitly offering the survivor-witness as a universal model for human conscience. But his method of doing so relied on invocations of the past that had little power in the English-speaking world.

The contrast between French popular interest in Rousset's project and Anglo-American indifference was never more evident than during the *Lettres françaises* trial itself, which began in November 1950 as the Korean War lifted US-Soviet tensions to new heights. For domestic audiences, the case was a front-page media spectacle. According to Rousset's press-clipping agents, from its opening session at the Seventeenth Correctional Chamber of the Seine to its conclusion in January 1951 the trial was discussed forty-nine times in *Le Monde*, fifty-two times in *Le Figaro*, thirty-two in *France soir*, thirty-six in *L'Aurore*, and thirty-eight in *Combat*. The communist press was even more voracious: seventy-three articles in *L'Humanité* dealt with the proceedings, fifty-eight in *Ce soir*. As for provincial papers, there were twenty-nine articles in *Nord-matin*, twenty in *La Croix du Nord*, thirty-three in Toulouse's *La Dépêche du Midi*, and seventeen in Marseille's *Le Provençal*.[141] The IRD was "astonished" and delighted by coverage elsewhere in Western Europe as well.[142] English-language reporting, however, lagged far behind. The *Times* of London offered a single brief note on the trial's outcome.[143] On the other side of the Atlantic, a February 15, 1951, letter to the editor of the *New York Times* signed by Hook, Arthur Koestler, Arthur M. Schlesinger Jr., Reinhold Niebuhr, Norman Thomas, Roger Baldwin, and George S. Counts protested that this "tremendous event—comparable in moral significance and surpassing in human scope the Dreyfus trial of a half-century ago—has remained almost completely unknown to the American public," garnering virtually no comment in any major paper or magazine.[144]

Rousset himself cannot have been overly surprised by the dearth of American and British popular interest in the trial, for—despite his pose as a latter-day Zola—he understood what set the Rousset Affair apart from the *fin de siècle* Dreyfus case, a legal battle whose global significance had arisen from the demand that the accused be perceived as an unmarked liberal subject rather than embodying any particular identity. "The moral importance of this affair," in contrast, Rousset informed the court, "comes from the fact that M. Pierre Daix is a former deportee of Mauthausen and from the fact that I am a former deportee of Buchenwald."[145] At stake, therefore, was the meaning of the Nazi camp experience for postwar, Cold War continental Western Europe—and for the camps' own survivors in particular. The *Lettres françaises* team and their lawyers Paul Vienney and Joë Nordmann agreed with this assessment, and devoted much of their time in court to reminding spectators of Daix's Resistance deportee credentials.

More broadly, both sides in the trial tried to make the most of the media spotlight by ignoring the narrow issue of libel and instead promoting larger narratives about the meaning of the past for the present. In line with the "peace movement" platform of contemporary international communism, the *Lettres françaises* team aimed to denigrate critics of Stalin as "warmongers" eager to render "peaceful coexistence" impossible and align France with the global forces of fascism in preparation for the next conflict.[146] Rousset, meanwhile, aimed to document not merely the existence of the gulag but its Nazi-like character. Yes, yes, other forms of oppression existed, he acknowledged, again vaguely invoking discrimination against African Americans. But he and Daix both knew from bitter, bodily experience that the *univers concentrationnaire* stood as "the greatest evil," which "must be destroyed." What was to be decided in the courtroom, therefore, was no less than "a question of humanity."[147]

The trial was not only composed of such grave pronouncements. As spectators whooped and jeered, speeches frequently gave way to name calling and other forms of verbal abuse by both sides: Rousset's "precursor was named Goebbels," charged Vienney; "You are a cynic and an idiot!" Rousset told Daix; Rosenthal shouted imprecations about Nordmann's "bad faith." The communists affected to disdain bourgeois justice and refuted the court's competence "to judge the interior regime of a foreign country"—particularly that of "the victors of Stalingrad."[148] They took evident pleasure in raising procedural objections and engaging in "interminable declarations"; with grudging admiration, *Le Monde*'s correspondent admitted Nordmann and Vienney's "ingeniousness" in the theatrical arts.[149] Rousset, meanwhile, was reluctant to be bested in the grandstanding department: as Simone de Beauvoir once cruelly observed, "the sound of his own voice exhilarated him."[150] Exasperated, the judge was reduced to pleading for "*un peu de silence!*" from both sides. Meanwhile, a steady stream of "violent incidents"—Morgan's ejection from the courtroom, scuffles among spectators, tense exchanges between the legal teams—provided rich fodder for the delighted journalists in the audience.[151]

Further color, along with whatever genuine solemnity entered into the case, came from the parade of former gulag inmates that Rousset had assembled as witnesses. Among them were prominent memoirists including Buber-Neumann, Elinor Lipper, Jerzy Gliksman, and Julius Margolin, other intellectuals, artists, and lawyers of Soviet, Polish, and Czech nationality, and a smattering of more humble figures. By far the most attention was garnered by the bombastic testimony of "El Campesino" (Valentín González), a communist Spanish Civil War hero who, upon fleeing to the USSR in 1939, had been imprisoned in Vorkuta. El Campesino and the others were "without hate and without fear," wrote Rousset's friend Georges Altman in the noncommunist leftist daily he edited, *Franc-Tireur*.[152] The communists begged to differ. "These witnesses were our enemies," Daix later wrote. He, Morgan, Vienney, and Nordmann "did not fight to win the trial, but to totally obstruct the exposés" of the men and women in the stand by suggesting they were motivated by "resentment and political hatred."[153] From within the PCF's worldview, it was evident that the witnesses were telling lies, since the Soviet penal system was "the most progressive and advanced in the world."[154] Rousset, meanwhile, waxed indignant on the witnesses' behalf: to accuse them of offering false testimony, to deny the veracity of their suffering, was to perpetuate the "crime against humanity" of which they had already been victims. Their words deserved reverence—and repetition by secondary witnesses, most importantly their brethren from the Nazi camps.[155]

After two months, the *Lettres françaises* case came to a close on January 21, 1951, with a victory for Rousset: the defamation charge was upheld, and Daix and Morgan were ordered to pay a fine and modest damages. The outcome had been preordained by their refusal to address the charges; hence they, too, publicly celebrated the verdict as a vindication, since Rousset was denied the full monetary compensation he had demanded.[156] (The court justified its leniency toward Daix by invoking "the sufferings that he endured during the war in the Hitlerian concentration camps.")[157] Yet the public relations triumph unmistakably belonged to Rousset—and to the anticommunist organs that supported him. "Justice is Rendered to David Rousset," reported *Le Figaro*, while *Le Parisien libéré* announced that "David Rousset Exits as Victor over 'Les Lettres françaises.'" "Claude Morgan and Pierre Daix Are Defamers," crowed *Le Populaire*. *L'Aurore* chose a similar front-page headline: "Claude Morgan and Pierre Daix Will Pay." The PCF position, it reported, was "condemned across the board in the trial of the death camps." Altman's *Franc-Tireur* was more solemn, reminding readers that "Freedom and human dignity did not in fact triumph in this trial, since there still exist concentration camps just about everywhere on the globe." Nevertheless, Rousset had "magnificently defended one of the rare causes worth fighting for in today's world."[158]

Such soaring humanist rhetoric on the part of an evidently partisan press organ points again to the overall interpretive problem posed by Rousset's "Appeal." In the end, is this story a proud epic about a man who, having suffered greatly, dared to bear witness on behalf of those still in agony? Or is it a Cold War period piece about an astute political operative and the propaganda campaign he mounted through evoking elevated ideals? The answer is, naturally, "both"—or, rather, "neither in full." One can take Rousset at his word that he launched his crusade "because I was a concentration camp slave, because I lived through this misfortune, because it has become the obsession [*hantise*] of my life," and yet still observe the anticommunist motives for and consequences of his action.[159] The gulag was not, after all, a wild fiction he invented but a real feature of the Soviet state; for this reason, Rousset's ethic of identification with its inmates and his Cold War politics cannot be neatly distinguished from one another. In any event, the historical significance of Rousset's "Appeal" resides not in the bare fact that it functioned as propaganda but in the way it mobilized victims' memory of the Nazi camps—and not, say, the language of human rights—to do so. In calling on Hitler's former political prisoners as witnesses to "the concentrationary universe," Rousset was not, as the communist cartoonist had charged, fiddling "to an American tune." He was playing a song unfamiliar and unbeguiling to Americans, pitched exclusively to the ears of societies that had experienced deportation as the signature evil of the Second World War.

Even in those places, the melody resonated differently for different listeners. The "Appeal" was a belligerent slander of the USSR and a betrayal of the dead to communist intellectuals, a devastating engine of schism to FNDIRP leaders, an exculpation of Western crimes and abnegation of revolutionary politics to Sartre and Merleau-Ponty, a moving defense of "concentrationary conscience" for many noncommunist Resistance survivors. And, to the men and women in this last category who would join Rousset in launching the anti–concentration camp movement, it was also something further: a founding document, marking the beginning of a new phase in the "aftermath" portion of their lives. It is to their story that we now turn.

# FORGING THE INTERNATIONAL COMMISSION

It was one thing to champion the notion that survivors of the Nazi camps ought to wage war on the "concentrationary universe," but quite another to forge an institution through which they might do so. This more challenging task was what Rousset and those who answered his call undertook in early 1950. They founded their commission in the absence of clear models. Of course, international nongovernmental organizations had long existed at the moment of the CICRC's birth, including many concerned with the plight of prisoners and forced laborers. Notable among them were the Anti-Slavery Society, the International League for the Rights of Man, and the venerable Red Cross.[1] Earlier initiatives such as the International Committee for Political Prisoners, founded in 1924 by Roger Nash Baldwin, also provided antecedents for the kind of consciousness-raising work that Rousset and his followers aspired to undertake, and other postwar groups—the Commission of Inquiry into Forced Labor of the Workers' Defense League, for instance—attacked similar targets. The CICRC, though, brought together not simply like-minded individuals but survivors of a collective foundational trauma, claiming the duty to stand as witnesses for humanity by virtue of their experience. In significant ways, therefore, it constituted a new sort of activist organization that could not simply take form: it first had to be imagined.

On January 24, twenty-odd French survivors representing different federations and *amicales* met in Paris at the home of Gabrielle Ferrières-Cavaillès, an ADIR leader, to begin that conceptual labor. They labeled themselves "The Deportees against the Concentrationary Regime" and set to work divvying up tasks. At subsequent meetings "work commissions" formed, and volunteers began assembling dossiers on various penal systems: Buchenwald survivor Gaston Weil took the Spanish case, Alfred-Serge Balachowsky the Soviet file, Jean Kreher that of South Africa, and so on.[2] Participants nominated officers, contemplated locations for permanent offices, and pondered the mechanics of membership dues. Most importantly, they issued a "fraternal" letter to "all organizations of former Nazi camp deportees existing in foreign countries, without discriminating among them in any way, asking them to proceed with the appointment of their Commissions of inquiry, with the goal of constituting the international Commission of inquiry of former Nazi camp deportees as rapidly as possible."[3]

Within the CICRC, the French commission's January 1950 "Open Letter" came to function as a much-quoted founding text, second in importance only to the "Appeal." Its existence—along with its stirring language of transnational unity and nonpartisan moral crusade—allowed members to tell a voluntarist and inclusive story about their group's coalescence. Upon the letter's dissemination, they asserted, the CICRC had sprung into being organically as Western Europe's survivors "resum[ed] contact . . . to once again fight against the same things that they fought against in the extermination camps during the Nazi occupation." As they joined hands across borders, at a stroke "a new resistance to the concentrationary regime crystallized."[4] This tale of open, artless beginnings within an extant community was appealing to contemporaries and is all the more seductive today since it fits smoothly with two idealistic narratives about the period: one that grounds the "European" project in the wartime fellowship of resisters, especially deportees, and another that locates the roots of contemporary human rights organizing in the dreams of Cold War–era nongovernmental groups that sought to "move the world away from a bipolar division toward an interdependent community."[5]

The problem with the CICRC's origins story—and hence with the sweeping interpretive accounts of the postwar moment it would appear to support—is that, like all such stories, it was a myth. This does not mean it was entirely false, but rather that it was partial, distorted, simplified, and engineered to obscure other, far messier histories. For instance, the "Open Letter" may have promised an apolitical human rights campaign conducted in a manner "entirely independent from public authorities"—but at the precise moment of its drafting, David Rousset was quietly seeking monetary support from American cold warriors by assuring them that his initiative would serve US aims. The majority of survivors involved in the commission were oblivious to these intrigues, but political calculations shaped the organization's early existence in ways that went beyond finances: they also governed the character of the coalition that assembled behind Rousset. In treating the unification of the CICRC as a natural resumption of solidarities born in the *univers concentrationnaire*, purveyors of the group's founding myth adopted a fairy-tale vision of the Nazi camps as arenas of international friendship, models for a future "European" or global community. In fact, the politics of Cold War anticommunism—not an easy renewal of concentrationary bonds, nor a shared "vision of one world"—ultimately did the most to determine who joined the group.[6]

The present chapter's exploration of this not-always-savory history challenges rose-tinted assessments of nongovernmental human rights advocacy in the post-war moment. It does not, however, thereby endorse the cynical position that European actors involved in international organizing in this period were blind pawns in a US-Soviet "shadow war of secret funding and Potemkin NGOs."[7] To view Rousset and his diverse followers in these terms would be to neglect their own agency as ideologically motivated actors and to deny the creativity behind their political mobilization of the survivor-witness identity. It would also fail to illuminate other central aspects of the CICRC's early months—for instance, participants' attempts to define "the concentration camp" (a task they resisted approaching instrumentally), their ambivalence regarding human rights, and, most importantly, their efforts to exclude "racial" victims from membership despite employing Holocaust historian Léon Poliakov as a secretary, researcher, and translator, and Drancy survivor Théo Bernard as a legal counselor. Thus rather than viewing the CICRC's early days according to a logic of front organizations and puppetry, the chapter shows that the group was forged through an ongoing, tension-ridden negotiation between the demands of Cold War politics and the imperatives of concentrationary memory as participants (including nonmembers such as Bernard) understood them. The commission's founding was, in one sense, yet another anguished attempt on the part of survivors to retrieve meaning for the polarized and difficult present out of the haunting losses of the none-too-distant past.

## Beyond France

When French deportees arrived at Ferrières-Cavaillès's apartment on January 24, 1950, to create an association, not all of them expected or desired for it to be international in character. Throughout the late 1940s, French survivors had conducted most of their collective activities within French groupings, many with the word "national" or "patriotic" (or both) in the title. One multinational federation of former political prisoners was founded in Paris in 1947, but this organization was controlled by the Kremlin via a Warsaw-based leadership; it garnered little interest among those in France who lacked ideological commitment to a specifically Marxist vision of internationalism.[8] Believing that their own country possessed "universal duties," noncommunist French survivors did not equate the obligation to defend global values with the necessity for transnational cooperation.[9] Moreover, they understood their past suffering as a sacrifice for the *patrie* and saw no need to perpetuate its legacy alongside foreigners. Thus many of them assumed that the commission Rousset called for would be exclusively French, a manifestation of heroic Gallic interventionism rather than cross-border collaboration. Léon Mazeaud's response to the "Appeal" was typical: "We liberated France; it is now up to us to liberate the world!"[10]

Mazeaud could be forgiven for failing to note that Rousset's call to arms had actually been addressed not only to French survivors but to "all foreign former deportees and their organizations."[11] After all, of the seven individuals it invoked by name, six were French. (The seventh, German Buchenwald chronicler Eugen Kogon, was widely viewed as Rousset's chief literary counterpart.)[12] Nationality had functioned in the Nazi camps as a segregating principle, and even such a determined cosmopolitan as Rousset had not returned from the Reich in possession of multiple foreign comrades who could now be rallied. In fact, he was exceptional in maintaining *any* relationships with non-French survivors. For many of his compatriots, the experience of such polyglot hells as Buchenwald and Ravensbrück had fostered outright hostility toward other Europeans. Martin-Chauffier commented acidly in *L'Homme et la bête* on the "smiling egoism" of Neuengamme's Danish prisoners, the "guile and vanity" of the Poles, and so on.[13] Rohmer, reflecting on Helmstedt, indicted the Dutch for being "too civilized to try to struggle" against the guards.[14] Tillion's 1946 criticism of Polish prisoners' behavior in Ravensbrück was so fierce that by the 1970s she was "ashamed" she had ever published it; the material was later silently expunged from *Ravensbrück*.[15] A contingent of priests, including Michel Riquet, did forge links of genuine European fellowship in Mauthausen and Dachau. But, as Riquet acknowledged, for most French survivors the camps were incubators of neighborly hatreds: "They returned more xenophobic than ever."[16]

In the years ahead, as proponents of the incipient European Community crafted an origins story partially grounded in the shared suffering of deportees, this uncomfortable history would be papered over by fantastical slogans such as "From the Europe of Dachau to that of Strasbourg!"[17] It is important to understand that such thinking was a retroactive effect of Cold War solidarities fostered by initiatives like the CICRC, not a cause of them. Rousset had never been a chauvinist—recall his steadfast refusal to interpret the concentrationary phenomenon in terms of German aberrance—and he did believe that continental victims of Nazism had undergone a "collective experience" that set them apart from the British and Americans.[18] But it was only his 1949 embrace of the Atlantic Alliance that turned him into a Europeanist, one who now argued that

"Western Europe should be unified economically" through a "great democratic movement" to counteract Soviet communism's "powerful influence on European workers and liberals."[19] In light of such newfound convictions, several months before issuing his "Appeal" Rousset began to wonder if it might attract survivors from "different European nations" despite having few personal contacts in those communities.[20] (He understood that his one genuine foreign comrade from Neuengamme, German communist Emil Künder, would disown him upon publication of the text—a fact that underlines the ease with which Cold War loyalties also trumped those rare transnational attachments that *did* exist among survivors.)[21] His decision to found an international movement, therefore, was not an effort to call upon bonds born in the camps but a bid to create new ones.

Rousset's vision of an anti-concentrationary project "conducted on the international plane" appealed to Anglo-American agents.[22] British intelligence officers, in particular, jumped at the chance to "broaden the base of this appeal by arousing interest in certain other European countries" and scrambled to translate Rousset's manifesto widely and put him in touch with survivors across the continent.[23] IRD agents were especially energetic in Belgium, where "we fortunately have special relations with the people who run *Le Peuple*," a Socialist daily; their efforts also spread to Italy, the Netherlands, and Scandinavia.[24] As such machinations unfolded, Rousset won French participants over to the notion of working alongside other Western Europeans. They acquiesced, assuming—correctly—that their own group would retain leadership of any broader coalition that developed. The "Open Letter" followed, furnishing a narrative of fraternal internationalization suitable for public consumption. It bore the signatures of thirty-three men and women, each technically signing as an envoy for an existing survivors' group (the FNDIR, the ADIR, and so on), and summoned foreign deportees to join on the same terms—that is, as delegates on behalf of their national organizations.

Partisan sympathies shaped the subsequent process by which Western European deportee federations decided whether to answer the French call. Unsurprisingly, communist-controlled groups were hostile, noncommunists more sympathetic. But matters were more complicated than that, first because some survivors' associations remained internally politically diverse, and, second, because the politics of anticommunism dictated different choices according to different national cultures of memory. An example may clarify this latter point. In January 1950, Rousset met with Sozialdemokratische Partei Deutschlands leader Kurt Schumacher, who had passed nearly a decade in the *univers concentrationnaire*, to seek his help locating West German participants. Rousset left the meeting buoyed, confident that representatives of the German Socialists' "working group" of former camp inmates would be ready to join the CICRC "within the coming month." This was not to be: months later Schumacher reported back that "the Commission did not raise much interest in Germany."[25] In truth, this response was hardly surprising, given the climate in Bonn. As Harold Marcuse has argued, the virulent anticommunism that accompanied the division of Germany and the end of denazification gave rise to a "reconceptualization of the concentration camp survivors as criminals and threats to the state."[26] In this context, moderate leftists could not mobilize concentrationary memory for anticommunist ends in the same way that they could elsewhere in Western Europe. Thus Rousset was compelled to start from scratch in his search for a delegation from the Federal Republic; it was only months later that he secured the participation of Christian democrats from the newly created, Düsseldorf-based Bund der Verfolgten des Naziregimes.[27] This group would prove to be unstable, discordant, embarrassingly hyperbolic in its denunciations of Stalin, and the cause of constant difficulties for the commission as a whole.

Cold War politics interacted with collective memory in a different way in the case of Belgian accession to the CICRC. At the moment the "Open Letter" was issued, Belgium possessed a single, inclusive umbrella federation for all camp survivors, the Confédération Nationale des Prisonniers Politiques et Ayants Droit (CNPPA). The CNPPA operated according to a "criterion of suffering" rather than patriotic sacrifice; that is, it united resisters with other categories of political prisoners and "racial" victims. It also bridged Belgium's regional and linguistic divides.[28] Like the similarly structured French FNDIRP, the CNPPA was already experiencing partisan power struggles by late 1949, and Rousset's initiative further fractured the group. Esterwegen survivor Luc Somerhausen and other communists on the confederation's executive board, following Communist Party instructions, at first managed to deflect discussion of the "Appeal" by counterproposing their own independent inquiry into "inhumane detention conditions" around the world.[29] "We are not children," one member commented, "and do not need to let our ourselves be guided by a French commission, or anyone."[30] International organizing was not necessary to defend "the principle of universalism"— in fact, working alongside an anti-Soviet ideologue such as Rousset would constitute a "violation" of it.[31]

In the end, however, and following the assurances in the "Open Letter" that the French were committed to investigating beyond the USSR, CNPPA's noncommunist bloc won out. A motion announcing Belgian willingness to "enter into contact with foreign Commissions in order to create an international Commission of inquiry" passed the confederation's national council on February 19 by a vote of 63 to 36.[32] The acrimony of the foregoing debates opened wounds that would not heal and that would ultimately divide the CNPPA no less surely—though a bit more slowly—than they had divided the FNDIRP. A schism opened in late 1951, with noncommunist secessionists forming a new, "exclusively patriotic"

Belgian Union of Political Prisoners whose rhetoric of suffering for the *patrie* and its "national democratic freedoms," while intended primarily to distinguish members from devotees of Stalin, also served to exclude racial victims.[33] Here, then, as in France, Cold War politics organizationally reconfigured the victims of the recent conflict, aligning noncommunists behind an elitist, patriotic vision of the deportation. Ironically, the creation of Rousset's International Commission served here as a catalyst for increasingly nationalistic uses of the concentrationary past.

In the meantime, Belgians emerged as central participants in the CICRC. Among them were Georges André, a medical doctor, World War I veteran, resister in the quasi-military "Secret Army," and survivor of Dora and Ellrich; André Alers, a Buchenwald survivor who now served as principal of the Athénée Royal Flamand in Brussels; and Maurice Bruyninckx, deported to Struthof and Dachau for disseminating clandestine journals. Most importantly, the CICRC gained its secretary-general, Père Damien (Henri) Reumont. Father Reumont, nearly sixty, was a member of the Capuchin order, a former missionary in Lahore, a philosophy teacher, and a leading militant in the worker-priest movement. He had been arrested in November 1942 for participating in the repatriation of French POWs and British aviators and deported to Esterwegen and Börgermoor concentration camps and Untermassfeld prison.[34] Upon his return to Belgium, he helped launch an experimental fraternity of priests dedicated to living, laboring, and preaching alongside the working class.[35] He was also a founder of the Belgian edition of the periodical *Témoignage chrétien*, which, while rejecting alliance with the Communist Party, was, as Jean-Louis Jadoulle puts it, "distinctly anticapitalist" and therefore within "the most progressive wing" of political Catholicism in postwar Western Europe.[36]

Reumont's engagement with the CICRC began when he penned a "Response to David Rousset" in the December 1949 *Témoignage chrétien* (Belgian edition) that expressed enthusiasm for the undertaking but insisted that inquiries be conducted "everywhere."[37] The Belgian priest's understanding of "witnessing" differed from that of the French Protestant-turned-atheist: for Reumont, to bear witness was to live in poverty and in the image of Christ.[38] Reumont was, however, passionate about the spiritual obligations of former camp prisoners. Still more to the point, by 1949 he had become fixated on the notion that "totalitarianism" threatened to transform "the whole world into a concentrationary hell."[39] He and Rousset entered into a friendly correspondence on their points of agreement and disagreement, and by the time the International Commission began to coalesce in 1950, he had emerged as the obvious choice to serve as secretary-general. This was, as Reumont put it, "*un job full-time!*" and one he would fulfill outstandingly over the coming years.[40] The CICRC would not have

lasted long without his cheerful management of correspondence, agendas, minutes, government and UN filings, travel arrangements, visas, and budgets, as well
as his knack for smoothing ruffled feathers: Rousset's own talents lay elsewhere.

The process of joining the CICRC was more straightforward in national
contexts that lacked a politically "mixed" federation like the CNPPA. The Netherlands' Vereniging van Ex-Politieke Gevangenen (National Union of Former
Political Prisoners, or ExPoGe), for example, had already purged its communist members in May 1949; the group also did not welcome "racial" survivors. It
proved eager to support Rousset.[41] ExPoGe was led by an anticommunist executive board, including the socialist publisher Karel van Staal, author of the memoir *De Hel van Buchenwald*, and his friend Cornelius van Rij, a distinguished
lawyer and European federalist. These men nursed strong resentments of CP
members' behavior in the camps; in a 1950 letter to Rousset, Van Staal identified
"Communist prisoners' terror" over other Buchenwald inmates as "the reason
for which I appreciate your action and your struggle."[42] Rousset, as we have seen,
did not share such sentiments; he also disliked the overall conservative bent of
the Netherlanders, later labeling their delegation the "*ultra* wing" of the CICRC.[43]
He was nevertheless grateful for their support, since Van Staal's publishing business and his editorship of ExPoGe's monthly *Aantreden* equipped his National
Committee with resources undreamt of by the French. It was a simple matter, for
instance, for Van Staal to send 560,000 letters seeking donations for the CICRC,
or to print 100,000 pamphlets on its work.[44] The rhetoric of these documents was
often crudely reactionary in ways that the CICRC's French publications never
were—but the semi-autonomy granted the Dutch permitted them to advocate
energetically for the movement, and in Rousset's eyes this was worth a great deal.

If securing Dutch adhesion helped the CICRC gain access to material
resources, locating a "Spanish émigré" delegation offered more intangible benefits: antifascist credentials and proof against Sartre's charge that Rousset had
"chosen his deportees." Rousset worked hard, therefore, to ensure the participation of Spanish republican exiles, several thousand of whom were Nazi camp
survivors. As it transpired, the Federación Española de Deportados e Internados
Políticos (FEDIP), founded in Toulouse in 1945, was delighted to join forces with
him since its members—anarcho-syndicalists, Trotskyists, other splinter-group
communists, socialists, liberals, and so on—had high hopes that Rousset would
target Francisco Franco's Spain. Uniformly anti-Stalinist, FEDIP members were
also already engaged in efforts to denounce the plight of a group of Spanish
republicans who, through a complicated series of events, had been imprisoned in
the Soviet Union's Karaganda gulag since 1941. In the spring of 1950, the organization selected its delegates to the International Commission; among them were
José Ester Borrás, a Mauthausen survivor and FEDIP's secretary-general, José

Calmarza (Mauthausen), José Domenech (Neuengamme), and José Rodes Bley (Dachau).

In the end, then, national dynamics governed the adhesion of different Western European survivors' federations to the CICRC. All who joined were motivated by anticommunism, to be sure—but the anticommunism of an anarcho-syndicalist Spanish Civil War veteran was quite unlike that of a Dutch socialist publisher with dark memories of Communist Party members' behavior in Buchenwald or a philosophically inclined Belgian worker-priest fearful of a world where "the State replaces God, man becomes a slave, and the law of the jungle replaces the law of charity."[45] What is more, disdain for Soviet-style communism was not, by itself, enough to drive survivors across the continent into the CICRC: only in contexts where national memory of the war years was compatible with the political vision propounded in the "Appeal" and "Open Letter" were those documents effective recruiting tools. We have seen Rousset's difficulties with German survivors; in other cases he failed entirely. Despite entreaties through socialist allies and other contacts, no Italian, Austrian, or Luxembourgeois participants materialized. Rousset fared better in his overtures to Scandinavian survivors' groups; nevertheless, it was not until two years later that a Norwegian delegation joined. The Danish only followed suit in 1953.

Thus by the moment the CICRC called its first conference in Brussels in October 1950, the organization was composed of five groups: the French, Belgians, "Spanish republicans," Dutch, and Germans.[46] In an attempt to underline the international character of the undertaking, Rousset insisted during this opening assembly that the Belgian capital, not Paris, serve as the International Commission's headquarters and the site for its roughly bimonthly meetings. He also declined to serve as CICRC president, bestowing this figurehead position on the aging, affable Dr. André. The inclusion of francophone Belgians such as André and Reumont in formal leadership roles did not, however, change the fact that the French—represented by Rousset, Tillion, and Balachowsky, along with Roure and Martin-Chauffier *in absentia*—dominated the assembly. Nor did self-congratulatory speeches about cross-border cooperation mask participants' differing agendas. Indeed, much of the meeting was devoted to complaints from the French and Belgian delegations that the Dutch and Germans, without permission, had recently associated their names with a nakedly partisan anti-East German "Manifesto."[47] As a genuinely international endeavor, Rousset admitted to André, the CICRC "up to now exists much more on paper than in action."[48]

But to other audiences, Rousset made thorough use of this "paper" existence. In a November 1950 letter to Jay Lovestone of the AFL, for instance, he boasted that the commission was now "the emanation of organizations which represent around 100 to 150,000 adherents" and, as such, could speak with authority in the name of deportees across the continent. The group was, he announced, the new mouthpiece of "the most elevated expression of the European Resistance."[49] In making such claims, Rousset was not only engaging in a sleight of hand by employing two contradictory logics of legitimation, one democratic and the other elitist. (The CICRC could claim to "represent" such impressive numbers only because it included groups such as the CNPPA containing many non-resister deportees.) He was also, like later proponents of "Europe" who used similar rhetoric, inventing the notion that there had ever *been* such a singular and self-conscious thing as a "European Resistance." Once again, collective memory of the war years was being reforged in the crucible of Cold War politics.

## Covert Operations

If Rousset's language of European unity told one story about the "internationalization" of the CICRC, the fact that he was employing it in a letter to a US labor organizer told another. At the same moment that the International Commission was coalescing, its leader was also busy reaching out to a second set of foreigners: Americans whom he hoped would back the new organization. Despite his acquaintance with several diplomats at the American Embassy in Paris and a warm rapport with his Montparnasse neighbor Harold Kaplan, head of the Marshall Plan's Mission France information division, it does not appear that he deliberately set out to procure US government funding.[50] In a November 1949 letter to the antifascist Italian writer Ignazio Silone about "how to finance all this" given his own "miserable resources," he even grimaced at the thought. "Obviously," he wrote, "no matter what, the Stalinists will say that it is State Department money. The essential thing for us is that it isn't, and that we can say openly and can publish precisely that it isn't."[51] In other words, if support were to come from the US, it would at least nominally have to come from private sources.

Already in late 1949, Rousset reached out to a long list of American non-communist intellectuals and activists, inviting them to sponsor his cause. He repeated his entreaties in person during a May 1950 trip to the States. Among the targets were Lovestone, his CIO counterpart Walter Reuther, Eleanor Roosevelt, Roger Nash Baldwin of the ACLU, Socialist politician Norman Thomas, and various "New York intellectuals" including Dwight Macdonald, Sidney Hook, James Burnham, Saul Padover, Max Ascoli, David Dallin, and *New Leader* editor Sol Levitas.[52] Convincing these contacts of the significance of his campaign was challenging for Rousset since, as Dallin informed him, "in this country the interest in the Soviet concentration camps is not overwhelming anymore. This was a sensation about three or four years ago; by now people know about their existence and new details do not arouse excitement."[53] In Western Europe, Rousset hastened to explain, the issue remained "primordial," thanks to remembrance of Nazi atrocity: "For countries like Belgium, France, Holland, Norway, the memory of the war is above all the memory of the concentration camps; public opinion knows exactly what concentration camps are, and that they are in every case the worst thing that could exist."[54] He assured Dallin, therefore, that exposing the gulag would destroy Soviet communism's appeal in "irrevocable and definitive" terms.[55] But for this to occur, "material support" from "the American milieu interested in these problems" would be necessary.[56]

The nature of this milieu was more complicated than Rousset likely understood at this juncture, since several of the figures he approached had recently begun working in witting collusion with the US government to combat communism. Burnham, for instance, a philosopher and ex-Trotskyist now fiercely turned against Marxist precepts, had begun to serve as an "expert consultant" to the year-old Office of Policy Coordination (OPC) in the summer of 1949.[57] The OPC, at this point a semiautonomous operation within the larger Central Intelligence Agency, was charged with a panoply of "covert activities," including propaganda efforts in "support of indigenous anti-communist elements in threatened countries of the free world."[58] For this reason, in 1948 it began to funnel money to Lovestone's Free Trade Union Committee as it worked to undermine Communist Party influence over Western European labor. By the time Rousset reached out to Lovestone, the FTUC had become the privileged conduit by which many thousands of "unvouchered" Marshall Fund dollars poured into countries such as France and Italy each month to fund anticommunist union organizing activities.[59]

Lovestone was able to grasp the importance of Rousset's project quickly, thanks to missives sent from Paris by the FTUC's representative in Europe, *éminence grise* Irving Brown. Born in the Bronx in 1911 to Russian-Jewish immigrant parents, Brown became a United Auto Workers organizer after graduating from NYU; during World War II he served as a lieutenant in the European theater and undertook missions on behalf of the CIA's wartime predecessor, developing his taste for both clandestine intrigue and all things European.[60] In late 1945, he arrived in Paris to act as the FTUC's "front man"—and, eventually (as the agency director's log put it), as "the cut-out through which CIA advances funds for the support of various Western European labor unions."[61] An admiring 1952 *Time* magazine article, titled "The Most Dangerous Man," quoted Brown likening himself and Lovestone to "reinforcing rods" in the "concrete" of homegrown European anticommunism. "Wherever we could find men who would fight," he explained, "we had to give them the knowledge that they were not fighting alone."[62] This ethos extended to supporting ventures that had little to do with labor, strictly speaking—for example, Rousset and Sartre's RDR. It was through providing clandestine support for foreign participants in that group's ill-fated "International Day of Resistance to War and Dictatorship" that Brown first met Rousset and began to wonder if he could "eventually be drawn towards a better political position"—that is, a more frankly pro-American one.[63]

Brown viewed the "Appeal" as cheering evidence that Rousset's political evolution had taken this hoped-for direction and was thrilled by the possibilities the initiative raised. "The slave labor issue must be met and some action taken on the Rousset movement," he wrote to Lovestone in January 1950.[64] While Lovestone agreed, for the time being this translated into little more than a contribution to Rousset's legal fund.[65] Brown's relationship with Rousset deepened that June, however, at the historic Berlin Conference during which the Congress for Cultural Freedom was founded. Covertly CIA-backed, the Congress was envisioned as an international association of anti-Stalinist writers, artists, and other intellectuals committed to championing the democratic value of freedom of expression. Both Rousset and Brown were tapped to serve on its executive committee; in that context, they discovered the potential advantages of an alliance and soon began corresponding with expansive familiarity.[66] For instance, a dense eleven-page letter from Rousset to Brown in August 1950 that ranged over the French politico-intellectual landscape situated author and recipient as comrades-in-arms, with Rousset referring repeatedly to "our" objectives, "our" media mouthpieces, and "our" role in the cultural Cold War as antagonists to PCF members and fellow-traveler intellectuals.[67]

Whether Rousset really felt a deep political kinship with Brown is questionable, for it appears obvious that much of this was flattery. The real purpose of his letter came at the end, when he renewed his request for AFL assistance in obtaining "considerable material means" to finance his upcoming trial and his commission-in-the-making.[68] Brown's response did not promise money but did propose a meeting to discuss "some of our mutual problems."[69] This and other encouraging noises from his direction seem to have rendered Rousset confident that funds would be forthcoming from the AFL—or, rather, from the newly founded International Confederation of Free Trade Unions (ICFTU), a nominally independent international group whose purse strings the AFL controlled.[70] He began preparing the ground accordingly within the CICRC. At the organization's October meeting, when rules for financing were laid out, it was agreed that although the commission could "not accept any subsidy either from governments or from political parties," it was permitted to seek help from "global labor organizations that are concerned with defending the rights of Man in the domain of labor."[71]

Rousset now began to make requests of the AFL in hard numbers. "I believe it would be very positive," he wrote to Lovestone, "if, out of a budget of 10 to 12 million French francs, the ICFTU could take charge of approximately 6 million."[72] (At 1950 exchange rates, this was a request for a bit more than $17,000 out of a total budget of between roughly $28,500 and $34,000.) Yet still no financing materialized, and the CICRC entered 1951 lacking any substantive source of support. In early February, a panicky Reumont wrote to Rousset that it was "time for your friends from the ICFTU to intervene, for I am at the end of my rope."[73] Lovestone, it seems, was reluctant to continue overextending his organization with commitments far removed from its core labor-related mission.[74] The archives are silent on how this impasse was resolved; perhaps Brown, who believed Rousset was "doing a very excellent job," prevailed upon Lovestone to see the task of backing him as worthwhile even if "extra-curricular."[75] Or perhaps the OPC intervened directly. What is certain is that, in the following weeks, payments finally began. On March 13, Reumont informed Rousset with relief that "Madame Brown"—Irving's wife, Lillie—had delivered him 135,000 Belgian francs (about $2,700).[76] Two weeks later, he had even better news: "I got a phone call this afternoon from Mr. Dale," who "will be waiting for me tomorrow to hand over the package that we have been expecting for some time." Reumont was jubilant, since the contents of this so-called package "assure that we will not break down."[77] Mr. Dale was Leon Dale, a CIA officer posted to Brown's Paris office.[78]

Thus began a funding relationship—or, rather, a series of funding relationships—that would last throughout the life of the CICRC. Much is unknowable about this alliance between European camp survivors and American cold warriors since, aside from a lone June 1953 memo from CIA operative Tom Braden listing the commission among "groups supported by the Agency," the American government's own records on the matter remain sealed.[79] It appears, however, that modest monies were funneled through the AFL and ICFTU until mid-1953. At this point, although Rousset maintained a relationship with Brown, the AFL "let us know that it could no longer help us as it had in the past."[80] Crisis for the CICRC was averted, however, thanks to Michael Josselson, the executive secretary of the Congress for Cultural Freedom. An Estonian-born Jew, a brilliant multilingual scholar, a former US military intelligence officer, and a CIA liaison since 1948, Josselson arranged for Rousset's organization to continue receiving support through the supposed good offices of a New York "fund-raiser," John J. M. O'Shea. Under a paper-thin fiction of donations obtained through "luncheon-meetings" with upstanding citizens to whom "slave-labor, wherever it may exist, is anathema," O'Shea moved significant sums into a Swiss account for the use of the CICRC and its increasingly ambitious publishing arm, the Centre International d'Édition et de Documentation—$198,437 in 1956, for example; $218,191 in 1957.[81] Rousset had no contact with O'Shea's shadowy donors, whom he politely referred to as the fund-raiser's "friends." But a letter that he sent to Josselson during a 1954 crisis (after taking pains for years to put nothing in writing) illuminates his real grasp of the situation. We will consider the contents of this missive at a later juncture; what matters here is that although the letter kept up the pretense that the CICRC was receiving "private funds"—"our Commission would not be able to accept any other origin"—Rousset noted that "it is, however, certain that M. O'Shea could no longer proceed with these regular collections if he ran up against a veto from his Government."[82] In other words, he understood the source of the money perfectly well.

However, from the 1951 delivery of Dale's first package to the moment in 1957 when O'Shea received precisely such a governmental veto, to disastrous effect for the CICRC, only a small circle was privy to the details of the group's financing arrangements. It likely included legal counselor Théo Bernard as well as Reumont. In public, Rousset occasionally admitted to AFL sponsorship; this was damaging enough, since the labor federation was viewed in left-leaning European circles as "archi-réactionnaire," and its most visible representative, Brown, was widely seen as a nefarious force.[83] Acknowledging the relationship earned the CICRC condemnation from some quarters, but on the world-weary advice of David Dallin— "Even if you refuse to accept any assistance from America, you will be called 'pro-American,' agent of Wall Street, American spy, in the sold [sic] of American monopolies, and finally a salesman for Coca Cola"—Rousset accepted this as a price to pay for Lovestone and Brown's aid.[84] However, he denied any charge that the US government lurked behind the AFL and issued frequent statements reassuring the public that the CICRC maintained no financial links with any state: "This rule, which admits no exceptions, guarantees [its] independence."[85]

Rousset made similarly righteous pledges over the years to the CICRC's own members. These seemed plausible in part because Reumont took care to limit participants' access to any figures liable to raise awkward questions. "Don't worry," he once wrote to Rousset. "In my meeting minutes I never cite numbers related to our budget."[86] Nor did he cite names. The arrangements with Brown and Lovestone and later with Josselson and O'Shea were conveyed to the plenary commission in the vaguest terms possible, as private fund-raising conducted by Rousset under his own "personal and moral authority."[87] Other information that, while not strictly financial, was nevertheless potentially compromising was also withheld; when Théo Bernard returned from an April 1953 trip to the United States, for example, he reported to the assembled membership that he had lobbied at the UN and consulted with "specialists on Russian questions" at Columbia University—but omitted mention of a detour to Washington, DC, where he had met with Louis T. Olom in the Office of Psychological Intelligence and other State Department officials.[88]

Greater honesty about such matters would probably not have troubled every CICRC participant. The Dutch, for instance, were frank in their appreciation for US power. It is unlikely, though, that all members of the Belgian, Spanish, and French delegations—Louis Martin-Chauffier in particular—would have remained affiliated with the organization had they had known the truth. Nor is it imaginable that the Spaniards would have knowingly embraced the use of a conservative Catholic "fund-raiser" whose previous job experience consisted of directing the pro-Nationalist American Spanish Relief Fund.[89] The majority of CICRC delegates were sincerely devoted to the notion that, as witnesses on behalf of mankind, they could engage in "defense of the defenseless, . . . speaking the truth in good faith and without hatred" while "refusing absolutely" to become a Cold War tool of the Americans.[90] Assured ad nauseam by Rousset that "the CICRC completely forbids itself from accepting State funding," they took the author of *L'Univers concentrationnaire* at his word.[91] They can be accused, perhaps, of naïveté or willful ignorance, but of little else.

It is important to stress most CICRC members' unwittingness of CIA involvement in their affairs. But knowledge of that unwittingness, by itself, does little to help answer the most pressing question raised by the existence of the funding relationship: how was the commission's work influenced by the US government? This problem can only really be addressed by examining what the group went on to do—and what occurred when its actions ultimately contravened American wishes. Some things, however, were clear from the outset. First, the fledgling CICRC needed no enticement from US operatives to engage in anti-Soviet activism: members were opposed to Stalinism for reasons of their own that grew out of Western Europe's internal midcentury politics. Second, their novel framework for condemning Karaganda and Kolyma as replicas of Buchenwald and Ravensbrück was not imposed on them by their backers; indeed, the notion that Resistance survivors could bear witness against a unitary, timeless "concentrationary universe" was alien to the Americans. As Rousset complained in early 1950, US cold warriors did "not at all grasp the importance" of his initiative until confronted with the staggering mass of press coverage it was receiving across a continent where, as he impatiently explained to them, *anciens déportés* retained "immense moral prestige" and "memory of the Nazi concentration camps remains extraordinarily *vivace*."[92]

Accordingly, Rousset behaved from the start as if his funders should be grateful for the favor that he was bestowing upon them, not vice versa. In his entreaties to the AFL and American intellectuals, he refused to position himself as a supplicant—instead, he demanded "moral and material support that is complete, absolutely complete," and warned against "underestimating the importance of our project."[93] So cocksure was he that by 1951 British IRD agents (from whom Rousset sought aid with publicity, evidence, and witnesses rather than direct financial assistance) threw up their hands: "Handling Rousset in his present mood is rather like handling a jumping cracker," wrote one exasperated official.[94] Rousset seems to have been more pliable in his dealings with Brown and Josselson, whom he viewed as "natural allies" to a greater extent than the denizens of London's Foreign Office.[95] He was, nevertheless, emphatic that he would not compromise his vision to suit their ends. His 1954 letter to Josselson not only made this attitude explicit but thanked the recipient for having respected it so thoroughly: "In four years (and this would surprise not only our enemies but many of our friends, who consider themselves clairvoyant and cynical)," he wrote, "you have never once suggested or proposed anything to our Commission, even though you could have. All the initiatives, always, have come from us.... You recognize the CICRC as sovereign in its decisions."[96]

It does not follow from this pronouncement that, as Tony Judt has sanguinely suggested, CIA involvement ultimately did little to shape nongovernmental Cold War endeavors like the CICRC.[97] The fact remains that the commission could not have functioned without its backers. And despite Rousset's claims to "sovereignty," he did not simply accept "packages" of money from his American liaisons and go his merry way: inevitably, these individuals became entangled in his enterprise. The archives offer fragmentary, tantalizing hints of their degree of involvement over the years: a flurry of correspondence to arrange a meeting between Rousset and Brown in the autumn of 1951; a note scheduling an early 1953 gathering among Rousset, Bernard, Josselson, and Brown "to seriously plan [Bernard's] New York voyage"; a 1955 letter from Rousset to Lovestone intricately updating him on the CICRC's China inquiry.[98] None of these materials suggest that the Americans exerted heavy-handed influence over the Frenchmen; Lovestone, Brown, Josselson, O'Shea, and their "donors" should not be conceptualized as puppeteers behind a curtain who controlled the CICRC's movements. They should, however, be understood as fellow players in its drama, from the opening scene onward.

## Defining the Concentration Camp Regime

In the autumn of 1950, as Brown and Lovestone were wrangling over whether they could "be of some assistance to this group," the Nazi camp survivors involved in the commission were occupied with their first shared task—namely, staking out the parameters of their new organization.[99] Armed with retrospective knowledge of the group's impending Cold War alliance, it is tempting to engage in a cynical reading of their early acts of self-definition: surely, participants fashioned whatever guidelines they believed would best facilitate condemnation of the USSR? But this was not the case. Anticommunism was one powerful motivating force for CICRC members, but it fails to explain their initial debates over the commission's identity and mission. However intense their political sympathies and antipathies, members were also driven to find meaning in their past suffering. In the end, the choices that they collectively made about which forms of victimization did and did not merit recognition had more to do with their desire to draw the proper lessons from Nazi violence than with their aspiration to censure Stalin.

Nowhere was this more evident than in the organization's divisive early conversations about a deceptively simple problem: what, precisely, was a "concentration camp"? It may seem surprising that the CICRC was troubled over this issue, since many of its adherents had already written books describing the Nazi *univers concentrationnaire*. Nevertheless, the group's definitional discussions proved contentious. It is, of course, true that the political stakes were high, since the characteristics the CICRC declared inherent to "concentration camps" would determine whether Stalin's gulag, Franco's prisons, or French Tunisian detention centers, respectively, could be identified as such. But the real discord had more fundamental origins: how could survivors fashion a cut-and-dry definition of the concentrationary universe they had endured that did justice to their unspeakably traumatic experience?

The answer proved elusive. A work of testimony could characterize the concentration camp as, in Rousset's well-known phrasing, "an amazing and complex machine of expiation," but poetic or metaphorical language was evidently inappropriate for the "juridical institution" the CICRC purported to be.[100] Nor was it feasible for the commission to adopt the makeshift solution of the American prosecution at Nuremberg—that is, using image and film to provide an otherwise impossible "explanation of what the words 'concentration camp' imply."[101] Another option tempted some members: refusing to address the issue at all. "We have no need—we, the former deportees—to define the concentrationary regime in advance of the inquiry," declared Léon Mazeaud. "We bear the terms of the definition in our flesh, in our blood, in our soul. We know too well the smell of man rotting—that, there, is the concentration camp. How could we pass by it without being nauseated? We are sure we will not be mistaken."[102] Mazeaud's defiant pronouncement later proved significant. But in the short term, it could not stand. The CICRC aspired to issue solemn verdicts on the "concentrationary" nature of present-day carceral systems. Thus it required concrete criteria regarding the characteristics that might merit the designation. Like it or not, participants were compelled to grope for a sufficiently categorical, legalistic rhetoric with which to encapsulate the essence of their past ordeal.

The French commission's "Open Letter" as well as the CICRC's "Fundamental Declaration" of October 20, 1950, might have led an observer to expect that the group would tackle the quandary by invoking human rights. Both of these documents employed the idiom. "The concentrationary problem," according to the "Open Letter," "places directly in question all the rights of man as they were proclaimed in the Charter, especially the right of the human person to bodily and moral integrity and the right to work."[103] The October text continued in this vein, asserting that the CICRC "bases its action on the Declaration of Human Rights adopted by the United Nations."[104] Consequently, some members did express interest in defining the concentration camp as (in Belgian member Martin Dehousse's formulation) "a system or regime *contravening the essential rights of the human person*."[105] It is easy to see the appeal of such a definitional tactic. For one thing, the language of human rights was now formally recognized, codified, and sanctioned by the UN. For another, at least as conceived by the UDHR, human rights operated in liberal terms centered on the claims of the sovereign individual. Not all CICRC participants were liberals, but—instrumentally speaking—a human rights framework that excluded social rights might have made it possible for the organization to denounce the Soviet gulag while looking past various Western penal and colonial labor schemes.

In the end, however, the commission adopted Rousset's circumspection about using the language of rights to condemn the camp universe. Members' reasons for doing so were based, once again, on a sense that talk of offended "rights" was inadequate to represent their own "concentrationary" injuries. "There is no equivalence between the two terms," Damien Reumont explained, since "not *every* violation of the rights of man presents a concentrationary character." It was "precisely" the task of the CICRC to draw a distinction between the staggering harms of the camps and mere human rights abuses, he added, whatever natural feelings of "indignation" might arise in response to the latter.[106] Others agreed. Though the "Open Letter" had proudly described survivors as the world's "most vigilant and tenacious defenders of the essential rights of man as they are enumerated in the Universal Declaration of Human Rights," ultimately members were not really interested in defending multiple enumerated rights. They hoped, rather, to preserve a singular boundary between "normal" abuses of human dignity and "concentrationary" evil—or, to put it in other terms, between Compiègne and Buchenwald.[107]

Thus participants agreed that the rhetoric of rights did not offer a way forward. As their discussions proceeded, however, they managed to agree on little else. Fatefully, French respondents to Rousset's "Appeal" had tasked Germaine Tillion and

Louis Martin-Chauffier with "defining the concentration camp, and defining *what is not a concentration camp*" in early 1950, before the International Commission came into being.[108] Martin-Chauffier, ill for much of the year, contributed little; Tillion therefore took on the assignment alone. Perhaps more than any other CICRC participant, the French anthropologist aimed for emotional detachment when she wrote about the camps in this era, trying desperately (as she put it later) to "forget myself" through cold analysis.[109] As a result, the draft text she circulated to her French, Dutch, German, Spanish, and Belgian counterparts in November 1950 was resolutely minimalist and disengaged from issues of victims' experience. Two "essential" characteristics defined the "concentrationary regime," Tillion wrote: "arbitrary privation of liberty" and "forced labor for the profit of the State."[110]

This bare-bones definition presented obvious advantages from an anti-Soviet perspective: Stalin's gulag, widely reputed to be less sadistic than the Nazi camps, could doubtless be shown to meet her two criteria. Nevertheless, her fellow survivors greeted Tillion's work not with delight at its strategic utility but with dismay at its inadequate rendering of their own sufferings. Rousset led the charge. A concentrationary regime, he asserted, was one "that brings about the dehumanization of man." Tillion's text, which referred only in passing to "debasement [*avilissement*]" as an "aggravation" of the crime in question, was insufficient.[111] Reumont was just as critical.[112] While Tillion and the Belgian priest both subscribed to a logic of absolute distinction between concentration camps and "normal" prisons, they disagreed about how to uphold this binary. According to Reumont, it could not be through reference to the profit-generating use of forced labor: this feature was not "specific" to concentration camps but was an element of many modern penal systems.[113] (He was correct: the humanitarian prison reform movement in post-1945 France took as a precept the injunction that prisoners "must work"; the UN-affiliated International Penal and Penitentiary Foundation declared in 1951 that prisoner labor "is considered a means of moral regeneration.")[114] Though he did not mention Jews, Roma, or other victim groups, Reumont also pointed out that the Nazi concentrationary universe had contained "extermination camps" for "those unable to work"; even in labor-oriented camps, he noted, "tasks were imposed on detainees that had no economic character, but whose purpose was uniquely to torment them and cause them to die." He was equally dubious of the notion that arbitrary detention could serve as a defining characteristic, asserting that the common-law criminals in Buchenwald had been arrested "justly" but that, nevertheless, "the regime they were subjected to was not just, because it was a concentrationary regime." Ultimately, he argued, the only meaningful criterion for identifying such a regime was "the *inhumane conditions* of detention" for prisoners.[115]

Tillion rejected Reumont's principle on the same grounds he had rejected hers: nonspecificity to "concentration camps." Ordinary prisons, she pointed out, robbed inmates of their dignity as well. "It is in the nature of all systems of detention," she wrote, "even those reputed to be 'democratic' or reputed to be 'civilized,' to torment, offend, wound the humanity of their victims. . . . These deplorable facts are part of the nature of all detention systems, though there can exist innumerable degrees within the enterprise of dehumanization."[116] Certainly the Nazi camps had ranked abominably high on the scale, but such an observation was an unstable basis for defining them. She dismissed Reumont's other points: "arbitrary" detention had many meanings beyond the absence of a trial, and while it was true that there might be "detainees who do not work" in "extermination camps," this outlying fact was not of sufficient importance to alter how concentration camps in general were defined. While she reluctantly consented to add "inhumane conditions of detention" to her list in a second draft, presented at the December 1950 meeting of the CICRC, she included an underlined caveat: "*The two criteria of forced labor and arbitrary arrest can suffice to characterize a concentrationary regime, even if the third criterion of inhumane conditions does not exist.*"[117]

In response, Reumont issued his final parry in February 1951: a "Note" addressed to the entire membership. This document insisted that dehumanizing treatment was the *only* "essential" feature of a concentration camp. The aim of condemning Stalin's gulag, Reumont acknowledged, was well served by Tillion's emphasis on "economic ends" and her refusal to take death camps seriously into account. (Here, though he again did not refer to Jewish suffering in his own voice, he quoted from Hannah Arendt's commentary on the grotesque "economic uselessness" of "transport[ing] millions of Jews to the east and set[ting] up enormous, costly extermination factories.")[118] But the utility of Tillion's definition for anti-Soviet purposes, Reumont wrote with emphasis, did not excuse its poor representation of "the *Nazi* concentrationary regime."[119] For him, despite his evident Cold War sympathies, the imperative to do justice to the past was the more important issue.

Though the bulk of Reumont's "Note" was combative, its conciliatory final pages did gesture toward a way out of the increasingly problematic stalemate in which the CICRC found itself. "We all give the word 'concentrationary' a very special meaning," he wrote, "using principles that we have drawn from our own experience." But perhaps members needed to abandon the frustrating effort to capture that "special meaning" in language. "Practically speaking," he reflected, it was less important that the CICRC's definition express the essence of Nazi evil than that it be usable in institutional contexts dominated by non-survivors. Tillion's three-point list did not satisfy him, but so long as the language on inhumanity was retained without caveat, he could concede that it had the advantage of flexibility. "If we are addressing the [International Labor Organization]," he mused, "we will emphasize the 'forced labor' aspect, since it is that aspect which interests them; if we are addressing the Commission on Human Rights, we will insist on the aspect of 'violations of man's fundamental freedoms,' etc."[120] Such reasoning convinced his exhausted colleagues. At the CICRC's April 1951 meeting, Tillion's "very concise . . . formulation" was finally accepted by the membership. A "concentrationary regime," declared the International Commission, was any internment system marked by "arbitrary privation of liberty; massive forced labor for the profit of the State; [and] inhumane conditions of detention."[121]

The notion that concentration camps could be identified on the basis of this brief, bloodless checklist was a far cry from Mazeaud's early claim that they were knowable on the basis of survivors' nausea at "the smell of man rotting." But in fact it was CICRC's members' subscription to his sensory, intuitive formulation that *permitted* them to adopt such anodyne criteria. As Rousset never tired of repeating, "A person cannot realize what a concentration camp is unless he himself has been there"; hence, in a sense, definitions were beside the point.[122] Indeed, they were dangerous. They implied that any intelligent observer—the "perfectly sincere people" of the Red Cross, for instance, nevertheless infamously duped by the Nazis at Theresienstadt in 1944—could identify a camp.[123] This would have obviated the need for survivors as expert witnesses and was therefore an idea that members protested at every turn—for example, insisting that "we will not recognize the authority of any inquiry [into concentration camps] led by the UN, nor its validity, if this inquiry is conducted without the participation of ex-*concentrationnaires*, because they alone are technically and morally qualified."[124] In the years ahead, therefore, though the CICRC made strategic use of its three-point definition in just the fashion Reumont had proposed, the text proved of negligible investigatory importance to the group. Believing, with Mazeaud, that "we bear the terms of the definition in our flesh, in our blood, in our soul," CICRC members determined whether penal regimes were "concentrationary" not by applying Tillion's list but by assessing whether victims' suffering resonated with their own experience. Thus, ultimately, both the commission's long debate over definitional principles and its swift, pragmatic conclusion served early notice that, whatever its Cold War commitments, the group's orientation toward the present would be largely dictated by participants' relationship to the past.

## The CICRC's Jewish Question

The CICRC members' 1950–1951 discussions about the nature of "the concentrationary regime" were inextricably entwined with their debates over a different issue: that of who could join their group. The survivors involved in the commission did not have any interest in a grassroots "mass membership" model like that later adopted by Amnesty International; nor, despite their prominence, did they conceive of themselves as a collective of "personalities"—as, for example, in the International Committee for Political Prisoners of the 1920s and '30s or the Bertrand Russell Tribunal of the 1960s and '70s.[125] Rather, they understood the CICRC and all of its subsidiary national commissions as identity-based assemblies composed of delegates, each serving as a representative for one community of camp survivors. Accordingly, they viewed the factor uniting them not as common anti-concentrationary *sentiment* but as shared concentrationary *experience*. What counted as a "concentration camp" therefore largely governed who was eligible to participate.

Matters were more complicated, however, because—in keeping with widely accepted postwar frameworks for conceptualizing Nazi violence and hierarchizing its victims—Rousset's "Appeal" had called not upon "*survivants*" but rather upon "*anciens déportés politiques.*" This ideational privileging both of deportation beyond national borders and of political imprisonment, when combined with members' anxiety to maintain an absolute distinction between "true concentration camps" and other forms of detention, meant that early CICRC participants confronted a welter of problems in seeking to delimit membership. These were not quickly resolved: since Europeans had been transported, imprisoned, set to labor, tortured, and brutalized in countless ways during World War II, the commission needed to address a seemingly endless series of specific queries. Could individuals who had been detained by their own national government rather than the Germans join? No. What of those who had been imprisoned in German-run but domestically located internment camps—Breendonk in Belgium, for example? No: "We are all aware of the severity of the detention regime at Breendonk," but this did not alter the fact that its inmates "were not sent to Germany" and thus were not, properly speaking, deportees.[126] And what of the German delegates, who had remained within their own state's territory while serving time in Dachau, Buchenwald, or Sachsenhausen? An explicit exception was made for them, as well as for Dutch resisters who had been imprisoned in Vught, an unusual SS-run concentration camp in the Netherlands. Non-Germans transported as volunteer or conscripted laborers? Certainly not: their claims to having been "deported" were regarded as positively blasphemous by some of Rousset's followers.[127] Members of French, Dutch, or Belgian resistance movements whose deportation to the Reich had ended in a prison cell rather than a camp? Against all logic of concentrationary "experience," but in line with their prestige as Resistance deportees, these figures were admitted.

All such questions, however, were overshadowed by a greater one: what of Hitler's "racial" victims? Could Holocaust survivors—say, former Auschwitz inmate Georges Wellers, who had responded enthusiastically to the "Appeal"—take part in the CICRC? David Rousset answered no. "The sole characteristic that I demand in order to belong to this Commission," he told reporters at a November 1949 press conference, "is to be a political deportee who is irreproachable in his political life."[128] Rousset, who made this statement while literally flanked by supporter Gaston Weil, a Jew who had been deported to Buchenwald as a resister, was not motivated by any desire to exclude Jews per se. His activist work throughout his life had always been undertaken alongside numerous Jewish comrades, from Georges Altman and Gérard Rosenthal to Roger Stéphane. However, he recognized the prestige that clung to Resistance deportees but not to "racial" survivors in most of Western Europe. To lay claim to the legacy of "the most elevated expression of the European Resistance," he understood, his organization would have to be composed only of political survivors.

Nevertheless, to bar Jewish Holocaust victims must have sat uneasily with the author of *Le Pitre ne rit pas*, not least because it made nonsense of the central claim of his enterprise: that "expertise" in concentrationary affairs arose from the simple fact of suffering in the Nazi camps. "Racial" deportees, too, were among those who knew "in [their] muscles" what the concentrationary universe had been; it was incoherent at best to declare that they were not equipped to bear witness to its continuation. Therefore, Rousset adopted a strangely inconsistent program in the following months: continuing to trumpet his intention of welcoming only "those who were truly in the Resistance" while proceeding as if he were oblivious to the exclusionary implications of this stance.[129] In June, for instance, he began firing off letters to distant contacts in Tel Aviv and Jerusalem seeking Israeli CICRC delegates. "I believe," he wrote, "that it would be of great importance for Palestinian former deportees to the Nazi camps to participate in the International Commission of Inquiry."[130] The following month, he demanded Israeli support in forceful and frankly threatening terms. In a letter to Julius Margolin, a Jewish gulag survivor now living in Israel, Rousset opined that to "compromise with the concentration camp system would be fatal for all of us, but above all, perhaps, for the Jewish people. . . . Such an attitude of 'neutrality' on the part of our Jewish friends would not only risk being utterly misunderstood, but could become—at least in today's sick Europe—an argument in favor of antisemitism."[131]

Rousset's unsettling entreaty to Margolin for "complete solidarity among former victims, Jewish or not," came to nothing. Its existence, however, does suggest that given a propitious opportunity he would have been willing to countenance the participation of Hitler's former "racial" victims in the CICRC.[132] It is likely fair to say, in other words, that his commitment to an elitist, Resistance-based membership criterion was never more than halfhearted. We cannot be sure, however; following his failed attempt to locate an Israeli delegation, Rousset fell silent for several years on the issue of Holocaust survivors' eligibility. In consequence, other participants stepped forward to define the organization's policy.

This they did in unmistakably exclusionary terms, seeking to replicate the "patriotic" rules that governed federations such as the FNDIR and the ADIR in France and ExPoGe in the Netherlands. Initially, ADIR members actually suggested that Rousset abandon the word *concentrationnaire* and refer instead to "people who have been locked up for the love of their country."[133] Meanwhile, the Dutch and Belgian commissions were categorical in their insistence that participants possess resistance credentials. Reumont emerged as a particularly intransigent defender of this principle. It was now evident, he wrote, that CNPPA members had been mistaken in their immediate postwar impulse toward unity among all categories of deportees: "We forgot," he wrote, "that *it is not the fact* of suffering together that profoundly unites men, but the *common ideal* for which they accept the suffering. . . . Moreover, we *submitted* to this community of suffering in the camps, where we shared an inhuman existence with criminals, common-law convicts, and people interned for reasons other than selfless patriotic activity." Shared traumatic experience "in itself," he now averred, was not sufficient to produce "a communion of hearts." Such fellowship was possible only among those whose sojourn through the *univers concentrationnaire* could be figured as heroic and self-sacrificial.[134] Reumont did not refer explicitly to "racial" deportees, but his lumping of "people interned for reasons other than selfless patriotic activity" together with the camps' hated criminal populations made his position clear.

This hierarchical reasoning—which, it bears repeating, barred victims of racial persecution but not Jewish resisters like Weil—triumphed without controversy in the CICRC. The commission's 1951 constitution made the rule official: "The only people who can be admitted as members of the association are those persons of either sex who were deported to Nazi concentration camps because of their patriotic, selfless, or anti-Nazi activity."[135] Thus the matter was settled—at least for the time being. It is important to underline, however, that the organization did not therefore abandon its claims to "represent" far broader groups of deportees. Indeed, commission members continued to lay numeric claim not only to the "racial" deportation's survivors but to Jews who had perished in the Shoah—averring, for example, that they were carrying out a sacred duty which "we owe as well to our dead, to our six or seven million dead."[136] That the vast majority of those millions would have been excluded from the organization had they lived was never mentioned. Thus CICRC participants legitimated their initiative through a process that involved not only occluding but also appropriating the legacy of the genocide.

The CICRC's history was also entangled with the afterlife of Jewish loss in ways that went far beyond rhetorical flourish, for the dramatis personae of the organization exceeded the official membership roster and included multiple individuals of Jewish origin. Most importantly, two of the movement's leading figures were Léon Poliakov and Théo Bernard, Jews for whom the Holocaust had been a cataclysmic, life-defining event. Born in Saint Petersburg in 1910, Poliakov had emigrated to France with his family at ten, fleeing Bolshevism. After a stint living in Germany, he returned to Paris in 1924, gained a law degree, and enlisted in the French military when World War II began. Captured by German forces, he escaped from a prisoner-of-war camp, regained Paris, and then passed into the southern "free zone" in October 1941. There, living under a false name, involved in various networks of Jewish resistance, and in constant motion between hide-outs, he managed to elude arrest. After the war, he was hired as director of research for the Centre de Documentation Juive Contemporaine (CDJC), a remarkable institution founded during the German occupation by Isaac Schneersohn and devoted to amassing systematic evidence of Nazi persecution of European Jewry. In this capacity Poliakov was appointed to assist the French team at Nuremberg. He found the trial "tedious" but was thrilled with the scholarly opportunities it afforded, retrieving three tons of material that helped him publish his first works on Nazi antisemitism.[137] He also assisted David Rousset on Le Pitre ne rit pas; the two men found that they got on well.

Thus in 1951, after a break with Schneersohn left Poliakov on "permanent vacation" from the CDJC and in awkward financial straits, he accepted an offer from Rousset to become his secretary—a job that amounted to serving as a jack-of-all-trades for the CICRC.[138] For the following four years, he performed a variety of duties: studying and translating Soviet penal codes, compiling information on abusive practices in the Eastern bloc, facilitating the organization's publishing operations, and carrying out various lines of foreign correspondence. Fluent in several languages and possessed of unparalleled knowledge on pertinent subjects, Poliakov was an invaluable asset; the CICRC quickly became dependent on his labor and expertise. But members acknowledged neither in any straightforward way, treating the pioneering scholar as a salaried subordinate instead of a partner.[139] Consider, for instance, what occurred in 1954 when the group decided to send Ravensbrück survivor Catherine Goetschel on a fact-finding mission to Bonn, Cologne, Hanover, Hamburg, Berlin, and Frankfurt to interview recent repatriates from Soviet camps.[140] Goetschel spoke no German, so Rousset determined that Poliakov would accompany her. In explaining the arrangement, he took pains to underline its hierarchical nature: Poliakov, he wrote to Goetschel, "is a charming and qualified man, and I am convinced that he will place himself entirely at your service . . . [but] it is evident that you alone are qualified to decide about everything involved in this voyage. . . . [Poliakov] may give good advice, but—once again—it is you who decide."[141] The CICRC's later report on Goetschel's thirty German interviews mentioned only that she had been accompanied by "an interpreter."[142]

It is true that Poliakov was not a former concentration camp inmate and therefore did not adhere to the CICRC's model of experientially acquired expertise. He was, however, widely recognized as one of the era's foremost authorities on Nazism and the camp system, especially after the 1951 publication of his *Bréviaire de la haine: Le III Reich et les Juifs* (later translated as *Harvest of Hate*), a then-unmatched analysis of the machinery of the "Final Solution." Though editors had been reluctant to touch the *Bréviaire*, which included frank discussion of Vichy's complicity, when the book was finally published by Calmann-Lévy it was greeted warmly. Academic critics recognized it as a "magisterial study . . . a top-tier historical work," and Sartre's *Les Temps modernes* endorsed Poliakov's "patient, nearly fastidious" research.[143] The *Bréviaire* received even higher praise abroad. Hannah Arendt's 1952 review for *Commentary*, for instance, stressed the unprecedented documentary value of this "excellent book."[144] For the CICRC, however, Poliakov's stature as a leading scholar of the camps was immaterial. He worked on the Jewish genocide, which CICRC members conceptualized as secondary to political deportation. What is more, his research was in their eyes inferior to the deep knowledge born of "lived experience." To have acknowledged Poliakov's authority would have been to abandon the bedrock principle that "only the deportees can understand the concentration camp regime."

Poliakov himself appears to have acquiesced to this dictum, commenting to Rousset on the gap between his own "pale" understanding gained from mere "reading" and that available through "direct human contact" with survivors. A lively missive he sent after his 1954 journey with Goetschel went to great lengths praising her "guts," "devotion," and "diplomatic acumen," and reassuring Rousset that "my role [was] confined to translating as best I could and indicating the exact spelling of names and places."[145] Though his liking for Goetschel seems sincere (recall that her Jewish husband had died in Auschwitz; one can surmise that she and Poliakov had much to discuss during their travels), this was hardly a generous description of his own weeks of intensive work. What is still more puzzling than his acceptance of the CICRC's dogma of concentrationary experience was Poliakov's silence on its exclusion of "racial" deportees from membership—a policy at odds with the case he made in the *Bréviaire* that "political" and "racial" survivors ought to now coalesce in a single "category of men and women" united in "tight fraternity."[146] Financial necessity, perhaps, helped reconcile him to the situation. So, too, did hatred of Stalin. Poliakov's Russian émigré identity, and the powerful anti-Soviet ideology that accompanied it, may have proved just as important as his identity as a Jew and a scholar of Nazism in this case.

Strange as Poliakov's position was, it contained fewer contradictions than that of Théo Bernard. Born in 1914, Bernard had become close to Rousset during their prewar youth as Trotskyist militants. The young lawyer was ambitious, brilliant (Rousset did not hesitate to use the term "genius"), and politically passionate.[147] On August 21, 1941, along with over forty prominent confrères, he was arrested by the French police as part of the infamous "Jewish lawyers' roundup" and sent to Drancy, a U-shaped, multistory complex just northeast of Paris.[148] First employed by the Germans as a police barracks, Drancy had only begun to function as a detention facility the previous day; Bernard was inmate number 229. In its early months the camp subjected roughly four thousand male Jewish prisoners to a punishing regime of starvation-level rations and brutal treatment. Beginning in mid-1942, however, as the "Final Solution" began in earnest on French soil, Drancy became a transit site—that is, a short-term holding dock for Jews of both sexes before their deportation. Bernard's own turn of phrase was apt: first under French police administration and then, after July 1943, under direct SS control, Drancy came to function as a "supplier for the crematori[a]" of Nazi Germany.[149] It served as the primary assembly point for the French "racial" deportation, and the great majority of the nearly seventy thousand men, women, and children who passed through it—two-thirds of them noncitizens—did so briefly, before being shipped on to their deaths.

Théo Bernard was not one of these deportees. Rather, he counted among the minuscule number who remained interned at Drancy throughout its existence—he was liberated from the camp after almost exactly three years on August 17, 1944. Bernard managed to avoid deportation in part through French citizenship and veteran status (he served in France's brief 1939–1940 campaign) and in part owing to additional strokes of fortune.[150] Chief among these was his appointment in late summer 1943 as *chef de service adjoint*, Bureau des Effectifs, within the "Chancellery" of the inmate administration recently imposed on the camp by the SS. This privileged position helped ensure his categorization as a "C-1" (a theoretically non-deportable cadre) in Drancy's internal hierarchy, and earned him the right to receive packages, take his soup directly from the kitchen, maintain a "normal haircut," and share his room with only two other prisoners.[151] One of his roommates was Drancy's "Jewish commander," the highest-ranking cadre of them all. In 1944, Bernard was even granted special license to leave the camp for twenty-four hours. "I was exempted from wearing the [yellow] star for the duration of the leave," he remembered decades later.[152]

However, Bernard's job also forced him to participate in the machinery of deportation. With, as Adam Rayski writes, the "evident intention of making them his accomplices," Alois Brunner and his SS henchmen required Drancy's inmates to carry out nearly every aspect of the preparations for transporting their fellow Jews east, from frisking them for valuables to cleaning the railway cars they would occupy.[153] Bernard's job as head of Effectifs made him responsible for maintaining tallies of the camp's ever-shifting population and, most distressingly, carrying out the "roll call" for each departure.[154] Thus, for instance, on the morning of July 31, 1944, he helped ensure that every one of the 1,024 adults and 297 children who composed the infamous Convoy 77, the final large transport from Drancy to Auschwitz, was present and accounted for at the moment of departure. Bernard carried out this "thankless task," according to his superior in the prisoner administration, with "a great deal of attentiveness and tact."[155] Most members of the convoy were gassed immediately upon disembarking; slightly more than two hundred lived to see the end of the war. Bernard himself, along with approximately fifteen hundred other remaining prisoners, was liberated from Drancy eighteen days later.

His postwar relationship to this terrible history was difficult. Bernard wrote and spoke about Drancy seldom; when he did, he avoided testimonial-style narration in favor of bitter, analytical, nearly anthropological description. In every instance, however, he dwelt in similar language on the fate of children. His 1946 article "Judenlager Drancy," a Marxist dissection of camp "society" on the model of Rousset's *L'Univers concentrationnaire*, opened with the image of "six-year-old heads of household, carrying blankets too heavy for a little sister," walking toward the fleet of buses that would take them from Drancy's gates to the Bobigny railway station, from which they would be conveyed onward to Auschwitz.[156] Twenty years later, he was still fixated on these grave little boys and girls "guiding their younger brothers and sisters by the hand, carrying blankets, carrying a chocolate bar that someone managed to give them" in the final moments. "One cannot forget this when one has seen it," he remarked, before a rare venture into the first-person singular: "I do not believe that anything worse ever existed. I even believe that the subsequent death of these children could not have been worse."[157] Bernard, like other prisoners, believed that the transports' shadowy destination was a labor camp or perhaps a ghetto; he did not, he insisted, imagine Birkenau.[158] Nevertheless, he admitted to feelings of "relief"—even "euphoria"—on the part of those who managed in each instance to remain behind, watching the buses pull into the distance. "It was not necessarily the best people who stayed, far from it," he noted tersely.[159]

No sources grant any insight into how Bernard understood his dark wartime experience to inform his postwar advocacy for the CICRC. We cannot know the means by which he squared his personal knowledge of *les déportés*, emblematized in his mind by the six-year-olds of Convoy 77, with the views of an organization that equated deportation with willing, politically motivated sacrifice. In one official document, Reumont misleadingly counted the CICRC's legal counselor among those who had "heavily participated" in the clandestine struggle against Hitler's Germany—but Bernard does not appear to have encouraged such representations, and he was uninterested in assimilating Jewish suffering into a narrative of patriotic combat.[160] Indeed, he brushed aside coreligionists' occasional attempts to pursue such a logic. Writer Jean-Jacques Bernard (no relation) might have tried to "get away from Judaism" by claiming that if he had died in the camps it would have been "for France," Théo Bernard wrote, but this would have been a lie: like it or not, he was "arrested as a Jew."[161] Bernard rejected the idea that Jews constituted a race and was scornful of the antisemitic mythology of international Jewish unity; national and class loyalties had divided Drancy into warring factions, he wrote.[162] Nevertheless, he understood the "racial" deportation as a distinct phenomenon targeting a recognizable group for their identity, not their actions. Perhaps a sense that the Jewish catastrophe was fundamentally distinct from the history of wartime political deportation actually helps explain his acceptance of the CICRC's exclusionary membership policies.

Whether Bernard endorsed or merely queasily tolerated the International Commission's effective ban on "racial" deportees, he would not have considered this the determining factor in his own status as a nonmember. He had not been deported, and he emphatically did not view himself as a concentration camp victim. Drancy, Bernard insisted, was "entirely different from the German camps," a "completely different thing" from the *univers concentrationnaire*.[163] (Some historians agree—though, without venturing too far into psychologizing speculation, we might wonder whether Bernard's vehemence on the point arose from an aversion to equating his own wartime suffering with that of the children on the buses.)[164] When he received Rousset's offer to serve as legal adviser to the newly founded CICRC, he accepted as a lawyer and a political ally, not as a fellow "specialist" in concentrationary suffering. Bernard became Rousset's right-hand man in administering the organization, participating in every plenary conference and nearly every informal leadership meeting; managing relations with the UN, the Council of Europe, and the ILO; orchestrating the mock trials of the Soviet and Chinese regimes; traveling alongside members to inspect Greek and Tunisian prison camps; publishing articles on the group's behalf; and lobbying continually for its interests in New York and Washington. But he undertook all these activities in a professional capacity—the CICRC did not call upon its lawyer to speak about what he had seen, felt, and done in Drancy. And, except for a handful of striking slippages into the first person—for example, he remarked in court in 1953 that "we [*nous*] who knew the camps . . . all retain terrible memories of them"—he did not volunteer to do so.[165] During his entire association with the commission, Bernard helped others to bear witness without identifying as a witness himself. He was the heart and soul of the CICRC, but, like the war's other "racial" victims, he could never be party to its "communion of hearts."

All foundings demand exclusions, and all projects undertaken in the name of memory entail selective forgetting. But the CICRC's creation involved especially tortured and intimate processes of rejecting certain individuals and certain pasts. The organization's relationship to the Jewish genocide was characterized not only by absence and denial but by appropriation, ambivalence, and haunting. It therefore has implications for our larger understanding of the relationship between Holocaust memory and postwar activism on behalf of global humanity. An earlier generation of scholarship posited a direct, causal connection between the two, suggesting that human rights, in particular, arose in answer to the cry of "Never again!" In the last decade, however, historians have become skeptical of this construction: "There was no widespread Holocaust consciousness in the postwar era," Samuel Moyn observes, "so human rights could not have been a response to it."[166] The story of the CICRC's founding as an anti-concentrationary organization that was composed exclusively of resisters but, behind the scenes, was actually run by a preeminent Holocaust historian and a Drancy survivor, points toward a reality more complex than is allowed for by either the old or new account. It suggests that concern for worldwide victims of state violence in the early postwar years, while not motivated by "Holocaust consciousness"—which indeed did not yet exist as such—may well have been driven by a sort of Holocaust *un*conscious. In the end, the small ghosts of Convoy 77 hovered over the anti–concentration camp movement's birth, each of them a disavowed "other" to the heroic political survivor redemptively constructed as a privileged witness on behalf of a still-suffering humanity.

In 1954, Damien Reumont contributed a retrospective article on the "spontaneous beginnings" and early years of the CICRC's history to *Associations: The Review of International Organizations and Meetings*. This short piece of self-puffery made a number of familiar claims about the group that this chapter has shown to be problematic (that it functioned as the "spokesman for the vast majority of survivors of the Nazi concentration camps," was "nonpartisan," and "base[d] its activities" on the Universal Declaration of Human Rights) or simply false (that it refused "governmental subsidy" since to accept it "would be, necessarily, to abdicate a measure of its objectivity"). The "nonpolitical," "first and foremost humanitarian" collective that Reumont described certainly sounded admirable.[167] But the real CICRC—the one whose "international" character emerged through Cold War compromise, whose cast of characters included Irving Brown and Léon Poliakov, whose funding relied upon furtive CIA cash drops, whose bylaws effectively banned Holocaust victims, whose members abjured the language of human rights and squabbled to define their object of inquiry—is of much greater historical interest. The process of its founding, far from being "spontaneous," involved a drawn-out series of choices reflecting the unexpected ways in which Western European memory of World War II's terrible violence both shaped and was shaped by postwar forces, most importantly the Cold War politics of anticommunism.

If Reumont's 1954 article blithely suppressed all this history in order to repeat the fable of organic, inclusive, apolitical moral unity, one assertion it contained was nevertheless true: the CICRC, he wrote, now possessed "a record of substantial achievement despite the relatively short span of its operation."[168] It is to this record that we can now turn our attention. By early 1951, the organization had taken concrete form, secured funding, and elaborated membership criteria. It had also now formally christened itself the Commission Internationale contre le Régime Concentrationnaire, rejecting Rousset's original formulation ("Commission of Inquiry") in order to stress members' commitment to "positive action" rather than mere "platonic investigation."[169] But it had not yet taken any such action. Members' promises to "suppress" or "abolish" concentration camps begged the question: even with the best will in the world—and even with American coffers open before them—what could a private collective of former victims possibly do to achieve such goals?[170] This query posed a greater difficulty to the movement than any of those we have yet considered. The following chapters take up the task of exploring how the group's members sought to use the concept of "concentrationary" internment and the identity of the expert witness to rise to the challenge of answering it.

# NUREMBERG RESTAGED

## The Soviet *Univers Concentrationnaire* on Trial

The question of what the CICRC might actually do to "suppress" concentration camps in the postwar world—and in the Soviet Union specifically—had been raised by skeptical observers from the moment of Rousset's 1949 "Appeal." That document, with its exaltation of survivors' visceral ability to identify camps by sight, sound, smell, and touch, had called for an "on site" investigation of Soviet detention conditions. Following its publication, Rousset had consistently maintained, with a straight face, that his next step would be to seek entry visas from Soviet authorities.[1] He declined to answer an audience member at his November 15 press conference who asked jeeringly, "Excuse me, Mr. Rousset, but suppose that by some extraordinary chance the Soviet government, through its embassy, refuses?"[2] The questioner may have been hostile, but the query was perfectly reasonable: the chances that the CICRC would be permitted into the USSR were nil. Thus as the International Commission's members came together in 1950, restless to embark on their first "positive action," it was unclear how they could carry out the key charges of the "Appeal": standing as witnesses to the "crime against humanity" of the Soviet gulag and condemning its "concentrationary" nature "before world opinion."[3]

The problem was a particularly sensitive one at this historical juncture. Following the landmark achievements of the postwar moment—Nuremberg's International Military Tribunal (IMT) and the subsequent Allied zonal trials, the founding of the United Nations, the Universal Declaration of Human Rights, the Genocide Convention—progress in "governing the world" and, in particular, creating global mechanisms of accountability for human rights violations appeared to have stalled indefinitely. The UN Economic and Social Council's 1947 declaration that the Commission on Human Rights would have no ability to act on the petitions submitted to it dealt an early blow to idealistic aspirations; the Soviet delegation's subsequent boycott of that commission meant that, as Samuel Moyn puts it, "the prospect of moving to legally enforce human rights across borders that a few observers still considered a live possibility as late as 1949 was dead by 1950."[4] As for international criminal law, by the end of the 1940s it was clear that Nuremberg would have no sequel in a permanent UN tribunal. Even prospects for a genuinely operational European Court on Human Rights appeared distant.[5] "The year 1949 resembles 1939," Henri Monneray, French assistant prosecutor at the IMT, wrote despairingly. "In the absence of international justice—that of Nuremberg seems to have disappeared without a trace—men once again realize their powerlessness."[6]

The CICRC took the impotence of international criminal law in the early 1950s as an opportunity rather than an impasse, seizing upon the courtroom as a symbolic space for bearing witness to otherwise hidden atrocities—and, more specifically, upon Nuremberg's rhetoric of "crimes against humanity" as an articulation of their own special duty to give voice to fellow victims. "Until now," Rousset announced in December 1950, "we have acknowledged the existence of crimes against humanity, but we have not yet created an institution capable of examining them, judging them, and organizing the struggle against them." Now the problem was solved: "The European Resistance, represented by the former political prisoners of the Nazi camps, has just created this institution" in the CICRC.[7] Since no supranational court existed that might put the "concentration camp universe" on trial, the International Commission itself would do so. Of course the group possessed no authority to prosecute acts of state: it could not impose sentences, compel changes in sovereign countries' legislation, or force detention facility closures. But, to be fair, no one had any such powers at this moment. The CICRC, as a collective of former Resistance deportees, at least possessed considerable moral authority. By announcing that it now considered itself an "international tribunal," and making clear that it would operate according to elaborately legalistic rules and procedures inspired by Nuremberg, the group only compounded its aura of gravitas.

Thus in May 1951 the commission put the Soviet Union "on trial" in Brussels for crimes against humanity. The mock trial was an extraordinary dramatic episode: for a full week, in a grand courtroom packed to the rafters with reporters and observers, Nazi camp survivors from throughout Western Europe earnestly acted out all the roles of a judiciary—judges, lawyers, bailiffs, clerks—as they listened to testimony against the USSR from a polyglot procession of former gulag inmates. The proceedings were punctuated by shouting matches and bloody brawls in the corridors, threats of diplomatic incidents, attempts to equate Nazi and Soviet "totalitarianism" in crude terms, and a great deal of Rousset's trademark grandstanding. They were also, however, marked by moments of heart-stopping pathos, as men and women haltingly, disjointedly recalled what they had suffered and seen in the Soviet camps to a panel of judges who had themselves once suffered greatly as well. Speaking in the name of "victims" everywhere, and invoking both the Nuremberg Charter and the Universal Declaration of Human Rights, the CICRC closed the hearings on June 1, 1951, by formally condemning the Soviet Union "before universal public opinion" for its "concentrationary regime" comparable to that of Nazi Germany.[8]

The CICRC's heavily publicized Brussels tribunal can be understood, first of all, as an ingenious Cold War propaganda stunt. With its parade of aggrieved witnesses, occasionally parodic aping of legal solemnity, and sweeping verdict, the trial was an extravagant chapter in what the British Information Research Department's 1951 midyear report called "the long-term operation of indoctrinating public opinion in the free world against Communism."[9] But labeling the event propagandistic is the beginning, not the end, of assessing its historical significance. Of greater interest here is the *form* that Rousset chose for his attack on the Soviet "camp universe": an international criminal tribunal. The CICRC's 1951 "trial" reveals the broad and ongoing influence of Nuremberg's juridical model for stigmatizing state-directed atrocities; in turn, it illustrates the essential role that Cold War motives played in the post-Nuremberg genealogy of Western European norms concerning the meaning of international justice, the nature of crimes against humanity, and the imperative to bear witness to victims' experience.

Of course, the CICRC's proceedings must be approached in a different register from those of Nuremberg. This is not because the commission tainted the lofty realm of international criminal law with the stench of base politics. The "fundamentally political nature" of the postwar Nazi trials (and of war crimes proceedings more generally) is universally acknowledged by scholars.[10] It is, rather, because—Rousset's outsize ambitions notwithstanding—the Brussels tribunal contributed nothing to the development of jurisprudence or legal doctrine. Myriad CICRC-affiliated lawyers took part—Théo Bernard, Paul Arrighi, Léon Mazeaud, Benjamin Stomps, P. J. Prinsen Geerligs, E. de Beer de Laer—but the ad hoc "trial" was (quite reasonably) ignored by the professional international legal community. Indeed, from a criminal law perspective the event was nonsensical: no individuals were in the dock. What is more, the provisions for meaningful defense were minimal, and the outcome was predetermined, lacking the element of "irreducible risk" inherent in real criminal hearings.[11] True, the event did not precisely constitute a show trial in the usual sense (since in a show trial, the court possesses the power to visit real punishment on the defendant), but it was certainly carried out for show.[12] It was, indeed, more show than trial.

And yet the ways that Rousset, Bernard, Balachowsky, Tillion, and the other survivors who composed the court chose to perform justice are revealing. Specifically, their tribunal may help us better understand the historical transition between what Lawrence Douglas has called the "aggressive war paradigm" of the IMT and the "victim-centered" and witness-oriented "atrocity paradigm" associated with the 1961 Israeli trial of German war criminal Adolf Eichmann and various post–Cold War international tribunals.[13] A decade before Eichmann arrived in Jerusalem, and a generation before the "reinvention" of international criminal law as "atrocity law," the CICRC embraced an "atrocity paradigm" in two ways.[14] First, it dissociated the concept of crimes against humanity from international warfare and took as self-evident the still unsettled notion that states could commit such crimes against their own citizens in peacetime. Second, and more importantly, the CICRC championed the radical idea that true justice for "humanity" was dependent on survivor-witnesses and their testimony. Freed from the constraints inherent in real criminal trials, the CICRC court rejected the Nuremberg model of "trial by document" and tried the USSR through the spoken words of its victims. Rousset's evocative dramaturgy allowed the 1951 "symbolic trial" to function as a deliberate, performative vindication of the practice of witnessing and as a plea for victims' voices to be heard in order for justice to be rendered. Thus the CICRC's proceeding against the USSR imitated the IMT, but with a crucial difference: this was Nuremberg restaged as justice by and for victims, where the voice of survivors reigned supreme. In this sense, and despite its complicated relationship to memory of the Jewish genocide, the Brussels tribunal ultimately helped herald "the advent of the witness" in the post-Holocaust West.[15]

## From Nuremberg to Brussels

Trials served as an important form of popular entertainment and political pedagogy in mid-twentieth-century Europe, and by the dawn of the 1950s courtrooms were well established as arenas in which to stage arguments about the desirability of Soviet-style communism. From the notorious Cardinal Mindszenty and Rajk prosecutions in Hungary to the Kravchenko affair in France and, finally, Rousset's suit against *Les Lettres françaises*, 1949 and 1950 had been full of court cases that inflamed Western Europeans' passions and succeeded, for good or ill, in shaping their views of Stalinism. Nevertheless, the CICRC's decision to put the USSR "on trial" in early 1951 was surprising. After all, as Rousset boasted, his own libel hearing had already functioned as "the trial of the Russian concentration camps."[16] However, the media blitz that greeted the *Lettres françaises* case appears to have convinced him that the juridical format, far from being exhausted, presented further opportunities. He had used the narrow charge of defamation to smuggle the crime of the gulag into a Paris court—but at the end of the day, the case had been nothing more than a municipal French civil suit, and the verdict pronounced at its close merely a nominal monetary judgment against one journal. Was there not, perhaps, a grander way to put Stalin's *univers concentrationnaire* in the dock?

The model Rousset had in mind by late 1950 was a spectacular one indeed: the justice rendered to Nazi leaders at Nuremberg. He was likely aware of prewar precedents for holding state actors symbolically accountable through "international citizens' tribunals," notably the Reichstag fire "counter-trial" held in London in 1933 and the 1937 Mexico City hearings on the Moscow Trials presided over by philosopher John Dewey. Indeed, several of his Trotskyist friends and acquaintances had participated in the latter.[17] But he never referred to it as an inspiration, even in private letters. Instead, the Allied war crimes tribunals occupied his thoughts—and those of other CICRC members and affiliates. Some had intimate memories of those post-1945 trials: Alfred-Serge Balachowsky, for instance, was enormously proud to have testified at Nuremberg; Léon Poliakov had assisted the prosecution; Martin-Chauffier had written extensively on the verdict.[18] Other participants had attended various subsequent proceedings. These included Rousset himself, who had sat in on the "curious mixture of rational jurisprudence and old-fashioned show trial" on display during the 1947 Soviet Military Tribunal for Sachsenhausen war criminals in Berlin.[19] It was an event he later recalled "with terror, for the justice rendered was of the most expeditious variety," but it clearly influenced his sense of the dramatic possibilities of international criminal law. (The Soviets called multiple victim-witnesses despite the coerced confessions of the accused, who uniformly pleaded guilty.)[20] Now, Rousset declared, the CICRC would serve as a successor to the postwar courts. It would transform itself into an "international tribunal," a "court of justice" on the standard of the IMT.[21]

It is not evident that any members of the International Commission (including the lawyers) initially possessed a strong understanding of the legal framework that had governed the Nuremberg prosecutions. Moreover, many of them had initially been harsh critics of the postwar proceedings. We already saw, for example, how Tillion viewed the British Ravensbrück trial as tragically "ill-adapted" to the task of censuring atrocities that were "unjudgeable within the ordinary forms of justice."[22] Martin-Chauffier had condemned the more lenient of the Nuremberg verdicts as a "scandal" and a "shame," remarking acerbically that "the juridical won out over justice. . . . We now know that the 'crime against humanity' costs [only] twenty years in prison."[23] Rousset, meanwhile, had argued in *Les*

*Jours de notre mort* that the concentrationary universe could only be captured through fragmented, experimental, and resolutely literary forms of testimony, defined in explicit contradistinction to the bloodless statements privileged in a legal context: "To debate the truth would be useless. Ours is in no way that of the courts of justice, of official paperwork, nor of photography."[24]

Nevertheless, by 1950 Rousset and his followers—especially the French men and women among them—had come to appreciate the broader cultural resonances that the Allied trials had assumed. In France, though the Anglo-Saxon legal norms that prevailed at Nuremberg caused a certain amount of confusion, and though the sentences were subject to some criticism for perceived leniency, survey data suggest that most viewed the IMT as a legitimate exercise conducted under "the most civilized possible conditions."[25] In French intellectual circles, support for the postwar international trials also became tied to support for the domestic purge of collaborators from French civic and political life, as both were subject to coordinated attack from a resurgent right—for example, in the 1948 treatise *Nuremberg ou la terre promise* by collaboration apologist and Holocaust denier Maurice Bardèche. Thus even early critics of the IMT found themselves, just a few years later, retrospectively defending Nuremberg as a continuation of the wartime struggle against Nazism and rhetorically linking its innovative legal instruments to Resistance ideals. Camp survivors were particularly vociferous. Rémy Roure, for one, asserted in 1949 that the IMT's work needed to be conceptualized as a "starting point" rather than a conclusion. "These projects, these dreams of international or global super-justice must not remain projects and dreams—they must finally become a tangible reality," he wrote. Roure, along with other noncommunist deportees, had retrospectively come to view Nuremberg as a triumph of civilization over barbarism and liberal legalism over totalitarian horror—a "signal" of what was possible in the realm of transnational jurisprudence. If Nazism's victims were not to have "suffered in vain," he lectured, this signal had to be heeded.[26]

The conceptual innovation of the International Military Tribunal most appealing to French Resistance–affiliated commentators by the end of the 1940s was its prosecution of Nazi leaders for "crimes against humanity." Retrospectively, they waxed eloquent over this "sanction . . . consecrated at the assizes of Nuremberg." In the "dark sky" of a postwar world full of "dread," Paris Court of Appeals prosecutor André Boissarie asserted, it was "the only brightness, announcing the fragile dawn of a clear and sure Justice that brings peace."[27] The French legal team at the IMT, led by François de Menthon, had defined the "crime against humanity" not simply as an "attack on human diversity as such"—Hannah Arendt's famous later phrasing, which essentially equated the term with genocide—but also as an unprecedented assault on "the dignity of the human being considered in each and every person individually."[28] This latter interpretation resonated strongly with David Rousset's indictment of the Nazi *univers concentrationnaire*; it was no accident, therefore, that his 1949 "Appeal" charged the architects of the gulag with "crimes against humanity." Rousset also employed this language on many occasions thereafter, and the phrase ultimately made its way into the CICRC's October 1950 "Fundamental Declaration." In the course of their bitter 1950–1951 debates over how to define "the concentration camp," Reumont and Tillion nevertheless concurred that its existence constituted a "crime against humanity."[29]

Thus in early 1951, the CICRC formally charged the USSR not simply with possessing camps but with having committed "crimes against humanity" according to "the definition . . . sanctioned by the Tribunal at Nuremberg."[30] Such offenses were enumerated by Article 6(c) of the Nuremberg Charter as including "murder, extermination, enslavement, deportation, and other inhumane acts committed against any civilian population" as well as "persecutions on political, racial, or religious grounds."[31] The phrase "and other inhumane acts" rendered this description non-exhaustive and perhaps even tautological, but such imprecision presented no difficulty for the CICRC. What mattered was that "crimes against humanity," unlike mere garden-variety human rights abuses, were understood as comprising the most heinous possible deeds. They were, in the words of the UN War Crimes Commission, those violations that "shock the conscience of mankind."[32] The very aim of the CICRC was to shock consciences—thus the charge appeared custom-made for the group's project of stigmatizing the USSR's "concentrationary universe."

In fact, however, it was not at all clear in 1951 that Nuremberg actually provided a precedent for condemning the Soviet state's peacetime abuses against its own citizens. Although the IMT is today most celebrated for bringing "crimes against humanity" into the realm of international jurisprudence, the charge was a relatively minor element of the Nuremberg proceedings, which were geared above all toward prosecuting the Germans for waging "aggressive war." Crimes against humanity were only recognized as such in Article 6(c) if they were committed "in execution of or in connection with" war crimes or crimes against the peace.[33] This condition, known as the "nexus requirement," meant that Nazi atrocities committed before 1939 against German nationals (including Jews) were not considered justiciable. The IMT's judgment on this issue referred *specifically* to the peacetime imprisonment of "political prisoners" in "concentration camps in circumstances of great horror and cruelty" as an example of a terrible atrocity that nevertheless categorically did *not* constitute a crime against humanity.[34] The restriction reflected the Allies' concerns about interference in their own unsavory sovereign affairs: as American lead prosecutor Robert Jackson explained,

"Ordinarily we do not consider that the acts of a government toward its own citizens warrant our interference. . . . We have some regrettable circumstances at times in our own country."[35] The nexus requirement was severed in Article II(c) of Control Council Law no. 10, which governed the zonal tribunals conducted by the four Allied powers; however, jurisdiction over crimes committed against German nationals in peacetime continued to provoke contention and uncertainty. Thus, as Devin O. Pendas writes, "crimes against humanity remained ambiguous in definitional terms" all the way through to the end of the postwar proceedings.[36]

The CICRC's members, by contrast, unambiguously rejected the nexus requirement. Because they interpreted "crimes against humanity" as extreme violations of the human status of individual victims rather than as attacks on the human race, and because they had no need to consider either the legal or the diplomatic implications of their stance, Rousset and his followers took it as a matter of course that state actors could and should be held accountable by the international community for atrocities against their own civilian nationals, including those committed outside the context of foreign war. Thus of the three categories of charges at Nuremberg, the group blithely announced, "We retain only crimes against humanity."[37]

Whether the CICRC rejected the link to aggressive war deliberately or in sheer ignorance of the complexities of Nuremberg's jurisprudence is uncertain. Either way, however, their choice is intriguing. It suggests first of all that perhaps revulsion toward political imprisonment and forced labor (and not only a desire to punish genocide) helped gradually push postwar public opinion toward acceptance of the idea that atrocities committed domestically, in peacetime, ought to be censured by international actors.[38] Still more to the point, it illustrates the central role that anti-Soviet sentiment played in this normative evolution. It was in order to condemn the gulag more spectacularly that the CICRC called its very existence a "crime against humanity," and it was thanks to Cold War side-taking that this label was greeted with widespread applause by the noncommunist political classes of Western Europe. In *Le Figaro*, for example, Henri de Linge predicted that the CICRC verdict "will attract the attention of the free world to these crimes against humanity. . . . Crime[s] against humanity, we wrote above. And it is indeed a matter of that."[39] Journalist Robert Tréno celebrated Rousset's plan as an overdue response to the USSR's "crime against Humanity . . . perpetrated under the pretext of socialism."[40] And following an impassioned speech by Rousset, the 1951 Congress of the Liberal International, under the leadership of writer and diplomat Salvador de Madariaga, passed a resolution calling on Westerners to "rise up against the affirmation that such events and such actions could be considered as a matter internal to countries and [their] governments."[41]

Basking in the approval of such observers, Rousset imagined that the tribunal he was creating would one day, "if authorized by the United Nations, become the permanent institution of inquiry on crimes against humanity."[42] The CICRC vowed to "employ the investigatory methods adopted by the Supreme Court of Justice at Nuremberg," and two prominent jurists from the French commission, Paul Arrighi and Léon Mazeaud, were appointed to elaborate working regulations for its proceedings.[43] Arrighi, a lawyer at the Court of Appeals in Paris and future founder of the Réseau du Souvenir (Memory Network), had long viewed the project of commemorating the "concentrationary universe" as inextricably connected to the imperative of obtaining justice against those responsible for it; he was proud to have testified at Philippe Pétain's 1945 treason trial.[44] Mazeaud was member of a distinguished legal dynasty and professor of private law on the Faculté de Droit of the Université de Paris. Both men had followed the Nuremberg trials; both understood the potential symbolic force of a verdict against the USSR issued by a self-proclaimed successor to the IMT, so long as that successor managed to be taken seriously. Thus the "Recommendations" they produced in the fall of 1950 employed a dryly legalistic idiom, avoiding rhetoric on suffering and horror to instead lay out "procedures" intended to "guarantee" the objectivity and transparency of the commission's tribunal.[45] This irreproachable body, as Arrighi and Mazeaud imagined it, would engage in an "orderly," "conscientious," and "impartial" quest for "the whole truth." "Personally," Arrighi wrote to Rousset, "I insist on the necessity of [our] directives being respected if you want the International Commission's work to avoid being the object of any criticism."[46]

The particular trial format that Arrighi and Mazeaud proposed was, unsurprisingly, modeled on continental law rather than on the actual practices of the IMT, where Anglo-Saxon traditions of adversarial jurisprudence had largely held sway. For instance, they divided the CICRC tribunal's work into two phases, the first a wide-ranging preliminary investigation directed by a *juge d'instruction* and the second an inquisitorial hearing in which judges (not lawyers) had the power to interrogate witnesses and present evidence.[47] The CICRC's members nevertheless believed that the document sufficiently emulated the Nuremberg Charter and embraced it enthusiastically, with only minor amendments.[48] To further stress the symbolic IMT precedent, the group appointed Balachowsky—the only one of their number who had officially testified at Nuremberg—as the tribunal's president. They also mimicked the structure of the International Military Tribunal by assigning a panel of four principal judges of different nationalities: Tillion for France, Catholic youth organizer and Sachsenhausen memoirist Franz Ballhorn for Germany, Secret Army veteran Martin Dehousse for Belgium, and Neuengamme survivor José Domenech for the exiles of "republican Spain."[49] The indefatigable Reumont sought still further inspiration from Nuremberg. "As far as procedure is concerned," he wrote to Rousset in March 1951, "I am in the middle of studying the statute of the International Military Tribunal and the rules of procedure of that tribunal," as well as scholarly treatments of it by Marcel Merle and Jacques Descheemaeker. He was optimistic that the CICRC could effectively simulate much of what he saw described: "We have here a solid foundation."[50]

On the question of jurisdiction, however, Reumont was full of trepidation, reluctantly admitting that he "did not see how we are legally qualified to proceed and to pronounce a judgment."[51] His concerns echoed those already expressed by writer Jean Cayrol, who despite his early enthusiasm for the "Appeal" had ultimately declined to participate in the inquiry it proposed: "What would be our sanction?" the Gusen survivor asked Rousset in late 1949. "Can one condemn a country to death, or even to forced labor? . . . Any judgment could only be derisory coming from a 'do-gooder' Commission."[52] As Reumont recognized, Cayrol's doubts about the CICRC's powers still remained pertinent a year later; by early 1951 the commission had not even secured recognition from the UN as a consultative NGO, much less been anointed as the standing international criminal tribunal of Rousset's daydreams. Making a virtue of necessity, Rousset championed the "private" nature of his proposed tribunal as an asset—this "original characteristic," he asserted, would allow it to avoid the concerns about sovereignty that might be aroused by a "*super-étatique*" United Nations tribunal.[53] Nevertheless, the fact remained that the CICRC's only juridical existence as of April 1951 was as a registered Belgian nonprofit association, not technically distinct from an Antwerp archery enthusiasts' club or a learned society of botanists in Bruges. Legalistic procedural rhetoric, no matter how elaborately conceived or loudly announced, could not change this fact.

Théo Bernard understood better than Reumont that the CICRC could not possibly possess any legal authority (and that "regimes" could not serve as criminal defendants); counterintuitively, this made the Drancy survivor more sanguine about such problems. Of course the commission had no real jurisdiction over "humanity"—but none was required for the successful dramatic staging of a "symbolic trial" intended to shape public opinion. The group's "*compétence*," he told Reumont, was "above all moral."[54] Moral authority, in the end, was the only variety currently available—and it was not worthless.[55] Although, as *France-Soir* put it, CICRC participants in the Brussels proceedings would be "more historians than judges," at least "the world, from here on, will know."[56] In more nakedly tactical language, the *New York Times* (far more interested in the CICRC's restaging of Nuremberg than it had been in the municipal *Lettres françaises* case) celebrated the camp survivors' appropriation of the rhetoric and rituals of the courtroom: "Totalitarian states have long known how to use trials as political weapons," the editors opined, so it was past time that "democratic forces" employed the "trial technique" as well.[57] Even absent criminal sanction, such a "technique" could possess a considerable pedagogical and stigmatizing effect.

Reumont ultimately accepted this logic of symbolic denunciation. So did Rousset, bowing to the reality that the United Nations was not poised to name him its *procureur général* for all mankind. "The value of the CICRC," he now declared, "does not come to it through the recognition of the UN. . . . Its moral value comes to it from the fact that it represents former political deportees. Our moral responsibility before the concentration camps is imposed on us by our conscience, and we must satisfy the moral demands that brought us together."[58] In an April 1951 memo he laid out the implications of his new position for the structure of the CICRC's tribunal. Most courts, he wrote, "represent the State or, in certain cases, a supra-state organization, an association of governments as at Nuremberg." But "the court of grievance in the context of the CICRC is something else completely"; this court would "represent at the same time" three distinct entities. The first was "public opinion": since the commission could not render judgment in the name of states, the hazy notion of a public with common standards would permit it nevertheless to speak on behalf of a collective, implicitly equated with the citizenry of the "free," democratic West. In truth, this idea marked only a partial departure from Nuremberg's precedent, where prosecutor Jackson and others had used the rhetoric of "civilization" to similar effect.

The second entity that the CICRC's court would "represent," Rousset wrote, was "the opinion of the European Resistance, which is troubled and demands that light be shed."[59] This statement was not only another effort to associate his organization with past heroics; subtly, it invoked a Resistance-based conception of the responsibility of private individuals to sanction wrongdoing when governments could or would not do so. In Vichy France, Resistance members had held that "justice" retained its meaning even when the only ones left to carry it out were isolated individuals operating outside the law. On multiple occasions during and immediately following the Occupation, resisters had even constructed ad hoc tribunals to enact solemn though extralegal judgment of collaborators and traitors. "For four years," as Albert Camus claimed in 1944, the Resistance had "judged not in the name of the written law, but in the name of the law of our hearts."[60] Now the commission's members would take up the charge, drawing their authority from their stature as political deportees.

Striking as Rousset's imagining of the CICRC's mock courtroom as a Resistance tribunal was, in truth it too did not stray far from the example of Nuremberg, where François de Menthon had demanded justice "above all in the name of the heroic martyrs of the Resistance" and where, if participants had not called upon "the law of our hearts," they had nevertheless judged the defendants for acts that, technically, at the moment they were committed, had not violated existing laws, only "unwritten" ones.[61] Thus it was Rousset's third claim to representation that marked his strongest departure from the IMT: the CICRC's tribunal, he wrote, above all "represents . . . the victims who accuse."[62] This Nuremberg's architects had emphatically not aspired to do; indeed, they had gone to great lengths to dissociate their court from the claims of injured parties, especially atrocity survivors, whom they viewed as irreparably "biased" and thus incapable of the serene impartiality required for a didactically effective international justice.[63] Rousset, thanks to his laudatory framing of victims as "specialists" with privileged access to truth, subscribed to a different logic. For him, justice concerning the *univers concentrationnaire* could never be realized in the absence of its former inmates' voices. Thus his pronouncement that the CICRC's tribunal would represent victims amounted to a rejection of Nuremberg's stance on this question; in fact, it anticipated by a decade the victim-centered staging of the 1961 Eichmann trial in Jerusalem.[64]

The Israeli court that tried Eichmann has been subject to much criticism—most famously from Karl Jaspers and Hannah Arendt—for acting on behalf of one victim group rather than "representing all mankind."[65] It is therefore worth underlining that in asserting that his court would operate "in the name of" concentration camp victims, Rousset did not believe he was narrowing its purview to the interests of a narrow category of individuals—as always, he was adamant that camp survivors would function as stand-ins for humanity as a whole. Hence his notion of restaging Nuremberg not only as a trial of the USSR but as a judicial proceeding enacted exclusively by former deportees. And hence, too, his deliberate ambiguity concerning the identity of the "victims who accuse." Were they the CICRC's own members or, rather, the gulag survivors called to Brussels to testify before them? Rousset saw no need to choose between these two formulations. Survivors of the *univers concentrationnaire* formed a bloc in his mind, and their transnational solidarity in suffering patterned the solidarity toward which the human race as a whole ought to aspire. Contemporary journalists covering the CICRC's initiative grasped and enthusiastically echoed this equation. De Linge, for example, opined that the mock tribunal's "sentence will be stronger than any juridical sentence, because it will be rendered in the name of humanity, in the name of all the victims of the concentrationary regime."[66] The Belgian daily *Le Soir*, meanwhile, rhapsodized that gulag survivors "pass before the world, before the conscience of the world, in Brussels," through the mediating mechanism of appearing in front of their brethren, "the martyrs miraculously escaped from Hitler's *bagnes*."[67]

As he composed the opening statement he would give as "*rapporteur*" at the trial, Rousset chose to employ similar language, explaining that he did not see himself as a prosecutor but rather as an empathic interpreter for fellow sufferers.

He would act, he vowed, "merely as the spokesman of the victims, the millions of men who today live in conditions entirely similar, as I will show, to those we experienced." Still more importantly, Rousset insisted that the chief moral imperative of a "crimes against humanity" court was to attend to victim-witnesses' *own* speech acts of testimony:

> It is our duty to give them this chance to speak about their lives and their misfortune [*de dire leur vie et leur malheur*]. My role is confined to this. I bring before you the charge of the victims. For the first time, men who suffered the concentrationary world are going to hear other victims of the concentrationary world. . . . I am, among our many comrades who experienced the life of the camps, the one who will interpret the speech of the victims of the Russian camps.[68]

Among the many exceptional ideas contained in these lines, the most striking is the claim that there existed a "duty" to provide a public tribunal for victims of atrocity to tell their stories. Though today this appears a self-evident goal of international justice, it was a radical claim in 1951.[69] The IMT had not only rejected the notion of conducting its proceedings "in the name of" victims but had been designed as a "trial by document" explicitly in order to allow minimal victim testimony. Jackson aspired to "put on no witnesses we could reasonably avoid," believing their statements would be vulnerable to attack under cross-examination and moreover that they might be viewed as vengeful, bitter, or mendacious.[70] Victims, in his eyes, could not be relied on for objectivity: to invite them to speak would be to convict the defendants "on the testimony of their foes."[71] Those on the prosecutorial team who (unsuccessfully) disagreed with him explained their position in strategic or dramaturgical terms, not by invoking any "duty" to victims themselves.

It is true that some of the subsequent American postwar proceedings known as the Nuremberg Military Trials (NMT)—notably the 1946 Medical Trial—relied more heavily than the IMT on survivor-witness testimony as a form of evidence. The NMT courts, however, certainly did not conceive of themselves as "representing" aggrieved victims. Lawrence Douglas, who admits that "the NMT's reliance on victim testimony remained quite modest," insists, nevertheless, that "the NMT program still deserves to be seen as emblematic of a larger shift toward privileging the voice and testimony of survivors."[72] If this is the case, then the CICRC's proceedings—in which a courtroom composed entirely of camp survivors invited fellow victims to "speak about their lives and their misfortune"— were positively revolutionary. The *New York Times* recognized this innovation in the moment—at the Brussels tribunal, it reported, each former victim would be treated as "an 'expert'" and "survivors' testimony" would be "regarded as 'evidence.'"[73] But Rousset aimed still higher. The impending trial, as he imagined it, would not simply permit victims to provide evidence. It would insist that the very purpose of international justice was to bear solemn witness to their testimony.

## Performing International Justice in a Polarized World

The CICRC's grand edicts of purpose always papered over a certain amount of sordid backstage scrambling, and the preparations for the Brussels trial were no exception. While publicly proclaiming the universal virtues of "witnessing," Rousset privately sought to procure a carefully curated set of gulag survivors to testify. As he had explained to a correspondent a year earlier, in relation to the *Lettres françaises* case, he did not personally care if a camp victim was on the "extreme right" or even a "monarchist," so long as he "could give of his camp experience a sincere, objective, precise testimony." But he had no intention of providing a "means of diversion" for communist critics, and therefore sought only "witnesses from the left who are former communists; socialists of all varieties; or else witnesses who are not, properly speaking, political; or Zionists."[74] The same principles applied to the Brussels trial. In February 1951, the CICRC unanimously elected the "morally irreproachable and unreproached" Frenchwoman Elisabeth Ingrand as the *juge d'instruction* to identify and interrogate witnesses, preparing them to take the stand.[75] Ingrand (née Dussauze), who had recently joined the French commission as an ADIR representative, possessed a doctorate in law and was later described by *Le Figaro* as a "tall, young woman whose very being exudes loyalty and scrupulousness."[76] Her appeal was obvious. But for an organization that fetishized "experience" as the foundation of expertise, she was an odd choice—she had been deported from France in 1942 for courageous Resistance activity (and for this was a bona fide member of the CICRC) but had been held captive in a series of prison cells and a labor battalion, not a camp. Thus, as she readily acknowledged, her knowledge of the *univers concentrationnaire* "properly speaking" was "limited because indirect."[77]

This awkward reality was not mitigated by the fact that Ingrand's role was actually restricted: to undertake the real legwork of locating witnesses, Rousset quietly employed a "technician" who had still less of a claim to lived experience of the Nazi camps.[78] This was former Menshevik leader and current US cold warrior David Dallin, who had long insisted that by "inviting as many witnesses as possible to appear" and testify under oath about the gulag, an international tribunal could serve as an effective anti-Soviet propaganda weapon.[79] Dallin would have preferred that this event take place under the auspices of the UN and that it employ Americans' favored language of "slave labor" rather than "concentrationary" abuses; nevertheless he readily consented to help the CICRC, which paid him for his services.[80] With Bernard's assistance, Dallin identified oral witnesses among former gulag inmates living in Germany and the US; he also suggested fruitful lines of inquiry that might be pursued with them. Rousset sought help elsewhere as well. German Elinor Lipper, author of *Eleven Years in Soviet Prison Camps* (1951), could not testify at Brussels since she had already taken the stand in Paris at the *Lettres françaises* trial, but she privately briefed the CICRC and produced a 228-item list of possible questions to pose to witnesses ("By what means were you transported?"; "Were you beaten, and if so by whom?"; "Were you together with common law criminals in your barracks?").[81] By May 1951, members felt themselves ready. The "court" was appointed, the press informed, arrangements made for film and audio recording, and "one of the most remarkable rooms in all of Brussels" reserved at the Palais d'Egmont.[82]

Much of this activity was made possible by CIA funds recently provided to the CICRC via the American Federation of Labor. It appears likely, in fact, that a favorable estimation of the propaganda value of the upcoming "trial" was precisely what finally pushed Rousset's American contacts into providing monetary support for his International Commission. There is, however, no evidence of American involvement in the inspiration, planning, or staging of the event. For instance, a March letter from Irving Brown to Rousset made no suggestions about the trial, merely neutrally (and mistakenly) noting that "if I understand correctly," the CICRC planned to hold it in April.[83] State Department officials in Washington and their counterparts at the US Embassy in Brussels were still more ill-informed; it was not until May 9 that Ambassador Robert Daniel Murphy alerted the secretary of state that the CICRC would shortly be holding a "conference" to "examine documentation new in its possession concerning existence of forced labor camps in Soviet Russia."[84] At this point State Department officials did recognize the opportunity at hand, directing Murphy to "report fully on these hearings."[85] He should provide a "daily summary," Dean Acheson instructed, as well as "material for producing pamphlets, feature stories, posters, and similar [International Press and Publication Division] products," especially "eye-witness reports about slave labor camps," "human interest stories," "pictures, drawings, illustrations, [and] cartoons," and "photographs of eyewitnesses and of the court procedure."[86]

Confident that their initiative would please Brussels as much as it appears to have pleased Washington, or perhaps lulled into complacency by their own assertions of supranational moral authority, the CICRC neglected to inform the Belgian government of its plans until a late date. This was a mistake. At the height of international tension over the Korean War, and in a period also marked by domestic crisis, Belgium's Christian democratic administration was greatly irritated to learn of the commission's planned stunt. And, as CICRC leaders now realized to their dismay, the fact that the trial was "private" provided no protection from state interference. Though the government could not legally ban a private meeting, it could easily withhold entry visas for the CICRC's planned witnesses.[87] Damien Reumont sent a pleading letter to Belgian foreign minister Paul van Zeeland in March; the proposed trial, he reminded Van Zeeland, "is an absolutely private initiative, having no official character," and "therefore cannot engage the responsibility of any Government whatsoever in any way." However, Reumont admitted, "we have perhaps committed an error in not *first* making contact with your office and in asking you, Monsieur le Ministre, whether you saw any inconvenience in the holding of a trial."[88] Could not the senior statesman see a way forward?

Van Zeeland appeared placated by this missive. He responded in April, "I believe that I can count on the members of the Commission that the sessions that will take place at the Palais d'Egmont will maintain such a character that they could not possibly cause incidents or problems in our international relations."[89] But days before the trial was to begin, crisis erupted again when the Soviet embassy protested. The Belgian government's position was delicate—it was still engaged in negotiations to repatriate the last of its nationals stranded in Soviet-controlled territory at the end of the war, it sought to maintain commercial relations with Moscow, and it hoped to put an end to the USSR's yearlong failure to replace its ambassador in Brussels, which the small country viewed as a humiliating slight.[90] The CICRC's proposed action threatened to disrupt all these endeavors. Thus, citing "the international situation" and "the possibility of diplomatic difficulties or, at the least, brawls," Belgian officials demanded that the CICRC abandon its plans and again threatened to bar witnesses' travel. Rousset, Reumont, and the others were thrown into a panic—to cancel the proceedings at this late date "would render the Commission ridiculous in the eyes of public opinion. . . . It would be the death of the CICRC."[91] But to hold the trial without witnesses was unthinkable. CICRC president Georges André rose to the occasion and contacted Van Zeeland as well as the ministers of justice and interior.[92] After "long and difficult negotiations," the Council of Ministers relented but warned that if "the witnesses give themselves over to attacks against the Union of Soviet Socialist Republics, these witnesses will be immediately expelled from Belgian territory and the Session will be suspended." A "trial of a Government or a State" would not be tolerated.[93]

This series of events undeniably highlighted the powerlessness of the CICRC before hostile government actors. Despite their pretentions to operate "outside" state power, the commission's members quickly realized that sovereignty could not be bypassed, nor diplomatic concerns waved away, simply by asserting the existence of a higher moral authority governing "private" action. One lesson here is clear: if Cold War–era governments were happy to seize on, nurture, and finance the projects of NGOs such as the CICRC when they served national priorities, they also possessed the ability to thwart initiatives misaligned with their interests. It is also important to note, however, the very real fears that the CICRC's project aroused. Even Belgian officials who were sympathetic to the group's aims (Van Zeeland, for one) appeared seriously to believe that a nonbinding mock trial had the potential to spark an international incident. In and of itself, a "trial of a Government or a State"—even one that lacked both jurisdiction and flesh-and-blood defendants—posed a threat to the precarious Cold War world order.

## Bearing Witness to Crimes against Humanity

When the CICRC's tribunal opened on May 21, 1951, to a courtroom over-crowded with 350 observers, presiding judge Balachowsky began the proceedings with words intended to calm the Belgian government's fears: "No political allusion against any country will be tolerated," he asserted, only "precise facts" related to "the problem that we are studying here."[94] Balachowsky's address situated the tribunal as an apolitical, even holy manifestation of the duty that survivors owed to those who had perished; early on, he called the assembled crowd to its feet for a "minute of silence," thereby dedicating the CICRC's "sacred task" to "our six or seven million dead, for if these dead could still speak, I do not think that they would consider for a single minute that the concentrationary regime could today still exist anywhere in the world."[95] This rhetoric anticipated prosecutor Gideon Hausner's famous appeal to "six million accusers" in his opening address at the Eichmann trial. But whereas Hausner's 1961 invocation of the dead strove to make the Holocaust visible, Balachowsky's 1951 words—spoken on behalf of an organization that did not permit "racial" survivors to join—assimilated Hitler's genocide to the suffering of Resistance deportees and, in turn, to that of Stalin's captives. Once again, it constituted an appropriation rather than a recognition of Jewish loss.

With "our" dead as silent witnesses, Balachowsky's discourse proceeded to establish the strange, hybrid idiom of the week's proceedings, half dependent on self-conscious proceduralism and legalistic rhetoric ("*instruction de dossiers*," "*droits de la défense*") and half on raw evocations of memory, loss, and bodily suffering. Following Balachowsky in order to present her preliminary findings, Elisabeth Ingrand echoed him in marrying a portentous insistence on impartial technique with references to knowledge born of agony. After averring that she had relied on "statistically proven methods" to select testimonies, she added: "We knew too well the gravity of the accusation being made, by virtue of having experienced ourselves, in our heart and in our body, all of the human suffering that it would imply if we were to discover that it was well-founded. It is precisely this dread, these memories, that move us in our work, and that have led us to adopt and follow with intransigence the rule of conduct we have traced since the beginning, which is that of absolute objectivity."[96] In this paradoxical formulation, objectivity remained a positive value but was born of shatteringly subjective involvement rather than disinterestedness or emotional distance. That is, *contra* the IMT, victims' ability to uphold universalistic standards flowed directly out of traumatic experience rather than being impeded by it. Rousset, the self-proclaimed "spokesman" for the Soviet witnesses about to take the stand, closed his own speech to the court in a similar vein. "Messieurs," he reminded its members, "you are not ordinary judges, you are men of Buchenwald and Auschwitz." (In fact none of them had been in Auschwitz, nor were they all men.) "You have lived the concentrationary world," he continued, "and you have this privilege over all others: you know—and I am persuaded, I am convinced, that precisely because you know, when you hear these men, you will understand."[97]

With Rousset's words, the "tragic march" of victim-witnesses began.[98] They included eighteen men and three women; nine were former Soviet nationals, while the rest were German (six), Polish (four), Czechoslovakian (one), and Bulgarian (one).[99] A handful had post-1945 experience of the gulag, though most had passed through it during the 1930s. Just as Rousset had insisted, none identified as frank rightists or fascist sympathizers; instead they were a mix of socialists, former communists, and various "apoliticals." As at the *Lettres françaises* trial, several were Jewish. Among the witnesses were common workers, a doctor, a professor, a former NKVD agent brought low, and a Russian Orthodox priest who addressed the court in full regalia, his beard flowing majestically. A few—Ukrainian literary scholar Hryhoriy Kostiuk, Polish journalist Wanda Brońska-Pampuch, German communist militant Susanne Leonhard—would later write important memoirs of their imprisonment.[100] Some testified in Brussels under their own names, some under pseudonyms. All spoke under oath. Several expressed gratitude for "the chance to testify in front of a free tribunal, to recount [our] sufferings and [our] secret life."[101]

The CICRC's procedure allowed the witnesses a good deal of latitude in this narration. Hours were devoted to discussions of hunger, cold, backbreaking labor, inadequate or nonexistent medical care, destroyed family units, and even prostitution, rape, and homosexuality in the gulag. The great guiding idea of the Nuremberg trials had been the notion that individuals, as persons, could be held criminally responsible under international law for acts of state. Nuremberg was not a fact-finding board, a truth commission, or a history classroom, but a legal tribunal at which, as Donald Bloxham reminds us, "the primary prosecutorial task was to gain convictions of the senior Germans who stood in the dock."[102] The IMT was thus constrained from permitting witnesses to speak on aspects of Nazi horror, however emotionally compelling, that did not help establish specific defendants' criminal liability. The CICRC, by contrast, was uninterested in establishing the responsibility of individual perpetrators (except insofar as members enjoyed making regular references to Stalin himself). "The essential guilty party here," as Rousset put it, "is the regime."[103] Free from the need to hold persons accountable, the CICRC's "trial without a defendant" could permit victim-witnesses' loosely structured stories to take center stage.[104]

These witnesses, it is true, were not well positioned to comment on the byzantine Soviet camp system as a whole; precisely as Nuremberg's prosecutors recognized, victims of state crimes generally possess no real knowledge of the high-level decision making that produced their personal ordeal, nor much insight into how that ordeal fits into a broader history. And indeed, the CICRC's witnesses offered fantastical narratives of the gulag's evolution over time, distorted descriptions of its geography, and inflated estimates of both its overall population and its mortality rate. Nicolai Antonov, for example, informed the court that seven hundred thousand prisoners had died building the White Sea–Baltic Canal in the early 1930s. (The true figure is contested but is likely closer to twenty-five thousand.)[105] Primarily, however, the witnesses spoke to the court about the day-to-day, sensory texture of their own experience of incarceration. By the CICRC's terms, so long as that experience could be shown to mirror members' own suffering in the Nazi camps, the Soviet Union was guilty of the "crime against humanity" of possessing a concentrationary regime.

The judges therefore took the opposite tack from that employed at Nuremberg and encouraged the witnesses to "*dire leur vie*" broadly, subjectively, and—so they claimed—spontaneously. To curb charges that testimony had been coached, Balachowsky banned the use of notes—witnesses had to speak extempore. Their unscripted, heartfelt words, announced E. de Beer de Laer, a Belgian lawyer serving as Rousset's assistant, "plunge us into a revolting atmosphere of degradation, of debasement of the human condition."[106] Working through translators, the court encouraged the men and women on the stand to give voice to their memories, and pressed them for physical details: How many spoonfuls of gruel did inmates receive each evening in Vorkuta? Did twelve-hour days salting salmon cause not only deadly fatigue but also painful skin ailments? What more could the witness say of the deplorable sanitary conditions in the Siblag camps of the Siberian Kuznetsk Basin? Did the guards rape female inmates in Kolyma?

Rousset's closing address praised the witnesses not for their exactitude in answering such questions but for their palpable "authenticity." He may have adopted the courtroom as a theater, but his understanding of "witnessing" remained tied to literary as opposed to legal constructions, and he was unconcerned with meeting the evidentiary standards of professional jurists. (During the *Lettres françaises* trial the previous year, he had explained that "the questions that I pose to my witness are not intended to make her recount the facts to demonstrate the truth, but rather to demonstrate the moral weight of these facts, by virtue of their *grandeur*, if I may say so.")[107] Driven by the universal human desire to relate "what they have suffered," the victims in Brussels had "answered questions in accordance with the truth of their experience"—and, to Rousset's mind, this subjective, embodied truth was the only one about the *univers concentration-naire* that mattered. "Each time," he insisted, "it was entirely evident, entirely visible, that the witness responded in accordance with his conscience, in accordance with his experience, with his integrity as a former deportee. You have been able to verify this and to follow it throughout the course of these public testimonials."[108] In other words, victims' words had made their suffering manifest, bringing it to life in order to permit others to "bear witness" to it as well. "The human concentrationary world," Rousset informed those assembled, "has been drawn [*dessiné*] before you by the witnesses."[109] In the absence of photographic or filmic images of the gulag, a medium had nevertheless been found by which Westerners could become *témoins oculaires* to its horrors. "It is this, indeed," Rousset stated, "which seems to me to be the significance of public testimony."[110]

Of course, the mock court did not actually give free rein to testimony. The "stage army" of witnesses had been minutely instructed beforehand, and when they took the stand the CICRC judges steered them toward subjects intended to confirm similarities between the Nazi and Soviet camps.[111] More literal-minded participants sought exact parallels: André, for instance, questioned Ludvig Golubowitsch on whether there were "*Nacht und Nebel*" prisoners in the gulag; Dehousse inquired about "triangles or distinctive symbols of different colors" on prisoners' clothing.[112] Interestingly, Balachowsky attempted at multiple junctures to lead Jewish witnesses into stating that antisemitism played a role in the Soviet detention schema. He especially pressed a German Jew named Friedrich Prenzlau: "I would like to ask him if he saw particular measures against Jews taken by the Soviet authorities, if there were really incarcerations of an antisemitic character comparable to those we knew in Nazi Germany."[113]

The witnesses obligingly did their best to satisfy such queries—Prenzlau provided a tame account of Jews in Karaganda denied a day off work for a religious holiday—but the effort failed. So, too, did lines of questioning intended to elicit stories of sadistic abuses by guards. Kostiuk, for example, assured Tillion that prisoners were "certainly" beaten, but drew back when she pressed the issue: "I can say nothing concerning myself, personally."[114] The response was telling: time and again, the witnesses frustrated CICRC members' requests that they testify only to what they had individually seen and done. Instead, they insisted on speaking on behalf of a remembered collective: "We experienced a permanent sensation of hunger"; "Our condition became more and more difficult"; "When we got out of the railroad cars, we were starving, thirsty, freezing, and we needed food"; "I saw terrible things; we were all witnesses to these cruelties."[115] Such pluralization of voice echoed the Nazi camp survivors' own earlier acts of literary witness—for instance, Louis Martin-Chauffier's choral evocation of "our" arrival at Neuengamme. But it was poorly adapted to the evidentiary norms of a courtroom, disrupting the performance of liberal legalism and the illusion that a real trial was taking place.

The witnesses' manifest pain while recounting traumatic episodes was also problematic for the "court." Many scholars have noted the disjuncture between the circling, fragmented, broken testimony often offered in the wake of trauma and the confident, clearheaded, rationally constructed "stories" privileged by the law.[116] "War crimes trials," Eric Stover writes, are "generally ill-suited" to atrocity victims' testimonial capacities—and vice versa.[117] The CICRC's trial bore out this observation. As Ambassador Murphy observed, with disappointment, witnesses' comments were often infused with "intense feeling" but "repetitious" and therefore less-than-ideal political theater.[118] Moreover, they threatened at many points to spill beyond the discursive boundaries the CICRC tried to set. "The story is not yet finished," one witness snapped when Rousset, eager to underline "analogous cases" in the Nazi camps, attempted to cut off his tale of a comrade's self-mutilation.[119] Balachowsky, presiding over the courtroom, sought to keep the depositions brief, but the speakers continually insisted that they had more to say; after all, as Nicolai Urguizof put it, "during the thirteen hundred nights that I passed in the camp, I and all the other detainees only thought of one thing, which was to have the possibility to say freely, in a free world, all that we experienced."[120] They did not want their chance, at last arrived, to be cut short.

Despite such tensions, however, the five days of witness statements ran mostly as a smooth duet between the "the slaves of the West" who constituted the court and "the slaves of the East" who testified before them.[121] "What remains new and enthralling in the courtroom in Brussels," enthused Pierre Scize in *Le Figaro*, despite the well-known facts under discussion, "is that the judges are here bringing their own memories of the Nazi camps face to face with the memories of Russian deportees."[122] The judges did also call four nonvictim witnesses, notably

Viacheslav Artem'ev, who used the pseudonym Vladimir Andreiev. This onetime Soviet official later participated in the anticommunist Russian Liberation Army (Vlasov's Army) that served under the Germans in World War II. He was able to discuss matters the victim-witnesses could not and which were hobbyhorses for many CICRC members—for instance, the supposed economic utility of Soviet prisoners' labor. But calling him to testify was an error. The communist press seized on the presence of this "war criminal" and "mercenary of Hitler" as further evidence that the trial was a fascist exercise, and mainstream journalists were distracted as well.[123] The revelation of Andreiev's participation in Vlasov's Army "cast a chill" over the proceedings, according to Le Monde's account. "What a magnificent instrument of propaganda has been handed to the Commission's adversaries," lamented Le Figaro.[124] Even CICRC members in the courtroom threatened to revolt—Domenech complained that the man's presence raised a "troubling question" about the entire proceeding.[125]

Rousset defended the calling of unsavory perpetrator-witnesses by again invoking the precedent of Nuremberg: "In this, we have followed the principle that seems to me to have been recognized and applied at the Nuremberg trial, where they heard the SS, the organizers of the camps, as technicians."[126] The comparison was dubious, since at the IMT and especially the zonal trials, the "organizers of the camps" had usually been defendants. Rousset was perhaps thinking of Auschwitz commandant Rudolf Höss, who indeed testified as a simple witness at Nuremberg—though Höss was called by the defense (and was later tried and hanged by the Polish Supreme National Tribunal). Rousset shrugged: here in Brussels, in any event, a "regime" and not a man was on trial. And since that was the case, Artem'ev and other perpetrators were "extremely precious witnesses. The Tribunal is not here in order to make a judgment about the moral quality of the witnesses."[127] Given his usual strident celebration of "witnessing" in itself as a supremely moral act, the argument struck a false note; sympathetic press commentators avoided defending it and hurried back to coverage of the "procession of former detainees" and their tales of labor, exposure, disease, and death.[128]

The CICRC also made a great show of inviting defense witnesses to address the court, eager to demonstrate evenhandedness. Members understood that the absence of any such witnesses was—in Rémy Roure's words—the "weak point" of their proceeding, threatening to tip the production from a credible dramatic re-creation of the IMT into a "parody of justice."[129] Since the Soviet government ignored Reumont's entreaties asking that it send representatives, the CICRC contacted five Western European communists who claimed to have toured "reeducation camps" during visits to the USSR: French jurists Paul Vienney and Joë Nordmann (recently Pierre Daix's lawyers in the Lettres françaises case), their confrère Marcel Willard (author of two books on the Moscow Trials), Belgian

Jean Fonteyne (also a lawyer, and a Buchenwald survivor), and French Resistance heroine Marie-Claude Vaillant-Couturier, well known for her testimony at Nuremberg regarding Auschwitz and Ravensbrück—as well as for her declaration at the *Lettres françaises* trial that the Soviet penal system was "the most desirable in the whole world."[130]

The invitation was disingenuous, since these five individuals—all already public opponents of Rousset—would never have dignified the proceedings with their presence. (Vaillant-Couturier would later become a great opponent of "crimes against humanity"; in the 1970s, Nordmann participated along with Rousset in the Russell Tribunal on International War Crimes.[131] He also, famously, prosecuted collaborator Paul Touvier for crimes against humanity under French municipal law. But all of that was far in the future—and moreover did not concern the USSR.) In a blistering letter to "the marionettes of Burnham play-acting a tribunal," the communists jointly rejected the offer to appear and announced that the trial was "an attempted diversion on the part of oppressive forces responsible for the atrocities of Korea and of Vietnam, of Spain, of Greece, and of Yugoslavia, for the racist crimes on the other side of the Atlantic, for the concentrationary regimes of black Africa and all the colonial penal colonies."[132] The CICRC's leaders ignored the particulars of this response and beatifically announced that the fact of their invitation, in itself, meant that the "rights of the defense" had been respected by their "court."[133] Communist Luc Somerhausen did arrive in the courtroom on May 21, where he demanded to be heard. But as he refused to be deposed by a tribunal he considered illegitimate, he was "gently" expelled as an "agitator."[134] Another group of Belgian communist deportees appeared a week later; an outright brawl between them and their anticommunist CNPPA counterparts ensued on the steps of the Palais d'Egmont, producing black eyes and bloodstained faces on both sides. "Trial Is Mock, but Not Punch in Reds' Noses," the *Chicago Tribune* gleefully reported.[135]

With no defense witnesses to hear, the CICRC's court was free to proceed to closing statements and judgment. In its final sessions, the purposive language of the tribunal shifted almost entirely toward moral condemnation; few references were made to fact finding. After all, as Beer de Laer remarked, it was "completely obvious" that the USSR maintained a prison-camp regime. The former Nazi camp deportees who now sat in judgment, he asserted, therefore ought not only proclaim their certainty that the gulag existed but "also express in the most formal terms the revolt that these condemnations provoke in free men; these horrors must not only be established, they must be stigmatized—that is the heavy but fruitful work that we expect from your justice."[136] Théo Bernard's closing statement went still further in this direction while also circling back to a Camusian, Resistance-inspired conception of justice. "Your Tribunal," he told the judges,

". . . is at the end of the day the Tribunal of the human conscience." Perhaps it could not render legal sanction, but it could apply "a law that is stronger than all of the legal laws. I demand the application of an unwritten law." This higher law, he lectured, "can only be put into effect if men themselves enforce it."[137]

The CICRC could in truth enforce nothing, but in their final verdict the judges did do their best to speak as voices of human conscience. In so doing, they made scant reference to their organization's formal three-point definition of a "concentrationary regime," falling back instead on the language of expertise gained through suffering. The testimony they had heard, Tillion, Domenech, Dehousse, and Ballhorn asserted, established beyond doubt that "the characteristics of the Soviet camps are indeed those of the concentrationary regime, as they follow from the experience inscribed in the flesh and blood of tens of thousands of former deportees of the Nazi camps." They conceded that certain differences existed between the Nazi and Soviet penal regimes: for instance, the latter lacked a program of "massive and methodical extermination comparable to that practiced in Nazi Germany, notably against the Jews and Romani put through the gas chamber." This was blunter acknowledgment of the genocide than CICRC members generally offered. But they proceeded to resolve the problem in familiar terms, insisting that, in the end, the *univers concentrationnaire* in all its guises was geared toward mass extermination. In the Soviet camps, they wrote, as in Buchenwald or Dora if not in Treblinka or Chełmno, "the extermination of detainees" simply came about "from progressive exhaustion due to inhumane work conditions and hunger" rather than gassing.[138]

Having asserted the identity between their own ordeal and that of the witnesses who had testified before them, the judges ended with a flourish. "Before universal public opinion," they unanimously denounced "the Soviet concentration camps, monstrous relic of a regime of slavery already condemned by History and which is excused by nothing." Their final words "solemnly recall[ed] the principles of the Universal Declaration of Human Rights, in order that human dignity be respected and Law be substituted for Force and arbitrariness in the relations between the State and citizens."[139] This closing invocation of the Universal Declaration marked a departure not only from the commission's own usual reticence about rights but also from the example of Nuremberg, where "human rights" had been mentioned only twenty-five times (versus 1,527 references to "aggression").[140] The CICRC judges' decision to pay this unexpected homage to the UDHR must be understood as yet another bid for legitimacy in the absence of real authority or tangible sanction, a last-gasp effort to connect their lonely performance of international justice to all available liberal norms and global institutions.

At this historic juncture, of course, the gesture was double-edged—it was precisely such pious invocations that rendered the language of human rights suspect or useless in the eyes of many postwar European leftists. For the fact remained that the CICRC's mock trial had been an anti-Soviet propaganda exercise. Even the participants were discomfited by the partisan nature of the proceedings. Tillion, who had freely signed the final judgment, nevertheless brooded over its contents. As 1951 drew to a close, she wrote to Dr. Adelaide Hautval, a much-respected Birkenau and Ravensbrück survivor, sending her a copy of the trial transcript. (Rousset had rushed it into print with Pavois, as planned, under the title *Livre blanc sur les camps de concentration soviétiques*). "This all touches on very worrying problems," Tillion confessed, "for it is extremely difficult to prevent these facts, which unfortunately are true, from being exploited in a partisan sense—and yet on the other hand, in my opinion, it is impossible to ignore an issue of such gravity. . . . I would very much like to discuss all this with you."[141] Here lay the crux of the problem: the Soviet Union really *did* possess prison labor camps. They really did constitute a gross human rights violation, a "crime against humanity." The court's judgment had been a just one. And yet it was not entirely clear to Tillion that, in pronouncing it, the CICRC had brought more justice into the world.

Because it constituted an attempt to mobilize every available tool to stigmatize the USSR's crimes against its own citizens, the CICRC's "trial" in Brussels helps make evident a set of contemporary assumptions in early-1950s Western Europe about international justice and "crimes against humanity." M. Cherif Bassiouni has noted that although the post-1945 history of international criminal law itself can be traced minutely, "it is difficult to measure or assess [Nuremberg's] impact . . . on the individual and collective values and attitudes that have developed since then."[142] The Cold War period, especially the fifteen years between the IMT and the Eichmann trial, appears as a particular blank spot in this story, scattered survey data on retrospective opinion about Nuremberg itself notwithstanding. The CICRC's mock trial provides one flash-point of illumination. Of course commonly shared beliefs about justice for atrocity cannot be extrapolated from the attitudes of Nazi camp survivors, some of them virulently partisan. Nevertheless, these individuals' attempts to shape public opinion by drawing on the rhetoric of "crimes against humanity"—with "humanity" constituted as a transnational community of shared victimhood—are highly suggestive. So, too, are the elaborate encomiums that greeted the "victims who make themselves judges, to their enormous moral credit."[143] For instance, it is interesting to note that nowhere—including in the Communist press—did the CICRC meet the objection that what the Soviet Union did to its own people in peacetime was its own business.

The point here is not that the world was won over by 1951 to a universalist ethics of transnational solidarity. It is, rather, that the language and rituals of international justice forged at Nuremberg were readily seized upon by that date as relevant and fitting instruments with which to wage the Cold War. Moreover, the CICRC did not merely borrow a handy idiom, then put it back on the shelf unaltered—rather, members refashioned the concepts they had appropriated in light of contemporary political concerns, and in relation to the specific violent practices in which they believed the Soviet Union was engaged. To better condemn the USSR, CICRC leaders privileged "crimes against humanity" as the signal legacy of Nuremberg, interpreted the charge as a condemnation of "concentrationary" assaults on human dignity, and resolutely freed it from the nexus requirement. Thus, a full decade ahead of the Eichmann trial, Rousset and his fellow survivors embraced Douglas's "atrocity paradigm"—not because of Holocaust consciousness (which they lacked) nor as the result of a sophisticated theory of international jurisprudence (they had none) but because of a pressing desire to equate past Nazi and present Soviet acts.

Still more importantly, the CICRC's "trial" advanced the "atrocity paradigm" in its wholehearted endorsement of victim-witness testimony. Indeed, it is difficult to imagine a stronger symbolic statement about the privilege that ought to be accorded to victims' voices than the commission's mock courtroom of Nazi camp survivors assembled to hear Soviet camp survivors "recount their sufferings and their secret life." Rousset's pronouncement that the tribunal was being conducted "in the name of" victims only spelled out what was already abundantly evident in the trial's theatrical production, its phantasmagoric reimagining of Nuremberg as a tribunal by and for those who had suffered. Here, again, a reverence for the spoken words of trauma survivors, which is generally associated with post-Eichmann Holocaust memory, was already present.

Disconcertingly, though, the commission's members adopted the position that testimony was sacred as an instrumental Cold War tactic while minimizing or appropriating the Holocaust rather than commemorating it. Thus the Brussels trial also complicates two widely accepted narratives of the post-1945 West: first, that which holds that the Cold War served as a temporary impediment to the development of norms and practices of international justice rather than playing a complex and ambivalent role in that development; and second, that which ties the "advent of the witness" directly to the explosion of Holocaust remembrance that began in the 1960s and 1970s. The CICRC's "trial" may have been a mock one, but its extraordinary staging suggests a need to revise those accounts—and to reconsider the 1950s as a period marked not only by undeniable absences but also by provocative, performative, and frankly political visions of justice for victims of "crimes against humanity." Strange as it may seem, David Rousset's project ultimately served as a bridge from Nuremberg to Jerusalem and beyond.

# 5

# INTO THE LABYRINTH OF FRANCO'S PRISONS

In 1952, the International Commission carried out its first investigations into detention conditions in the capitalist world, targeting Spain and Greece. Inquiries into the two Western nations most commonly accused of maintaining "concentration camp regimes" had been long promised—under pressure from critics, Rousset first suggested them a fortnight after issuing the November 1949 "Appeal." Subsequently the French commission's 1950 "Open Letter" to survivors elsewhere in Europe made the commitment formal, thereby rendering Rousset's project acceptable to several eventual participants. These included Louis Martin-Chauffier, José Ester Borrás and other representatives of the "Spanish republican" community, and Resistance heroine Elisabeth Ingrand, who agreed to serve in her crucial role as *juge d'instruction* for the Brussels trial only after receiving Rousset's "assurance that no possibility existed of the Russian case being handled alone," without Western counterparts.[1] Spurred on by such voices and eager to establish his commission's nonpartisan bona fides, Rousset made a priority of the Western cases from the instant the CICRC pronounced the USSR guilty of "crimes against humanity."

The work the organization undertook in 1952 to determine whether Spain and Greece maintained "concentrationary regimes" looked different from its spectacular hearing against the Soviet Union. This was in part because the governments in question reluctantly granted Rousset's followers in-person access to their internment facilities, a concession that—in line with the CICRC's bylaws—precluded them from undertaking mock courtroom proceedings. The group's privileging of on-site inquiry as a mechanism by which an embarrassing public "trial" might be avoided was evidently strategic, but it also reflected members' beliefs about their own expertise and duties. Since the CICRC was premised on the idea that Nazi camp survivors possessed a special ability to *see* concentrationary dehumanization at work, its founding documents specified that Hitler's former victims ought to serve humanity not simply as "witnesses" in a metaphorical sense but as literal, visual eyewitnesses. Members eagerly embraced this agenda, even though it at first appeared impracticable not only in the USSR but globally: in the early 1950s, the prospect of submitting domestic detention facilities to outside inspection was hardly more congenial to Madrid or Athens than to Moscow. Cold War politics, however, facilitated a process by which the Greek and Spanish governments were gradually cajoled, tempted, and shamed into providing the commission access. Ironically, therefore, despite the CICRC's anti-Soviet origins, it was in the West that the group most fully enacted its model of memory-driven "witnessing" as a response to ongoing carceral abuses.

The practical workings of that model can best be understood through examining the CICRC's Spanish investigation, undertaken in May 1952 by Ingrand, Lise Børsum, André Alers, and Jean de Swart, with assistance from Rousset. Their inquiry is of special interest, beyond that of the Greek case, for several reasons. First, it produced revelatory knowledge about ongoing political repression in the authoritarian Iberian nation. As Catalan historian Ricard Vinyes puts it, "in the heart of the Francoist years," in a *Livre blanc* as well as articles, interviews, and United Nations testimony, the CICRC "presented to the world for the first—and only—time" a comprehensive, internal view of Spain's carceral universe. Its findings are still mined by specialist scholars; they deserve to be known more widely.[2] Second, the history provides uncommonly rich material for considering how state agents sought to instrumentalize nongovernmental actors in the early Cold War, and vice versa. Francoist bureaucrats' decision to admit the commission—one they would come to regret—is revelatory of how the era's polarized politics created unexpected openings to challenge Western states' impunity, even as they also hamstrung the UN from serving as an effective arbiter for such challenges.

Third, because of Spain's strange status in the post-1945 European imagination as a living relic of the continent's catastrophic interwar affair with fascist ideology, the CICRC's mission there offers a striking illustration of the transformations that antifascism underwent in this era, as figures such as Ester, Calmarza, and Rousset himself—all opponents of Franco since the 1930s—grappled for new terms with which to condemn his regime. The CICRC's Spanish mission was not merely an alibi for its anticommunist agenda—it was also an attempt to keep faith with members' pre–World War II commitments in radically changed circumstances. While the discourse of "totalitarianism" provided one key tool for this project, so too did Rousset's binary framework of "concentrationary" versus "non-concentrationary" detention—which the Spanish exiles on the commission, who had by this point survived myriad carceral institutions (including, not least, the wretched internment camps of late Third Republic France), were now compelled to embrace as an instrument for stigmatizing their homeland within the constraints of Cold War politics.

Fourth, and most important, the history of the commission's Spanish adventure sheds light on both the power and fragility of the notion that ethical judgment could arise from the memory of suffering. In many ways, the mission appeared to affirm CICRC members' assertion that as former prisoners of the Nazis they were uniquely positioned to evaluate postwar forms of state violence; after all, the astonishing fact of their admission into the political prisons of a peacetime state—an autocratic one—was largely thanks to their claims to moral authority as Resistance deportees. And once the group arrived in Spain, delegates' determination to "bear witness" through comparing the suffering of Franco's prisoners to their own past victimization drove them to overcome substantial obstacles. In particular, it encouraged them to see the Spanish political prisoners they encountered as kindred spirits and therefore to act as "collectors of voices" (in Vinyes's words) in their impassioned pursuit of first-person testimony.[3]

However, the inquiry also exposed perils in invoking memory of Nazi atrocity as a basis for postwar judgment. To begin with, in July 1952 one of the investigators was unmasked as a false survivor. The CICRC dealt with the revelation of his lack of "concentrationary" experience through obfuscation, exposing the limits of its dedication to truthful *témoignage* and making itself vulnerable to discrediting attacks. Though this affair was damaging, the process by which the remaining delegates drew conclusions from their voyage exposed even more fundamental problems with the notion that Hitler's former victims now constituted a privileged class of "experts." As the investigators themselves quietly acknowledged, the "imposed optic" of concentrationary memory ultimately hampered their ability to evaluate Francoist political detention on its own terms.[4] The organization's negative final verdict on the question of whether or not Spain was currently operating a "concentrationary regime" indisputably served Cold War ends. But its content was not the result of any calculated abandonment of the CICRC's standards—to the contrary, it arose from the application of those standards. Thus it was in Spain that some members tentatively began to wonder if their comparative mandate might impede meaningful criticism of ongoing persecution rather than encourage it.

## Why Spain?

By the moment in 1949 when David Rousset first vowed to request access to Spanish detention centers, Spain had exited the period of greatest terror spawned by the 1936–1939 Civil War and its aftermath. The war years were marked by intense levels of violence on the part of both republican ("Loyalist") factions and—to a greater degree—General Francisco Franco's Nationalist military rebels: the former carried out roughly fifty thousand rearguard executions, the latter somewhere between seventy thousand and one hundred thousand before 1939, and an additional twenty to thirty thousand after. More importantly for our purposes, between 1936 and the early 1940s the Francoists incarcerated hundreds of thousands of combatant and civilian "enemies" in unthinkably overcrowded prisons and a vast constellation of penal colonies, slave labor battalions, and squalid, hastily converted warehouses, schools, hospitals, and barracks.[5] Some of these facilities evidently qualified as "concentration camps" according to the CICRC's three-point definition (or, indeed, any definition) and were at times identified explicitly as such by Nationalist leaders, though the term was applied in a haphazard fashion.[6]

Franco's military victory did not mark an end to his use of mass detention as a tool of political repression and purgative terror. In fact, quantitatively speaking, the high point of internment came only after 1939. By its own count (which may have understated the truth), his regime held 280,000 people in its penitentiaries alone in 1940.[7] Forced labor continued; torture and rape of internees were endemic; death rates from malnutrition, abysmal hygiene practices, and sheer cold were high.[8] The system did, however, evolve over the decade. Large-scale paroles and sentence revisions began in the early 1940s; by 1942, due not only to these policies but also to executions and other prisoner deaths, the official detainee population had declined to 124,423.[9] Given that the country's pre–Civil War internment facilities were equipped to hold only a quarter of that number, conditions did not quickly improve. But the 1945 defeat of the Axis powers, which terminated what Stanley Payne calls the "semifascist" period in Spanish history and forced Franco toward a more conventional Catholic authoritarianism, did contribute to a further easing of repression.[10] The government technically put an end to the reign of martial law in 1948 and limited the use of military tribunals to try accused "rebels" in 1949. By 1952 only some 829 political prisoners (labeled "*anteriores*") were still serving sentences related to wartime offenses, though thousands more remained jailed for post-1939 political crimes.[11]

In the eyes of CICRC members, Spain stood out as the most urgent target of inquiry for their organization after the Soviet Union. This was partly due to the influence of the commission's Spanish exile delegation. José Ester Borrás, José Calmarza, José Rodes Bley, Ignacio Iglesias, and José Domenech were passionate opponents of Franco's regime. The men were of varying political backgrounds: Ester, for instance, was an anarcho-syndicalist, while Calmarza, a former civil servant, identified as a republican moderate, and Rodes had been a leader in the non-Stalinist communist Partido Obrero de Unificación Marxista (POUM). All of them, however, fled across the Pyrenees into Southern France during the *retirada* (retreat) of early 1939 after Catalonia fell. They joined a flood of Spanish men, women, and children—514,337 by the French Ministry of Interior's count—seeking refuge in the neighboring republic.[12] France's government, under Édouard Daladier, was ill equipped and ill disposed to manage this tide of bodies, hastily opening Argelès-sur-Mer, Saint-Cyprien, and other primitive internment camps on France's southwestern beaches as well as "specialized" camps such as Gurs and Le Vernet further inland.[13] The function of these crowded, miserable facilities would shift many times in the months and years ahead. For example, German refugees and domestic political "undesirables" arrived at Gurs in 1940, and thousands of Jewish foreign nationals (including Hannah Arendt) were subsequently interned there.[14] French detention of Spanish refugees persisted as well, however, despite heavy pressure for them to repatriate—perhaps 125,000 Spaniards remained in metropolitan France at the moment of the 1940 armistice, the future members of the Federación Española de Deportados e Internados Políticos among them.

During World War II, roughly fifteen thousand of these Spanish republican exiles landed in the Nazi *univers concentrationnaire*, overwhelmingly in Mauthausen. They arrived via varied trajectories. Many, having joined French foreign military regiments at the outbreak of hostilities, were captured with their units in 1940, imprisoned in POW camps, and then transferred to concentration camps.[15] Such was the case for Calmarza, who after six months in Stalag V-D in Strasbourg was "transformed" into a political deportee and shipped to Mauthausen, where he survived for four and a half years.[16] Others, arrested for acts of resistance or criminality, passed directly from French internment facilities to German camps. In November 1941, for instance, Rodes was condemned by military tribunal to fifteen years' hard labor for "Communist activity." He eventually landed in Eysses penitentiary, Vichy France's most important prison for political convicts.[17] On May 30, 1944, Eysses was turned over to the SS, which deported over twelve hundred of its inmates, including Rodes, to Dachau. Ester, meanwhile, resisting in the "Pat O'Leary network" alongside a number of other Spanish anarchists, was freed after an initial internment in Le Vernet in 1941 but recaptured by the Gestapo in late 1943. Upon his arrival at Mauthausen he became an organizer in the camp's clandestine prisoner network and sat on the Spanish "committee of national union" forged in the spring of 1944.[18]

The FEDIP, founded in Toulouse in 1945, brought together roughly seventeen hundred Spanish survivors of such labyrinthine journeys through the carceral worlds of midcentury Europe.[19] With Calmarza as president and Ester as assistant secretary-general, the organization welcomed Nazi camp deportees of all parties (though, in practice, communists did not participate) and existed primarily for purposes of mutual aid, fulfilling a significant social function as France's "Spanish colony" took on aspects of a permanent exile community.[20] However, the FEDIP also conceived of itself as a lobbying group for persecuted compatriots worldwide. One of its targets was the USSR, where an unfortunate group of Spaniards had been imprisoned in Karaganda since 1941. But its actions were primarily directed against Francisco Franco's "tyranny," "oppression," "barbarity," and "destruction of human dignity" back in Spain.[21]

The Spanish exiles' determination to stigmatize the ruler of their homeland in global opinion was heightened by geopolitical shifts of the early 1950s. In the immediate postwar years, Spain held a pariah status in the international community, symbolically enforced by the UN's 1946 call on member nations to withdraw their ambassadors from the country. But by the end of the decade, spurred by strategic considerations, Western governments commenced steps to normalize relations with the Iberian regime. The "Spain lobby" in the US gained momentum year by year, restoring contact with Madrid by piecemeal measures while wearing down President Truman's resistance to doing business with "a collaborator of Mr. Hitler's."[22] The French, meanwhile, first moved toward rapprochement with their neighbor through commercial and financial accords in 1948 and 1949. The FEDIP responded to such activity with frantic efforts to mobilize human rights discourse against Franco: in a "dossier" submitted to the UN in November 1950, members offered a side-by-side "confrontation" between each article of the Universal Declaration of Human Rights and an item of Francoist legislation contravening it.[23] An accompanying letter to Secretary-General Trygve Lie begged the UN not to help "whitewash the regime of Francoist Spain."[24]

Spain would not gain UN membership until 1955, but it was clear to FEDIP members by the end of 1950 that their efforts to instrumentalize the UDHR against Franco had been futile. Mere days after they submitted their "dossier" to Lie, the United Nations reauthorized the dispatch of ambassadors to Madrid. The US and France both normalized relations within weeks; in July 1951 the US opened negotiations for a military pact as well. The FEDIP voiced disgust with (in Ester's words) "the lack of courage of certain so-called democracies"; it did not, however, abandon its activism.[25] Rather, reasoning that Franco would now be under heightened diplomatic pressure to conform to humanitarian standards, members sought new tactics to publicize the plight of comrades still persecuted by his regime. Setting aside the language of "human rights," so evidently ineffectual, the organization now embraced Rousset's favored idiom, expressing its hope for his commission to affirm that "the government of General Franco has put in practice—and puts in practice still—a concentrationary system as it has been defined by the CICRC."[26]

By accusing Spain of "concentrationary" abuses, FEDIP members hoped to suggest that Hitler's legacy lived on under the Iberian dictator whom he had once helped bring to power. This strategic aim had the virtue of narrative clarity. It is worth underlining, however, that its pursuit demanded acceptance of the CICRC's understanding of the term *concentrationnaire*, which excluded from consideration the various *French* internment facilities through which many Spaniards had passed between 1939 and 1944. This represented a real concession on their part. Ester, Calmarza, Rodes, and the others may have agreed with writer Arthur Koestler's assertion that if, "in Liberal-Centigrade, Vernet was the zero-point of infamy, measured in Dachau-Fahrenheit it was still 32 degrees above zero."[27] But to claim that, nonetheless, Le Vernet, Gurs, and their French counterparts had indeed been "concentration camps" was within the bounds of mainstream discourse in post-1945 France.[28] Participating in Rousset's project demanded that FEDIP members abstain from using such language—and thus that they accept a vision of World War II–era political internment that elided Spanish suffering in France. Rousset never denied historic French wrongdoing, but his geography of the "concentrationary universe"—now powerfully reinforced by Cold War imperatives—had always excluded his own country's institutions. Thus no Spanish CICRC participant (indeed, no CICRC participant of any nationality) ever voiced a suggestion that Franco's prisons might productively be compared to, say, Eysses or Gurs. The commission's approach to memory dictated that the only ethically meaningful points of historical reference for the post-1945 world were the German SS camps.

Unwillingness on the part of the French leadership of the CICRC to confront the implications of Spanish members' complex personal histories of imprisonment should not be confused with lack of sympathy for their struggles or a Cold War–inflected unwillingness to censure Spain. Members of the Spanish federation—whose French "Committee of Protection" included CICRC figurehead Rémy Roure alongside such luminaries as Sartre, Camus, and Mauriac—understood that French political survivors were virtually unanimously arrayed against Franco. Indeed, several of the CICRC's founders belonged to a generation of antifascists for whom acts of republican solidarity during Spain's Civil War had constituted a prelude to the Resistance activities for which they were eventually deported.[29] Louis Martin-Chauffier, for example, had helped to lead the Comité Franco-Espagnol, a Loyalist aid group, and authored articles and pamphlets intended to convince fellow French Catholics that "there are not two Spains. There is an army against a people, an international fascist conspiracy against a democracy."[30] His views remained the same at the dawn of the 1950s. In allowing for the rehabilitation of "the Hitlerite Franco," he wrote disgustedly, the UN had betrayed its Charter—and France, along with the United States, had abandoned the "grand principles" for which World War II was waged.[31]

David Rousset, meanwhile—then a Trotskyist—had actually been in Barcelona in the early months of the Civil War, working with a Moroccan delegation to the Central Committee of Antifascist Militias. He was proud of this history, considering himself "intimately" tied to the Spanish republican cause "not only by the solidarity of principles but by that of common action."[32] In the 1950s, Rousset continued to protest ongoing Spanish persecution of antifascists: "The combatants of 1936," he wrote, "remain symbols of the last great workers' fight for a socialist revolution in freedom. For this reason, all the blows that are still struck against them today, all the murders that are still perpetrated against them, are blows against what remains of liberty in the world."[33] Despite his evolving pro-American sympathies, Rousset also persisted in denouncing cultural and diplomatic concessions that indirectly legitimized Franco.[34] And he categorically condemned his own government's steps toward renewed relations: "It is our greatest duty to say clearly and loudly that any compromise with Franco and his regime, any collusion with what he represents, is a weakening of democracy. . . . Freedom and democracy cannot be defended through compromises of any kind with totalitarianism of any kind."[35]

This final phrase was a telling one: if the David Rousset of 1936 had found Franco guilty of "fascism," in 1950 he altered the verdict. The word *totalitaire*, earlier used by French intellectuals as a loose synonym for *fasciste*, had by now become a coded means to indicate moral equivalency between Hitler's Germany and Stalin's USSR. It signaled, in shorthand, a belief that the great tragedy of twentieth-century Europe was the rise of the all-powerful, antidemocratic, anti-individualist state apparatus, under any ideological banner. Identifying Spain, too, with this label became standard practice among French noncommunist leftists by the early '50s—it permitted them to censure Franco's dictatorship without thereby adopting a posture congenial to the Parti Communiste.[36] Camus, for example, who in 1944 and 1945 described Spain as "fascist," by 1948 grouped it with the Soviet Union as an exemplar of "a type of political society which has come into being, or is coming into being, on the right and the left, according to the totalitarian model."[37] Altman's *Franc-Tireur*, meanwhile, protested the return of ambassadors to Madrid ("the Spanish Munich") by "quickly enumerating what the regimes of Franco and Stalin have in common"; the list included "prison and camps for adversaries" who challenged their respective bids for "totalitarian power."[38] Similarly *Preuves*, the French journal of the Congress for Cultural Freedom, appealed in March 1952 to "international solidarity against totalitarianism" to decry Franco's continued use of political executions.[39]

Unlike his allies in the US, David Rousset was never drawn to the discourse of "totalitarianism" as a means of denouncing Stalin: since he arrived at his Nazi-Soviet equivalency through invoking the "concentrationary" nature of both regimes, other conceptual frameworks for conflating them were superfluous to his project. (Recall that the "Appeal" had not employed the term *totalitaire*.) However, he found the language useful in discussing Spain: it permitted him not only to avoid the PCF's perilous fascist-antifascist binary but also to transform any condemnation of Francoism into a fresh opportunity to tar the Soviets. "Franco and those who serve him are in reality Stalin's best allies," he insisted: however distant communist ideology might be from "the political and philosophical conceptions of Franco," the Soviet and Spanish governments were analogous—indeed, united—in their "totalitarian" disregard for individual freedom.[40] Rousset, it is true, was not preoccupied with political detention in Spain in the same way that he was with the gulag. But he did despise Franco's government, and he came to see that its targeting by the CICRC could serve to highlight embarrassing similarities between Soviet detention facilities and those of a right-wing dictatorship.

Rousset was also delighted to observe that announcing a Spanish CICRC inquiry placated portions of the French intellectual left. For example, Emmanuel Mounier, venerable editor of *Esprit* (where the "Appeal" had been condemned as propaganda), reached out to him in February 1950 volunteering to publish the CICRC's eventual findings on Spain. The invitation was, admittedly, lukewarm: "Since you individually have been mixed up in certain polemics," Mounier wrote, any material *Esprit* printed would have to be "signed impersonally by the committee."[41] It also went nowhere, since Mounier died two months later. All the same, the overture bolstered Rousset's hope that targeting Spain might help him gain valuable allies. Lashing Stalin ever more tightly to Franco, he reasoned, would allow him to continue assailing the USSR while nevertheless blunting Merleau-Ponty and Sartre's charge that he had "chosen his deportees."

Despite mild discomfort among State Department officials about the "political ramifications" of Rousset's newfound zeal regarding Spanish prisons, overall his American and British contacts felt similarly.[42] Gerard Corley-Smith of the IRD openly cheered at the prospect of a Spanish CICRC inquiry: "The association of the USSR with Spain would be remarkably fruitful," he claimed.[43] The British were also pleased to realize that if Spain and Greece agreed to on-site inspections, the USSR would be visibly isolated in its refusal to allow the CICRC access to its detention facilities. "I do not have to point out the propaganda value" such a state of affairs would produce, wrote one embassy official.[44] On the American side, Irving Brown likewise rejoiced. Adjudging "the Franco crowd" to comprise "not as totalitarian a regime as the Soviets" but one nonetheless corrupted by "the spirit of totalitarianism," he and Lovestone welcomed pressure on Spain's treatment of political opponents. More importantly, they agreed, Rousset's maneuver would "put the Russians on the spot."[45]

Such prospects were, of course, realizable only if Francoist officials actually agreed to inspection by a foreign committee of Resistance deportees, an outcome that at first appeared extremely remote. Spanish Nationalist leaders, who had cut off Red Cross access to prisoners in August 1938, did not have a favorable view of outside investigators. While proclaiming great pride in their "modern and humanitarian" penitentiaries, Franco's ministers interpreted Rousset's proposal to investigate in Spain as a slight to Spanish sovereignty.[46] No state that "holds its independence in high esteem" could submit to such an exercise, argued one diplomat.[47] The regime was also alarmed by the presence of "red" exiles on the commission, and by Rousset's own political biography (as they misunderstood it). Amid a flurry of memoranda warning against this "former communist" of "Jewish origin," the Ministry of Foreign Affairs preemptively suspended his personal visa in November 1950.[48] The CICRC then attempted to approach the Spanish through a less threatening representative, Reumont. But matters did not improve. In fact, this overture backfired spectacularly: the Spanish contacted allies at the Vatican to pressure the Belgian priest (unsuccessfully) to resign from the CICRC.[49]

Nevertheless, the commission's leaders eventually managed to gain an invitation into Spain's penitentiaries. It was their spring 1951 mock-judicial proceeding against the gulag that produced this surprising about-face. Madrid was frightened by the "trial": Spain, it was now clear, might be subject to a similar shaming procedure if it continued to reject requests for in-person access. Moreover, the tribunal's hostility to the USSR convinced Spanish embassy staff in Brussels that the CICRC's purported desire to root out "concentration camps" worldwide was, in truth, no more than a "formula for attacking Russia." Rousset's proposed investigation of Spanish detention facilities, explained Franco's ambassador to Belgium, the Conde de Casa Miranda, was merely an alibi against charges of partisanship. Spain therefore possessed a golden opportunity: it could instrumentalize Rousset to generate an alibi of its own. "The Spanish government finds in its path," Casa Miranda argued, at a delicate moment in its refashioning as a respectable member of the Western community, "an organization firmly on the left, democratic, pro-American, with an enormous global reach, ready to certify and proclaim the nonexistence of concentrationary regimes in Spain, against the opinion of millions and millions of people, especially in North America." This good fortune demanded seizing.[50]

The CICRC's battle was not won through the conversion of Casa Miranda, since officials in Madrid remained preoccupied with anxieties over sovereignty and status. "Spain," they maintained, "was not a colony and did not have to submit to an inquiry nor to justify itself against imaginary accusations before examining magistrates."[51] By January 1952, negotiations were again in stalemate;

the Spanish delegation to the CICRC, complained Ester, "[has] the impression that the International Commission is taking forever in its haggling with the Spanish government." In response, members voted "not to prolong indefinitely these so-far sterile negotiations with Madrid" and—after one last effort at dialogue—to proceed toward a mock trial "as it had done for the USSR."[52] This ultimatum worked. In March Rousset was invited to travel to the Spanish capital with Bernard to carve out a set of "accords" with Franco's Ministry of Justice. The resulting agreement contained some uncomfortable compromises for the CICRC—for instance, a delegation of survivors would only be permitted to enter Spain "as private persons" rather than representatives of the commission, which Spain refused to recognize. Rousset and Bernard accepted this concession in return for a guarantee they considered more vital: a go-ahead to travel widely and visit "all facilities," not only those proposed by government agents.[53]

This point was nonnegotiable for the CICRC because it already possessed a long list of Spanish detention centers and penal colonies whose inspection it considered mandatory. This had been compiled by the FEDIP using information solicited from the larger Spanish exile community, part of years' worth of efforts the organization invested in laying groundwork for the inquiry.[54] FEDIP members could not openly help investigate their homeland—CICRC rules barred such conflicts of interest, and moreover Franco's government would never have countenanced it. But behind the scenes they took a leading role. In addition to charting the carceral geography that their fellow survivors should explore, they proposed a "work plan" to ensure the voyage was carried out "with efficiency" and crafted a questionnaire to be used in interrogating inmates.[55] Most importantly, they compiled a thick dossier of survivor testimonials on Francoist detention from an array of former Spanish prisoners now living in France. Though these statements varied in style—some were intimate accounts of their authors' political biographies, others brief third-person summaries of oral interviews—taken together the texts composed a rich collage of the Nationalist repression and an invaluable resource for the non-Spanish CICRC participants charged by Rousset with journeying to Spain.

These were four men and women hailing from four different member-nations: Elisabeth Ingrand of France, André Alers of Belgium, Jean de Swart of the Netherlands, and Lise Børsum of Norway. Ingrand we have already encountered; Alers was a CICRC stalwart; as for De Swart, a Catholic entrepreneur and a leading figure in the Dutch commission, we will shortly have occasion to consider his credentials carefully. Børsum, meanwhile, was a recent addition to the commission, to which a Norwegian delegation representing the Norsk Samband av Politiske Fanger had only just acceded.[56] A Ravensbrück survivor and memoirist, a prolific journalist, an indefatigable activist, and a staunch anticommunist (by the time she joined the CICRC she had already published a book on the gulag), Børsum immediately became one of the commission's most active participants, adding another female deportee voice to those provided by the French ADIR contingent.[57] Rousset insisted on her inclusion in the Spanish venture, believing it "would highlight the international character of the [CICRC] and have a beneficial psychological effect."[58] Traveling separately, the four investigators each arrived in Madrid between May 5 and May 7, 1952—as did Rousset, present to ensure that Spanish officials abided by the "accords." This would prove arduous work.

## The CICRC's Spanish Odyssey

Difficulties arose between the Spanish government and the International Commission's delegation immediately upon its arrival in the country. One "absolutely unexpected" early crisis could have been foreseen by an investigatory body less green than the CICRC: upon meeting the mixed-gender delegation, Spanish authorities, citing both the law of the land and Catholic "custom and morals," announced that it forbade the entry of female investigators into male prisons.[59] The edict paralyzed the inquiry for days but was eventually resolved through parleys with Ministry of Justice officials.[60] Other challenges were not, however, so easily resolved—in particular those related to the actual substance of the prison visits. Whatever each side's hopes of instrumentalizing the other, the aims of the Spanish government and the CICRC were in conflict. Francoist officials, wracked by ongoing qualms about the wisdom of permitting a non-state entity to police their affairs, hoped for the inspection to be a cursory tour of formal appointments, under cover of which the commission could certify that Spain was blameless and the USSR uniquely felonious. Meanwhile, although CICRC members did view Spain through a Cold War prism according to which Stalin's crimes outweighed Franco's, they nevertheless were deadly serious about bearing witness to the suffering of political prisoners wherever possible. Once admitted to the country, the investigators—especially Ingrand, who had been poring over Spanish penal codes and FEDIP testimonials for months—had no intention of proceeding in bad faith. Thus the two sides clashed early and often over the basic parameters of the inquiry.

Unsurprisingly, a key sticking point was the integrity of inmate testimony. Despite Rousset's "accords" with the government, Spain's general director of prisons, José María Herreros de Tejada, announced during an "extremely difficult" May 8 meeting his "formal rejection" of the principle that CICRC investigators be permitted to conduct interviews using independent translators and without prison personnel present.[61] On this the CICRC could not compromise: in its view, inviting prisoners to testify in the presence of their guards would be not only evidentiarily worthless but sadistic. After a strained debate, Herreros de Tejada grudgingly agreed to unsupervised interviews in Madrid prisons but declined to guarantee that his authorization would hold elsewhere in the country or even to put it in writing. Over the next two weeks, as the delegates traveled from the capital region south to Seville, El Puerto de Santa María, Alicante, and Valencia, then back to Madrid, they "were forced constantly and often, in difficult conditions, to impose the application of this agreement" with hostile local officials.[62]

At this point De Swart and Alers threw up their hands and left the country. Børsum and Ingrand, however, were determined to persist. They were far from the end of the FEDIP's list, and Ingrand was keen to travel to penitentiaries north of the capital that harbored a handful of young French *résistants* who had quixotically crossed the Pyrenees following the 1944 liberation of France to attempt a parallel overthrow of Franco.[63] The two women penned an ultimatum to the Ministry of Justice demanding that written authorization for confidential detainee meetings be provided within forty-eight hours.[64] On May 27, this document finally materialized, bearing Herreros de Tejada's signature; thereafter, in circumstances that they judged by and large satisfactory, Børsum and Ingrand completed the mission, traveling north to Cuéllar, Langreo, and nearby Tudela, along the coast to Santoña and Bilbao, then south again to Burgos, Madrid once more, and finally, on June 5, Barcelona. They returned home exhausted. "In three weeks, we covered nearly 5,000 kilometers," Børsum noted. "The door of each prison barely closed behind us before we found ourselves back on the road."[65] In the aggregate, from the full delegation's arrival in Spain to Ingrand and Børsum's departure, they had toured seventeen prisons and five penal colonies containing a total of fourteen thousand detainees.

The procedure the CICRC representatives followed at each of these sites involved two modes of "expert witnessing." First, they minutely inspected the premises for resonant traces of German practices. Their method was partly reliant on visual observation but also drew on the power of memory associated with other senses. "We stuck our noses into buckets in the hospital," Børsum recounted in a series of articles that she penned for the left-leaning Norwegian paper *Dagbladet* later that year. "We inhaled and smelled the restrooms and the kitchens."[66] The repellent odor of the toilets in one penal colony, she asserted, "reminded us, in an ominous way, of the worst of the Nazi bunkhouses."[67] Such moments of horrified recall were rare, however, since Spanish officials engaged in elaborate stagecraft regarding food, sanitation, work regimens, and recreation policies in their facilities. An inmate account later smuggled out of San Miguel de los Reyes described four days of frenetic painting and cleaning ahead of the commission's visit, and Børsum reported that similar efforts had clearly been undertaken everywhere: prisoners in "spanking new uniforms" milled about "improvised workshops"; tempting puddings simmered in just-painted kitchens; trees hastily imported into a desolate courtyard "were falling over lamentably."[68] On occasion, she wrote, "we were so obviously expected that it approached a comedy," noting one particularly "abominable" serenade from a trumped-up "prisoner orchestra."[69] She and the other CICRC members were little troubled, though, since they remained confident of their own ability, as survivors, to see through any "camouflage" of conditions. "It would be very easy to fool a Commission," Børsum asserted coolly, "except when it is made up of former [Nazi] prisoners."[70] They—and they alone—were "*gens de métier*" for the task at hand.[71]

Second, the delegates made use of their hard-won permission to solicit victim testimony from detainees. By the end, counting interviews conducted both before and after the departure of Alers and De Swart, the group was able to speak through translators with sixty-five prisoners, sixty-three of them male. Forty-four were political detainees sentenced by military tribunal, including ten "*anteriores*." (Members of this latter group, reported Børsum, now confined for upward of thirteen years, were unaccustomed to speaking about themselves and provided "unclear" answers; when "finally their tongues came untied," they struggled to produce the "plain and simplified" testimony privileged by the commission.)[72] Forty-six of the interviews took place in conditions the CICRC considered acceptable: a single witness at a time, chosen by the delegates based on their perusal of prison records, and—most importantly—the absence of prison personnel.[73] Even in these cases, however, the process was not ideal. For example, the investigators were aware that questioning internees in a prison director's office was unlikely to inspire trust, but they often lacked other options. A letter later smuggled out of El Dueso Prison, moreover, confirmed their suspicion that interviewees were later pressured to reveal, "Spaniard to Spaniard," how they had responded to queries.[74] The delegates also longed for more time with each prisoner than the quarter hour generally allotted. "We barely discovered a face—a personality—behind the mask of toughness when they each had to go," wrote Børsum wistfully.[75]

Despite such frustrations in their efforts to access witnesses' voices of subjective truth, the CICRC delegates thoroughly succeeded on another front: by the end of the mission, they could speak with confidence on the distribution of political detainees in Spain, the procedures by which they had been arrested, the sentencing norms to which they were subject, the length of terms they actually tended to serve, and their use as laborers in "redemption through work" programs. Most importantly, the delegation was able to estimate the past and present size of the imprisoned population. At the end of the Civil War, they determined, "without any doubt, the number of prisoners and detainees greatly surpassed 300,000." Though those dark days were past, roughly thirty thousand men and women remained incarcerated—whether in penitentiaries, prisons "*de partido*," work battalions, militarized penal colonies, or "special establishments" for "vagabonds"—and approximately seven to eight thousand of them qualified as political prisoners by the CICRC's lights.[76]

More than anyone else, Ingrand was responsible for this investigatory triumph. "The more I got to know [her]," wrote an admiring Børsum, "the more I had to acknowledge that the Spanish were right to be disinclined to allow women into the prisons. She had an extremely piercing and clear spirit, and never gave up on getting to the bottom of things." Ingrand "knew the Spanish penal code better than any Spaniard" and, against officials who greeted the women with cellophane-wrapped bouquets and obsequious flattery, deployed her "iron will" to prevent the inquiry from degenerating into a "courtesy call."[77] Her specialty, it seems, was the swift and efficient perusal of partial, chaotic registers to reconstruct the history of political detention at individual penitentiaries along the commission's journey. She combined the information gleaned from these archives with the FEDIP testimonials, her own prisoner interviews, data provided by the Ministry of Justice, and conversations with local administrators to arrive at the most authoritative knowledge of the scope of Spanish political internment then possessed by any outsider.

That Ingrand had once been imprisoned in a series of Nazi prison cells rather than concentration camps "properly speaking," a fact that had troubled her during her 1951 stint as *juge d'instruction* in Brussels, presented no difficulty during the Spanish mission. The facilities now under investigation were prisons and labor colonies, and in these, she could legitimately claim to be a "specialist" in the experiential sense privileged by Rousset. In the end, however, it was not Ingrand's memories of her handcuffed solitary confinement at the Gestapo's Cologne headquarters in 1943, vivid though they might have been, but her legal expertise, research acumen, and aptitude for precise empirical reasoning that enabled her to take the lead in the commission's project of bearing witness to the Francoist prison universe. Thus, paradoxically, the very rigor of her work in Spain exposed the questionable premises of the group's model of epistemological authority gained through suffering.

A second and graver challenge to that model arose in the case of a different delegate. Jean de Swart had joined the Dutch and subsequently the International Commission in 1951 as a survivor of Vught. In the summer of 1952, however, as a result of his attempt to receive reparations from a private Dutch foundation charged with indemnitizing surviving political prisoners, the truth emerged: he had never been in that or any SS camp. De Swart, records showed, was indeed briefly imprisoned in 1943 for black market trading (of food, gin, cigarettes, cigars, and razors, but not—as he later tried to claim—arms for the Resistance). However, he was released without charge. Fellow members of the Dutch commission were still more outraged to learn that De Swart had not been a resister at all but, if anything, a minor collaborator, administering canteens for the National Labor Service throughout the war and, in 1941, selling a batch of electrodes to the Germans. His request for reparations argued that he deserved compensation, first, for the black market goods confiscated from him upon his arrest and, second, for losses incurred when he was forced to return an "abandoned" house he had purchased during the war to its rightful Jewish owner. The claim was summarily rejected, "these operations having nothing to do with the Resistance."[78]

Dutch commission leader Karel van Staal delivered all of this distinctly unwelcome news to Rousset on July 10, 1952, after the Spanish investigation was over but before its conclusions were made public. De Swart was immediately dismissed from the group, producing a sulky letter of resignation that conceded, "If in the statutes of the CICRC it states that it is necessary to have been in a concentration camp, then I cannot be a member."[79] Rousset was not personally sorry to lose the man—he had been a divisive, troublesome presence during the Iberian investigation before abandoning it midstream. Though the documentary record is murky (for reasons which will become clear momentarily), it appears that he was also responsible for persuading Alers to depart from Spain in mid-May, leaving Ingrand and Børsum to forge on alone. Once the truth was known, Alers felt himself the victim of "a shameful moral fraud," issuing an apology to the entire organization.[80] But however little regretted was De Swart's departure from the ranks of the commission, the fact of his participation in the inquiry remained.

That De Swart had been a member of the Spanish delegation—had, in fact, served as its nominal "president"—was not merely embarrassing. More importantly, it challenged the CICRC's logic of experiential expertise derived from suffering. Whereas De Swart's Dutch compatriots were the most indignant over his trumped-up Resistance credentials, judging his black market activities a blemish on their organization's honor, Rousset was only affronted that the man had never been in a Nazi camp. Camp survivors alone, he wrote to Van Staal, were capable of carrying out the sacred duty of investigating whether the *univers concentrationnaire* lived on in the postwar world: "We have affirmed from the very first day that we are the only experts, the only ones truly qualified to resolve this question, precisely because we experienced concentrationary conditions. . . . This is why the members of the National Commissions and the International Commission are chosen strictly, exclusively, from among those who survived the Nazi concentration camps and are universally recognized as having done so." De Swart's distressing case now threatened to "destroy entirely" these foundational claims.[81]

Thus the CICRC took drastic steps. On July 12, Rousset decreed that "[De Swart's] name must be eliminated from the report on Spain, which must be edited as if he did not participate in it."[82] The Dutch investigator thereby disappeared from the CICRC's Spanish *Livre blanc* and was never mentioned in participants' public commentary on the case, including their later UN testimony. "This affair," wrote Reumont (too optimistically, as it would turn out), "is thus definitively resolved."[83] The group's use of blatant mendacity to achieve such a "resolution" highlights the underlying fragility of its reliance on memory as the basis for judgment.

## From Witnessing to Judgment

Despite the unhappy De Swart business, Rousset considered the venture in Spain a success. "I believe," he wrote to Reumont, "that the voyage achieved all of its objectives."[84] Indeed, he and the group's other leaders felt that its very occurrence marked a milestone in the history of international accountability for political prisoners' treatment, as a sovereign nation provided foreign inspectors access to its detention facilities and private interviews with its detainees with the understanding that the conclusions would be publicized globally. But as the inspectors returned to their respective countries in early summer, they faced a different challenge: producing those conclusions.

Elisabeth Ingrand took primary responsibility for drafting the report. She presented her initial thoughts to a special meeting of the French commission convened on June 17.[85] Fellow ADIR member Catherine Goetschel spoke at the same gathering about Greece, having recently returned from a three-week sojourn there with Georges André, accompanied by Théo Bernard. Goetschel, an enthusiastic early proponent of a CICRC inquiry in Greece, had noted in 1950 that many "very diverse" sources indicated that Makronisos Island was a "Greek concentration camp" whose detainees "had been arrested in an arbitrary fashion" and were now "subject to a perfectly odious system of 'political reeducation.'"[86] Greece had begun to dismantle this system following its civil war, however, and by the time of Goetschel's 1952 voyage with André, only traces of its horrors remained. Although tortures and large-scale "brutalities" had taken place in the "recent past," Goetschel and André concluded, "the detention camps that now exist in Greece do not present the characteristics of concentration camps."[87]

It was evident that Ingrand would not be able to draw such straightforward conclusions about Franco's prisons. She and her fellow delegates had been revolted by much of what they encountered in Spain: arrest for political motives was "frequently accompanied by serious acts of police brutality"; provisions for defense were "practically nonexistent"; political prisoners were mixed willy-nilly with common-law criminals and consequently at their mercy; food was scarce in some locales, medicine in others, and heat nearly everywhere; hygiene was "absolutely insufficient" for penal colony inmates.[88] Describing these conditions presented no difficulty for Ingrand and her colleagues, but expository description was not the only task before them. Rather, the group was compelled to fulfill the CICRC's mandate—that is, to translate their multiform, sensory acts of witness to the Spanish prison system into a yes-or-no judgment on its "concentrationary" nature.

One reason Ingrand, Alers, and Børsum struggled to issue a singular statement on this problem was the diversity of conditions they had encountered. Local variations were so large, declared a frustrated Børsum, that "it is impossible to provide a general assessment of penitentiary institutions in Spain."[89] But the challenge of generalizing about Spain's heterogeneous facilities paled next to the difficulty of comparing them to the Nazi *univers concentrationnaire*. The delegates understood that such an act of comparison was the point of their visit and, indeed, the CICRC's raison d'être. As Ingrand wrote, the organization did not exist simply to evaluate detention systems in general terms but "to determine if, in a particular country, there exists or not a concentrationary regime." And as survivors themselves, their criteria for the "concentrationary" were necessarily "defined . . . in accordance with Hitler's Germany, which was a typical concentrationary regime, where all of these characteristics were pushed to the extreme." This "point of departure," which equated the paradigmatic or "typical" object of ethical concern with the historically "extreme" case of the Nazi camps, was "an inevitable one," Ingrand hastened to add, reluctant to undermine the commission's very premise. But it posed "a double risk of error": "First would be to consider acceptable everything which does not reach the degree of intensity of the Hitlerian concentrationary regime. . . . Inversely, [the second error] would be to consider concentrationary everything which does not seem acceptable."[90]

With this statement, Ingrand recognized that conditions of incarceration could fail to meet the criteria for "concentrationary" abuses while still demanding condemnation—that circumstances might be neither black nor white, in other words. Unfortunately, she and the other delegates had few conceptual tools at their disposal to interpret shades of gray. For one thing, they were personally unacquainted with any "normal" carceral institutions. Børsum, for one, confessed frankly that she had never been inside a Norwegian penitentiary and possessed no idea of prevailing Western practices vis-à-vis sanitation, food, and medical care.[91] Conceiving of themselves as defenders of political prisoners rather than advocates for inmate rights more broadly, the delegates were also apparently unaware of International Penal and Penitentiary Commission minimum standards for detainee treatment, which had first been "noted" by the League of Nations in 1934 and were under revision at the UN at the moment of the Spain voyage.[92] Without the ability to draw on a language of multiple norms or rights that might be abrogated to different degrees, and without any interest in generating a radical critique of imprisonment as such, the delegation could not escape the either/ or logic of "the concentrationary" (Buchenwald, not Compiègne; Dachau, not Drancy; Mauthausen, not Gurs). And in practice, as Ingrand now realized, this logic dictated offering exoneration to any but the most egregious imaginable offenses against imprisoned subjects.

This was, in the end, the choice that she and her comrades felt compelled to make. Franco's penitentiaries, they agreed, fell short of the "concentrationary" standard. In prose composed by Ingrand and edited by Alers in the autumn of 1952, the group offered a grudging admission (buried midway into their "conclusions") that "in no case were concentrationary conditions of the Hitlerian type [all] brought together" in a single Spanish prison or work colony.[93] They stressed that Franco had operated "true [véritables] concentration camps" in the recent past and might easily do so again. "Without it being necessary to change a single paragraph of the law," Børsum underlined in Dagbladet, such camps "could reemerge at any time in Spain."[94] The Ravensbrück survivor (who found the "atmosphere" in at least one Spanish prison "nearly Nazi") added that if "what we saw cannot, in the end, be called a concentration camp system," it nevertheless possessed some "characteristic traits of a concentration camp system."[95] She and the other delegates recognized that such qualifiers did not alter the verdict, however, and remained frustrated with the binary choice thrust upon them.

Of course, from David Rousset's perspective this either/or determination was an *intended* feature of the discourse of "concentrationary" atrocity, not an unforeseen consequence. By asserting that a chasm, not an ethical gray zone, separated states that maintained concentration camps from those that did not, Rousset was able to sweep past the existence of carceral abuses in the noncommunist world to assert its absolute superiority over the USSR. And this is precisely the use he made of Ingrand's report. "It is a first general observation of our work," he wrote in March 1953, "that the most pernicious tendencies, those most favorable to the appearance of the concentrationary world, are today on the decline in Western Europe." While insisting that he remained a staunch anti-Francoist despite the delegation's verdict ("It is still possible today, thank God, to oppose a regime for other reasons"), Rousset suggested that growing Western engagement with Spain, far from constituting a scandal, was helping Franco's autocracy to evolve: "With difficulty, tortuously, slowly, the pressure of free public opinion is forcing open the hinges" of the country's prison doors. In this vein, he made much of the fact that, in the end, the Spanish government had permitted its internees to bear witness. "Today," he asserted, "the dossier of the West is open." Now "when will we be able to collect the depositions of the men of Kolyma?"[96]

Rousset's anti-Soviet instrumentalization of the delegation's verdict, then, was blatant. But he and other CICRC members were evidently unprepared for just how uncomfortable it would feel to declare Spain free of "concentration camps," given their own earlier antifascist commitments and the undeniable historic ties that existed between Franco and Hitler. Rousset dwelt rather too lingeringly on his "love" for the country, his participation in its Civil War–era struggles, and his "haunting" experience of the recent voyage.[97] As for the delegates, they insisted on "reminding" readers of their report of "the limits of the mission that was entrusted to them." In so doing, they offered a muted but unmistakable criticism of the CICRC's entire project. "Given the very terms of its mission," they wrote in a remarkable passage, "the Commission had to refer to the actual term of comparison that it had available"—that is, to Nazi Germany's concentrationary universe, as the authors remembered it. "These conclusions," they insisted, "therefore only possess their exact significance if this imposed optic is taken into consideration."[98] This oblique comment was intended as an apologia for the verdict. But whether or not the delegates realized it, their words also functioned to suggest more generally that the comparative deployment of memory might constrain, not facilitate, present-oriented processes of intellectual comprehension and ethical judgment. As such, the text constituted the first suggestion by CICRC members that the "imposed optic" of the concentrationary paradigm was anything less than illuminating. It would not be the last.

## Spanish Testaments and Tribulations

The delegates put the finishing touches on their *Livre blanc sur le système pénitentiaire espagnol* (White book on the Spanish penitentiary system) in September 1952. Though it would not be published until the following spring, they began presenting it to select audiences that fall. At 236 pages, the text comprised much more than the delegation's conclusions—also included were a thickly documented introduction outlining the negotiations with Franco's government; a summary of the delegates' methods and journeys (meticulously detailed except for the systematic excision of De Swart); a point-by-point consideration of Spanish law as it pertained to penal matters as well as an analysis of de facto procedures; and a historical account of the Nationalists' use of political detention. The book concluded with a lengthy set of appendices containing juridical codes and statutes, Ingrand's calculations of the past and present size of the interned population, and thirty-seven political prisoners' testimonials.

These final materials were selected exclusively from the survivor-in-exile statements provided by the FEDIP: the delegation prudently declined to publish its interviews with current inmates. Their own report, however, referenced the oral testimony they had collected—stripped of identifying details—and they stressed the convergence between exiled survivors' accounts and the words of those who still languished behind bars. "I believe that [current Spanish prisoners'] living presence is there in our book," proclaimed Rousset, eager to stress his solidarity with them. He also leveraged his on-the-ground contact with prisoners during the voyage into ammunition against his familiar nemesis: "Sartre, with that audacity in irresponsibility which is the dominant trait in his character, once wrote that I had chosen my deportees," he wrote. "Certainly, I was at the prison of Puerto de Santa María . . . while he was congratulating himself in Vienna [at the Soviet-backed 1952 World Peace Conference] with the purveyors of camps and gallows . . . I prefer my choice."[99] Beyond his political aims in flaunting his participation in the inquiry, Rousset did appear genuinely proud of the *Livre blanc* as an act of witness on behalf of Spanish republicans. So, too, did the three delegates. In Alers's words, it "put a beautiful end to a particularly arduous and delicate labor."[100]

Nevertheless, Lise Børsum predicted that, aside from themselves, "no one is going to be happy" with the text's strained conclusions.[101] She was correct. During a closed-door Paris reading of the findings in November, Spanish exiles were bitterly disappointed to learn that Franco's regime had been deemed non-concentrationary. José Maldonado of the Republican Left declared the report "weak." Wilebaldo Solano of the POUM concurred, and remarked that "the weakness of the conclusions could serve Franco."[102] Anarcho-syndicalist Marciano Sigüenza took the floor at a press conference held by Rousset months later to protest that the commission had committed a grievous error: "Spain itself"—not only its prisons—"is a vast concentration camp."[103] Ester and Calmarza were more resigned in their response. As CICRC participants, they understood the commission's restrictive "definition of a concentrationary system."[104] And Ester reflected that, after all, the full text of the *Livre blanc* contained plentiful criticism of Franco. Copies, he told Rousset, should be smuggled into Spain—and especially its penitentiaries—in large quantities, so that antifascists there might take heart, "knowing that the voice of former concentration camp inmates does not cease to ring out in their favor."[105] But his earlier hopes that the inquiry would equate Franco's regime with Nazi Germany were dashed.

If Spanish republican exiles were dissatisfied with the commission's work, Francoist administrators were apoplectic over it. The primary trigger for their ire was not the *Livre blanc* but Ingrand's October 17, 1952, testimony before the United Nations and International Labor Organization's Ad Hoc Committee on

Forced Labor. Her presentation was an exceptional event, and its occurrence demands some explanation before considering the Spanish response. The Ad Hoc Committee had come into being in March 1951, following years of American pressure. Crafted in the context of strong anxieties among European imperial powers over potential attacks on colonial labor practices ("we are against immolating the Colonies for the sake of a very doubtful advantage in the cold war," one British official wrote), the committee was originally outfitted with the narrow, obviously anti-Soviet mandate of studying forced labor schemes "employed as a means of political coercion or punishment for holding or expressing political views, and which are on such a scale as to constitute an important element in the economy of a given country."[106] Chaired by Sir Ramaswami Mudaliar, it solicited documentation from member nations and also welcomed testimony from nongovernmental specialists. Rousset was desperate to be included in this latter group. "It is absolutely indispensable," he wrote to Reumont, "that our International Commission be recognized by the UN's Commission and be able . . . to participate in its work." The issue was of "primordial importance" for the reputation of the CICRC.[107]

Rousset need not have worried. Upon the Ad Hoc Committee's formation, the US government set in motion efforts to ensure that it receive damning information on Soviet practices from "independent" NGOs. In a November 1951 meeting with David Dallin, Bertram Wolfe, Toni Sender, and other American anticommunists, Walter Kotschnig of the State Department underlined the particular importance of "utiliz[ing] . . . non-Americans such as David Rousset" for this purpose, "to avoid the impression that the forced labor item was 'set up' by the US."[108] His machinations likely helped ensure that the CICRC received an invitation to address the Ad Hoc Committee at its autumn 1952 session. In the meantime, Kotschnig also supported the Nazi camp survivors' group in its bid for B-level consultative status with the UN's Economic and Social Council (ECOSOC), the highest possible categorization for a single-issue NGO.[109] The CICRC at last gained this designation at the June 1952 ECOSOC session (the Soviets voted against; Uruguay abstained), thereby acquiring the right to address that body orally and through circulated written statements.

B-level status was not required to testify before the Ad Hoc Committee, but it certainly elevated the CICRC's standing ahead of the October audience. The group's leaders were jubilant: "The Commission will no longer be confused with a more or less well-organized propaganda organization, for it has shown itself to be an assembly of true experts," rejoiced Reumont, who promptly ordered stationery vaunting the new label.[110] Meanwhile Théo Bernard reminded members that the recognition implied arduous duties.[111] He and Rousset accordingly began to prepare for the upcoming hearing by assembling a massive file of English-language documentation on Soviet forced labor. In a flurry of late-September correspondence, the two men organized thousands of pages of evidence, largely out of materials provided to them by the Americans and the British. These included legislation, maps, administrative charts, victim statements, and a "bibliographic essay" of published works treating the subject.[112]

While preoccupied with their upcoming anti-Soviet testimony, Rousset and Bernard nevertheless operated with a longer-term ambition in mind: to pursue a "politics of presence" at the UN.[113] Strategically, they believed, cultivating the International Commission's image as a fair-minded contributor to the workings of the global institution was more important than scoring quick Cold War points. It was for this reason, at least in part, that Rousset insisted that members address the Ad Hoc Committee regarding the CICRC's recent investigations in Spain and Greece: "I believe it is of extreme importance that we give depositions on these two countries," he wrote to Bernard. "I am convinced that we will be the only ones to do so among [the NGOs] that are going to be heard in October"— a fact "of great interest."[114] Bernard agreed—and recognized the greater symbolic significance of the Iberian case. "It is indispensable that we appear entirely impartial on the political plane," he responded. "Whence the importance, first of all, of the Spanish dossier."[115]

Elisabeth Ingrand therefore readied herself to address the committee. On October 17, she, Rousset, André, and Bernard appeared in Geneva before Mudaliar, Paul Berg (Norway), and Enrique García Sayán (Peru), claiming to "morally and organizationally represent a hundred thousand former political prisoners of Western Europe."[116] Unaware that the Ad Hoc Committee was already familiar with the CICRC's work—it had actively modeled its own "quasi-judicial" procedures on the Brussels "crimes against humanity" trial—the members prefaced their testimony with an introduction of their organization.[117] The International Commission was "unbiased and humanitarian," André declared, was possessed of singular expertise, and was interested in abolishing forced labor regimes wherever they existed—that is, in the East or West.[118] His own statement on the Greek case was brief, however, and the majority of the CICRC's five-hour hearing was taken up by Rousset and Bernard's presentation on the Soviet gulag. It was only in the final half hour that Ingrand gave her conclusions regarding Spain's use of political prisoners' labor. From 1938 or 1939 until 1945 or 1946, she charged, "the state of affairs . . . could be compared with either the description that we have heard of the USSR this morning or, within limits, with what we knew in the German regime."[119] Now matters had improved, she continued, but serious concerns about prisoners' rights remained. "Work was not systematically exacted," a summary of her report reads, "but where exacted it was hard as prisoners were used mainly for such projects for which free labour was not forthcoming. . . .

Conditions varied from 'normal' for a penal settlement in a poor country to 'miserable.'"[120]

Because the Ad Hoc Committee was not charged with determining if states were "concentrationary" but only with discovering whether they employed unfree labor, such observations—delivered with Ingrand's practiced confidence, a raft of documentary evidence, and a lawyerly command of the Spanish penal code—did not resonate with Mudaliar and his colleagues as exculpatory. In fact, committee members were manifestly troubled, as Rousset noted with pride in reviewing the day's hearing.[121] He applauded the "very substantial interest" that Ingrand's report elicited, informing CICRC members that "our recognition as a nongovernmental organization . . . has been confirmed in its importance" and that "this will have very positive consequences for our future work."[122]

Rousset was unconcerned that Ingrand's criticism of Spain would blunt charges against the USSR or embarrass the capitalist bloc, and these apprehensions did not plague the CICRC's allies, either. The Americans and British had greater worries on another score: the Ad Hoc Committee's unexpected recent decision to abandon its narrow mandate and, as Sandrine Kott writes, "to take into account varieties of forced labor resulting from ethnic, social, and economic relations unfavorable to workers," not just from political repression.[123] US intelligence was, accordingly, more concerned about how the committee would treat convict labor in America than about any criticism it might level at Franco. The British, meanwhile, were preoccupied with fears that negative findings on Portuguese Angola could be used "as a stick to beat all 'Imperialistic' powers."[124] Forced labor in Angola was not "defensible," the Colonial Office admitted (noting past efforts "unobtrusively to get the Portuguese to pull their socks up"), but Britain could not afford to break the "general 'Colonial Front'": "a scandal about one Colonial Power has the effect of besmirching all the others."[125] Thus British officials devoted flurries of correspondence to the Ad Hoc Committee testimony of Charles W. W. Greenidge, president of the London-based Anti-Slavery Society, who spoke on October 16, 1952, about Portuguese crimes, and little to that of Rousset, Bernard, André, and Ingrand the following day. Indeed, it seems Ingrand's testimony was barely noticed by either London or Washington.

But Madrid was paying attention—and was far from pleased. The Spanish government, informed of the CICRC's conclusions earlier that month, belatedly recognized that the decision to cooperate with the commission had been a grievous error. Encouraged to hope for a *gran triunfo de opinión* by allies abroad, Spanish officials had awaited a brief, positive statement confirming the absence of "concentration camps" in their country.[126] Instead they found themselves confronted with a long, painfully critical report that not only attacked many current Spanish practices but also provided shocking historical statistics. The findings were "erroneous, false, and badly intentioned," raged Manuel María de Barandica y Uhagón, a lawyer in the Ministry of Foreign Affairs. It did Spain no good to be declared non-concentrationary if the verdict was accompanied by so many reproaches and qualifiers. Barandica was particularly vexed against Ingrand: "The insincerity and wicked intention of that lady is evident."[127] But how to explain her perfidy when she had been perfectly amenable during her passage through the country? Enlightenment soon appeared from an unlikely source: Jean de Swart, "friend of Spain."[128]

De Swart paid a visit to Franco's embassy in The Hague on February 1, 1953, and made a series of fabricated declarations that, the gratified Spanish ambassador remarked, "shed a great deal of light on this matter." Now expelled from the CICRC and embittered against Rousset, De Swart claimed, first, that the delegation's Iberian voyage had been a "pleasure trip, during which the idea was to splurge on the high allowances paid by the Commission." He, De Swart, had battled valiantly to hold down costs but had been defeated in this endeavor by the spendthrift women, who sought to exploit the "elevated outlays" on offer from the group's secret bankrollers: the Masonic order. According to De Swart, freemasonry's anticlerical, cosmopolitan principles had "undermined" the commission, which had originally been a noble anticommunist initiative. The Protestant members of the delegation (Børsum, Rousset, and Ingrand) were all Masons, he asserted, and had sought during their time in Spain to make contact with their hidden brethren "on the basis of signals provided by Paris." Their determination to slander Spain's penitentiary system arose from their blind determination to "follow instructions from the Lodges." Thus, De Swart explained, because of his own efforts to dictate "an objective and favorable report" in line with "reality," he had been summarily expelled from the group.[129]

Spanish officials, noting with emphasis that De Swart was "*Catholic* by religion," willingly consumed this fantastical narrative.[130] As the object of a personal obsession on Franco's part, Freemasonry had been ferociously persecuted during the Civil War and outlawed in Spain since 1940. De Swart's charge that Rousset, Ingrand, and Børsum had been acting in its name perfectly accounted for their "bad faith," Barandica and other ministry bureaucrats believed.[131] They understood, however, that accusations of this sort would not discredit the CICRC's conclusions in the eyes of UN actors; ultimately more useful, therefore, was the simple fact of De Swart's dismissal from the CICRC. Thus on February 17, 1953, Foreign Minister Alberto Martín Artajo issued a formal protest to the Ad Hoc Committee, pointing out that Ingrand's testimony had omitted mention of the fourth participant in her delegation. This absence, he charged, had an obvious explanation: De Swart's admiration for Spain's model penitentiaries was "completely at variance" with the negative findings that his "sectarian and biased" fellow investigators had been determined to advance.[132]

Martín proceeded to dispute the commission's UN testimony on several more specific points. Spain did not maintain a *"régime d'exception,"* he asserted, and "no category of delinquents has ever been the object of arbitrary treatment." The handful of prisoners still serving sentences related to Civil War–era offenses had been tried for "the most execrable infamies, crimes, rapes and pillages, which revolt all honorable men equally." Current detainees, he continued, numbered only 23,461, not 30,000, and included fewer than 4,000 "politicals." (Tellingly, Martín was mum about the CICRC's far more damaging estimate of the prisoner population circa 1940, complaining only that it had not "tak[en] into account the fact that emergency measures were required to restore order in the country.")[133] As for the delegates' criticism of detainees' living conditions, he demanded to know what they had expected: "luxury hotels"? Still more fundamentally, he complained that "the comparison made with concentration camp regimes which may have existed in other countries is considered offensive and unfounded."[134] Though the CICRC might have ruled that Spain did not maintain a Nazi-style concentrationary system, the very airing of the question was an outrage.

When the Ad Hoc Committee's findings were finally published in a June 1953 *Report*, Martín's letter placed Rousset and his followers in an awkward position. On the basis of the CICRC's testimony, the *Report* concluded that Spanish legal codes made possible "a system of forced labor imposed in the name of political coercion" and offered additional censure of Franco's criminalization of dissent.[135] But the committee also chose to include, as potentially exculpatory evidence, the full text of the Spanish rebuttal. Faced with this publicly humiliating questioning of their motives and competence, CICRC members felt compelled to respond. The result was a lengthy missive to the Spanish foreign minister signed by Ingrand, Alers, and Børsum late that year. The bulk of their letter constituted a systematic defense of their conclusions, buttressed with damaging details omitted from the original report. But the text also, belatedly, attempted a forthright treatment of the De Swart affair. The Dutchman's name was missing from their testimony, the three remaining delegates wrote, for a reason "absolutely lacking in any connection to the Spanish inquiry": his confession that he was "statutorily incapable of being a part of the CICRC." They expanded on this contention by way of responding to Martín's complaint about their comparative historical orientation. Judgment of present detention facilities against past ones, wrote Alers, Ingrand, and Børsum, was the very point of their organization: "The aim of the CICRC, uniquely composed of former *concentrationnaires* of the Nazi camps . . . is, indeed, to research . . . systems analogous to that which its members suffered" and which they were now "more competent than any other person" to recognize.

"It is, by the way, because he did not have the experience of this Nazi concentrationary regime that M. de Swart declared himself unqualified to be a part of the CICRC," they wrote.[136]

For obvious reasons, any ambivalence that had haunted the Spanish *Livre blanc* about the limitations of the CICRC's framework was purged from this response. In fact the letter celebrated survivors' special capabilities in unproblematized terms—pointing out, for example, that the "mental operation" of holding prisons to the standard of "luxury hotels" was "improbable indeed for former *concentrationnaires* investigating as such."[137] But did not the fact that, until his unmasking, De Swart had easily passed among them as a fellow survivor undermine the delegates' claims to expertise conferred by experience? And did not the omission of his name from their report amount to an act of false witness on the part of a group putatively committed to testimony above all else? These questions were not entertained by Ingrand, Alers, and Børsum, who instead insisted flatly on their own "good faith," "strict objectivity," and personal "honor" in contrast to De Swart's treachery.[138] Though it worried Bernard for reasons of precedent ("Should we get into the habit of responding [to national governments] on issues of substance? I believe not"), the delegation's militant defense of its work delighted most CICRC members. Submission of the statement to the UN permitted them to feel they had issued the final, triumphant word in the dispute.[139]

In truth, the CICRC's self-declared victory over Martín's charges owed less to its combative response than to a Spanish decision that further squabbling would be "counterproductive," given that the issue had "ceased to interest public opinion."[140] The wisdom of this strategy was confirmed by the tepid reception ultimately given to the Ad Hoc Committee's work despite the best efforts of the US and its friends, including the CICRC. Whatever its gestures toward evenhandedness, the *Report* was unequivocally harshest regarding the Soviet gulag; hence the CIA registered plans to "insure [its] maximum exploitation" as Cold War "ammunition," and Tom Braden, chief of the International Organizations Division in the agency, assured Director Allen Dulles that Rousset's organization "has been alerted and will begin a well-publicized campaign to the effect that the UN findings are formal substantiation of the charges [against the USSR] that it has long been endeavoring to call to the attention of world opinion."[141] But this campaign could find no receptive audience: as Théo Bernard noted bitterly in *Preuves*, the Ad Hoc Committee's *Report*, with its disapproving treatment of colonial work-brigade conscription, had "embarrassed or disturbed a great number of governments, not all in the camp of totalitarian states."[142] Imperial powers' displeasure, along with a reluctance to antagonize the USSR in the delicate moment following Stalin's death, inhibited the willingness of ECOSOC members even to discuss the *Report*, and momentum around the issue at the UN evaporated.[143] CICRC participants were deeply disappointed. In November 1953 they privately vowed not to allow the Ad Hoc Committee's torch to go cold. Their own organization, they declared, was ready and willing to launch a broader campaign of on-site investigations "in its place."[144] The work of eyewitnessing that members had begun in Spain could—and would—serve as the starting point for a universal mission.

As they turned their attention elsewhere in the coming years, CICRC members' engagement with Franco's prisons did not end. Though their collective fervor on the issue was diminished by Elisabeth Ingrand's 1954 departure from the commission (occasioned by her husband's appointment as ambassador to Colombia), her friend Germaine Tillion took over sending care packages of cigarettes, Nescafé, vitamins, Gruyère, and so on to the handful of French nationals ("your *protégés*") who still languished in Spanish penitentiaries.[145] More publicly, the group put out regular grim updates from the FEDIP on Franco's ongoing abuses: "No attenuation of the arbitrary [arrest and detention regime] denounced by the International Commission following its on-site inquiry three years ago has taken place," Calmarza announced in a late 1954 article, for example.[146] In the 1960s, after the commission's collapse, former members including Tillion, Roure, and Arrighi joined erstwhile foes such as Sartre and Joë Nordmann in the Western European Conference for Amnesty for Spanish Political Prisoners and Exiles. Rousset, meanwhile, maintained his opposition to Franco beyond the dictator's death by supporting the International Tribunal against the Crimes of Francoism in 1984.

The Nazi camp survivors' real contribution to exposing the Spanish general's crimes, however, was made three decades earlier. Børsum had been correct that the *Livre blanc* would please no one, but historians have been kinder than the exiled Loyalists of the 1950s, recognizing that the investigation constituted a milestone despite its ambivalent conclusion. As Javier Rodrigo puts it, "For the first time on the part of an organization with an international character, the CICRC was able to denounce how Francoism was politically and socially constructed on top of a cellar full of reprisal victims, internees, executed people, and the excluded."[147] The thirty-seven prisoner testimonials that the group published, writes Vinyes, constituted "the first 'historical verbalization' of the *franquista* repression." First-person accounts of Franco's prisons had been aired previously (most famously Arthur Koestler's *Spanish Testament*), but the CICRC, aided by the FEDIP, did something different. It laid on offer a critical mass of victim-witness voices—male and female; young and old; elite and humble; *anterior* and *posterior*; anarchist, socialist, Trotskyist, and liberal. Scholars also still

cite the longitudinal data that Ingrand unearthed on the Spanish prisoner population, celebrating her "notable empirical vocation."[148]

This is not to suggest that historians of Spain have been inattentive to the
shortcomings of the 1952 investigation. Vinyes offers an especially eloquent critique, commenting that the CICRC's adoption of the Nazi case as an absolute
"paradigm" did not only present the "double risk" that the delegation recognized. It also threatened "to block comprehension of punitive systems within
the societies that created them," in all their internal historical complexity.[149] To
the examples he himself adduces in support of this point, we might add another:
Lise Børsum's description in *Dagbladet* of the "familial well-being" that characterized a women's prison (the only one the delegation visited) where she saw a
four-year-old sleeping peacefully beside his mother. It is profoundly understandable that a woman torn away from her own daughter in 1943 and transported
to Ravensbrück, where newborns were generally murdered, concluded that there
reigned in this penitentiary, in contrast, "an atmosphere of pure humanity."[150]
But Børsum's article failed to confront the fact of a four-year-old living out his
days in prison on its own terms, or to grapple with the implications of this tiny
prisoner for a global analysis of the Spanish repressive apparatus.

As we have seen, a vague consciousness that holding up the Francoist prisons
of the 1950s against the Nazi concentration camps of the 1940s was an inadequate way to make sense of them haunted the Spanish delegates' conclusions.
However, it did not yet lead them to rebel against their "imposed optic." To
compare Franco's repressive regime with that of Hitler, however much it limited
the possibilities for internal analysis of the Spanish system, nevertheless made
some historical sense—and certainly dovetailed with the commission's own
understanding of Francoist Spain as a remnant of Europe's ill-fated midcentury
experiments. Configuring Spain as a recognizable kind of "totalitarian" autocracy similar not only to Nazi Germany but also to the USSR permitted CICRC
members to make sense of the abuses they registered there without internal crisis.
This framework—which would cease to be available to the organization later in
the decade when it was confronted with abusive detention practices in French
Algeria—left Rousset and his followers convinced that they had borne faithful
witness on behalf of Franco's prisoners even as they absolved Spain of operating
a full-blown "concentrationary regime."

Moreover, aided by the FEDIP's input and by their own political educations
in the 1930s, the CICRC investigators possessed a modicum of *knowledge* about
Spain—its political system, its social organization, its culture—at the outset. This
provided them with some ability to situate the country's prisons, as they stood in
1952, within various synchronic and diachronic contexts, and to confront these

facilities as one element in a larger history of violence. It also permitted them to exercise well-informed skepticism regarding Spanish authorities' claims—for example, that inhumane conditions were temporary aberrations or that political prisoners were "terrorists" who deserved their fate. Such skepticism was deepened by sentiments of long-term political solidarity with Spanish republicans and enhanced still further in Ingrand's case by the empathy-inducing presence of young, idealistic *French* resisters within Franco's prisoner population. Thus, though the CICRC may have proudly attributed its ability to see through official Spanish lies to its own members' status as concentration camp survivors, other forms of understanding and affective identification were at least as important. For all its strangeness, Spain in 1952 remained a land populated by recognizable ghosts of the very recent continental past—and for this reason, as 1953 began, the CICRC's mystique of expertise derived from experience still awaited its real test.

# TRIUMPHS AND TENSIONS ON THE GLOBAL STAGE

By the time the dust settled on the CICRC's Spain investigation, almost four years had passed since David Rousset's "Appeal" galvanized survivors of the Nazi camps into action against the ongoing existence of the "concentrationary universe." Their organization was now in its institutional heyday. Between 1953 and 1956, CICRC representatives became a constant presence at the UN and the ILO, forged a partnership with the International Confederation of Free Trade Unions, and collaborated on an ad hoc basis with nongovernmental groups ranging from the Red Cross to the newly founded International Commission of Jurists. Members also developed warm relationships with Western governments: the Danish Parliament ceremonially hosted the opening session of their twentieth plenary conference in June 1954, Queen Elisabeth of Belgium received them in December that year, and they were feted at the Élysée Palace by French president René Coty in May 1955. Flush with funding from the mysterious Mr. O'Shea, the commission not only continued carrying out investigations but also publicized its findings extensively, founding its own International Center for Edition and Documentation and publishing a handsome *Bulletin*, later transformed into a quarterly journal titled *Saturne* with editions in French, English, and (briefly) Japanese.

Despite the hustle and bustle, however, the CICRC stood at a crossroads in the mid-1950s, faced with difficult questions concerning the ongoing relevance of its mission and the universality of its ethical framework. By the time of Joseph Stalin's death in 1953—and even more dramatically as the decade progressed—the survivors' movement found itself confronting a global landscape of political repression, imprisonment, and forced labor whose shifting contours undermined its foundational logic. State violence was by no means on the decline in the mid-1950s, a period marked by bloody wars of decolonization in Africa and Asia and waves of political repression in Eastern Europe. But the forms that such violence took in these years, which were also marked by massive contraction in the Soviet camp system, tended to defy easy comparison with Hitler's "*crime majeur*" as the CICRC understood it. Moreover, as time passed, the "emotional resonance" of wartime political deportation and incarceration faded for Western European publics—and new ways of conceptualizing Nazi atrocity, more focused on racial persecution, began to compete with the commission's model.[1] David Rousset's original "Appeal" had been cast as an equation between the emblematic past suffering of resisters sent to German camps and the present suffering of distant victims; now the equation was destabilized, and with it the "expert" status of the men and women who had responded to his call. Thus, just at its point of greatest activity, the commission began to splinter from within.

The cracks were most visible in the CICRC's confrontation with three different problems in the mid-1950s, each of which challenged members' assertion that their past experience retained fixed meaning. The first involved the commission's cultural competence to investigate beyond Europe. Rousset championed the desirability of inquiries targeting North African and Asian locales, insisting that "the experience of the Nazi camps is not, alas! unique to the West and is not limited to those with white skins. It is, on the contrary, an experience with universal value and which permits us to gauge internment conditions very accurately, wherever they exist."[2] But other members of the commission were less confident, voicing new doubts about whether their own ordeal granted them any particular competence to evaluate unfamiliar regions of the world. For now, Rousset managed to prevail over his colleagues; hence the CICRC investigated on-site in French Tunisia in 1953 and put the People's Republic of China "on trial" in 1956. But the concessions that he made along the way, both to allow the inquiries to proceed and (in the Chinese case) to avoid the appearance of Western finger-wagging, weakened his position and threw into doubt the relevance of "concentrationary" experience to new global problems.

Meanwhile, persistent tensions over how to remember Jewish suffering in World War II also troubled the commission, disrupting both its claims to universal moral jurisdiction and its strategic efforts to condemn Soviet terror. In the final months of Stalin's life, for instance, while scores of observers in the West rushed to depict rising antisemitic persecutions in the Eastern bloc as an echo of Hitler's projects, CICRC members stubbornly refused to draw the parallel: their idiosyncratic conceptualization of the similarity between the Nazi and Soviet camp systems still depended on an elision of racially or religiously motivated violence. By 1954, Rousset tardily and tentatively reconsidered, working with Bernard and Poliakov to refashion the Jewish Holocaust as a usable past for the commission. But his efforts could only go so far while the organization's membership policies remained tethered to a Resistance-centric schema of deportation memory. Thus as the CICRC was confronted anew in the post-Stalin years with the task of squaring its vision of the past with its agenda for the present, it was brought up short once again by the uncomfortable question of whether witness status could be afforded to Nazi Germany's "racial" victims.

While members were wrestling with such difficulties, the Soviet repression of the Hungarian Revolution in the autumn of 1956—a campaign that shocked the world but could only be described as *concentrationnaire* by stretching language to its breaking point—abruptly posed a third challenge for them. The CICRC responded to the crisis in Hungary with a barrage of high-profile actions, gaining momentum as former critics were compelled to concede that Soviet communism should indeed be rejected on the basis of moral outrage at its treatment of political dissidents. At the same time, however, Budapest's flames illuminated major inherent weaknesses in the commission's model: the rigidity of its backward-glancing comparative framework and the passivity of its praxis of witnessing. In a context of widespread Western revulsion with Soviet repressive methods, invocations of "the concentrationary universe" were no longer necessary as a clever mode of attack on the USSR; in fact, attempts to defend strained parallels to Nazi practices proved superfluous to the general outcry against Soviet aggression. Moreover, the CICRC failed to influence the unfolding of the crisis—and, for an anguished David Rousset, this fact threw into question the entire notion that "bearing witness" constituted a meaningful response to state violence. By late 1956, it was less clear than ever how participants could continue to link their own past experience to a coherent vision for a troubled, changing world.

## Survivor Expertise and Suffering beyond Europe

Following the completion of its Spanish and Greek investigations in mid-1952, the CICRC found itself at loose ends. The group maintained open dossiers on several cases, including Tito's Yugoslavia, an object of ferocious attack from Western communists thanks to its leader's "deviation" from the Stalinist model. But in November Rousset reported that his negotiations with the Yugoslav government had reached an "impasse" since "Belgrade absolutely refuses to admit an on-site inquiry." In front of the assembled international membership, he backed Théo Bernard's intransigent position regarding the next step: "The Yugoslavs must know that, if necessary, we will not shy away from a public trial like that of the

USSR."[3] In a letter to his British contact Corley-Smith about this "delicate" matter, however, Rousset admitted he had no intention of staging such a hearing: the undertaking would be "very inopportune" since "we would risk, despite all our efforts, seeing ourselves actually be used by the Cominformists, directly or indirectly." Rousset insisted that he still hoped to hold the Yugoslavs accountable for their detention regime, thereby serving "the interest of truth."[4] But his statement about the Cominform—especially when viewed in light of the fact that the CICRC never proceeded with the inquiry—demonstrated the pragmatic limits of his ethical universalism.

In the same moment, however, Rousset staked out a position as a militant defender of "universalism" understood in a different sense, one that aided rather than undermined his political agenda. This brand of universalism was founded upon the self-consciously antiracist notion that non-European bodies deserved protection from "concentrationary" suffering as well. Beginning in 1952, Rousset undertook a personal crusade to expand the CICRC's geographic purview. Multiple factors motivated him: his belief that "concentration camps" constituted a unified global phenomenon; his support for colonial independence movements; his belief that anticommunists would lose the cultural Cold War if they did not condemn Western imperial violence; and finally his growing conviction that China posed an even greater threat on the world stage than the USSR. On the basis of such considerations, the CICRC's founder began to reorient the group toward Africa and Asia as its momentum slowed in Eastern Europe. The first concrete result was an on-site CICRC investigation in the French protectorate of Tunisia in early 1953.

The impetus for the Tunisian endeavor came via a 1952 petition from Mahmoud Messadi, assistant secretary-general of the Union Générale Tunisienne du Travail (UGTT), concerning mass arrests, "concentration camps," assassinations, and other French abuses targeting nationalist activists in the troubled territory.[5] The UGTT was closely tied to Tunisia's major anticolonialist party, the Néo-Destour. It was also a categorically noncommunist body that had recently joined Irving Brown's ICFTU, and Rousset, who possessed prewar ties to North African labor, was sympathetic to its cause.[6] He responded warmly to Messadi, and in March 1952, at his urging, CICRC members agreed to consider the possibility of an on-site inquiry in Tunisia.[7]

Rousset began at this point to build behind-the-scenes governmental support for the proposed mission. But it was Damien Reumont, as CICRC secretary, who was charged with formally managing the affair. The Belgian priest, not sharing Rousset's anticolonialist orientation, proved a hostile interlocutor for UGTT members, whom he suspected of instrumentalizing the CICRC "for political ends."[8] Meanwhile, the communiqués he sent to France's Tunisian resident-general Jean de Hauteclocque struck an extravagantly respectful tone. In regard to Hauteclocque's dismissal of the UGTT's charges as "entirely tendentious," for example, Reumont signaled his agreement: "This information does nothing but confirm the opinion that I already had of events occurring in the Residence; however, I needed these official details to support my opinion, and to allow me to answer accusations bandied about or accepted by a press that is biased or insufficiently informed."[9] When Hauteclocque assured him in October 1952 that most prisoners had been released in the wake of "very liberal reforms," Reumont was congratulatory: "I need not tell you, Excellence, that we have always been convinced that the measures taken when serious troubles were erupting in Tunisia were dictated by the desire to reestablish order, to separate the rebels, and that they would only be maintained as long as necessary. . . . This, I believe, ought to mark the end of our intervention."[10]

After Reumont reported on these developments at the CICRC's November meeting, members appeared ready to "close the file" on Tunisia.[11] UGTT secretary-general Farhat Hached, however, forced it back open with an indignant letter charging that Reumont had been "seduced" by Hauteclocque. Tunisian "concentration camps," he insisted, were "overflowing with trade unionists and patriots."[12] At this point, although the evidence is unclear, it seems likely that Rousset personally intervened to insist an investigation was necessary.

This necessity became still more urgent in his eyes when, days later, the UGTT's secretary-general was assassinated by a colonialist terrorist group (probably supported by French intelligence services). Hached had recently been seated on the ICFTU's executive board; as Anthony Carew writes, his death gave that organization its "first martyr."[13] Brown and his colleagues protested to the French government, the UN, and the ILO, aiming to broadcast noncommunist leftist solidarity with the Tunisian independence struggle and thereby prevent an "ungodly alliance" linking Arab nationalism with Stalinism.[14] Rousset, who condemned Hached's murder as "the most scandalous political crime of our times," shared this goal.[15] Drawing on well-connected contacts in the community of *anciens déportés*, he managed to secure an interview with France's President Vincent Auriol, to whom he argued that a demonstration of the government's willingness to countenance an impartial inquiry would help calm the roiling waters of Tunisian society. Auriol, according to Rousset, admired the commission and vowed "to facilitate our efforts as much as possible." Thanks to his help, Hauteclocque was compelled by Robert Schuman's foreign ministry to welcome a CICRC delegation in January 1953.[16]

Rousset was aware of Reumont's reluctance regarding Tunisia, and in the days ahead of the mission he attempted to convince him of the prestige that would accrue to their organization through being entrusted with such a sensitive task. Auriol wanted to eliminate abuses in Tunisia, he wrote to Reumont, even if Hauteclocque did not; "the French climate" was "a far cry from the climate of the French authorities in Tunis."[17] Reumont was appropriately impressed, and came around to championing the inquiry as "an important business"—though now he began to fret that his obsequious early correspondence with Hauteclocque and rebukes to the UGTT might be included if the CICRC were to issue a Tunisian *Livre blanc*. The former missionary hastened to explain himself to Rousset: "In truth, I admit to you that I was very cautious in this affair, fearing first of all its politicization, fearing next that the members sent to Tunisia for an inquiry would judge the situation *in abstracto* and not take account of the whole ambiance—the traditions, the customs, the reactions of these populations. I lived through all that in the Indies."[18] Of course, the CICRC had been founded on precisely the notion that detention regimes anywhere in the world *could* be judged in the abstract, thanks to the universal standard of "concentrationary" evil. Here, instead, Reumont appeared to suggest not only that political expediency mattered when judging the internment practices of imperial powers but also that such judgments might be shaped by consideration of the lower living standards and strange "customs" of colonized peoples. "Abstract" observations were inappropriate in colonial settings, his words implied, since norms defining appropriate treatment of prisoners were different there.

Rousset rejected such logic wholesale but held his tongue (and later forgot, or pretended to forget, that Reumont ever espoused a position he found so distasteful).[19] The on-site investigation proceeded. CICRC president Georges André, his fellow Belgian Maurice Bruyninckx, and Benjamin Stomps of the Netherlands, accompanied by Rousset and Bernard, arrived in Tunis on January 17, 1953, and remained for ten days. They toured the Tatahouine military internment camp, then home to 131 detainees; a number of recently emptied camps (Remada, Bordj le Boeuf, Mareth, Ben Gardane, and Zarour); a civilian-run triage center; a remote village where five UGTT leaders had been forced to reside; two civilian-run prisons; and—after some tense wrangling over access—the Tunis military prison. Inmate interviews (primarily with detainees suggested to the CICRC by the UGTT) revealed harrowing stories of abusive arrest practices, insufficient food and medicine, and undignified lodging conditions, particularly at Bordj le Boeuf. Above all the men protested their basic situation: they were penned up behind barbed wire, like common criminals, for their political beliefs. Future UN General Assembly president Mongi Slim noted, for example, that he had been imprisoned in Tatahouine for seeking authorization to hold a Néo-Destour convention. At Bardo prison, the delegation departed to prisoners' choral chant of "*Régime politique, régime politique*" and nationalist songs.[20] Despite their grievances, however, detainees confirmed the observation of the

American consul general in Tunis: anxiety over the CICRC's impending visit had produced "sudden and drastic improvements in living conditions at the camps" and had forced the closure of Bordj le Boeuf, the installation most susceptible to the epithet "concentration camp."[21]

Noting these positive developments, and taking account of both the small overall number of detainees and the absence of systematized forced labor, the commission's members determined that "the regime of political detention in Tunisia is not a concentrationary regime."[22] In truth, given the CICRC's criteria, no other conclusion to the investigation was possible. While the delegation carefully avoided Reumont's frank cultural relativism, its maximalist definition of the *univers concentrationnaire* accomplished the same end. Certainly, members criticized French practices in Tunisia: "arrests under illegal conditions" and "*véritables tortures*" were taking place in the protectorate, they asserted, offering copious documentary evidence alongside moving documents of victim testimony—including one detainee's artistic rendering of his own torture.[23] A scathing legal brief by Bernard even warned that though Tunisia was not "a concentrationary regime in the sense that former Buchenwald deportees mean it," the protectorate did show the "beginning signs" of transformation in such a direction, "and this is already too much."[24] But Bernard's stern commentary was overshadowed in subsequent press coverage by the "not guilty" verdict. "No Concentrationary Universe in Tunisia, Declares David Rousset," *Combat*'s headline declared. *L'Aurore* underlined that Rousset's organization had once again established Western superiority: "Only the USSR Still Knows the System of Forced Labor."[25] As Slim wrote to Rousset in March 1953 in a bitter, insightful letter on behalf of his fellow Tatahouine internees, "Everything is relative!"[26]

It would have been clear to any reader of the *Livre blanc* that the commission was never likely to condemn a Western colonial regime as *concentrationnaire*. Nevertheless, the Tunisian inquiry did set a precedent for CICRC investigation of such territories. It also served formal notice of Rousset's new insistence that his organization consider the plight of victims without "white skins"—and his conviction that members' status as Nazi camp survivors provided them with sufficient expertise to do so. Despite Reumont's early foot-dragging, the Tunisian inquiry was shepherded along by Rousset so autocratically that no real opportunity arose for other CICRC members to weigh in on this latter issue. In short order, however, it became clear that they did not unanimously back his position. The circumstance that pushed the disagreement into the open was Rousset's growing interest in conducting an inquiry targeting the People's Republic of China.

Rousset had never visited China, had no training in its history or culture, and spoke no Asian languages. Yet beginning in 1952, he became obsessively preoccupied with Mao Zedong's use of camps as sites of forced labor and pun-ishment.[27] Far-off China's ability to serve as a "projection screen" for postwar French intellectuals, who saw in it whatever they wished, may partly explain his fascination.[28] Moreover, Rousset was highly attuned to "China's prestige for underdeveloped countries," which he assessed as "much greater" than that of the USSR.[29] But above all it is evident that he came to believe—and believe quite fervently—that the People's Republic was a "concentrationary" state with a vast political prison camp system parallel to that of Nazi Germany.[30] To address the Chinese *laogai* (labor camps), he lectured CICRC members in late 1952, would be "to assume, in the most rigorous sense, the tasks that we have posed for our-selves since the beginning: that is to say, alerting the opinion of the world to the situation produced for mankind by the existence of a concentrationary regime. We have largely assumed these tasks in the domain that is most directly our own, that is to say our Western world; we have a duty of assuming them on the human scale, which is the scale of international opinion."[31] Only by turning toward Asia, he asserted, would the International Commission fulfill that duty and live up to its name.

Rousset, then, fixed his sights on Mao quite early. But his resolve to put the People's Republic "on trial" increased as the decade progressed. The Chinese case, he discovered, possessed the power to spark fresh intellectual polemics about communism, now harder and harder to come by. In the 1950s, even before the Budapest repression provoked a wave of disillusionment with the USSR, the mood of the French intellectual scene began shifting away from revolutionary idealism. Maurice Merleau-Ponty's "*prise de conscience*" about Stalinist crimes, resulting in his gradual abandonment of Marxism, quietly began in 1950; the "new liberalism" he eventually espoused echoed the CICRC in its focus on indi-vidual political liberties, whose defense Merleau-Ponty now insisted was "not only and not necessarily a defense of capitalism."[32] Robert Antelme, meanwhile, was expelled from the PCF not long after the "Appeal" and withdrew from pub-lic controversy over communism. And Pierre Naville reached out to Rousset, his former Trotskyist comrade, in 1953. "When will we see each other again—I mean, in order to understand one another?" he asked. "You know that I wish for this."[33] As for Claude Bourdet, he made peace with Rousset the following year in a gesture of approval for CICRC statements censuring French police violence in Morocco.[34]

Jean-Paul Sartre and Simone de Beauvoir, however, proved impervious to the reconciliatory tendencies of the mid-'50s—and their admiration for Mao's China helped to deepen Rousset's own critical fixation. Sartre prefaced the Henri Cartier-Bresson photo essay *D'une Chine à l'autre* in 1954; in 1955 he and Beau-voir toured the PRC together.[35] Upon their return, Sartre published a glowing commentary in *France-Observateur*, praising Mao's "admirable moderation" and insisting that "terror is an unknown word in China."[36] He granted a similar essay to the Beijing-based *People's Daily*, a party organ. Rousset reacted as a bull to a red flag, insisting that Sartre's obeisance toward the Chinese state was an act of moral treason. In a China dotted with prison camps, he wrote, "terror is a fact." By denying this elementary truth and instead offering "odious twaddle on profound humanitarianism," Rousset charged, his onetime friend was "writing exactly what the [Chinese] government wants him to write." Thus, whatever his pretensions to radical oppositionalism, he was no more than "a scribe for established power," "one of those intellectuals who become voluntary lackeys for entrenched tyranny with singular ease."[37] Sartre refused to counter these attacks from a man he now considered a stooge of American capital—"You don't respond to Rousset," he wrote, "you let him earn his daily bread as best he can"—but Rousset correctly calculated that putting Mao's regime "on trial" would eventually force the *Les Temps modernes* team to answer his charges.[38]

Other CICRC members, however, uninvested in French intellectuals' feuds, were not sure that such a faraway state was a feasible target. Norwegian Lise Børsum led the charge. There was still work to accomplish closer to home, she wrote in December 1952: "In our opinion, the [organization's] goals in Europe are not fulfilled until we have researched whether there are concentration camps in *all* the countries of Europe, including the countries of Western Europe." Did the group possess sufficiently "universal" expertise to eventually work outside the continent? Børsum was ambivalent, skirting the problem of whether the Nazi camps provided a template for understanding all global systems of political detention. "We are of the opinion," she wrote, "that with its present apparatus, and with its current experience, the CICRC is not up to the task of resolving the problem in Asia in an effective manner."[39]

French members of the CICRC dismissed this statement of reservation without engaging the underlying issue of cultural competence. Pasteur Institute scientist Alfred Balachowsky, Rousset's most enthusiastic supporter regarding China, lectured Børsum that "the International Commission never had the intention of limiting its activity geographically."[40] Rousset himself simply ignored her missive. Preliminary steps toward an investigation continued, and in early 1954 Rousset and Balachowsky undertook a long voyage to multiple sites in Asia, including Hong Kong, Singapore, Bangkok, and Tokyo, to collect exiles' testimony. With their eyes fixed toward a "trial," they also sought help amassing Chinese legal codes and other documentary evidence from the Vatican, the IRD, French diplomats, the AFL, and the ICFTU, with whom—thanks to Irving Brown's work as intermediary—the CICRC formally partnered on the project in June 1955. A "courageous" Rousset was "fighting in many ways a long battle and should get our support," Brown insisted.[41] US State Department officials also offered assistance, anticipating findings that could be mined to good profit: "Rousset and INFO he has collected in past [have] been extremely useful [in] US propaganda efforts especially in UN," John Foster Dulles's office telegraphed to Bangkok. Thus the Department would "appreciate any assist[ance] [the embassy] can give Rousset."[42]

Not all the CICRC's own members, however, were as eager to help. In late 1954, as it became clear to Børsum that the initiative was steamrolling forward, she relaunched her objection, now supported by both the Norwegian and Danish delegations—and now in frontal attack on Rousset's principles. The "lessons" imparted in Buchenwald and Ravensbrück were *not* universal, she argued. To address political repression in contemporary China, "we reckon that our experiences in the Nazi camps do not suffice"—and, in fact, "do not give us any more of a standard [*plus de critère*] to judge the situation in Eastern countries than that of any human being from the Western countries endowed with a healthy moral responsibility."[43] Børsum suggested, therefore, that the organization "concentrate its energies on the parts of the world where the white race is responsible for conditions," pointedly proposing British Kenya as well as South Africa, Indochina, and Argentina. "It is only when we have brought order to our own ranks," she wrote, "that we will have the right to busy ourselves with the same problems in the rest of the world."[44]

Rousset rejected these arguments *in toto*, incapable of interpreting Børsum's position as a good-faith objection. The Scandinavian delegations, he speculated, must have been perverted by "strong Communist pressure" to turn a blind eye to Mao's crimes.[45] (This charge was incoherent, since Børsum, a committed anticommunist, was demanding not only Western European inquiries but also expanded investigation in the Eastern bloc and renewed appeals to the USSR itself.) Possibly, Rousset also mused, racism was preventing the Scandinavians from taking Chinese suffering seriously. "I confess," he wrote to Reumont, "that I do not understand the argument that consists of saying that our experience in the Nazi camps is not valid for the Asian countries. It is a very strange borrowing from the arsenal of the colonialists," who in Tunisia two years earlier had suggested that "it was necessary to judge the conditions of the camp of Tatahouine in relation to the usual living conditions of Tunisians, and that these people, of course, were accustomed to particularly harsh or miserable circumstances." (The reference here to "colonialists" functioned as a polite erasure of Reumont's own adoption of precisely this position during the Tunisian affair.) "If the Norwegian argument doesn't have this meaning, then I don't see at all what they're trying to say." Surely it could not be that Børsum and her compatriots really believed that Nazi camp survivors' experience lacked "universal value" as a source of expertise in internment.[46]

Rousset did concede, however, that managing the optics of an inquiry into Mao's China posed a challenge. Putting the regime in the dock in a fashion that aroused regional memories of the 1946–1948 Tokyo Trial of Japan's World War II leaders could, he recognized, potentially be construed as a haughty and hypocritical imperialist exercise. But this insight did not lead him toward Børsum's position that the project should be abandoned. Rather, he announced at the start of 1955 that since "an exclusively European tribunal would not possess sufficient moral credit before the Asian world," the CICRC would "modify" its past procedures to create a "mixed" courtroom. With the help of the ICFTU, he explained, the Nazi camp survivors of the CICRC would locate five or six Asian and African counterparts "chosen for their competence, their high morality, and their political independence" to sit alongside them as judges. "If possible," he stated, these participants would be *ex-concentrationnaires* "from the Japanese camps, for example."[47] (He meant survivors of Japan's wartime prison camps, not Japanese-American survivors of US civilian internment, of which he was by all indications oblivious.) But this vague idea proved impossible to implement. In the end, the non-Europeans selected to take part in the inquiry—a Tunisian, a Pakistani, two men from the Philippines, one from Thailand, and one from Japan—were simply noncommunist labor activists.[48]

By inviting these men to join them, the CICRC leaders aimed to increase the "universality" and global appeal of their tribunal—to demonstrate that "we are today all part of a *univers solidaire*, founded on the same principles, responding to the same criteria. . . . Races, colors, diverse historical circumstances are no more than surface fires."[49] But this gesture of Cold War cosmopolitanism was double-edged, since it also constituted an implicit acknowledgment that Western European camp survivors did not actually possess a singular ability to speak on behalf of fellow "concentrationary" victims anywhere in the world. Thus, well before the commission's China hearing opened, it was clear that its staging would not replicate that of the 1951 Soviet mock trial, where the judges had drawn their moral authority from their identity as "men of Auschwitz and Buchenwald."

Rousset did still hope, however, that the Chinese trial would match the earlier proceeding in brio. Aiming to ensure maximum visibility before Asian audiences, he enlisted the British Foreign Office to help secure a locale for the trial in one of the continent's major cities. In a flurry of correspondence, IRD officials ruled out Bangkok as "notoriously totalitarian" and Tokyo and Manila as too evidently within the American sphere of influence.[50] Singapore remained under consideration for months, thanks to the efforts of IRD director John Rennie (later head of MI6), but Colonial Office administrators blocked this possibility. "In the present spirit of the Geneva talks," they determined, conducting the trial in British territory might produce "official repercussions which could be embarrassing to the Colonial Office."[51] Rousset himself also recognized that the 1955 "Big Four" Geneva Summit had yielded a wave of Cold War détente that dampened the appeal of his variety of politico-legal theater.[52] In response, he made an startling concession, offering to hold a closed-door session if this would help him secure access to an Asian capital. But even this idea proved a nonstarter. Burma was nixed when it was pointed out that the notion of holding "secret" sessions there was laughable: "Rangoon is not a place where even eleven foreigners can lose themselves in the crowd."[53] Hope for Ceylon collapsed in autumn, as did a last-ditch effort to interest Pakistan.[54] The CICRC was thus confronted with a dismal empirical rebuke to its pretentions to universal moral jurisdiction. Unhappily, the leadership turned back toward European sites. In the end, Rousset announced that the China hearing, like the Soviet one years earlier, would take place in Brussels. A chamber was reserved at the Hôtel Métropole in that city's Place de Brouckère.

Notably, the trial's relocation to supposedly neutral ground did not mean that Rousset's offer to hold a closed session could now be rescinded, since even in Belgium officials feared "political repercussions" from a one-sided public indictment of Mao.[55] Throughout 1955, as Børsum continued to agitate against the momentum toward a trial, she especially protested the prospect of secrecy. "This trial," she wrote in November, if it was to take place at all, "ought to be open."[56] Here she echoed the discomfort of many members.[57] In response, Rousset insisted that he had attempted to "do the impossible to allow for an open trial" but had found the way blocked.[58] The rejections he had encountered, he suggested, "testify very clearly, in their way, to the decisive importance that world opinion accords to concentrationary questions.... What do you expect? We are inconvenient people: we don't chatter about culture, we concern ourselves with camps."[59] Thus, "in the current circumstances," the CICRC was compelled to carry out its task of witnessing differently from before. "It is not up to us to hold a public trial; but it *is* up to us to tell the truth about the Chinese regime," he lectured members.[60]

His sheer tenacity at last wore down Børsum's defenses. As 1956 dawned, she not only ceased to protest the forthcoming Brussels proceedings but agreed to sit on the "Special Commission of Inquiry" at the Hôtel Métropole alongside Goetschel, André, Van Rij, Calmarza, Balachowsky, Ballhorn, and the Asian and African labor representatives. Over the course of eight closed-door sessions beginning on April 20, directed by Rousset, Bernard, and Gérard Rosenthal, this group worked through a massive dossier of translated Maoist laws and decrees, studied maps of the PRC's "camp universe," and perused Chinese Communist Party communiqués, speeches, and resolutions. Most importantly, it heard scores of victim statements on the cruelties of the *laogai* and reviewed many more similar written depositions. The presence of the non-European judges blocked

Rousset from framing the event as a confrontation between past and present victims—he was forced instead to employ a general language extolling the virtues of private individuals challenging the state. Nevertheless, camp survivors who took part recorded powerful feelings of identification with Chinese "concentrationary" suffering. "I cannot stop myself," wrote Goetschel, "from saying a word about the emotion that listening to these witnesses brought out in me. I rediscovered in their comportment the natural quality with which many [Ravensbrück] comrades speak of their deportation, that language we can understand."[61] On April 30, the panel issued its conclusion: China's system of political detention had "the characteristics" of "an authentic concentrationary regime."[62]

With help from Goetschel and other members—including Børsum—Rousset set to work publicizing this result. Despite the closed courtroom, he was pleased to note, the endeavor produced "a large echo in the international press."[63] The eventual publication of a two-volume *Livre blanc* in both French and English offered further opportunities for promotion and polemics, and doubtless Rousset was particularly gratified that Simone de Beauvoir's 1957 book on China, *La Longue marche*, devoted a full chapter to rebutting his "partisan" allegations.[64] The PRC, according to Beauvoir, did not punish individuals for political opinions—certainly not with "concentrationary" detention. Its penal system was humane, its treatment of counterrevolutionaries "concretely prudent and moderate."[65] Her "inanities" offered great grist for the CICRC's mill, allowing the organization and its defenders to again adopt the ringing rhetoric of the era of the "Appeal": Rosenthal ended a response to *La Longe marche* in *Saturne* by suggesting that "intellectuals, however engaged they might be," possessed a "heavy responsibility" not to "cover up abuses and massive acts of violence." Mao's China, he reminded Beauvoir, was not an abstract thought experiment about communism but a real place containing "the flesh and the blood of six hundred million beings." Borrowing the title of her own famous 1945 novel about wartime France, he called his article "The Blood of Others."[66]

Rousset, with Rosenthal, clearly believed that the CICRC had laid claim to an antiracist moral high ground by insisting that the "blood" of Mao's victims ought to matter equally to that of Westerners. "Solidarity" had dictated the China inquiry, he stated, and in carrying it out the commission had defended "the freedom of all, the dignity of every person," demonstrating that "the movement of emancipation across the entire planet is one."[67] This universalizing rhetoric was disingenuous: a political agenda had dictated the CICRC's targeting of China, just as it had dictated the group's silence on Yugoslavia and its tragic dismissal of Børsum's plea for a Kenyan inquiry. Nevertheless, by insisting first on the Tunisian investigation and subsequently on the Chinese one, Rousset had indeed made an effort—after his own partisan lights—to carry through on the notion that the *univers concentrationnaire* was a phenomenon of relevance for mankind as such.

Paradoxically, however, the compromises that the CICRC made in order to allow the China inquiry to proceed also weakened the group's claims to universal authority. Inviting third-world trade union representatives to sit in judgment of the Chinese detention system belied the idea that former deportees, alone, could serve as witnesses for camp victims anywhere in the world. Holding a closed-door session, meanwhile, undercut the organization's long-term privileging of public testimony. And its effort to speak a comprehensible language of moral condemnation to Asian audiences who knew little about Buchenwald or Dachau muddled its clarity of purpose as an anti-concentrationary collective. In the end, as a result of ICFTU pressure, Rousset was even forced to leave his beloved neologism off the cover of the Chinese *Livre blanc*: only on the title page was "concentrationary institutions" added to "forced labor" as a subject. "It is this aspect—forced labor—that interests the ICFTU and the ILO above all else," Bernard gently explained.[68] This was true—but it begged the question of why the camp survivors' movement needed to exist at all. If Rousset had triumphed in the battle with Børsum over the global relevance of Western Europeans' "Nazi camp experience," it was no means clear that he was winning the larger war.

## The Jewish Membership Question Revisited

As the universality of the CICRC's framework was challenged by its African and Asian investigations, it was also undermined by persistent tensions over the memory of World War II. Throughout the early 1950s, questions about the relationship between "concentrationary" regimes and Jewish suffering—and hence about the CICRC's own restrictive membership policies—seemed to crop up at every turn. This was in part because of the centrality of the commission's paid Jewish staffers, Léon Poliakov and Théo Bernard, to its day-to-day work. It was also because of a slowly growing emphasis on Hitler's racial genocide in European elites' discussions of World War II: as the 1950s progressed, it became less feasible in France, Belgium, or the Netherlands to continually invoke the German "camp universe" without ever mentioning Jews.[69] But, most of all, it was a function of the shifting nature of Soviet and Eastern European state violence in these years. By 1952, genocide was no longer quite so manifestly the "wrong atrocity" for Cold War anticommunists to highlight and denounce—a difficult fact to accept for those CICRC members still attached to Resistance-centered modes of memorializing the recent past.

Problems began for the organization toward the end of Stalin's life, as Western attention was transfixed by a series of high-profile antisemitic episodes in the USSR and its satellites. A key moment in this history was the November 1952 trial of Rudolf Slánský in Czechoslovakia, during which fourteen defendants, eleven of them Jews, were charged with a "Trotskyist-Titoite-Zionist conspiracy" against the Communist Party. Just weeks after the sentencing and execution of these "clever cosmopolitans who have sold out to the dollar," *Pravda* announced the arrest of a "terrorist" group of Jewish doctors in the USSR itself, accused of undertaking a "fifth column" conspiracy in league with an "international Jewish bourgeois nationalist organization" (the American Jewish Joint Distribution Committee).[70] While the so-called Doctors' Plot played out, Jews were also purged from various positions in multiple Eastern European communist parties.

As Gennadi Kostyrchenko underlines, "official antisemitism in the multinational and nominally still internationalistic Soviet Union" was never "all-encompassing," even at its late-Stalinist height.[71] Just the same, these events caused consternation in the West, unnerving even prominent true believers: Pierre Daix later claimed that in 1952, France's best-known female communist, Elsa Triolet (born Ella Kagan in Moscow), privately concluded, "They're Hitlerites!"[72] Thus it would appear at first glance that the CICRC, an organization premised on comparison of Nazi and Stalinist violence, had a golden opportunity on its hands. Certainly, other cold warriors seized the occasion. Addressing the American Jewish Committee (AJC) in January 1953, former US high commissioner for Germany John J. McCloy lamented that "we may be on the verge of a full repetition of the Nazi disgrace in the form of antisemitic persecution. . . . Those who escaped Hitler's concentration camps are now headed for Stalin's."[73] The Congress for Cultural Freedom employed similar language in a petition to the United Nations: "Thus, under a new guise, the most hideous of the political lies kindled by Nazism reappears: antisemitic racism." The Slánský trial and other recent events "constitute an encouragement to racial genocide," wrote the signatories, who included Bertrand Russell, Ignazio Silone, and Upton Sinclair. And this, they incorrectly claimed (in a striking act of misremembrance that again demonstrates the importance of anticommunism in shaping the legacy of the postwar Nazi trials), was "the crime for which a certain number of National Socialist leaders were condemned to death at Nuremberg."[74] Still closer to home for Rousset and his followers, Léon Poliakov called for the Centre de Documentation Juive Contemporaine to undertake a campaign against "Stalinist antisemitism" to expose "the close kinship between the two totalitarianisms." The CDJC, Poliakov proposed, could "pinpoint the similarity" between current Communist propaganda and past Nazi motifs.[75]

David Rousset was aware of all these machinations. In fact, he passed Polia-kov's proposal along to Irving Brown, commenting that "it will be very interesting to follow [this] affair."[76] But he had no intention at this juncture of doing any-thing besides following it, as an observer. His organization may have charged the USSR with repeating Nazism's crime against humanity, but it did not view "racial genocide" as Hitler's chief misdeed. In fact, the CICRC's combat against ongo-ing concentrationary internment depended on treating antisemitic persecution as a non-defining feature of the German camp universe. Still more to the point, members' claims to expert authority, grounded in experience, were necessarily lim-ited to the issues surrounding states' use of mass incarceration and forced labor to subjugate resisters and dissidents. The trial and execution of Rudolf Slánský and his supposed coconspirators simply did not fall within this remit. Accordingly, and ironically, CICRC members found themselves constrained from joining in the chorus of condemnation targeting the return of the repressed in the Eastern bloc.

The group's leaders were reluctant, however, to be left out entirely—particularly because, following the 1951 "guilty" verdict in Brussels, they lacked any obvi-ous means to maintain pressure on the USSR. Members hoped initially to build on the momentum of the mock trial with similar hearings on political deten-tion in the Eastern bloc states, but the dossiers they assembled concerning Bul-garia, Hungary, Poland, Romania, and Czechoslovakia were too thin to proceed. More information surfaced on the German Democratic Republic; this initiative, though, was crippled by continual chaos within the commission's West German delegation.[77] Consequently, though the CICRC continued to publish on the gulag, it struggled to garner fresh attention for what felt like old news. Hence on December 2, 1952, the day before the Slánský defendants were hanged, Rousset and Bernard met to discuss "the prospects that the Prague trial could open up for our activity."[78]

The key problem for the two men was how the Czechoslovakian proceed-ing could be portrayed as "concentrationary" and therefore fair game for their organization. They hit upon an odd way forward: addressing the trial in a highly abstract, legalistic idiom based upon one of the CICRC's three formal criteria for identifying a "concentration camp," the "arbitrary privation of liberty." Following their meeting, Bernard drafted a *mémoire* to circulate at the UN (under André's and Reumont's signatures, not his own). When individuals were arrested and tried without genuine safeguards for their defense, he wrote, as in the "spectacu-lar trial" in Prague, "a strong presumption exists for the survival of the concen-trationary regime," regardless of whether the condemned parties were later sub-ject to forced labor or dehumanizing internment conditions. Bernard then raised a laundry list of procedural questions about the Slánský case: "On the order of which judicial authority and for what infraction were these men arrested? Which impartial jurisdiction decided that the charge was sufficiently serious to keep them detained? In what conditions did they learn about the accusation, and could they defend themselves at the preliminary inquiry?" Buried deep among the many queries stood a notable item: "In what measure was the declaration of guilt influenced by considerations of politics, of race, or of religion?"[79] But the text did not refer directly to Jewishness as a defining characteristic of the Slánský defendants, and Bernard certainly did not join other Western denouncers in accusing the trial's engineers of "antisemitism."

The inhibited language of Bernard's *mémoire* can, in part, be explained as a function of genre and audience: a United Nations circular was no place for a nongovernmental organization to bandy accusations of "racial genocide." In fact, new 1952 UN rules barred NGOs from alleging country-specific abuses at all—thus, colorless as it was, the CICRC text was rejected for distribution until Bernard stripped it of any direct reference to Czechoslovakia.[80] He had learned his lesson by April 1953, when he addressed the Committee on Non-Governmental Organizations with what the *New York Times* described as a carefully vague "general discussion" of "arbitrary arrests."[81] But UN regulations were clearly not the only thing holding the International Commission back from more inflammatory language. Other CICRC documents, intended for general readers, were just as elliptical as Bernard's *mémoire*. For example, one press release on the Slánský case noted "the resurgence, notably in the countries of Eastern Europe that were occupied by Nazi Germany, of massive violations of individual liberty."[82] The reference to former Nazi occupation was not accidental, but neither was it a direct invocation of Theresienstadt—and this at a time when other observers were loudly announcing that "two and a half million Jews are in danger of extinction" as Stalin threatened to repeat (or complete) Hitler's genocide in Eastern Europe.[83]

Even before Stalin's death, then, the desire to respond to new forms of state violence in the USSR and its satellites clearly began to place strain on the CICRC's intellectual framework of "concentrationary" suffering. But since the group remained principally focused on the gulag, still a significant object of Western European interest and still at its demographic height, the problem was not yet acute. The situation changed in March 1953 with Stalin's passing. Within weeks, the USSR's new head of the Ministry of Internal Affairs and State Security (MVD), Lavrenty Beria, enacted a major amnesty and effectively halved the gulag population of roughly 2.5 million, releasing 1.2 million inmates. A wave of strikes and revolts centered in the special camps from 1953 to 1955 helped ensure that Beria's policies were not reversed upon his downfall; in fact, over the remainder of the 1950s and especially after 1956, releases accelerated, the gulag administration was dissolved, and detainee labor—long unprofitable—was granted a much-diminished place in the Soviet economy.[84]

Rousset greeted these transformations of the Soviet camp system with self-congratulatory rhetoric: "Certainly," he wrote, "I would never argue that the liberations of prisoners are due to our efforts alone. But we have hit the target, we have struck the weak spot, and in so doing we have contributed to fortifying the Soviet Government in its decisions—this seems certain to me."[85] If the evolution of the Soviet camp system permitted the CICRC's founder to boast, however, it also posed a problem for his organization: as the gulag shrank, how could a group founded to condemn its existence remain relevant? Casting about for answers to the question, members of the commission focused as usual on their vocation of facilitating victim-witness testimony. It was at this moment, for instance, that the organization dispatched Goetschel to interview newly repatriated West German and Austrian survivors of the Soviet camps. A widely publicized "Letter to Beria," meanwhile, renewed Rousset's demand for access to the USSR itself. "If the regime has authentically changed in Russia," he wrote, "then it is necessary to give voice [donner la parole] to the survivors of Kolyma. It is a good thing that an officer of the MVD is announcing the closing of the camps. But it is necessary that the former slaves tell the world what those camps were."[86]

The "Letter to Beria" netted the CICRC a burst of media coverage, but attention was fleeting.[87] By mid-1954 the organization again found itself without a clear and urgent language for comparing current Soviet actions to past Nazi violence. At this point, abruptly—long after the "anticosmopolitan" campaign had ended and other cold warriors had abandoned the issue—Rousset decided at last to attack the Eastern bloc regimes for antisemitism. When the CICRC next approached the UN, he informed members in July, "we also ought to make a note of the antisemitic trials now going on in the popular democracies, which the press practically ignore."[88] This was the first time he had identified antisemitism, as such, as an issue the organization might address. Rousset subsequently asked Poliakov, long ago stymied in his efforts through the CDJC, to begin assembling a "dossier" on "antisemitic" trials in Romania, Bulgaria, and elsewhere.[89] As the CICRC founder now explained to an AJC representative, "What matters to us, above all else, is to bring together all of the documents establishing the discriminatory nature of these trials. It must be established that the Jewish character of the accused plays an important role in the procedure and in the condemnation."[90]

This new rhetoric on Rousset's part marked a sharp departure from Bernard's 1952 mémoire, whose linguistic gymnastics had been necessary precisely to avoid discussing the "Jewish character" of the Prague defendants. The tactical advantages of the changed approach were clear; less so was how it remained within the mandate of the International Commission against the Concentration Camp Regime.[91] But Rousset declined to explain himself, calling on the organization to condemn communist "antisemitism" without explaining what this had to do

with "concentration camps" as the CICRC understood them—and without specifying what sort of expertise a group composed exclusively of former Resistance
deportees possessed on the issue. Had the new campaign taken off in a serious
way, this strategy of intellectual avoidance may well have proved untenable. However, the issue of Eastern bloc antisemitism simply did not have legs by 1954; the
whole effort turned out to be short-lived. While it lasted, moreover, the labor
involved was not undertaken by members who might have posed inconvenient
questions but by Poliakov and Bernard. Attendees at meetings received assurances that "M. Bernard continues to busy himself with this affair"; they did not
otherwise discuss it.[92]

In truth, by 1954 Poliakov and Bernard were responsible for much of the
CICRC's daily business. Reumont carried out his duties from his home in little
Banneux-Louveigné, Belgium, and the group continued to hold plenary meetings in Brussels; it also maintained Belgian headquarters for legal purposes. But
the real "work team" operated out of France.[93] In recognition of this fact, Rousset
began that autumn to seek a proper Parisian organizational office; the following
year a suitable location was rented at 5 rue Daunou near the Opéra. Poliakov was
at the center of research operations in Paris, his tasks so intensive that he took on
a secretary of his own. Bernard, meanwhile, worked hand in hand with Rousset
on every aspect of the commission's operations and also served as its public face
at the United Nations and in the international press. When Rousset decided to
launch a campaign against anti-Jewish "discriminatory measures" in the communist world, it was only natural that these two would spearhead it.[94] Nevertheless, the resulting situation did present a strange spectacle: a former Drancy
inmate and a historian of the Final Solution attacking "the racial character" of
Eastern European justice on behalf of a collective that did not welcome survivors
of Hitler's "racial" deportation to join its ranks.[95]

Poliakov and Bernard themselves did not covet membership in the CICRC.
But other Jews did. In 1953, the Association Indépendante des Anciens Déportés
et Internés Juifs (AIADIJ)—a group that included such notable Jewish survivors
as sociologist Michał Borwicz—petitioned for admission to the CICRC via its
subsidiary French commission. Germaine Tillion, then serving as president of
the French group, reviewed the request submitted by AIADIJ secretary-general
D. Berkhauer and appears to have discussed it with other French members, jot-
ting notes on follow-up questions to pose ("what kind of deportees?" "arrested
where?").[96] Ultimately she informed Berkhauer that his association was not qualified to join the French delegation because "unless I am mistaken, a great proportion of your members were arrested in Poland," noting unhelpfully that "there is
no Polish Commission among us."[97] It might at first glance appear that her logic
depended more on national categories than on hierarchical distinctions between

"racial" and "political" deportees: after all, some members of the AIADIJ had been partisan fighters. But at stake was the French commission's status as an elite emanation of the French Resistance. It was because of participants' commitment to a patriotic schema for remembering the deportation that they could not envision including survivors originally arrested in Poland, even if those individuals now lived in France.

Interestingly, Tillion did inform Berkhauer that there might be a future opportunity for certain Jewish survivors to involve themselves in the CICRC's work since (employing a polite French term for Jews, not Israelis), "there have been various discussions about creating *une Commission israélite*" within the organization.[98] In other words, it was conceivable that Holocaust victims could someday participate in the CICRC—but as a distinct group, permitting the existing country-based contingents to maintain their purity as collectives of resisters. No such arrangement materialized, however, and the commission continued as before. It is important, once again, to underline that this was not the result of ignorance or callousness among members about the extent of past Jewish suffering. Tillion's own 1954 "Réflexions sur l'étude de la déportation" was, as Francois Azouvi comments, "impeccable" in delineating the nature and extent of Jewish losses during World War II.[99] But knowledge of the Holocaust did not translate into an impetus toward inclusivity vis-à-vis its survivors. As the French deportation was commemoratively sanctified in these years through Resistance-centric official projects—from postage stamps to a National Day of Remembrance, government fund drives for the eventual Natzweiler-Struthof Memorial, and publication of the state-supported anthology *Tragédie de la déportation*—the CICRC's leading French members saw little reason to compromise or confuse their identity as a collective of heroic combatants for *la patrie*.[100]

David Rousset, who had originally assured Berkhauer that he was "convinced" the AIADIJ's application would be "very favorably looked upon," stood as the major exception to this rule.[101] Though he did not contest Tillion's decision, it is clear he would have handled the matter differently. Perhaps his sympathies were swayed by the prospect of incorporating more individuals of Eastern European origin into the CICRC, an attractive one for both propagandistic and research purposes. Or perhaps, with his impressive knowledge of "Jewish resistance" in the Warsaw Ghetto (on which he had published multiple articles), he viewed the Polish Jews of the AIADIJ as something other than simple "racial" deportees.[102] Neither of these factors, however, appears determinative. The fact of the matter was that Rousset had ceased to care whether individuals on the commission had suffered as a result of "crimes of doing" or "crimes of being," so long as they had once been imprisoned in a Nazi camp.

Rousset's evolution on this question was unsurprising—and not simply because by the mid-1950s he was conducting the commission's work with the help of predominantly Jewish supporters, from Bernard and Poliakov to Brown, Lovestone, and Josselson. His concept of the "concentrationary universe" had always offered the potential of delineating an undifferentiated survivors' community on the basis of shared suffering. His early insistence that CICRC participants had to possess Resistance credentials was not ideological; it was governed pragmatically by the prestige that political deportees possessed in 1949 France. Once the commission was established, he ceased to belabor the issue. We saw, for example, that his outrage over the 1952 De Swart affair—quite unlike that of De Swart's Dutch colleagues—sprang from the impostor never having been inside the *univers concentrationnaire*, not from his manufactured record of anti-Nazi valor. For Rousset, the CICRC's true authority derived from its members' passage through the crucible of "the camps"; the motive behind their original arrest was immaterial. And by 1954 he had come to believe that discussion of Hitler's victimization of Jews, *qua* Jews, was no longer strategically harmful in attacking Eastern bloc regimes.

One sticking point did remain as Rousset moved toward reopening the question of "racial" survivor membership in the CICRC. This was how to square Jews' remembered experiences with claims to equivalency between Nazi and Soviet concentration camps—for, despite the diminution of the Soviet forced labor system, making such claims remained the organization's central task. In an early 1956 essay in *Saturne*, Rousset outlined his solution to the problem. He began by admitting that "Birkenau remains beyond comparison [*Birkenau demeure incomparable*]." But Jews had not only experienced extermination facilities during World War II. They had been incarcerated in "normal" camps like Neuengamme and Dachau as well. Borrowing language directly from Poliakov—who finally quit his CICRC job in late 1955 when he secured academic employment, but who remained an important interlocutor—Rousset suggested that these camps could be conceptualized as Dantesque hells comprising multiple "circles" of intensifying suffering, with Jews "occupy[ing] the dark pit upon which all other circles rest." The Soviet gulag, too, contained circles upon circles, Rousset wrote: "inequality in hardship" was "the universal golden rule of the crime against humanity," not a German particularity. In the Soviet camps, however, it was political prisoners who occupied the "dark pit." The CICRC's founder thus offered a startling formulation: "In the USSR, the 'political' is the Jew of the Nazi camps."[103] From this, it logically followed that Jewish racial deportees belonged in the CICRC. Their suffering closely matched that of Soviet political prisoners, even if the reason behind their deportation differed.

Thus in April 1957 Rousset announced at a CICRC meeting that he intended to seek a delegation of Jewish "racial" survivors for the commission. "Those who were arrested and interned in the camps for a racial motive," he declared unambiguously, "are experts in concentrationary matters just as much as the others."[104] His plan was to locate representatives in Israel—a concession, perhaps, to participants who wished to maintain the existing composition of their national delegations, but also a savvy political choice at a moment of widespread French sympathy for that country in the wake of the Suez-Sinai crisis. Through Bernard, Rousset explained to his colleagues, he had begun to seek contact with a Haifa-headquartered "national organization of former Nazi camp internees." The announcement was met with strident opposition, particularly from the Dutch. "We want to know," Karel van Staal stated baldly, "if it is a matter of Jews persecuted for racial motives or for motives of resistance to Nazism. The Dutch organization will not accept those who were interned for a racial motive."[105] In this tense conversation, as in the earliest days of Rousset's crusade, two contradictory logics of legitimation clashed against each other: was the commission a collective forged in shared human suffering, or was it an elite corps of *résistants* whose passage through the Nazi camps had provided them with proof of patriotic heroism? CICRC members simply could not agree on the answer to this fundamental question. In fact, they never resolved it. Beneath the surface, the commission was beginning to fracture over who and what the group represented when it claimed to speak in the name of memory.

## Rethinking the CICRC's Mission after the Hungarian Revolution

The issue of Jewish membership remained sensitive for the International Commission in its final years. But conflict on this point never gave way to full-blown crisis, perhaps because Rousset and his followers were consumed by other challenges. One of these was the late 1956 Soviet invasion of Hungary to suppress a revolt against that nation's Moscow-backed government. The CICRC reaped great propaganda benefits by condemning the military repression in Hungary, which the survivors' organization portrayed as an occupier's act of terror against patriotic *résistants*. At the same time, however, the event drew members into the dangerous business of mobilizing against acts of state violence that could not really be described as "concentrationary." Moreover, as the French intellectual left realigned in the aftermath of the fighting in Hungary, Rousset and his colleagues were transformed from lonely voices of witness into marginal participants in a crowded field of protest. The CICRC's purpose became less clear in a context in which *everyone* was outraged about Soviet crimes—and in which *no one* understood those crimes as centrally involving "concentration camps." Still more dispiritingly, the institutional failure of Western international actors to aid the Hungarian fighters made clear to the commission's members—and especially its founder—that an ethics of accountability toward "victims wherever victims are to be found" was irrelevant to Cold War realpolitik.[106]

Events in Hungary in October 1956 initially electrified Rousset. Aided by Poliakov's equally erudite replacement, exiled Czech semiotician Jiří Veltruský, Rousset was already closely attuned to rumblings of discontent in the Eastern bloc, which gained momentum following Nikita Khrushchev's famous February "secret speech" criticizing Stalin. In July, for instance, Rousset spoke at a rally in support of striking workers in Poznań, Poland, and opened *Saturne* to a celebratory analysis of their efforts by Bernard. "In burning police files," Bernard wrote, "the workers of Poznań have weighed in decisively in the fight against the concentrationary regime."[107] Within days of the October 23, 1956, uprising in Budapest, Rousset organized a meeting with *Le Figaro* editor Pierre Brisson to propose an article demanding "solidarity with the Hungarian insurrection."[108] This piece was published on October 30, then republished in longer form in *Saturne*. Titled "Le silence n'est plus tolérable" (Silence is no longer tolerable), it announced that as the blood of laborers and students ran in the streets of Budapest, Western Europe's intelligentsia faced a moment of reckoning. "Silence has become unsupportable," Rousset wrote. "Unsupportable for everyone. The insurrection demands of all honest men a public and unequivocal rupture with Stalinism."[109] On November 3, *Le Figaro littéraire* published statements of support for Rousset from Albert Camus, Pierre Emmanuel, Stanislas Fumet, Robert Aron, Pierre Gascar, Gabriel Marcel, Jules Monnerot, Roger Nimier, and Charles Vildrac, as well as Martin-Chauffier.

Rousset took care in "Le silence n'est plus tolérable" to insist that the current crisis in Hungary was linked to the struggle against "the concentrationary universe" that the CICRC had been waging for seven years. "The Polish and the Hungarians," he wrote,

> have not hesitated to name their chief enemy: the political police, the security forces, and their apparatus of prisons and of camps. Never in history has the struggle for bread been so intimately associated with denunciation of the arbitrary, of the camp and of the prison. When Merleau-Ponty and Sartre publicly broke with me, they signed this sentence: 'The truth is that even the experience of an absolute like the concentrationary horror does not determine a politics.' How well the insurrection answers them, is it not true?[110]

Rousset thus construed the Hungarian Revolution as above all a stand against
state terror. In so doing, he aimed not only to shape readers' interpretation of
the struggle but also to justify preemptively his own "apolitical" organization's
fierce engagement in favor of the insurrectionists. If the protests in Hungary
were, at heart, strikes against "concentrationary horror," the CICRC would be
acting within its existing mandate to offer full-throated support.

The unfolding of the Hungarian Revolution over the following days complicated this crisp narrative, for it offered a repellent spectacle of state violence
that could nevertheless only tenuously be connected to the theme of concentrationary suffering. As Western observers were held rapt by reports chronicling
the military dismantling of the Hungarian resistance, it made increasingly little
strategic sense for the CICRC to protest this very visible repression by referring to unseen prisons and camps. Hence, as Rousset admitted to the assembled
membership in Brussels, "The events in Hungary pose a problem concerning
the present orientation of the CICRC."[111] The delegations were not in agreement
over how to proceed. The Scandinavians were reluctant to act in "too energetic
or radical a fashion," as Rousset sourly observed (blaming, as usual, "crude and
vulgar" communist influence); meanwhile, the Dutch proposed wildly aggressive
measures "without hesitating, under the circumstances, to run the risk of a Third
World War."[112] Overall, though, members were committed to offering an institutional response. They also had sufficient resources to wade into the fray—in fact,
John O'Shea cabled Rousset a discretionary $7,500 "for use in special Hungar-
ian actions."[113] But to intervene as "specialists," the CICRC's survivor-members
either had to lay claim to a new authority regarding assaults on human dignity
that were not "concentrationary" in nature, or alternatively to paint the acts of
Soviet troops as falling within the CICRC's existing purview.

Rousset chose the latter course. The Soviet method of re-subjugating Hungary was *concentrationnaire*, he proclaimed: revolutionaries were not only being
killed on site but also, and more importantly, being deported to "concentration
camps" in the USSR. To advance this interpretation of events, Rousset undertook a two-pronged mobilization centered first on the French public sphere and
second on the United Nations. In Paris, the CICRC organized a November 13,
1956, pro-Hungary rally in the name of "former Resistance deportees to the Nazi
camps." Rousset served as ringmaster for this event, flanked by Martin-Chauffier,
for whom the Hungarian repression sparked a redoubled involvement in the
commission's work. The rally, which drew roughly fifteen thousand spectators,
was addressed by a panoply of speakers who stood beneath an enormous banner emblazoned with the words, "FREEDOM FOR HUNGARY. STOP THE DEPORTA-
TIONS."[114] The Vélodrome d'Hiver served as the setting for this pageant, and
both Rousset and Martin-Chauffier embraced the symbolism of denouncing

Hungarian "convoys of deportees to the death camps" in the bicycling arena that in 1942 had served as a way station to Auschwitz for thousands of Jews.[115] The assembly even issued a resolution declaring that Soviet acts in Hungary "constitute a true crime of genocide," a term the CICRC would not have employed half a decade earlier.[116] Ultimately, however, the rally's organizers did not portray the Hungarian insurrectionists primarily as new Holocaust victims but rather as successors to the valiant French Resistance struggle against the Germans. These "combatants for freedom" were being deported, speaker upon speaker charged, for "resistance against a foreign aggressor."[117]

The Vel' d'Hiv rally received widespread, respectful media coverage. "All the daily press, without exception, gave long accounts of the demonstration," and some featured "large front-page photographs," the CICRC's internal report proudly noted. "Even the Communist press was obliged to mention it."[118] This was true—and yet in a month of incessant, overheated discussion of Hungary the gathering did not stand out. Indeed, on the night it took place, more spectators (apparently around twenty thousand) attended a soccer match at the Parc des Princes organized as a benefit for Hungarians.[119] In intellectual circles, meanwhile, mid-November conversations were dominated by the sensational news of Sartre's break with the PCF. Condemnations of the USSR by long-standing anticommunists such as Rousset were hardly noteworthy. Moreover, with graphic images of violence in the streets of Budapest available on television and in newsreels, the charge that the invaders were also engaging in behind-the-scenes deportations proved superfluous. Thus the rally was quickly forgotten, subsumed by the ongoing flood of denunciations.

Meanwhile, the commission also attempted to insert the issue of deportation into the conversation on Hungary at the UN. On November 17, 1956, Rousset sent a telegram to Secretary-General Dag Hammarskjöld in the name of "deportees and combatants of the European Resistance to Hitler's Germany" demanding "urgent action to put a stop to the deportation of Hungarian *résistants*."[120] Subsequently, by a "very happy coincidence," the French UN delegate charged with addressing the General Assembly on Hungary turned out to be Senator Edmond Michelet, a longtime member of the French commission. Michelet agreed, as Théo Bernard reported, "to be our spokesperson."[121] He began his December 4 speech by referring to himself as "*un ancien de Dachau*," establishing an authority of experience he then buttressed by invoking the CICRC, "a body associated with the United Nations . . . and grouping together 100,000 former deportees." The commission's members, Michelet lectured, were uniquely well positioned to understand that "a process we thought was forgotten forever" had now begun again. As in the dark days of wartime France, police were awakening resisters with brutal dawn raids, snatching them unceremoniously from their homes, and shoving them onto cattle cars for "that mournful transport toward unknown, always fearsome destinations." In Dachau, Michelet reflected, he had encountered many brave "Hungarian patriots." Now these men who "had known the horrors of the Nazi camps are about to go back—if they have not already done so—to some other sinister space of the concentrationary universe."[122]

The International Commission attempted to lend substance to Michelet's accusations in its habitual way: through victim-witness testimony. Just before the speech, Théo Bernard flew to New York armed, as he later told it, with a "dossier of testimonies with verified, certified signatures, constituting juridical proof of the existence of the alleged deportations."[123] In fact, he arrived with only five such documents in hand; Rousset sent him nine more over the course of his stay in the US, but he had difficulties photocopying them in sufficient numbers.[124] Moreover, as the UN's Special Committee on the Problem of Hungary later pointed out, the testimonies were evidentiarily weak: "None of the refugees who had signed these statements had actually been taken to the USSR."[125] Bernard originally hoped to fly witnesses to New York to address UN representatives themselves but then recognized that this would be "useless": "the Hungarian question is [already] so much on the front page of the newspapers," he told Rousset, "that the presence of witnesses would not have added anything."[126] In an atmosphere saturated with various rhetorics of condemnation for Soviet "imperialism," "massacres," "fascism," and "atrocity," the project of testifying to this latest instance of the *univers concentrationnaire* was robbed of its urgency. There was no starring role for the CICRC to play here—and, more broadly, no clear case to be made for the continued relevance of "concentrationary" suffering as a singular criterion for political judgment.

Still more dismaying to Rousset and his followers, the UN's handling of the Hungarian affair exposed the insignificance of its victim-centric vision to the practical business of the Cold War. With the Security Council effectively hamstrung by Soviet veto power and further divided by the contemporaneous Suez crisis unfolding in Egypt, the General Assembly finally issued a November 4, 1956, vote calling on the USSR to end its intervention; by this point, a second wave of Soviet-led military action had begun, US unwillingness to intervene directly had become evident, and the denunciation was essentially symbolic. The General Assembly went on to issue a barrage of further censures, some of which even included language about "deportations," but these were meaningless in the face of a fait accompli. Meaningless, as well, were its pleas that neutral UN observers be permitted to "enter the territory of Hungary, to travel freely therein, and to report their findings to the Secretary-General": the newly installed János Kádár government in Budapest simply ignored them.[127] CICRC members understood perfectly well that the UN, "not disposing of any supra-national authority," could not actually function as an enforcer of global human rights norms; their lobbying in New York and Geneva had always been performance art geared toward influencing Western perceptions, not a bid for the UN itself to curb Soviet abuses.[128] Nevertheless, they appear to have been genuinely stunned by the organization's impotence in this case, experiencing it as a cynical betrayal of the moral imperative that justified their own Cold War allegiance: solidarity with victims of Soviet repression. The UN, Martin-Chauffier stormed, was standing by, "powerless and practically mute at one of the greatest crimes of history."[129] Bernard mourned its "tragic powerlessness" as well.[130] The United Nations, he concluded, was "a made-up story, one that is now at an end."[131]

Rousset, meanwhile, more irate than elegiac, published a public letter in *Le Figaro* railing against the impotence of not only the UN but the entire Western world—including his own organization. This December 15 tirade, titled "Notre impuissance est devenue angoisse" (Our powerlessness has become anguish), denounced "our cowardice, the incredible cowardice of free peoples," in the face of "the crime against humanity that the Russians are perpetrating in Hungary."[132] Most of his spleen was vented at "the White House" for abandoning the revolutionaries to their fate when, Rousset believed, more could have been done. He went so far as to suggest that US inaction had discredited the Atlantic Alliance for noncommunist Western European leftists like himself: "If its goal is not to defend the independence of peoples, the safeguard of democratic freedoms and workers' freedoms, then why would it hold the least interest for us?" Likely enough, he predicted, "on the day when Paris is in flames . . . Eisenhower's successor, with all necessary moral firmness, will cry on our graves" rather than lifting a finger. The Hungarian Revolution's downfall, the article made clear, had undermined Rousset's faith in the strategic allegiances that had long sustained the CICRC. It had exposed for him the gap between America's pragmatic priorities and his own profoundly moral and ideological understanding of the Cold War. His response to this revelation, he announced, striking a Sartrean note, was "nausea."[133]

If "Notre impuissance est devenue angoisse" marked a shift away from its author's habitually measured tone toward the United States, it constituted a still more stunning reversal for Rousset in another sense: the text rejected "witnessing" as a sufficient response to state violence. In fact, as the contemptuous reference to "crying on our graves" suggests, its structuring binary was between authentic, tangible action and self-satisfied, empty expressions of fellow feeling. "I am ashamed of our indignation," Rousset wrote. "I am ashamed of our declarations. Because, in the end, faced with this people fighting ceaselessly in the most extraordinary agony ever known to history, we remain spectators." In these circumstances, he insisted, it was "better to remain silent than to write, since we can only weep before the wailing wall." Such claims recast empathic witnessing as mere comfortable bystanding or after-the-fact hand-wringing, dismissing its value as a form of political action. Rousset made this point with still more force in another line: "We are paying ourselves in words," he wrote, "although everything demands of us that simple solidarity of entering into combat." He intended the final term literally. Reverting to the revolutionary vocabulary of his youth, he closed the article imagining "volunteers for freedom . . . creating their international brigades to fight by the side of their Hungarian comrades."[134]

Of course, the CICRC's founder did not actually launch himself into paramilitary organizing for the Hungarian cause—Budapest was not Barcelona, 1956 was not 1936, and Cold War antitotalitarian commitments, however deeply felt, did not translate into the same forms of struggle as interwar antifascist ones had. What is more, Rousset's dismissal of "words" was offered in the form of them: had he truly believed that mere speech acts about Hungary were useless, he would not have written "Notre impuissance est devenue angoisse" in the first place. But this performative contradiction should not distract from the significance of the text as a critique, even a repudiation, of projects that had occupied its author for many years. Rousset's ability to maintain that the CICRC was a noble and coherent answer to a universal calling had survived many challenges. But faced with the annihilation of the Budapest insurgency, he appears to have lost confidence that the "witnessing" the commission had engaged in constituted a meaningful form of action in a still-violent world. Was the organization helping to create a *univers solidaire* to replace the *univers concentrationnaire*? Or was all its work, in the end, no more than the shedding of pointless, pious tears on victims' graves? These questions echoed in the air as the commission turned toward Algeria, presaging its final crisis.

# FROM AUSCHWITZ TO ALGERIA
## The Limits of Memory

While CICRC members' eyes were turned east in 1956, the storm that would ultimately wreck the organization was brewing to the south, in French Algeria. David
Rousset had been paying attention to the Algerian War from the beginning—and,
in particular, to a trickle of reportage in the left-wing press ominously claiming
that supporters of the Algerian Front de Libération Nationale (FLN) were being
confined to "internment camps." Once the Hungarian crisis faded, he set to work
convincing his fellow survivors that "the methods of repression in Algeria pose
a problem that the CICRC cannot ignore."[1] On April 6, 1957, the commission's
membership fatefully voted to investigate political detention in the "crown jewel"
of French empire. On June 18, following negotiations with two successive governments, Georges André, Lise Børsum, Cornelius van Rij, Louis Martin-Chauffier,
and Germaine Tillion flew across the Mediterranean. As the battle of Algiers
raged, they undertook an unprecedented journey through a growing archipelago of prisons, detention centers, and military triage camps. With the exception
of International Red Cross teams, who presented their findings exclusively to
French officials, they were the only non-government-appointed witnesses ever
to inspect these facilities formally.

Their endeavor was a success on many levels. Members pierced a veil of official secrecy to produce critical knowledge about the role of political internment
in France's undeclared 1954–1962 war. They spoke hard truths about the widespread French use of torture, gaining new respect on the left. And they further
advanced the norm of international accountability for states' repressive treatment of their own subjects. But such success came at a high cost: in the end, the

mission destroyed the organization. This was first of all because the decision to investigate in Algeria soured Rousset's relationship with his American backers. Long supportive of the CICRC's efforts to both the east and west, the New York "fund-raiser" John O'Shea warned the group away from this mission. As Rousset interpreted his position, the politics of international interference in what France desperately insisted was an internal disturbance within a sovereign state were too explosive for O'Shea's "friends."[2] Rousset, who was not only a principled anticolonialist but also a staunch advocate of the Cold War necessity of noncommunist support for Arab nationalism, pushed ahead with the project all the same, perhaps assuming that he would be forgiven after the fact. This did not ensue. Whatever their own criticisms of French policy in Algeria, US government actors were dismayed by the initiative. In late 1957 they informed Rousset that they would be severing their ties with the CICRC, ending a connection that after Hungary was proving increasingly burdensome.

This loss of financial backing was devastating to the commission, but the group did not expire only because its subsidies disappeared. Rousset and his followers could have soldiered on were it not for the effects of the 1957 investigation on participants themselves, especially key French members of the organization. Some quit in protest of the "inopportune" turn toward scrutiny of their own country, unable to accept the undermining of *Algérie française* as a consequence of Rousset's universalizing logic.[3] Others, though willing to criticize France, came to feel that viewing its violence in Algeria through the optic of "the concentrationary universe" obscured as much as it illuminated. As the delegation's conclusions proved distressingly open to instrumentalization by French military apologists, Martin-Chauffier and later Tillion concluded that seeking echoes of Nazi practices was an unsatisfactory way to combat the state atrocities occurring in Algeria, which possessed a distinctly French genealogy and did not actually much resemble the crimes committed at Neuengamme or Ravensbrück. They also became impatient with an activist protocol demanding full-bore identification with victims rather than simple compassion. The precept that the other-in-pain could be recognized as such only if his suffering was deemed indistinguishable from members' own past anguish did not, it now became clear, facilitate a sufficiently vigorous response to violence directed at Muslim Algerians. Similar problems had dogged the group for years, most of all in Tunisia. But in Algeria the stakes were higher and the inadequacy of the CICRC's framework more acutely felt, particularly as metropolitan French antiwar activism coalesced around the signal issue of torture, not camps.

Faced with the twin challenges of defunding and members' "loss of interest" in "these concentrationary questions," David Rousset fought valiantly for his organization's survival.[4] Even so, he, too, gradually came to question the utility of the anti-concentrationary project in the era of decolonization. While the CICRC's founder maintained his insistence on the relevance of the *univers concentration-naire*, he distanced himself from the organization's second structuring concept, that of *le témoin*. The agony of Budapest in 1956 had already shaken Rousset's faith in "witnessing" as meaningful political action; now the Algerian War shattered it. Nonpartisan testimony to human suffering might compel France to wage a marginally more humane imperialist war, he came to believe, but it would not further the cause of Algerian independence—which he endorsed. This was a revolutionary goal that would have to be fought for by avowedly political means.

This chapter on the CICRC's confrontation with decolonizing warfare, then, is not only about members' achievement in demanding international oversight for a Western democracy's "police operations" against internal "terrorists." It is also about the crumbling of the organization's financial, political, and epistemological foundations, the collapse of its unity, and its eventual demise. The story it tells about World War II memory during the Algerian War is consequently less uplifting than that offered in most scholarship, including Michael Rothberg's account of how French camp survivors' remembrance of their own suffering spurred their demands for justice on behalf of persecuted Algerians after 1954.[5] Undoubtedly, references to World War II offered an emotionally resonant idiom with which to denounce French violence in North Africa a decade later.[6] The CICRC's investigation demonstrates, however, that drawing parallels between past German atrocities and present French ones was not necessarily a politically productive exercise for survivors. It was certainly not one upon which they cooperated harmoniously: ideology, not experience, determined individual deportees' responses to the Algerian War. And, in the end, it was only by jettisoning the rigid paradigm of the past that CICRC members such as Tillion were able to stake out their most trenchant responses to decolonization. Thus the Algerian conflict did herald a new era in the remembrance of Nazi criminality—but not by directly heightening French Holocaust consciousness, as Rothberg suggests. Rather, Western European survivors' efforts to address colonial atrocity destroyed their Cold War consensus about the German camps' archetypal status as institutions of political repression and about the universal, antitotalitarian "lessons" that those camps offered mankind. Robbed of this grounding, the CICRC could no longer stand.

## Opening the Algerian Dossier

Political internment constituted an integral apparatus of the state of exception that France created in Algeria beginning in the nineteenth century. As Sylvie Thénault writes, the practice of extra-juridical confinement "permeates the long term of the years from 1830 to 1962."[7] But if such violence was nothing new in 1954, its realm expanded dramatically over the course of Algeria's war of independence, as France constructed or repurposed an array of facilities to imprison "suspects." The proliferation of these camps was simultaneous to the process by which the French military and police implemented the use of torture against thousands of Algerians. But they were not—generally speaking—torture sites: individuals came to them after interrogations elsewhere.[8] Their purpose within a conflict viewed by the French as an ideological battle was in part prophylactic—internment was intended to prevent nationalist "contamination" of communities by cordoning off individuals with dangerous sympathies.[9] It was also reeducative, at least in fits and starts, and camp officials periodically launched "psychological action" schemes to inspire "realization of the duty required of French Muslims" among internees.[10] Finally, the camps functioned as something resembling prisoner-of-war installations for a war that could not speak its name. Unwilling to recognize the Algerian "rebels" as combatants under international law but unable in practical terms to prosecute them all as common-law criminals, France depended on administrative internment to sideline opponents as it struggled to regain control of the territory.

The camps' legal justification, a dubious one, initially rested on emergency legislation. On April 3, 1955, five months after the FLN attacks that launched the conflict, the French Assembly declared an "*état d'urgence*" in France's trans-Mediterranean departments, beginning in Kabylia and the Aurès. Law No. 55–385 granted extraordinary powers to French authorities, including the ability to issue individual edicts of "compulsory residence" in a "determined location." Article Six of the law stipulated that "compulsory residence must permit those subject to it to reside in an urban area or in immediate proximity to an urban area.... In no case will compulsory residence be permitted to produce the creation of camps."[11] Maurice Bourgès-Maunoury, minister of the interior, explained that the legislation was expressly "designed to avoid the barbed wire and the camps that we unfortunately knew." Neither he nor Algerian governor-general Jacques Soustelle, he assured the Assembly, "have the intention of interning thousands of people."[12]

Meanwhile, Soustelle's administration was already building or redeploying sites to do just that. Less than three months after the state of emergency was declared, Inspector General G. Ciosi toured these "localities," which the government—following a long French tradition of euphemism regarding internment camps in both metropole and empire—would soon label "*centres d'hébergement*" (roughly, "accommodation centers").[13] Ciosi's report to his superiors was categorical: France had created a camp system in Algeria. "The absence of barbed wire cannot deceive," he wrote, "and it would be childish to want to play with words. Therefore, we are everywhere in violation of the law."[14] When Prime Minister Edgar Faure dissolved the National Assembly in December 1955, annulling the state of emergency, the gap between reality and legality became still more evident. His successor, Guy Mollet, attempted to regularize the situation. Upon being granted "special powers" in March 1956, he issued a decree authorizing civilian administrators to "make all arrangements to assure the subsistence and the accommodation of people confined to compulsory residence."[15] By this point thousands of internees were amassed in "centers" throughout Algerian territory. Though "camps" were still theoretically verboten, officials matter-of-factly used the term in internal correspondence; after all, they were referring to isolated agglomerations of prisoners housed in tents or barracks, under armed guard, and—whatever Ciosi claimed—often surrounded by barbed wire fences.

As resident minister Robert Lacoste surveyed these facilities upon taking over from Soustelle in 1956, terminology must have been the least of his worries. The early *centres d'hébergement* were primitive, and problems with hygiene, food, personnel, and infrastructure abounded. Members of Lacoste's administration were also anxious about an expanding network of military-run detention camps, though they felt themselves by and large powerless to regulate it. In a March 1957 meeting, Captain Bianconi (an administrator with civilian responsibilities despite his military rank) sighed that, unfortunately, "the interdiction [of such camps] is impossible, for if this solution were accepted, we would risk inciting the army to eliminate suspects by some other means."[16] This chilling admission of resignation in the face of military lawlessness signaled much larger problems for the French Fourth Republic, and Lacoste subsequently did make an effort to impose oversight upon the army's detention regime. His decree of April 11, 1957, stipulated that prefects be made cognizant of arrests carried out by military personnel within twenty-four hours and that suspects be detained no longer than one month in the military camps, to which he affixed the label "*centres de triage et de transit.*" As Thénault observes, the primary result of these ineffectual strictures was to normalize "the militarization of internment."[17] Army camps quickly became more populous than civilian-administered centers: internal government documents from a few weeks apart in late summer 1957 give a figure of 5,750 *hébergés* compared to 9,834 occupants of *tri et transit* facilities.[18]

Little information about conditions at any of these locales was available to the metropolitan public. In 1956 the National Assembly did authorize a delegation of the Commission of the Interior to investigate allegations of problematic practices in the Oran department, but its March 1957 report, far from elucidating the situation, was devoted to defending the regime of exception. "To demand the protection of a judge or lawyer" for internees, it stated, "or to do away with exceptional procedure and go back to traditional rules, would in fact end up favoring [nationalist] clandestine action and rendering it invulnerable. The arrest of a member of a clandestine network is quasi-impossible within respect for the habitual laws."[19] One member of the delegation, Léon Hovnanian, refused to sign this declaration and attempted to organize a follow-up inspection; Lacoste's ministry effectively blocked his initiative by refusing to guarantee Hovnanian's group protection from right-wing protesters.[20] It also responded negatively to requests from Irving Brown for an ICFTU visit to the *centres d'hébergement*.[21]

Despite internal grumbling about "foreign intrusion" in "a territory of complete and total French sovereignty," subsequent French leaders did honor the decision made by Prime Minister Pierre Mendès France in February 1955, three days before his government fell, to permit the International Committee of the Red Cross (ICRC) access to the Algerian detention camps.[22] ICRC teams toured the camps in the spring of 1955, in spring 1956, fall 1956, spring 1957, and on six further occasions through 1962.[23] If Mendès France appears to have issued his invitation out of genuine concern over military "excesses," his successors bowed to precedent, reconciling themselves to ICRC interference by recalling that the organization's "policy of discretion" dictated that it disclose its findings only to the French government.[24] By welcoming Red Cross inspections, one Ministry of Interior official pointed out, France gained a "pretext to refuse the entry of [other] missions," notably the Red Crescent, and demonstrated its "liberal policy" without risking embarrassment.[25] Indeed, despite sharp criticisms contained in the ICRC reports, their confidential nature left the French free to assert at the United Nations that "the minutes of these missions . . . confirm that France has nothing to reproach itself for in its attitude toward those who fight against it."[26] To point out this dynamic is not to condemn the ICRC's rule of silence, which was in line with its own humanitarian goals. It is simply to underline that, as of June 1957, the French government had revealed virtually nothing to the metropolitan or global public about the internment regime in Algeria.

Given this near-absence of information, the leadership of the CICRC became attentive to the problem quite quickly. David Rousset began to consider the possibility of an Algeria investigation in the autumn of 1955, possibly alerted by Irving Brown to Algerian labor organizers' complaints. He was further gripped by an exposé headlined "Internment Camps Exist in Algeria" that appeared in *Témoignage chrétien* in January 1956. The piece was written by Denise Barrat, a Catholic anticolonialist radical whose Jewish family of origin had been murdered at Auschwitz. It was unsigned, but no knowledge of its author's identity was necessary to understand her reference to "sinister memories" as she presented two documents describing Djorf, a *centre d'hébergement* in the Constantine region. One, a letter from detainees, referred to the *centres* as "concentration camps" and "forced labor camps." The other, a leaked note from Djorf's director, described conditions as "extremely miserable."[27] Rousset appealed to *Témoignage chrétien* for further information, requesting a meeting with Barrat. Events then proceeded quickly. In the January–February issue of *Saturne*, he announced that the CICRC had "opened the Algerian dossier."[28]

Rousset's decision to address internment in Algeria did not likely strike him as a momentous one at first—and certainly not a step toward ruin. Despite Reumont's initial reluctance, the CICRC's previous foray into North Africa had neither produced conflict within the organization nor drawn much outside fire. Certainly, some readers had taken offense at the 1953 Tunisian *Livre blanc*: the pro-colonialist newspaper *Tunisie-France*, for instance, raged that "even if the analogy between Bordj-Le-Boeuf and Buchenwald or the Siberian mines did not cross your mind, you had better believe that the simple fact of your coming here has given credence to this calumny."[29] The Tunisian resident-general's administration had also objected to "inexactitudes" in the conclusions.[30] In 1954, it even seized a trans-Mediterranean shipment of three hundred copies of the *Livre blanc*. But Mendès France's minister for Tunisian and Moroccan affairs intervened to resolve the affair, affirming what Rousset already understood: the CICRC's reprimands may have ruffled feathers in Tunis, but, counterbalanced as they were with an exculpatory verdict on the "concentrationary" question, they had not earned the organization enemies in Parisian halls of power.

Thus in its first article on the Algerian situation three years later, the CICRC came out with guns blazing. Denouncing "flagrant illegalities in the means of arresting and detaining Muslim Algerians, both in the metropole . . . and in Algeria," the author (probably Bernard) mentioned "grave abuses" during interrogations on both sides of the Mediterranean but focused overwhelmingly on "the existence of internment camps" in Algeria. Complaints about insufficient rations were widespread, the existence of forced labor could not be ruled out, and demands for better hygiene and medical care "appear very common." Even had conditions in the camps been excellent, moreover, Algerians were landing in them by way of a blatantly unlawful process: "The Governor and the prefects intern [people] even though they have at their disposal only the right to send [them] into compulsory residence." And now that the state of emergency had been annulled, the "illegality . . . was aggravated and extended." In light of these alarming facts, the author announced, the CICRC "will pursue examination of the Algerian dossier in a systematic fashion. It will receive with the greatest interest all documents and testimonies that interested parties or observers can transmit to it."[31]

This article generated outrage among some of the commission's French members, signaling the corrosive effects that the Algerian conflict was to have upon an alliance of survivors whose shared anticommunism had long masked their ideological diversity on other counts. The first to protest was Dr. Charles Richet, one of the CICRC's earliest adherents. In a letter to Georges André, Richet angrily insisted that there was no need for the group to concern itself with conditions in the *centres d'hébergement*, since "compared with those of Auschwitz or Buchenwald, they are sentimental children's stories [*berquinades*]." By suggesting that the *centres* fell within the purview of an anti-concentrationary organization, he charged, the *Saturne* piece had provided ammunition to "the enemies of the French Army—those in Algeria, and even more so those in Russia, and still more those in Paris." No one, Richet declared, "reproves unjustified abuses more than me." But if, since the hostilities began, French forces had killed or harmed fifty or so innocent "natives" who found themselves in the wrong place at the wrong time, this was nothing compared to the numbers massacred by the other side. The CICRC, Richet counseled, would do better to concern itself with FLN crimes.[32]

A few days later, Rémy Roure expressed his dismay as well. Roure, unlike Richet, remained an active CICRC participant and a personal friend of Rousset. He was also a proponent of empire, believing that "France would be insignificant without its overseas extensions."[33] Now, in a series of frank notes, he told Rousset that hunting for abuses in Algeria was "at the least inopportune."[34] The CICRC's real mission was to "target above all the concentration camp system as applied by totalitarian governments. . . . But the investigation that has begun concerning Algeria throws into relief, first of all, just or unjust accusations against France. . . . Your reasoning in regard to principles is, as far as I am concerned, too absolute."[35] Hence Roure resigned from the commission. Rousset begged him to change his mind but remained unmoved by his argument. "From the start," he wrote, "we have affirmed that we would establish the truth everywhere that a problem arose, without being preoccupied with social, political, or historical considerations. In other words, we have always judged that no such considerations could justify a concentrationary system."[36] Of course, Rousset had compromised this standard on many occasions: the disagreement between him and Roure, as both men understood, stemmed not from a clash between politics and pure ethics but from a political difference of opinion about colonialism. Roure left the CICRC, a momentous loss.

A third member of the movement, one still more central to its operations, was also troubled by the *Saturne* article. This was Tillion. Having lived for much of the 1930s among isolated populations in the Aurès, Tillion was involved in efforts to limit the violence of the Algerian War from the start.[37] Most significantly, in 1955 she was recruited by Soustelle (a fellow anthropologist by training) to help launch the "Social Centers," hybrid vocational institutes, community empowerment associations, and social service providers intended to promote Franco-Algerian solidarity.[38] Tillion worked passionately toward this aim. The

FLN's revolt, in her eyes, was propelled by the "pauperization [*clochardisation*]" of the Muslim population and best addressed through a vigorous reformist program of economic and human development within the context of an abidingly French Algeria.[39] While she condemned colonists' abusive deeds over the centuries, Tillion insisted that independence was a false solution: to break ties with France would spell economic disaster for the Algerian people.[40] The only way out of the impasse was through reconciliation. From this premise, Tillion concluded that broadcasting French atrocities was ill-advised: it could only deepen the existing rift. "I do not speak willingly either of our crimes or of Algerian crimes," she wrote in 1957, since it was counterproductive to finding "a method of association that saves both sides."[41]

Such sentiments—shared in the war's early years by many French intellectuals, including some who later became leading anti-torture crusaders—left Tillion skeptical about Rousset's new direction.[42] Broadly speaking, she was not opposed at this point to approaching the Algerian War from the standpoint of a Nazi camp survivor. Her subtle and anguished late 1956 analysis of the unfolding tragedy, *L'Algérie en 1957*, was penned at the request of the ADIR; Ravensbrück deportees distributed copies in pamphlet form before it was published as a book. Tillion, whose analysis of the Nazi camp universe had always been resolutely economic, was willing to link its history to pre-1954 Algerian "pauperization": Hitler's "concentrationary system," she wrote, could be "considered an extreme rationalization" of the same exploitative dynamic that had driven Algerians to despair.[43] But engaging in such reflection was different from suggesting, even indirectly, that France might be constructing literal "concentration camps" in Algerian territory. This latter project struck Tillion as dangerous, though she did not contemplate abandoning the CICRC. Instead she set to work ensuring that the materials included in a follow-up March–May 1956 *Saturne* dossier would highlight humane internment practices and French officials' determination to remedy remaining shortcomings. As she collected documents from contacts in the former Soustelle administration (including Soustelle himself, who was enraged by Rousset's initiative), she especially sought evidence of "improvements" to the *centres* over time. Good news, she wrote to Ciosi, was vital: "You know how much our country is insulted on a daily basis."[44]

Ciosi assured Tillion that *Saturne* readers could rest easy: "the material conditions of existence" in the camps were "today not only acceptable, but *in every respect* very obviously superior to the average living standard of the people constrained to residence there."[45] David Rousset did not draw such encouraging conclusions from the documents Tillion produced. In his opinion, the administration's materials actually "confirm[ed] . . . for the most part, the declarations of the complainants." They referred to obligatory labor and violent mistreatment, revealed problems with medical care, and, most seriously, left no doubt about the "arbitrary character of the internments." To be sure, Rousset told Tillion, evidence such as Ciosi's original 1955 report (excerpts of which *Saturne* published, unsigned) did suggest that the most egregious abuses were local affairs, reproved by higher echelons of officialdom. Nevertheless, the CICRC would have to investigate—and it was "indispensable" that the initiative come from French members. The inquiry need not be a "spectacular" event, he wrote; "it is not a question of denouncing, etc. It is a question of seriously examining the problem, in such a way that we can make concrete proposals to the French Government for modifications and reforms, if this proves necessary." Such an effort would serve Tillion's politics, he intimated, by demonstrating French solidarity with Algerians.[46] It is unclear if she was convinced in the moment, but in April 1957 she joined the vote in favor of a CICRC inquiry into conditions of detention in French Algeria.

By this point, Rousset had been working behind the scenes for nearly a year and a half seeking appropriate petitioners to request that the mission take place. In late 1955 he entered into dialogue with the most important French antiwar organization to date, the Comité d'Action des Intellectuels contre la Poursuite de la Guerre en Afrique du Nord, hoping the CICRC might investigate at its behest.[47] This was not to be, for if Rousset's determination to launch an Algerian investigation alienated old friends such as Roure, it did not thereby reconcile him with remaining enemies on the French intellectual left. As Comité cofounder Edgar Morin later recalled disgustedly, his communist and Sartrean colleagues balked at any association with "the ignoble Rousset" or his "infamous Commission."[48] Rousset took their rejection with good humor, but the consequences were grave: had the CICRC gained the backing of this dynamic oppositional group, its eventual findings might have been deployed to maximum effect by figures like Daniel Guérin who viewed violence in Algeria through an explicitly anti-imperial lens.[49] Rebuffed by the Comité, however, Rousset was compelled to fall back instead on a familiar "apolitical" network of support, the community of French noncommunist camp survivors. In the end, the petition asking the CICRC to intervene came from the FNDIR, UNADIF, ADIR, and the Association Nationale des Familles de Résistants et d'Otages Morts pour la France.

The CICRC's previous attacks on the USSR may have hurt it with the Comité, but they proved a boon in its dealings with Mollet's government. Mollet guaranteed the commission not merely access to Algerian territory but—according to Rousset's triumphant account—"conditions of total independence and full freedom of action" to conduct unsupervised inmate interviews at any detention facilities members wished to visit, even those not "officially known" to exist.[50] The prime minister's cooperation is puzzling, since Rousset was by this point on the record supporting full independence as "the authentic aspiration of a great portion of the Algerian population," a position that was anathema to the administration. He was also signatory to a March 1957 petition to the government concerning "widespread" French atrocities.[51] Moreover, Mollet had already hit upon a seemingly lower-risk response to accusations of wrongdoing: the appointment of a handpicked Commission of Safeguard for Individual Rights and Liberties—complete with a token *ancien déporté* participant, none other than Charles Richet.[52] The composition and conclusions of a CICRC delegation could not be controlled in the same way as a government-appointed body. But Mollet, author of a public letter celebrating Rousset's stance during the Hungarian Revolution, evidently viewed the organization as an unworrisome ally.[53] The CICRC had never found a Western power guilty of operating a "concentrationary regime," and its broadcasting of the absence of "concentration camps" in Tunisia four years earlier had been positively useful to the French government. Organs of the press supportive of Mollet's Algeria policy exhibited no concerns about his wisdom in permitting the investigation. As the centrist Catholic *La Croix* noted matter-of-factly, "France doesn't seem to have much to fear from this report."[54]

Robert Lacoste, according to Martin-Chauffier, accepted his prime minister's accord with Rousset "while grumbling." After Mollet's government fell on June 13, his Radical successor Bourgès-Maunoury maintained the agreement, if "very reluctantly."[55] (He may have been reassured by the involvement of Tillion, who was friendly with members of his cabinet.)[56] The CICRC's American financial backers, however, were reluctant to support the initiative. Without access to relevant CIA archives, their position cannot be fully explained. The US government may not have operated during the Algerian War as the backroom FLN sponsor of paranoid French colonialist fantasy, but, broadly speaking, it was exasperated by the Fourth Republic's waging of the endless, divisive conflict. Allen Dulles of the CIA, having concluded in January 1957 that the French would inevitably have to leave Algeria, was unhappy to see their imperial stubbornness fuel anti-Western sentiment in the meantime.[57] His brother's State Department likewise viewed Mollet's approach to "pacification" with dismay. Nevertheless, given France's "transcendent importance" to Cold War security objectives, America could not afford to push its ally into neutralism or NATO withdrawal.[58] Thus throughout the war the US administration provided important military aid for the French and steered well clear of publicly questioning arrest, interrogation, or detention procedures in "sovereign" French territory. The prospect of funneling money into an international investigation of these sensitive matters—carried out by a group still regularly accused of being on the State Department's payroll—likely struck the CIA as undesirable.

Any conclusions we can draw about CIA actions pursuant to this judgment are provisional, since they rely largely on documents written by Rousset months later, including a narrative of the affair in a December 1957 letter to O'Shea. It is worth underlining, therefore, that Rousset may have misunderstood or misrepresented American motives. According to his account, the investigation in Algeria was carried out against US backers' clearly articulated wishes. "Your friends did not want an Algerian inquiry. They let me know this very firmly," he wrote.[59] Indeed, O'Shea explicitly warned him that, in proceeding, the CICRC was risking the loss of all funding. Rousset believed that the Americans were driven by understandable concerns: "They did not want to create additional difficulties for a government that is a friend."[60] But he was unsympathetic to such logic, responding that "the CICRC could in no case yield before this veto." And if O'Shea's "friends" abandoned the group in retaliation? Well then, "I would be sorry about it, but even faced with such an eventuality, to yield would be to hand in our resignations." The CICRC, as "an absolutely independent institution," would not be dictated to by outsiders.[61] And, in particular, it would not be dissuaded from carrying out its task in Algeria.

This uncompromising stance was in line with Rousset's convictions, but he may have also assumed that American opposition to the investigation was nominal, since it was widely believed in France that the US government favored the FLN. The CICRC's founder had in any case always interacted with his benefactors as if he was granting a service rather than receiving one—and he had emerged unscathed from his one previous clash with them, likewise concerning French violence in North Africa. This occurred in 1954, when the CICRC formally protested the killing of fourteen Moroccans in French police custody in Oujda. The funders expressed their displeasure through the intermediary of Michael Josselson; Rousset's response was witheringly dismissive. This was a matter of "fourteen dead men, not a bushel of fleas," he wrote. "You fear difficulties with the [French] Government? We have never held that consideration as decisive. And as it happens, I believe, you are mistaken. The difficulties are coming the Government's way from these blinkered policemen and these imbecilic, enraged colonialists—and the Government knows it."[62]

In 1957 Rousset again brushed aside American objections. He asked Karel van Staal for a subsidy from the habitually flush Dutch commission that would permit the Algerian voyage to proceed with minimal American funds; when this was granted, he began composing the investigative delegation. It was a heterogeneous group: Georges André, CICRC president; Lise Børsum, who had long pressed for the commission to focus on Western Europe's colonies; and Dutch jurist Cornelius van Rij, recently "president" at the China mock trial.[63] Tillion and Martin-Chauffier joined these three as observers, barred from formal participation by dint of their nationality. On June 18, 1957, all five climbed aboard the plane that would take them from Paris to Algeria—where, with the important exception of Tillion, none had ever set foot. Their charge: to determine whether "a structure presenting the characteristics of a concentration camp system could develop here."[64]

## Colonial Violence as Concentrationary Violence?

The CICRC delegation, sun-dazzled and disoriented, started their trip with three days of polite bureaucratic wrangling in Algiers. Their real work began on June 21 at the Barberousse prison and Beni-Messous triage center. Over the following two weeks they visited nine prisons (which housed formally charged or convicted individuals, not administrative detainees), nine military triage and transit camps, and all seven extant "*centres d'hébergement*," as well as Algiers's Hôpital Parnet à Hussein-Dey. At each facility, the delegates met with authorities, inspected the premises, and conducted confidential detainee interviews (three at Paul-Cazelles, six at Djorf, four at Dellys *camp de tri*, and so on). By the end of the trip, they had completed ninety-two such sessions and received written materials from other inmates. Members of the group also held additional meetings, most importantly with Dachau survivor Paul Teitgen, who now served as secretary-general of the Algiers police (though he would soon publicly resign, dismayed by torture).[65] The ceaseless activity proved draining, but—as Martin-Chauffier observed admiringly—the three principal investigators were tireless. As for Tillion, "fatigue has a curiously invigorating effect on [her]."[66] The French ethnographer's own scrawled notes—a cryptic amalgam of detainee names, camp populations, inmate complaints, administrators' claims, shorthand observations, reminders to herself ("See Teitgen about the Chafi brothers"), and shopping lists for political prisoners she knew personally from her Social Centers work ("milk butter sugar cheeses jam chocolate")—produce the same impression.[67]

Tillion's encounter with the prisons and camps inspected over the course of the voyage was clearly mediated by her previous experiences in Algeria. By contrast, the three official delegates possessed virtually no knowledge of the territory's complex social, cultural, geographic, and religious makeup, its political and ethnic divisions, or its long history of imperial rule and anti-imperial resistance. This did not mean, however, that they arrived in Algeria without preconceived notions: their expectations were conditioned by favorable beliefs about France. André, it must be said, was a strange leader for a mission purportedly oriented toward consideration of whether Belgium's neighbor was engaged in building "concentration camps." As Tillion recalled, "He adored the French army—he was in ecstasy before the French army—he was a Francophile as one can [only] be in Liège."[68] In a daily journal chronicling the voyage, later published in *Saturne*, Martin-Chauffier agreed: "France, for Dr. André, is a beloved and untouchable person, such that the mildest criticism or the slightest reservation becomes a blasphemy." Indeed, he wrote, all three delegates "love France very much. This sentiment is so acute that they would be sorry if their scrupulous honesty led them to any judgment that included a reprimand."[69] As for his own predispositions, Martin-Chauffier considered himself an opponent of colonialism and was willing to criticize his government's Algeria policy—but within the context of promoting an improved *Algérie française*.[70] Demanding "a return of France to her principles," he held out hope that, in time, "a single Algerian people could be born."[71]

French officials sought to convince the delegation that the only obstacle to such a happy resolution lay with the nationalists. They respected Rousset's agreement with Bourgès-Maunoury, and—with the exception of one sub-prefect who subjected the visitors to a tirade about Parisian intellectuals and "your friends" in the FLN—they treated André, Børsum, Van Rij, Martin-Chauffier, and Tillion well everywhere they went.[72] But into the inspection team's vacuum of contextual understanding, Lacoste's representatives poured a simple cause-and-effect narrative according to which the camp system was a desperately improvised, fundamentally humane response to the nationalist fighters' barbarity. To hammer home the point, the resident-general insisted that the delegates visit the site of the infamous "Melouza massacre," a slaughter of hundreds of villagers carried out by the FLN a month earlier in M'Sila Province, where the smell of carnage still hovered.[73] The strategy was effective. The following day, an indignant André wrote to Rousset that the situation in Algeria was "horrible for French people and non-FLN Muslims." For fighting nobly against the "bandits," he opined, "hats off to your compatriots."[74] In Algeria, then, more so than in Spain or even Tunisia (where the UGTT had played a crucial mediating role), CICRC participants were susceptible to the state's framing of administrative detention as a measure taken to combat sheer criminality rather than a form of political repression properly speaking.

André and his fellow investigators did take seriously their charge of inspecting conditions in the *centres*. The CICRC's narrow, remembrance-driven mandate, however, did not ultimately facilitate a critical approach to this task. Consider, for example, the group's June 22 visit to the most isolated of the civilian camps, Paul-Cazelles, languishing in the desert of Aïn Oussera two hundred kilometers south of Algiers. Paul-Cazelles was overflowing that summer with nearly two thousand inmates. "Swarming with mosquitoes and scorpions," and "baking like a cake in the sun" in 106-degree heat, the installation initially raised alarms for the CICRC's team of survivors. "Barbed wire, watchtowers, military guard—nothing is missing," Martin-Chauffier wrote. "[It has] all the appearances of the Nazi concentration camps that all five of us once knew." But the inspectors were quickly mollified: "In the interior, however, nothing of the sort." Detainees were "not forced to work," received letters, were decently fed (as always, the delegates sampled the food), and "do not undergo any abuses."[75] The draft version of the CICRC's *Livre blanc* on Algeria (never published, for reasons discussed below) stressed that the infirmary was "that of an army in the field," not that of Buchenwald.[76] Confirming that the sights, sounds, smells, and tastes of the *centre* did not match memories of their own past agonies, Louis Martin-Chauffier wrote, the delegates "all agree[d]" that even Paul-Cazelles, "the worst Algerian internment camp," had "no relationship with the Nazi concentration camps with regard to the conditions that are provided for detainees."[77]

The CICRC delegation was obviously correct to conclude that Paul-Cazelles was not Dachau or Auschwitz. But the observation was banal, not a miraculous insight only available to survivors. And it hardly offered cause for celebration. In truth, Paul-Cazelles was wracked with such severe administrative, financial, and infrastructural problems and such grave detainee abuses at the point of the CICRC visit that, weeks later, it was slated for closure.[78] The delegation missed most of this. Martin-Chauffier's description of the camp's "humane" director in his "Journal de Voyage," for instance, contrasts sharply with the ugly portrait of this "brutal, impulsive, violent, scheming" man painted in an internal government report written that same summer.[79] Of course Martin-Chauffier did not have access to confidential information on the director's misdeeds. Nevertheless, the case remains illustrative of larger problems with the CICRC's framework of "concentrationary" expertise and witnessing. The commission's delegates did not intuitively "see" more than non-survivors might have as they passed through the French internment centers, and what they did notice had to be filtered through comparison to Nazi Germany's very different camp system—all in order to provide the predictable answer to the single question that governed their work.

The German concentrationary standard not only set an impossible benchmark for a "guilty" verdict. It also mapped poorly onto the geography of French repression in Algeria. Everywhere they went, the delegates found themselves interviewing prisoners who wanted to discuss not the rations in Bossuet or the hygiene in St. Leu but rather the torture they had undergone *before* they entered the formal internment system. At the Tizi Ouzou prison, for example, the CICRC members were pleased to observe that the premises were "very orderly and clean" and that a doctor visited frequently. They hoped that dental visits might be instituted, as well. But when it came time to conduct interviews, the detainees did not wish to discuss teeth cleanings. Rather, they related events that had taken place months earlier, prior to their incarceration. One interviewee, arrested in January by the Chasseurs Alpins infantrymen, described being strangled with a scarf, electrocuted with a battery, drowned with a hose, and beaten. Another listed "electricity, water, hanging" as tortures he had undergone. A third showed André his ripped-away big toenail and the scar from electricity that encircled his penis.[80]

With their habitual respect for victim testimony, the CICRC investigators took such claims seriously and recorded detailed notes on each story. In a set of tables on graph paper that listed names, professions, arrest dates, tortures undergone, and injuries sustained, they even attempted to impose order on the bewildering and heartbreaking choral tale of suffering. Occasionally, the delegates expressed some private doubt about the accusations they heard, or speculated about the truthfulness of the victim ("Bears the trace of four scars . . . which he attributes to burn marks from electricity. It's possible . . ."). But most of their jotted comments were matter-of-fact: "Bears scars on both wrists (consequence of hanging)"; "Rope knots have left a scar on his right wrist"; "He was subjected to electricity (head of the penis, testicles, ear, skull, and neck). He presents scars on the ankles and wrists."[81] Any uncertainty they might have still harbored after collecting such observations disappeared during a meeting with Pierre Lambert, chief civilian administrator of the Oran region, who admitted that torture was indeed being used "to save innocent lives."[82]

Yet it was unclear what the delegation was to do with its distressing new knowledge. Several CICRC members had undergone brutal interrogations prior to their deportations; the practice of torture need not, theoretically, have fallen outside the organization's claims to authority by virtue of experience. In fact, three years earlier, Norwegian delegate Axel Middelthon had submitted a motion to the commission denouncing "all forms of torture" as denigrations of human dignity and calling on his fellow survivors to combat such violence even if it was committed "outside of the concentration camps."[83] But other members had rejected this proposal as a dilution of their mission, with Rousset taking the lead: survivors, he declared, "cannot take responsibility for the struggle against all aspects of the oppression of man," since "if we enlarged the well-defined sector in which the CICRC is competent, it would as a result lose its effectiveness and its reason for existing."[84] Beyond this pragmatic concern for defending his organization's institutional niche, Rousset simply did not believe that torture, "as serious as it is," was a threat to humanity on par with "concentrationary" abuses.[85] To testify against it was a good deed, even a duty, for all people. ("Since torture indubitably exists," he once wrote, "and there is no such thing as 'just' or 'unjust' torture, if I am silent about it that means I am accepting . . . a compromise with the crime.")[86] But it was not a moral imperative uniquely incumbent on *survivors* as such. Their vocation as eyewitnesses was spatially circumscribed by the barbed wire fence of "the camp."

In Algeria, the results of this restriction became clear. Confronted for two weeks with a parade of detainees covered in gruesome scars, lesions, and bruises, the delegation's members responded, bizarrely, by assuring themselves in each instance that the damage had been done *somewhere else* and was therefore tangential to their researches. At each stop, they dutifully recorded inmates' stories of outrageous brutalities, then moved on to tasting the food, touring the infirmary, inspecting the bedding, and quizzing the commandant about dental care. The disjuncture between such investigative activities and the ethical emergency occurring in French Algeria at this moment was such that Tillion left the foreign delegates increasingly to their own devices as she pursued more urgent projects—including, eventually, her now-famous secret meetings with FLN leader Saadi Yacef that may have helped produce a short-lived "truce" in the use of certain forms of violence by the two sides.[87] Martin-Chauffier, meanwhile, became frankly distraught over torture as the journey unfolded. Ordered by Dr. André on June 28 to remain in Algiers and recover from the rigors of travel (he had long struggled with poor health), he acquiesced "with joy." At last, rather than participating in another tedious round of camp visits that "can hardly now bring me any surprises," he would be able to "pursue my research on tortures and disappearances."[88] On July 3, after many meetings and with a troubled spirit, he flew home.

## Decisions and Discord

Three days later, in Paris, Martin-Chauffier joined the other exhausted travelers as well as Rousset, Bernard, Reumont, Goetschel, Calmarza, and Charles Coppieters't Wallant, a Dutch participant then serving as CICRC treasurer, at the commission's office to begin composing their conclusions. The group intended to publish a full-length Algerian *livre blanc* "as soon as possible."[89] In the short term, however, it needed to release a brief summary of findings. Since none of the delegates had concluded that the Algerian camp system was *concentrationnaire*, this should not have been a difficult task. But the encounter with French Algeria, in all its agony and complexity, had made evident that larger questions loomed beyond the usual yes-or-no query governing the inquiry. Individual participants were shaken in their previous certainties; both Tillion and Børsum used the word "shattered" to describe their emotional state at this juncture. The latter confessed that she could scarcely wait to escape the "nervous atmosphere" that enveloped the Rue Daunou office and return to Norway.[90] The tension was palpably divisive:

not only were the political stakes of this investigation higher than any previous one, but participants' political sentiments were far more disparate. Thus the drafting-by-committee process proved painful, and the document that emerged from it was internally inconsistent in voice and content.

Signed on July 21, released to Mollet, Bourgès-Maunoury, Lacoste, and France's president René Coty on July 22, and published in full on *Le Monde*'s front page on July 27, the CICRC "Conclusions" struck a generally severe tone.[91] The delegates addressed torture and disappearances directly—in fact, two sections of the report were organized under these headings. Their text did not traffic in euphemisms. "*Tortures*" outlined delegates' "conviction" that paratroopers, gendarmes, and police "have inflicted on arrested persons mistreatments and often genuine tortures (by electricity, by water hose, by bathtub, by hanging)." "*Disparitions*," meanwhile, cautiously but unmistakably suggested that arrestees reported missing, escaped, or "killed during an attempt to flee" might instead have been executed or tortured to death.[92]

These portions of the text were brief, but the report was expansive when it came to matters recognizably within the CICRC's field of expertise. The camp regime in Algerian territory, it maintained, was constructed on arbitrary and illegal premises. An understated passage on the triage centers, for example, noted that the commission "has been unable to find out in virtue of which legal text the administration can detain for a month a person who is subject neither to a committal order nor to a decree of internment." Once such a person was nevertheless detained, "no avenue of judicial recourse, no means of defense," was made available to him. The situation was, if anything, worse in the civilian-administered *centres*, where "the duration of the internment is unlimited" and prisoners, charged with no crime, might remain unenlightened for months or years about the reasons for their committal. Taken as a whole, the CICRC asserted, the present system of extrajudicial arrest and detention in Algeria did not provide "sufficient protection for the safeguard of man's freedom."[93]

Much of this critical text was Bernard's handiwork—no other CICRC participant grasped the Algerian legal situation as thoroughly as he did, and the former Drancy inmate had few illusions regarding his country's capacity for carceral violence.[94] But it was the German *univers concentrationnaire*, not the internment facilities of France's own none-too-distant past, that served as the CICRC's vital reference point. And however much some members appreciated Bernard's contributions (Børsum, for one, breathed a sigh of relief when he edited away "idiocies and banalities" drafted by other participants), it was the delegation that ultimately determined the verdict.[95] Hence the report could only offer the expected pronouncement: the Algerian camps, it declared, "do not constitute a concentrationary regime in the proper sense of the term."[96] This was hardly an enthusiastic exoneration. As Thénault points out, moreover, it was justified with a grudging double negative: "conditions of detention" in the *centres*, the delegates stated (just lines before the list of torture methods employed at pre-detention sites), were "not inhumane."[97] However lukewarm the judgment was, though, it constituted the most politically salient element of the text. As one British Foreign Office staffer observed, employing a double negative of his own, it meant that "the report as a whole," whatever criticisms it contained, was "by no means too unfavorable to France."[98] In the commission's black-and-white vision of a world comprising "concentrationary" and "non-concentrationary" regimes, France remained safely in the latter grouping.

It could not have been otherwise. As Maurice Duverger wrote in *Le Monde* just days before the CICRC "Conclusions" were released, concentration camps marked "the line of demarcation that separates democracy from dictatorship" in the post-1945 European imagination.[99] This imagination remained anchored in continental categories impervious to imperial reality. French rule had never even approximated "democracy" for millions of Algerian subjects, but this was immaterial to the country's classification (by noncommunists like Rousset and his colleagues) as a democratic, liberal, constitutional state. The notion that it would possess a *régime concentrationnaire* or anything approaching one was therefore unthinkable—concentration camps were totalitarian institutions, and political prison camps the apparatus of authoritarian rulers. Hence, despite offering a systematic critique of the Algerian internment system, the CICRC's report ended incoherently by pronouncing its authors "convinced" that any "errors" were "not widespread." As for why even localized abuses had occurred, the authors adopted the French government's language of emergency. In "an extraordinary situation and under the fire of an armed rebellion often accompanied by barbarous acts of terrorism," they explained, "measures taken" were "not always in conformity with principles of respect for the rights of man recognized by the French government and all democratic nations."[100] (In a draft, Tillion originally proposed "and all Western governments in normal situations." She thought the better of that particular formulation and crossed it out.)[101] As evidence of France's basic underlying rights-centric values, the delegates pointed to the fact of their own visit: "The care brought to bear by French authorities to maximally assure the delegation's freedom to investigate," read their final line," "is a guarantee that where breaches of the principle of freedom may have been committed, such breaches cannot become the rule of the repression."[102]

This closing sentence offered an affirmation of the CICRC's core belief in international accountability regarding political internment. It can also be read, however, as an overly hopeful assertion that if French state actors had recognized commission members' democratic "freedoms"—to travel, speak, write, dissent—then surely they would do the same for Algerian Muslim nationalists. Such a slippage was symptomatic of participants' continuing trouble with the challenge that colonial warfare posed to their essentially benevolent view of the West, and also to their persistently nonracialized understanding of how state violence tended to select its victims. The resultant ambivalence of the report as a whole left it open to pro-governmental exploitation despite its critical elements. *Le Monde* and *Combat* joined the *New York Times* and other English-language press organs in reporting both the positive and negative content of the "Conclusions" comprehensively. Meanwhile, *France-Observateur*, *Demain*, *L'Express*, *Franc-Tireur*, *Le Canard enchaîné*, and the communist papers *L'Humanité* and *Libération* (these last two swallowing their disdain for the CICRC) exclusively trumpeted the report's condemnatory portions, focusing on torture.[103] In the flood of coverage that the "Conclusions" provoked, however, both these approaches were subsumed by congratulatory readings.[104] The Socialist paper *Le Populaire*, for example, reported the CICRC findings under the headline "Algeria: 'No Concentration Camp Regime,' Certifies the Delegation of Former Deportees."[105] The story that followed did not mention torture. On the right, *L'Aurore* rejoiced that the CICRC had provided "precise facts" favorable to France to counter "vague allegations of Arab orators."[106] *Le Figaro*'s July 27 account was frankly tendentious, pasting together laudatory statements without context. Its August 9 issue was not much better—an article titled "There Is No Concentrationary Regime in Algeria" did allude to physical "abuses" but insisted that they were not "systematic."[107]

In *Témoignage chrétien*, Pierre Emmanuel raged against such "strange mutilation" of the CICRC's findings. "What caution, or what complicity," he wondered, had led his fellow journalists "to work over this text—a terrible text in its serene objectivity—so that it has the appearance of saying to all the vacationers of France, of Navarre, and of the Palais Bourbon that there's nothing here worth whipping a cat over, much less a paratrooper?" In Emmanuel's eyes, the camp survivors of the commission, "not only witnesses but judges," had acted to defend "the human race" without regard for base political considerations. They had been thwarted by a partisan and dishonest press. "If the French had a little bit of memory," he concluded, "their normal state would be nausea."[108]

Emmanuel's sentiments were understandable, but matters were more muddled than this. In fact, by the time he wrote, two members of the expedition who had ample "memory" but who supported France's continued presence in North Africa had themselves taken action to undermine the commission's collective testimony. Georges André held an August 8 press conference in Brussels at which he declared that, "as a private individual," he believed incidents of torture in Algeria were "much less numerous than some have claimed" and that, overall, "the accusations leveled against the French authorities in Algeria are excessive [*abusives*]." André also attacked the FLN at length, describing its atrocities and—venturing here into explicitly political terrain—dismissing its claim to represent widespread nationalist sentiment. "It is absurd to speak of a revolt of the Algerian people," he insisted; most "only ask to live peacefully" under continued French rule.[109] The French press, along with European Algerian publications such as *L'Echo d'Alger*, printed large excerpts from these "private" comments under headlines reminding readers that the speaker was president of the CICRC.[110]

Lise Børsum played a similar role to André's, though her underlying motivations were different. In August, the Norwegian socialist was wrong-footed by an Agence France-Presse report that quoted selectively from comments she had made in her own country's press, giving the misleading impression that she was an opponent of French rule in Algeria.[111] In an effort to prove that this was not the case, Børsum granted multiple interviews to French outlets in which she more or less justified the army's methods, including torture, as necessary to counter Algerian violence. Statements reported in *La Croix* were representative: "A democracy finds itself in a nearly hopeless situation in confronting terrorism," Børsum asserted. "[The CICRC's] task only touched on a minimal aspect of the Algerian tragedy, while the entire territory is struck by a disaster without end. Daily life is saturated with panic. Terrorists throw bombs everywhere. . . . They prefer to kill their own compatriots and their families, in a manner so cruel that it is necessary to go far back in history to find a similar cruelty."[112] Børsum's horror at FLN atrocities was heartfelt. But by suggesting that liberal democracies might be exempted from such norms as the prohibition on torture of their own citizens when confronting terrorism, she uncritically reproduced the government's logic of emergency. She also echoed its false claim that French violence in Algeria was exclusively defensive. This was a familiar line in France by mid-1957—Françoise Giroud at *L'Express* referred to it derisively as the "He started it, Teacher!" justification—and the anti-torture movement was already accustomed to parrying it.[113] But even the savviest activists could do little with the CICRC's "apolitical" testimony once André's and Børsum's personal comments were reported.

French government officials, meanwhile, found many uses for the commission report. These were strictly propagandistic; little indicates that they took the "Conclusions" as a cue to modify their actions. (One individual exception is Paul Teitgen, who cited them in his September letter of resignation.) The director of the Central Service of the *centres d'hébergement* noted in mid-August that his office never even "officially received" a copy from the resident-general.[114] But if Lacoste did not bother to provide camp administrators with the CICRC "Conclusions," he was happy to quote the document publicly. By this point, the official Commission of Safeguard had also finished its work, with some of its handpicked members reaching unexpectedly grave conclusions regarding torture; accordingly, the government blocked its findings for many months—and might have continued to do so forever, were they not eventually leaked in *Le Monde*. Under fire in the National Assembly over the matter, Lacoste quoted the final line of the CICRC report celebrating his government's embrace of oversight. "That's not all [the CICRC] said!" shouted Union Progressiste representative Robert Chambeiron. "It condemned and recognized tortures," added his colleague Pierre Cot. Lacoste shook off these interruptions by citing Børsum's interviews. This impartial Norwegian, he informed the Assembly, could affirm that the CICRC's inquiry "was conducted on the initiative of French authorities."[115] Overall, he concluded, "I can say that France has coped with humanity and with honor. Our action has been internationally checked and inspected." Conservative Félix Kir ended the discussion by asserting that the foreign investigators' compliments confirmed a simple truth: "In the eyes of the universe, France remains the pilot nation who, tomorrow as much as in the past, will steer peoples on the paths of civilization, peace, and liberty."[116]

Government representatives also selectively flaunted the CICRC "Conclusions" at the United Nations, the most crucial and contentious arena of their struggle to manage international responses to the conflict.[117] Speaking to the General Assembly on November 30, 1957, Foreign Minister Christian Pineau rebutted a Syrian delegate's demand for UN inspection in Algeria by insisting that sufficient international oversight had already been exercised by Rousset's commission. Pineau was himself a Buchenwald survivor and had denounced "concentration camps" in Algeria in the National Assembly in 1955.[118] Now, however, with his own Socialist party embedded in France's governing coalition, he quoted carefully from the CICRC "Conclusions" to stress the absence of a "concentrationary regime" in Algeria and assure UN delegates that "all means were being applied" to eliminate any scattered abuses. Like Lacoste, he emphasized the report's final line as proof of France's liberal norms. "In reality," he lectured, "France remains one of the places in the world where the control of public opinion over politics is exerted most strictly."[119] The fact that his fellow survivors had been permitted to conduct their inquiry proved it. No further investigation could be necessary after one conducted by these witnesses before other men.

Michael Rothberg points to figures such as Paul Teitgen as proof that personal remembrance of Nazi inhumanity tended to stimulate identification with Algerian suffering a decade later.[120] The story of the CICRC's Algerian inquiry, capped off by Pineau's use of it in his UN testimony, suggests that this represents a partial reading of the evidence. Survivors of the Resistance deportation were indeed well represented in the antiwar and anti-torture movements that developed in France during the 1954–1962 conflict, but it is unnecessary to invoke memory to explain their presence. These were politically engaged, intellectually prominent figures with experience confronting state power. Meanwhile, *anciens déportés* sympathetic to the French presence in Algeria drew just as forcefully on their authority as survivors to justify intensely apologetic positions on current French practices. For every Teitgen, there was also a Pineau; for every Rousset, a Richet. Memory, it transpired, was a powerful rhetorical weapon with which to wage the Algerian War, but it was not the lever for a unified, coherent response to its violence among survivors. In fact, the CICRC's confrontation with the war's atrocities definitively destroyed its members' belief that concentrationary trauma itself could dictate a common outlook on the post-1945 world. "The truth is that even the experience of an absolute like the concentrationary horror cannot determine a political position," Sartre and Merleau-Ponty had once chided Rousset. "When one comes back to life, for better or for worse . . . one chooses one's loyalties."[121] In this context, their analysis was correct.

## The Algerian Crucible and the Demise of the CICRC

By the fall of 1957, despite the rifts that the Algerian investigation had exposed within the CICRC, it was not yet obvious that the experience would spell the organization's end. In fact, David Rousset was ebullient about the report's reverberations in the press: "None of our other inquiries has had such a global impact," he rejoiced. He was particularly pleased that French Communist Party members had cited the torture findings. "Our worst enemies are disarmed," he exulted in early November. "If they accept the CICRC's authority in the Algerian affair, they must also accept it in other affairs the CICRC is working on." It is evident from such commentary that Rousset, now busily trying to complete the Algerian *Livre blanc*, still imagined that the inquiry had strengthened rather than eroded the commission's position as a cultural Cold War combatant.[122]

Rousset did remember that his American supporters had threatened to cut him off for carrying out the voyage. As he wrote to O'Shea, however, "I was able to believe, in light of the results obtained by this inquiry, and in particular the moral authority of the CICRC being so visibly and greatly reinforced, that this difficulty was smoothed over." Months later, he realized that he had miscalculated. The French government may have found ways to instrumentalize the report, but the commission's American backers remained "full of bitterness about this Algerian affair."[123] In a November 26 letter, O'Shea announced that "we are not certain that the budget for the fiscal year that begins July 1, 1958, will permit us to subsidize your activities on the present scale" since "it is difficult to sufficiently control certain aspects of our common work." O'Shea referred to "the use of our funds for aims not asked for—and sometimes not wanted—by us." Various unpleasant prospects now loomed. "We may be obliged," he claimed, "to reduce our current budget by half, or even to limit our financial aid to projects specified in advance . . . rather than a regular subsidy."[124]

Rousset was stupefied. "Your friends are perfectly within their rights" to withdraw their money, he retorted, but to do so would be folly. The Algerian investigation, far from harming their investment, had protected it: the CICRC's credibility and hence it effectiveness as a Cold War instrument depended upon its freedom to target Western powers. And communists' citations of the Algerian "Conclusions" represented a "capitulation" of great consequence. Overall, he claimed, "this inquiry exposed us to an audience that we have never previously known with the European left and in African and Asian countries. In other words, with precisely the world that your friends are extremely eager for us to influence." Though such arguments were intended to calm American concerns, Rousset declined to strike a deferential tone: the CICRC's backers could not and would not interfere in its decisions about where to investigate, which were dictated by members' conscience as camp survivors. "To have renounced the inquiry in Algeria would have been [for the CICRC] to disavow its own convictions," he wrote. The mission had been a moral necessity. Rousset also violently rejected O'Shea's suggestion that future payments cover only preapproved projects: "The CICRC could in no case accept financing that was constrained by political, administrative, or technical conditions. . . . To have the money, for example, to publish *Le Monde concentrationnaire soviétique* but none at all to dispense for an inquiry in Algeria, in Tunisia, or in the United States would compromise the CICRC to the very point of its existence."[125]

As other members of the CICRC's inner circle became aware of the unfolding financial calamity, Rousset did soften this stance somewhat. A "Resolution" co-signed with André, Reumont, and Coppieters't Wallant on March 8, 1958, proposed a meeting every three months with O'Shea's representative in Paris. At each such meeting, Rousset would propose "allocation of funds for a general type of spending such as: general administration, publication of *Saturne*, inquiry in a particular country," and so on. In the event that the Americans were unwilling to cover any specific expense, the representative would let this be known immediately so that a different sponsor could be found.[126] Rousset considered this proposal "the extreme of possible concessions" the CICRC could make without destroying its independence. But his overture was not sufficient.[127] On May 6, O'Shea informed him that, "as it is apparently impossible to satisfy my donors' natural desire for assurances concerning the expenditure of their contributions, we are regretfully obliged to withdraw our support at the end of the first six months of 1958."[128] The unthinkable had happened. The CICRC had been cut adrift.

Over the next year and a half, with the commission in financial disarray—thus ruling out publication of the Algerian *Livre blanc*—Rousset engaged in a series of unsuccessful attempts to secure new sources of revenue. The collapse of the French Fourth Republic following a military coup in Algiers on May 13, 1958, and the subsequent founding of Charles de Gaulle's Fifth Republic initially appeared propitious to his cause: the CICRC had friends in the new administration, notably the incoming minister of justice, Edmond Michelet.[129] The commission could not (or, rather, not openly) accept money from a single national government, but Rousset imagined that, with French support, a group of European countries could be persuaded to finance its efforts collectively, giving it "a status in its own domain comparable to that of the International Red Cross."[130] Michelet, aided by his *conseiller technique* and fellow Dachau survivor Joseph Rovan, made heroic efforts to further this unlikely plan among high-level officials. Meanwhile Rousset composed fervid letters to various figures—including de Gaulle—arguing that the CICRC's work could improve humanity's lot while also advancing France's interests.[131] Despite an anodyne letter from France's new president admiring the "seriousness," "objectivity," and "importance" of the commission's prior inquiries, these efforts yielded nil.[132] The *univers concentrationnaire* was far from the de Gaulle administration's major concerns. The Fifth Republic's architects also subscribed to an increasingly managerial and technocratic understanding of "expertise," distant from the CICRC's championing of embodied, intuitive knowledge born of experience. Thus Rousset's twin claims that "the concentrationary fact" remained the chief problem facing the world community and that *anciens déportés* alone could address this challenge both fell on deaf ears.

What is more, in the aftermath of the Algeria inquiry, the CICRC's leading French participants began to turn away from these two foundational ideas themselves. Certainly the loss of funding was devastating to the organization, but even those involved in attempting to remedy the financial collapse admitted that it was not, on its own, terminal. In Germaine Tillion's words, the movement's death had a "double" cause, which she sought to explain to Lise Børsum in an extraordinary 1960 letter. Tillion insisted that, money troubles aside, "a second reason" for the death of the CICRC "is, in my opinion, more determinative. This is loss of interest" among a French membership overwhelmed and disoriented by the ongoing Algerian crisis. "In France," Tillion wrote, "we have so many worries that we are not focused on these concentrationary questions. As for me, all my time is now taken up by Algeria and by trying to help Algerians."[133]

This final claim was true: Tillion was consumed at this point by the conflict. Why, though, could the CICRC not serve as the vehicle for her engagement?

Tillion pointed to the disjuncture, now clear to her, between the forms of violence tearing Algeria apart and the commission's exceedingly limited mandate. Torture, she explained to Børsum, constituted the true emergency in *Algérie française*: "For the moment, this is a much graver and more urgent problem than [political] detention, where—in contrast—everything has been done to make the regime very humane."[134] Other elements of French counterterrorism likewise struck her as more pressing targets for protest than the detention camps: state-sanctioned executions, for instance, which were a central object of criticism in her 1960 book on the war, *Ennemis complémentaires*. By the time she wrote to Børsum, she had also become concerned over the so-called "regroupment centers" managed by the military's *sections administratives spécialisées* to facilitate the forced resettlement of large swaths of the Algerian rural population. These camps, inhabited by roughly two million men, women, and children by war's end, had already been more populous than the *centres d'hébergement* in 1957, but their inhabitants were more akin to refugees than political prisoners. Thus the CICRC had never even considered inspecting them. Now, freed from the constraint of only seeking out abuses that mirrored Ravensbrück, Tillion came to view their construction as the "most decisive event for the future of Algeria" that had taken place in the course of the war.[135]

Multiple scholars have suggested that Tillion's activism during the Algerian conflict was driven by memory of her own experiences in World War II—and, throughout the later decades of her life, Tillion encouraged this interpretation.[136] However, in dispassionately considering the trajectory of her engagement, it is clear that the project of understanding French violence in Algeria was not facilitated for her by comparative invocations of memory. As she implicitly recognized in the letter to Børsum, posing "these concentrationary questions" had inhibited rather than enhanced her ability to "help Algerians" in the period of the CICRC inquiry; her insistence that the *centres d'hébergement* were not similar to Ravensbrück had been intellectually honest but politically unhelpful and ethically beside the point. Tillion's greater frankness about her own country's atrocities after 1957 was in part a consequence of disillusionment after France violated the "truce" she brokered with Yacef, but it also followed her recognition of the limited utility of her own ordeal as a yardstick for approaching the pain of others. "Experience," she wrote in 1964, was only useful in "guiding the imagination" under the condition that "one gets outside of oneself [*on sortir de soi-même*]."[137] Thus if she did continue to suggest, vaguely, that some French people who had sacrificed greatly during World War II were more attuned than others to Algerian "hardship," she avoided looking to the past in more specific terms.[138] The eventual death of the CICRC seemed to relieve her. She informed Børsum in her 1960 letter that she had a new project in mind, an "Association against Torture." This group, she stressed, would be organized differently from the CICRC: "It would not only be composed of former deportees."[139] Memory of their own earlier suffering, in other words, would not guide its members' response to the suffering of others in the present.

Louis Martin-Chauffier, in the aftermath of the 1957 voyage, likewise grew dissatisfied with the CICRC's exclusive focus on the *univers concentrationnaire* and its exaltation of survivors' memory. Relieved when he was compelled to quit the circuit of camp visits and turn his attention instead to torture, he continued along this trajectory when he returned to France, throwing himself into the agitation building around the recent "disappearance" of communist mathematician Maurice Audin in Algiers after an arrest by First Regiment paratroopers.[140] He informed *Saturne* readers that he would have signed on to the official CICRC delegates' "Conclusions," "but while adding, 'to be continued.' Not to supplement an inquiry so well led, but rather—as one might guess in reading these notes—to enlarge its object" by considering problems beyond political internment.[141] Hence, charged by Rousset in late 1957 with composing an "appraisal" to "complete" and "reinforce" the delegation's "Conclusions" for the still-envisioned *Livre blanc*, Martin-Chauffier instead drafted a long study of torture, explaining that there was "no need" to retread the same ground as Børsum, André, and Van Rij.[142] His numerous published articles in this period focused on what happened to "suspects" like Audin in the indeterminate zone of time and space "between arrest and 'deposit' into a triage camp"—that is, precisely the subject that the commission's strict focus on formal facilities had barred his colleagues from addressing head-on.[143] François Mauriac, for one, understood the implications of Martin-Chauffier's commentary for how to read between the lines of the official CICRC report: "We must conclude," he wrote sarcastically, "that concentration camps have a good side: at the point we are at, they fill the role of humanitarian institutions. . . . But unfortunately, before reaching this refuge of the camp, this haven of mercy, it sometimes happens that, as Martin-Chauffier discreetly puts it, 'people get lost along the way.'"[144]

Martin-Chauffier himself was never so acerbic as Mauriac. He retained great respect for the CICRC colleagues with whom he had traveled (especially Tillion) and was careful at all points to speak highly of their "valuable testimony"—and of the commission's testimonial mission in general.[145] As the CICRC began to collapse in 1958, he even attempted to help save it by volunteering to serve as editor-in-chief for a reimagined, revitalized *Saturne* that might pay its own way in sales. Nevertheless, a letter he wrote to Rousset laying out his vision for the journal's future also reveals his new rejection of the group's longtime structuring principles: it made no reference to the *univers concentrationnaire*, to political detention, or to survivors. "To improve the review without thereby altering its originality," Martin-Chauffier wrote, "we must first expand its subject to everything that concerns, in sum, man in society." He had already secured a handful of potential contributors, including Edgar Morin, Jean Cassou, and Georges Friedmann; none were *anciens déportés*.[146]

In preparation for his new role, Martin-Chauffier also conducted a survey of *Saturne* readers. Many of the 526 respondents expressed sentiments similar to his own. With the exception of one "simple Resistance deportee who would rather forget the horrors of the camp," the survivors among them did not wish for the Nazi concentrationary universe to fall into oblivion. In fact, several requested more articles considering "problems concerning former deportees" and providing "a reminder of their sufferings." They saw no need, however, for the journal's contemporary subjects to be narrowly inspired by memory. Readers demanded coverage of myriad topics outside the CICRC's existing remit, from the US penitentiary system to Latin American dictatorships, "decolonization," "disarmament," the plight of "Arab refugees," the "deterioration of parliamentarianism" in France, and—especially—torture and terror in Algeria. Some expressed ideological criticism—"sterile and outdated anticommunism" was a representative charge, and a suggestive one given the self-selecting nature of the *Saturne* readership. Even an exclusively noncommunist set of respondents, it seems, had limited enthusiasm at this juncture for Cold War shibboleths. In a France at war (and a Fourth Republic in terminal crisis), they were "more preoccupied by our own problems." Others explicitly expressed dissatisfaction that the review was "too exclusively devoted to that form of crime against freedom that the concentration camps constitute." Were not "other kinds of offenses against human dignity" equally worthy of protest? Anise Postel-Vinay, deported alongside Tillion to Ravensbrück in 1943, drew attention to the Algerian "Conclusions" to make the point. The text had "disappointed" her, she wrote. "You didn't have to be afraid to get to the bottom of the horrors: 'conditions of internment' are only one link in the chain."[147]

Summarizing the reader responses in January 1959, Martin-Chauffier noted that Algeria was "the burning subject among all others for the French," just as it was for him personally. Thus he interpreted the survey results as a positive referendum on his decision to "extend the field of our researches beyond the concentrationary problem, strictly speaking," and as a directive for the journal, going forward, to "condemn everything, in this boiling world in transformation, that threatens man in his imprescriptible rights and in his sovereign spirit."[148] What this may have looked like in practice is unknowable. With funding still beyond reach and member interest collapsing, the CICRC disbanded late that year. *Saturne* was never published again. Martin-Chauffier, who eventually became a reluctant advocate of Algerian independence, confronted the terrible violence of the war's final years on his own, outside the confines of the anti–concentration camp movement.[149]

And what of David Rousset? He clung to some of the commission's foundational principles to the end. Concentrationary internment was incommensurable with other crimes, he continued to maintain, and survivors' memory of the Nazi camps provided them with a universal standard for judging the world's carceral regimes. Even after the CICRC had for all intents and purposes ceased to exist, he insisted stubbornly that it remained "the only group that is truly qualified" to investigate political detention in the post-1945 world.[150] In one respect, however, his confrontation with the violence of decolonization did lead him to repudiate the project that had consumed a decade of his life. Continuing down a trajectory that had begun for him with the Hungarian Revolution, Rousset rejected bearing witness as a universally adequate form of engagement, a sufficient means of taking part in the ongoing drama of the present-day world. He had recognized even before the investigation that it was impossible to contain his ardor about the Algerian War within the CICRC's putatively apolitical bounds: "I am the only one up to now to have published an analysis of the dossier of internees and prisoners in Algeria," he pointed out in January 1957. "But it would be to commit another error, no less grave, to find here a pretext to be silent about the essential matter, that is to say about politics."[151] Testifying to prisoners' suffering would not substitute for other forms of commitment, struggle, and judgment. While the CICRC continued to exist, Rousset argued that his "elementary right to have the freedom to express myself personally on political questions" simply had nothing to do with the organization.[152] But—despite his distress—the death of the CICRC freed him to pursue this "essential matter" much more openly and extensively.

He did so primarily through the medium of journalism, penning editorials for major publications including *Le Monde* and *Le Figaro*, as well as francophone journals such as *Afrique action*, throughout the remainder of the war. His major themes were the urgent necessity of negotiation with the FLN—which he insisted was France's only possible interlocutor, for better or worse—and the desirability of widespread decolonization. Late in the conflict, Rousset also militated in print against the far-right Organisation de l'Armée Secrète as it attempted to disrupt the process of independence and destabilize de Gaulle's government, a position that required him to attack the pusillanimity of politicians such as Lacoste in a way that would never have been possible while he still needed to curry their favor for the CICRC.[153] Within the substantial body of texts he produced in this period, only a single 1961 piece was devoted to internment. It was not concerned with human suffering and was not written from the viewpoint of the *ancien déporté*. Instead, it called for France to liberate its Algerian prisoners as an act of "political wisdom," as many were seasoned FLN leaders whose presence on the outside would be helpful in advancing the peace process.[154]

After the war ended, Rousset served as a correspondent for *Le Figaro littéraire* and *Nouvelle Candide*, reporting optimistically on the newly independent Algeria. Describing his brisk schedule of North African travels in a cordial letter to Georges André in September 1962, he wrote, "It goes without saying that these voyages have nothing to do with the concentrationary questions that occupied us for so many years."[155] This offhanded dismissal of a major portion of his life's work may well have masked deep feelings of loss. Rousset, though, even in his immediate postwar books of testimony, had always been a man fundamentally oriented toward the present and the future. As ever, he turned his eyes forward. As ever, he chose his loyalties.

# EPILOGUE

In the 1958 edition of *The Origins of Totalitarianism*, Hannah Arendt revised her famous reflections on concentration camps written a decade earlier. Arendt still believed that the camp was "the most consequential institution of totalitarian rule" ever created. She also continued to assert, citing Rousset, that such sites "serve as the laboratories in which the fundamental belief of totalitarianism that everything is possible is being verified." Into the 1958 *Origins*, though, she inserted a new passage on the memory of Hitler's concentrationary system in the post–World War II period. Here she insisted that "the horror, or the dwelling on it," had failed to serve as "the basis of a political community." Efforts to ground a new internationalism "on the common European experience of the concentration camps," Arendt wrote, "have foundered in much the same manner as the attempts following the first World War to draw political conclusions from the international experience of the front generation. In both cases it turned out that the experiences themselves can communicate no more than nihilistic banalities."[1] According to this grim analysis, survivors' remembrance of their ordeal had ultimately led nowhere.

My intent in writing this book has not been to endorse Arendt's perspective. Members of the International Commission against the Concentration Camp Regime drew far more than "banalities" from their passage through the Nazi camps, and their crusade was in no sense a nihilistic endeavor. It is true, however, that by the end of the decade their community had foundered, as members confronted the limits of their effort to marshal concentrationary memory on behalf of global humanity. Just as Arendt argued (and as Sartre and Merleau-Ponty had also once insisted, in their own way), the shared experience of victimization did not provide survivors with an enduring basis for unified political action. Nor did the aspiration to deploy the memory of Nazi evil for exemplary, present-oriented purposes translate into an unproblematically "universalizing" moral project. CICRC members, like all postwar Europeans, actually remembered World War II's violence in particular ways that permitted some comparisons and analogies while blocking recognition of other potential connections between past and present—and, crucially, disallowing a frank discussion of real differences between the two. The commission's singular construction of the meaning of the Nazi camps served it well in its early anti-Soviet initiatives—no surprise, since it had been forged for precisely such purposes. But when members turned their attention elsewhere—and when, contemporaneously, the forms of state violence that the USSR was using began to shift—the whole intellectual scaffold began to totter. In the confrontation with internment and torture in French Algeria, it broke down completely. The group could not adapt to the changed political circumstances presented by France's terrible decolonizing conflict while continuing to defend the timeless relevance of its binary categories.

The CICRC's eventual collapse points toward the perils of constructing moral universals on the basis of historically specific traumas, however epochal they may have been, however transparent their lessons may appear. More broadly, it also indicates the fragility of ethico-political appeals to the authority of lived experience. A melancholic David Rousset acknowledged the problem himself in a 1961 letter to Edgar Morin: "The truth," he wrote, was "that experience of a certain depth is not directly communicable; that men are imprisoned in their own tragedy and are uninterested in their neighbor's tragedy; that victims are just as odious with regard to other victims as their masters; and that to move beyond this condition requires either a great deal of love or a creative effort at reflection."[2] The suffering of others, Rousset suggested, was not really accessible via memory of one's own losses. To comprehend it required strenuous processes of compassion and imagination rather than spontaneous acts of identification.

Two years later, Rousset apparently set these concerns aside when, with the Algerian War over and France again largely oriented toward continental affairs, he made a last-gasp effort to revive the CICRC. This time, Rousset imagined the group as a joint undertaking of German and Soviet camp survivors, explaining the idea as a further expression of his hope for "full solidarity" among all concentrationary victims across borders. "Our fraternity," he wrote to former gulag inmates in a new "Appeal" in *Le Figaro*, "has taken the profound sense of our sharing in the same knowledge, through having lived through the same ordeal, the same suffering, the same society. . . . [W]e are, the ones and the others, survivors. And survivors of the two greatest concentrationary systems that history has yet known." Together, they could undertake a mission of "detection, prevention, and teaching" on "the planetary scale," preventing the recrudescence of horror through bearing continued witness to "the incomparable depths of the concentrationary universe, the immense social and human impact of this crime among all crimes."[3]

If the original "Appeal" had landed like a bomb in a crowd, this reworked version was a mere stone dropped in water. French political and intellectual life in 1963 simply lacked the explosive tensions over communism and carcerality that had existed in 1949.[4] What is more, the author of *L'Univers concentrationnaire*—like other political survivors—no longer possessed the stock of cultural capital he once had. With Charles de Gaulle back in power, the legacy of the French Resistance was becoming institutionalized and fused with the state. France's community of *anciens déportés de la Résistance* was still highly esteemed in the mid-1960s, but its members were not called upon to serve as the country's chief symbols of unbroken national honor through the dark years now that de Gaulle—the "man of June 18, 1940"—could fill this role himself. Individuals like Rousset, whose pre-deportation activities as a *résistant* had been non-martial and tied to left-wing politics, barely registered in the new Gaullist version of history, according to which, as Henry Rousso writes, "the Resistance was above all a military action."[5]

A further difference also distinguished 1963 from 1949. In the wake of the Eichmann trial in Jerusalem and various other milestone literary, cultural, and political events of the late Algerian War years, the "concentrationary" model for understanding Nazism's *crime majeur* was slowly beginning to be replaced in France and elsewhere with a conceptual framework more heavily focused on extermination—in particular, the Jewish genocide.[6] To posit an abrupt paradigm shift in the nature of Western remembrance of World War II's violence would certainly be to overstate the case: as the history related in this book shows, the emergence of what we now call "Holocaust consciousness" was already under way in the 1950s, and it would intensify in a complex series of fits and starts over the next three decades.[7] Nevertheless, the genocide unmistakably did become more central to French collective memory in the early sixties. Consider François de Menthon, the prosecutor whose celebrated opening address at Nuremberg had referenced Jews only in passing, singling out "Resistance martyrs" instead as the war's emblematic victims. Now, in the preface to a 1961 *Dossier Eichmann* produced by the Centre de Documentation Juive Contemporaine, Menthon called the extermination of Europe's Jewish population "the most monstrous crime of Hitler and of National Socialism" and the one that "will remain in History the exceptional crime, the symbolic crime." As the paradigmatic example of humanity's capacity for evil became the extermination of "the race of Israel, because they belonged to the race of Israel and for no other reason," the era of possibility for the CICRC's comparative project came to a close.[8]

If efforts to mobilize concentrationary memory for present-oriented purposes became unfeasible in an era of more genocide-centric remembrance, the legacies of David Rousset's vision of expert witnessing nevertheless lived on in unexpected ways. Notably, the work he and other political survivors carried out in the 1940s and 1950s to invest the act of testimony with heroic qualities, as an extension of the Resistance project, was one precondition for the eventual "advent of the witness" for Jewish survivors. It was by drawing on participants' enormous postwar prestige as patriotic resisters that the CICRC had been able to insist so influentially that other victims who possessed no such credentials—Chinese *laogai* inmates, Spanish *anteriores*, Tunisian nationalists—also had to be heeded as brave, resilient, and dignified bearers of remembered truth. Ironically, then, the commission's exclusionary membership policies facilitated its ability to generalize a set of positive associations around the figure of the victim-who-testifies, thereby helping to produce the initial conditions of possibility for cultural and legal recognition of Holocaust survivors as "witnesses" too. For this reason, although the commission's ambivalent relationship to Jewish survivors primarily reflects the social imaginary of its own era, it also constitutes a prehistory to the later rise of the Shoah victim as the modern West's quintessential "*homme-mémoire.*"[9]

The CICRC also helped to forge a path for future humanitarian and human rights projects oriented around the task of bearing third-party witness to ongoing suffering, chiefly by insisting that truthful *témoignage* rather than revolutionary *engagement* was the chief duty of committed intellectuals. Groups initially geared toward denouncing the plight of political prisoners such as Amnesty International and the Groupe d'Information sur les Prisons (GIP) are particular cases in point.[10] It seems likely that the CICRC served as a concrete source of inspiration for the two men who helped Michel Foucault to organize the GIP in 1971, both of whom knew Rousset well: historian of the Nazi genocide Pierre Vidal-Naquet and *Esprit* editor Jean-Marie Domenach.[11] Amnesty was not likewise directly linked to the CICRC, but the organization nevertheless echoed many of Rousset's principles in its espousal of ethical minimalism, its discourse of apoliticism or antipolitics rooted in disappointment with earlier revolutionary dreams, its privileging of testimony, its focus on prisons as paradigmatic institutions of authoritarian power, its emphasis on negative liberties—in particular, the right to dissent—and, last but not least, its activist orientation toward knowledge production, on-site inquiry, and public reportage.[12]

Despite this family resemblance, Amnesty and other international NGOs such as Human Rights Watch that gained prominence in the post-1968 era were not direct descendants of Rousset's erstwhile commission. They were rights-based initiatives, as the CICRC had emphatically not been, and therefore possessed a very different ethical, legal, and intellectual framework for condemning state violence. Yet it does not follow from this that the CICRC's history is therefore irrelevant to how scholars ought to approach the much-contested genealogy of human rights. On the contrary, the saga of the commission's rise and fall may help illuminate why Western Europeans' embrace of the language of the Universal Declaration of Human Rights was so belated, demonstrating that one factor was the competing existence in the 1940s and 1950s of more compelling moral vocabularies. Samuel Moyn has written that human rights triumphed in the 1970s because it was at last "widely understood as a moral alternative to bankrupt political utopias."[13] But the platform of rights did not emerge as a lone alternative to maximalist, overtly political visions of global humanity such as Leninist Marxism. It also won out over *other* supposedly apolitical internationalisms geared toward protecting bodies from suffering. In the postwar intellectual terrain of recently occupied countries such as France, the Netherlands, and Belgium, the idiom of defending victims of the "concentrationary universe" in the name of the patriotic martyrs of Nazi atrocity initially appeared to offer a more persuasive way to articulate the need for supranational oversight of state violence than the project of protecting "rights"—not to mention a more provocative counter to revolutionary leftist visions of utopia. The eventual collapse of this project can thus be viewed as one chapter in the disjointed chronicle of how human rights eventually emerged as the dominant discursive framework for asserting and protecting human dignity.

Former CICRC stalwarts were not individually central to the human rights revolution of the 1970s and beyond. Many died before it began. Cornelius van Rij passed away in 1960, Karel van Staal in 1961. In 1965 Damien Reumont succumbed to a "long and painful" illness with "admirable resignation and serenity."[14] Rémy Roure died in 1966 and Edmond Michelet in 1970. Others remained involved in various domestic and international activist projects on a more modest scale than during the CICRC's heyday. Théo Bernard, for example, collaborated with his old courtroom opponent Joë Nordmann in a legal battle against "racial hatred" in the form of anti-Arab prejudice.[15] An aging Martin-Chauffier likewise increasingly framed his political engagements as antiracist interventions rather than acts of anti-concentrationary combat. In January 1972, he warned fellow survivors of a growing "racial xenophobia" in France; the following year, he sarcastically condemned the French right for its flirtation with racism "as an abstract doctrine, of course, and completely independent of the millions of Jews who were victims of this 'theory.'" In May 1975, he marked the thirtieth anniversary of Bergen-Belsen's liberation not with an homage to Resistance martyrs but with reflections on his "horror at what racism, in all its forms, seeks to destroy."[16]

Germaine Tillion's activist commitments, meanwhile, took many forms after the Algerian War. For one thing, she was the only former member of the CICRC who remained substantively preoccupied with incarcerated populations, helping to develop the Fifth Republic's prison education system. Her exceptionality in this regard is not surprising: she had always been more concerned than any other participant with "the excesses of all penal systems, in general," including those for common-law criminals.[17] In the 1970s, as her ethnographic career flourished, Tillion also agitated against global slavery, poverty, and gendered oppression: "Do human rights also concern women?" she demanded in 1978.[18] Like Martin-Chauffier, Tillion spoke more and more often about the perils of racial hatred; she was particularly vocal in reminding her compatriots that "Hitler, in the middle of the twentieth century, carried out the most monstrous massacre in history" in the name of "race."[19] Over the years—and through multiple revised editions of *Ravensbrück*—Tillion continued to grapple with the relationship between that massacre and the suffering she herself had endured as a Resistance deportee. "Ravensbrück," she wrote in 1989, "was only a spoke on a wheel, the immense revolving concentrationary wheel. At its center, there was the flame of the Jewish genocide."[20]

David Rousset pursued a course different from that of Martin-Chauffier or Tillion after the CICRC's breakdown, continuing his evolution away from *témoignage* and toward explicitly political combat. After a transitional period in journalism he joined France's Gaullist movement, becoming what was known as a *gaulliste de gauche*. He was won over, he claimed, by the president's "Algerian policy" and "resolute opposition to the war in Vietnam."[21] Rousset was even elected to the National Assembly as a representative of the Isère department in 1968. There he sat on the Commission des affaires culturelles, familiales et sociales and intervened in debates over education policy and union bargaining rights. Rousset also championed the cause of youth protesters. These included his son Pierre, active in a leftist groupuscule called the Jeunesse Communiste Révolutionnaire and jailed for several weeks in July 1968. David Rousset, labeled "a sort of overweight Danton" by the bemused author of a long *New York Times Magazine* profile, agreed with his son that revolutionary change was necessary in France—but insisted that it could be initiated "from the summit."[22] "Deep Gaullism," he declared, "expressly condemns capitalism. . . . And that is why *we are with the students today and not against them*. We speak in the same spirit as the revolting and revolutionary students. We bear the same anxiety and the same desire."[23] Once the excitement of '68 passed, however, Rousset lost patience with the rote business of parliamentary politics. He separated from the Gaullists in 1971 and quit the legislature entirely in 1973, after a single term.

From this point forward, Rousset entered a period of relative obscurity. He continued to author new books on historic Soviet violence and current world politics, but they gained little attention compared to his earlier work.[24] His marginalization persisted following the French publication of Aleksandr Solzhenitsyn's *Gulag Archipelago* in 1974: Rousset might have experienced a sense of "strange and total communion" with its author, but his idiosyncratic ideological affiliations placed him outside the antitotalitarian discourses now developing among France's "new philosophers."[25] Thus, for example, André Glucksmann's influential 1975 book on the Soviet camps, *La Cuisinière et le mangeur d'hommes*, did not mention Rousset—in fact, it misrepresented Sartre and Merleau-Ponty's 1950 response to his "Appeal" as an element of their quarrel with Camus.[26] Rousset also became extraneous to academic and popular conversations about Nazi atrocity, thanks to his increasingly unfashionable insistence that a "functional identity" existed between extermination centers and concentration camps.[27] Except for an extraordinary 1967 public debate with Pierre Vidal-Naquet over the particularity of Jewish victimhood, scholars of the genocide did not overtly criticize the author of *L'Univers concentrationnaire* for this position.[28] After all, Rousset had always acknowledged the staggering immensity of Jewish losses during World War II.[29] But as time went on and the "extermination paradigm" gained force, he slipped out of mainstream public discussion about Nazi violence. His former prominence as an interpreter of concentrationary society, along with his role as leader of the most consequential survivors' movement of the postwar period, was largely forgotten.

The story of the International Commission's historic rise and fall did not quite end with this slide into oblivion, however. In the 1990s, after the collapse of the Soviet Union, the CICRC tentatively entered a surprising new phase of its afterlife. First, Rousset's "concentrationary" model for understanding Nazi criminality began to enjoy what Moyn has called a "potent European renaissance" as world events sparked fresh intellectual interest in dehumanizing forms of internment—both as a historic phenomenon of Soviet power and as a seemingly omnipresent and recurrent feature of modern societies.[30] Second, for a handful of scholars and other authors in search of twentieth-century moral heroes untainted by compromise with either communism or fascism, figures such as Rousset and Tillion took on new appeal as historical icons. Thus, in some quarters, these aging Resistance deportees were now celebrated as witnesses to the century's horrors, combatants for truth and justice in an era of lies and violence, and symbols of hope in circumstances that would have led others to despair.[31] The CICRC, according to its post–Cold War admirers, had dared to draw universal lessons from the Nazi camps when others had not. In a process that itself revealed the selective functioning of collective memory, the partisan nature of the commission's allegiances and the exclusions upon which its universalism had been premised were rendered invisible in these new accounts. What mattered now was only that members had been on the "right side" of history.[32]

Praise for the CICRC has continued in recent years even as its deeds have slowly begun to pass out of living memory. The last of the group's leading members to die was Germaine Tillion, who passed away in 2008 at age one hundred. In 2015, Tillion was symbolically reburied in France's Panthéon as a national hero. In a poignant speech marking the occasion, President François Hollande announced that the Ravensbrück survivor's moral courage—her refusal to "join any party except that of the suffering flesh of humanity"—had been most evident when "with David Rousset, she denounced the concentrationary universe beyond the Iron Curtain."[33] Rousset, sadly, did not live to hear the president invoke his name that spring day at France's secular shrine: he had died of a cerebral hemorrhage in late 1997, at age eighty-five. His passing, too, was met with a wave of respectful remembrance and acclaim from observers on all sides, in sharp contrast to the polarized reactions that his activities had once inspired. "Through his works, through his life as a whole, David Rousset leaves behind a true moral testament," opined *La Croix*.[34] Jean-Michel Krivine, reclaiming Rousset for the Trotskyist far left, hailed his "passion and his loyalty to the generous ideal of his youth."[35] *Libération*, meanwhile, honored his "pioneering" role as "the first to describe the concentrationary universe."[36] And a warmly phrased obituary in *L'Humanité*, the communist daily that had once accused him (correctly, as it turned out) of working in secret collusion with American intelligence, referred unblinkingly to his vital work exposing "the Soviet concentrationary system." The title of the piece, above all, served notice of how much the political landscape had changed in the decades since the "Appeal." "David Rousset," it read. "Death of a Great Witness."[37]

# Notes

**ARCHIVAL ABBREVIATIONS**

AA          Fonds André Alers (in CEGESOMA)
AB          Fonds Alfred Balachowsky (in IP)
ADB         Archives Diplomatiques, Brussels
AGA         Asuntos Exteriores (dossier Dirección de Europa, 1950–1952–53,
            01–95, Organización Mundial Congresos y Conferencias. El movimiento
            anticoncentralista en relación con España), Archivo General de la
            Administración, Alcalá de Henares, Spain
AN          Archives Nationales, Paris
ANOM        Archives Nationales d'Outre-Mer, Aix-en-Provence, France
BDIC        Bibliothèque de Documentation Internationale Contemporaine,
            Nanterre, France
BNA         British National Archives, Kew
BNF         Bibliothèque Nationale de France (Richelieu), Paris
CDJC        Centre de Documentation Juive Contemporaine, Paris
CEGESOMA    Centre d'Études et de Documentation Guerre et Sociétés
            Contemporaines, Brussels
CF          Fonds Commission Française contre le Régime Concentrationnaire
            (in BDIC)
DR          Fonds David Rousset (in BDIC)
GT          Fonds Germaine Tillion (in BNF)
HIA         Hoover Institution Archives, Stanford University, Stanford, California
IB          Irving Brown Papers (in MMA)
IISH        International Institute of Social History, Amsterdam
IMEC        Institut Mémoires de l'Édition Contemporaine, Caen, France
IP          Institut Pasteur, Paris
JE          José Ester Borrás Papers (in IISH)
JL          Jay Lovestone Papers (in MMA or HIA)
LMC         Fonds Louis and Simone Martin-Chauffier (in IMEC)
LS          Fonds Luc Somerhausen (in CEGESOMA)
MMA         George Meany Memorial AFL-CIO Archives, University of Maryland,
            Silver Spring
NARA        National Archives and Records Administration of the United States,
            College Park, Maryland

**INTRODUCTION**

1. David Rousset, "Au secours des déportés dans les camps soviétiques: Un appel de David Rousset aux anciens déportés des camps nazis," *Le Figaro littéraire*, November 12, 1949. This appeal and other texts by Rousset are reproduced in David Rousset, *La Fraternité de nos ruines: Écrits sur la violence concentrationnaire (1945–1970)*, ed. Grégory Cingal (Paris: Fayard, 2016); David Rousset and Émile Copfermann, *David Rousset: Une vie*

*dans le siècle, fragments d'autobiographie* (Paris: Plon, 1991). This and all other uncredited translations throughout this book are my own.

2. Déclaration de Gérard Rosenthal, Sténotypie (Cabinet Bluet), fasciscule 4, Cour d'Appel de Paris, 11ème chambre, Audience du 10 juin 1953, F/Delta/1880/56/3/2, DR BDIC.

3. Suzanne La Follette, letter to David Rousset, January 16, 1951, F/Delta/1880/56/1/2, DR BDIC.

4. An exception to this variety of reading is Thomas Wieder, "L'affaire David Rousset et la figure du déporté: Les rescapés des camps nazis contre les camps soviétiques (1949–1959)," in *Qu'est-ce qu'un déporté? Histoire et mémoires des déportations de la Seconde Guerre Mondiale*, ed. Tal Bruttmann, Laurent Joly, and Annette Wieviorka (Paris: CNRS, 2009), 311–331.

5. Hannah Arendt, "The Concentration Camps," *Partisan Review* 15, no. 7 (July 1948): 742–763, at 742.

6. Tzvetan Todorov, *Mémoire du mal, tentation du bien: Enquête sur le siècle* (Paris: Laffont, 2000), 164.

7. Rousset, "Au secours des déportés."

8. Annette Wieviorka, *Déportation et génocide: Entre la mémoire et l'oubli* (Paris: Plon, 1992); Pieter Lagrou, *The Legacy of Nazi Occupation: Patriotic Memory and National Recovery in Western Europe, 1945–1965* (Cambridge: Cambridge University Press, 2000); Regula Ludi, *Reparations for Nazi Victims in Postwar Europe* (Cambridge: Cambridge University Press, 2012).

9. David Rousset, "Le sens de notre combat," in Paul Barton [Jiří Veltruský], *L'Institution concentrationnaire en Russie (1930–1957)* (Paris: Plon, 1959), 15.

10. David Rousset, "À propos des changements qui auraient lieu dans la société soviétique (III)," *Saturne* 6 (January–February 1956): 6–33, at 14–15.

11. Samuel Moyn, *The Last Utopia: Human Rights in History* (Cambridge, MA: Harvard University Press, 2010). For rebuttals of the persistent myth that human rights quickly triumphed in postwar Europe thanks to Holocaust memory see Marco Duranti, "The Holocaust, the Legacy of 1789 and the Birth of International Human Rights Law: Revisiting the Foundation Myth," *Journal of Genocide Research* 14, no. 2 (2012): 159–186; Samuel Moyn, *Human Rights and the Uses of History* (New York: Verso, 2014), 87–98.

12. Human rights discourse of course relies implicitly on appeals to memory too, but demands its systematic decontextualization: see Daniel Levy and Natan Sznaider, *Human Rights and Memory* (University Park: Pennsylvania State University Press, 2010). On World War II memory and French humanitarianism see Eleanor Davey, *Idealism beyond Borders: The French Revolutionary Left and the Rise of Humanitarianism, 1954–1988* (Cambridge: Cambridge University Press, 2015).

13. David Rousset, *L'Univers concentrationnaire* (Paris: Fayard/Pluriel, 2011), 36, 181.

14. For a revelatory recent history of concentration camps worldwide see Andrea Pitzer, *One Long Night: A Global History of Concentration Camps* (New York: Little, Brown, 2017). There is an extensive, contentious body of scholarship on the historical relationship between colonial concentration camps and the Nazi model. A still more polemical literature considers whether the Soviet gulag inspired the Germans. For an overview of these debates see Nikolaus Wachsmann, "Comparisons and Connections: The Nazi Concentration Camps in International Context," in *Rewriting German History*, ed. Jan Rüger and Nikolaus Wachsmann (New York: Palgrave Macmillan, 2015), 306–325. Wachsmann concludes that proponents of both types of arguments for influence "turn faint parallels into firm precedents, and loose connections into causal links" (318). On the issue of similarity between camp systems (as distinct from influence) see notes below.

15. Rousset, "Le sens de notre combat," 15.

16. Rousset, *L'Univers concentrationnaire*, 186–187.

17. Carolyn J. Dean situates Rousset's project in a longer genealogy in *The Moral Witness: Trials and Testimony after Genocide* (Ithaca, NY: Cornell University Press, forthcoming), chap. 2.

18. Rousset, *L'Univers concentrationnaire*, 181; Rousset, "Au secours des déportés," emphasis in original. On the discursive power of appeals to the "authority of direct experience" in relation to Europe's other great twentieth-century trauma see Jay Winter and Antoine Prost, *The Great War in History: Debates and Controversies, 1914 to the Present* (Cambridge: Cambridge University Press, 2005), 174. See also Joan W. Scott, "The Evidence of Experience," *Critical Inquiry* 17, no. 4 (Summer 1991): 773–797, at 790; Martin Jay, *Songs of Experience: Modern American and European Variations on a Universal Theme* (Berkeley: University of California Press, 2006).

19. Rousset, "Au secours des déportés," emphasis in original.

20. Ibid.

21. "CICRC 5ᵉ Session," April 1–2, 1951, GT BNF.

22. Rousset, "Au secours des déportés." On NGO expertise, and on the link between expert status and "witnessing," see Peter Redfield, *Life in Crisis: The Ethical Journey of Doctors without Borders* (Berkeley: University of California Press, 2013), 98–123; Michal Givoni, *The Care of the Witness: A Contemporary History of Testimony in Crises* (Cambridge: Cambridge University Press, 2016).

23. David Rousset, *Les Jours de notre mort* (Paris: Fayard/Pluriel, 2012).

24. Samuel Moyn, "In the Aftermath of Camps," in *Histories of the Aftermath: The Legacies of the Second World War in Europe*, ed. Frank Biess and Robert G. Moeller (New York: Berghahn Books, 2010), 49–64, at 54.

25. Ibid. As Moyn notes, Rousset's "concentration paradigm" has resurfaced in certain strands of theoretical literature, for example Giorgio Agamben's *Remnants of Auschwitz*, trans. Daniel Heller-Roazen (New York: Zone Books, 1999). However, Rousset's vision was distinct from Agamben's: he rejected the idea that Auschwitz was "everywhere" as a dangerous conflation of what was, to his mind, the essential distinction of the post-1945 world. His crusade against "the camps" was not an element of a broader critique of carcerality, social control, or modernity. It should therefore also be distinguished from recent approaches to the biopolitics of "encampment"—for instance, Michel Agier, ed., *Un monde de camps* (Paris: La Découverte, 2014).

26. François Bondy, "Le combat de Persée," *Preuves* 13 (March 1952): 45–47, at 45.

27. Annette Wieviorka, *The Era of the Witness*, trans. Jared Stark (Ithaca, NY: Cornell University Press, 2006), 88. See also Samuel Moyn, "Bearing Witness: The Theological Roots of a Secular Morality," in *The Holocaust and Historical Methodology*, ed. Dan Stone (New York: Berghahn Books, 2012), 127–142; François Azouvi, *Le Mythe du grand silence: Auschwitz, les Français, la mémoire* (Paris: Fayard 2012).

28. Pierre Emmanuel, "L'hymne des témoins" [1945], in *Babel* (Paris: Desclée, De Brouwer, 1951), 250–259, at 257.

29. On the gulag's demography see Steven A. Barnes, *Between Death and Redemption: The Gulag and the Shaping of Soviet Society* (Princeton, NJ: Princeton University Press, 2011); on that of the Nazi camps see Nikolaus Wachsmann, *KL: A History of the Nazi Concentration Camps* (New York: Farrar, Straus and Giroux, 2015). Much scholarly polemic over totalitarianism hinges on comparison between the two camp systems. For recent appraisals see Wachsmann, "Comparisons and Connections"; Dietrich Beyrau, "Camp Worlds and Forced Labor: A Comparison of the National Socialist and Soviet Camp Systems," in *The Soviet Gulag: Evidence, Interpretation, and Comparison*, ed. Michael David-Fox (Pittsburgh: University of Pittsburgh Press, 2016), 224–249. Mark Mazower offers a consideration of the atypicality of National Socialist violence and consequent

problems with using it as a "benchmark," in "Violence and the State in the Twentieth Century," *American Historical Review* 107, no. 4 (October 2002): 1158–1178. For a diffuse effort to situate the Nazi project within a global "century of camps" see Joël Kotek and Pierre Rigoulot, *Le Siècle des camps: Détention, concentration, extermination. Cent ans de mal radical* (Paris: Lattès, 2000).

30. On French awareness of the gulag before the 1950s see Pierre Rigoulot, *Les Paupières lourdes, les Français face au goulag: Aveuglements et indignations* (Paris: Éditions universitaires, 1991).

31. David Rousset, "Au secours des déportés."

32. La Commission Française d'Enquête, "Lettre ouverte aux organisations de déportés à l'étranger," reproduced in Commission Internationale contre le Régime Concentrationnaire, *Livre blanc sur les camps de concentration soviétiques* (Paris: Pavois, 1951), 230–234, at 233.

33. François Mauriac, "Au secours des déportés dans les camps soviétiques," *Le Figaro*, November 14, 1949.

34. Despite Arendt's reliance on his depiction of the Nazi camps, Rousset was not a significant figure in the elaboration of totalitarian theory: he was uninterested in the concept and rarely employed the term. On the idea of totalitarianism in the 1940s–1950s see especially Abbott Gleason, *Totalitarianism: The Inner History of the Cold War* (New York: Oxford University Press, 1995); Anson Rabinbach, "Moments of Totalitarianism," *History & Theory* 45, no. 1 (February 2006): 72–100; Udi Greenberg, *The Weimar Century: German Émigrés and the Ideological Foundations of the Cold War* (Princeton, NJ: Princeton University Press, 2015); James Chappel, *Catholic Modern: The Challenge of Totalitarianism and the Remaking of the Church* (Cambridge, MA: Harvard University Press, 2018). On post-1968 French antitotalitarianism see Michael Scott Christofferson, *French Intellectuals against the Left: The Antitotalitarian Moment of the 1970s* (New York: Berghahn Books, 2004); Stephen W. Sawyer and Iain Stewart, eds., *In Search of the Liberal Moment: Democracy, Anti-Totalitarianism, and Intellectual Politics in France since 1950* (New York: Palgrave Macmillan, 2016); Julian Bourg, *From Revolution to Ethics: May 1968 and Contemporary French Thought* (Montreal: McGill–Queen's University Press, 2007).

35. M. Merleau-Ponty and J.-P. Sartre, "Les jours de notre vie," *Les Temps modernes* 51 (January 1950): 1153–1168, at 1155.

36. For an argument that human rights could only "break through" once détente-era activists rejected "the bleak Manichean worldview that divided states into friends and foes" see Jan Eckel, "The Rebirth of Politics from the Spirit of Morality: Explaining the Human Rights Revolution of the 1970s," in *The Breakthrough: Human Rights in the 1970s*, ed. Samuel Moyn and Jan Eckel (Philadelphia: University of Pennsylvania Press, 2013), 226–260, at 255. Literature on NGOs often narrativizes a historic turn "away from strident anticommunism" toward true universalism: e.g., see Howard Tolley, *The International Commission of Jurists: Global Advocates for Human Rights* (Philadelphia: University of Pennsylvania Press, 1994), 49.

37. "Conference of the Unforgetting," *Economist*, May 26, 1951, 1225.

38. Commission Internationale contre le Régime Concentrationnaire, *Livre blanc sur le travail forcé et les institutions concentrationnaires dans la République Populaire de Chine*, vol. 1 (Paris: Centre International d'Édition et de Documentation, 1957), 25.

39. See especially Dwight A. McBride, *Impossible Witnesses: Truth, Abolitionism, and Slave Testimony* (New York: NYU Press, 2001); Alexandra Garbarini, "Document Volumes and the Status of Victim Testimony in the Era of the First World War and Its Aftermath," *Études arméniennes contemporaines* 5 (2015): 113–138.

40. CICRC, *Livre blanc sur les camps de concentration soviétiques*, 156. Carolyn J. Dean offers a somewhat different interpretation of Rousset's deployment of testimony and assessment of its historical significance in *Moral Witness*, chap. 2.

41. Germaine Tillion, letter to Lise Børsum, December 15, 1960, folder "CICRC Commission française, correspondance, 1950–1960," GT BNF.

42. Avishai Margalit, *The Ethics of Memory* (Cambridge, MA: Harvard University Press, 2002), chap. 5; Tzvetan Todorov, *Les Abus de la mémoire* (Paris: Arléa, 1995), 31. For critiques of Todorov's treatment of Rousset as embodying "exemplary memory" see Carolyn J. Dean, *Aversion and Erasure: The Fate of the Victim after the Holocaust* (Ithaca, NY: Cornell University Press, 2010), 80–89; Samuel Moyn, *A Holocaust Controversy: The Treblinka Affair in Postwar France* (Waltham, MA: Brandeis University Press, 2005), 165–166.

43. Michael Rothberg, *Multidirectional Memory: Remembering the Holocaust in the Age of Decolonization* (Stanford, CA: Stanford University Press, 2009), 5 and 179.

44. Michael Rothberg, "Introduction: Between Memory and Memory; From Lieux de mémoire to Nœuds de mémoire," *Yale French Studies* 118/119 (2010): 3–12, at 11; Rothberg, *Multidirectional Memory*, 193.

45. Charles Richet, letter to Georges André, March 18, 1956, F/Delta/1880/99/ 4, DR BDIC.

46. Like other historians who study recipients of CIA funding, however, I ultimately rely most heavily on the organization's own records to reveal "strong traces" of the clandestine relationship: see Hugh Wilford, *The Mighty Wurlitzer: How the CIA Played America* (Cambridge, MA: Harvard University Press, 2008), 9. My own Freedom of Information Act requests to the CIA were denied.

47. Robert Darnton, "In Search of Enlightenment," *Journal of Modern History* 43 (1971): 113–132, at 132; Dominick LaCapra, *History and Criticism* (Ithaca, NY: Cornell University Press, 1985), 91–93.

48. Akira Iriye, *Global Community: The Role of International Organizations in the Making of the Contemporary World* (Berkeley: University of California Press, 2002), 65.

49. Tony Judt, *The Burden of Responsibility: Blum, Camus, Aron, and the French Twentieth Century* (Chicago: University of Chicago Press, 1998); see also Tony Judt, *Past Imperfect: French Intellectuals, 1944–1956* (Berkeley: University of California Press, 1992).

50. Neal Oxenhandler, *Looking for Heroes in Postwar France: Albert Camus, Max Jacob, Simone Weil* (Hanover, NH: University Press of New England, 1996).

51. Wieviorka, *Era of the Witness*.

52. CICRC, *Livre blanc sur les camps de concentration soviétiques*, 19; Didier Fassin, *Humanitarian Reason: A Moral History of the Present* (Berkeley: University of California Press, 2011), 166. See also Nicolas Guilhot, "The Anthropologist as Witness: Humanitarianism between Ethnography and Critique," *Humanity* 3, no. 1 (Spring 2012): 81–101.

53. Luc Boltanski, *Distant Suffering: Morality, Media, and Politics*, trans. Graham Burchell (New York: Cambridge University Press, 1999), 35–54.

54. Statement of Léon Mazeaud, transcript, "Conférence de presse donnée par M. David Rousset mardi 15 novembre 1949," F/Delta/1880/53/2, DR BDIC.

## 1. SURVIVORS AS WITNESSES IN POSTWAR FRANCE

1. When the war in Europe ended, approximately 1.5 million French citizens found themselves in the territory of the former Third Reich, including 950,000 prisoners of war.

2. Serge Klarsfeld, *Le Mémorial de la déportation des Juifs de France* (Paris: Klarsfeld, 1978); Annette Wieviorka, *Déportation et génocide: Entre la mémoire et l'oubli* (Paris: Plon, 1992). The majority of those deported and dead were foreign Jews lacking French citizenship.

3. Fondation pour la Mémoire de la Déportation, *Le Livre-mémorial des déportés de France arrêtés par mesure de répression et dans certains cas par mesure de persécution*, vol. 1 (Paris: Tirésias, 2004), 17 and 53–54. The Fondation worked with the following definition of "*déporté*": "any person arrested and displaced against his will, outside the borders of France, in the Nazi concentration camp system and in the prisons of the Reich or of its allies" (16). It further distinguished between "repression" deportees and "persecution" (i.e., racial) deportees, primarily limiting its own work to counting the former. By including additional categories of individuals—notably, those arrested in the annexed territories of Alsace-Moselle, as well as Spanish republican refugees transferred from prisoner-of-war camps to concentration camps—the *Livre-mémorial* tallied a total of 86,048 people deported as a measure of repression; the Fondation continues to revise this number upward on its website, http://www.bddm.org/liv/index_liv.php/.

4. Bertrand D'Astorg, "Réflexions d'un survivant," *Esprit* 139 (November 1947): 691.

5. Louis Martin-Chauffier, speech at 42 rue des Martyrs, n.d. [April 14, 1947], MCH13, LMC IMEC. See also Alina Bothe and Markus Nesselrodt, "Survivor: Towards a Conceptual History," *Leo Baeck Institute Year Book* 61, no. 1 (November 2016): 57–82.

6. On the postwar development of "the witness" as a self-conscious identity for survivors (by and large construed as Shoah survivors) see Annette Wieviorka, *The Era of the Witness*, trans. Jared Stark (Ithaca, NY: Cornell University Press, 2006); Annette Wieviorka, "From Survivor to Witness," in *War and Remembrance in the Twentieth Century*, ed. Jay Winter and Emmanuel Sivan (Cambridge: Cambridge University Press, 1999), 125–141; Margaret Taft, *From Victim to Survivor: The Emergence and Development of the Holocaust Witness, 1941–1949* (London: Vallentine Mitchell, 2013); Zoë Vania Waxman, *Writing the Holocaust: Identity, Testimony, Representation* (Oxford: Oxford University Press, 2006). See also Dominick LaCapra, *History in Transit: Experience, Identity, Critical Theory* (Ithaca, NY: Cornell University Press, 2004).

7. On the profusion of references to *témoignage* in postwar French literature see Yannick Malgouzou, *Les Camps nazis: Réflexions sur la réception littéraire française* (Paris: Classiques Garnier, 2012), 68; on resisters' *témoignage* beyond the deportee community, Laurent Douzou, *La Résistance française: Une histoire périlleuse. Essai d'historiographie* (Paris: Seuil, 2005), 83–134. On the problematic nature of the concept of "primary witnessing" see Dominick LaCapra, *History and Memory after Auschwitz* (Ithaca, NY: Cornell University Press, 1998), 21.

8. Within the vast literature on testimony's evidentiary status see especially Shoshana Felman and Dori Laub, *Testimony: Crises of Witnessing in Literature, Psychoanalysis, and History* (New York: Routledge, 1992); James E. Young, "Between History and Memory: The Voice of the Eyewitness," in *Witness and Memory: The Discourse of Trauma*, ed. Ana Douglass and Thomas A. Vogler (New York: Routledge, 2003), 275–283; Michael Bernard-Donals and Richard Glejzer, eds., *Witnessing the Disaster: Essays on Representation and the Holocaust* (Madison: University of Wisconsin Press, 2003); Geoffrey Hartmann, ed., *The Humanities of Testimony*, special issue of *Poetics Today* 27, no. 2 (Summer 2006).

9. Samuel Moyn, "In the Aftermath of Camps," in *Histories of the Aftermath: The Legacies of the Second World War in Europe*, ed. Frank Biess and Robert G. Moeller (New York: Berghahn Books, 2010), 49–64, at 54.

10. See Wieviorka, *Déportation et génocide*, 79–118; Annette Wieviorka, *1945: La découverte* (Paris: Seuil, 2015); Olga Wormser-Migot, *Le Retour des déportés: Quand les alliés*

*ouvrirent les portes* (Brussels: Éditions Complèxe, 1997); Marie-Anne Matard-Bonucci and Édouard Lynch, eds., *La Libération des camps et le retour des déportés* (Brussels: Éditions Complèxe, 1995).

11. French citizens did not pass from concentration camps into long-term residence in displaced person camps. For overviews of liberation, repatriation, and resettlement beyond the French case see Dan Stone, *The Liberation of the Camps: The End of the Holocaust and Its Aftermath* (New Haven, CT: Yale University Press, 2015); G. Daniel Cohen, *In War's Wake: Europe's Displaced Persons in the Postwar Order* (New York: Oxford University Press, 2011); Ben Shephard, *The Long Road Home: The Aftermath of the Second World War* (New York: Knopf, 2011).

12. Wormser-Migot, *Le Retour des déportés*, 285.

13. See Sune Persson, "Folke Bernadotte and the White Buses," in *Bystanders to the Holocaust: A Re-evaluation*, ed. David Cesarani and Paul A. Levine (London: Frank Cass, 2002); Sarah Helm, *Ravensbrück: Life and Death in Hitler's Concentration Camp for Women* (New York: Nan A. Talese, 2014), 593–610; L'Amicale de Ravensbrück and L'Association des Déportées et Internées de la Résistance, *Les Françaises à Ravensbrück* (Paris: Denoël/Gonthier, 1971), 295–321.

14. Edmond Michelet, *Rue de la liberté: Dachau 1943–1945* (Paris: Seuil, 1955), 234.

15. H. L. J. P. [Henri, Léon, and Jean-Pierre] Mazeaud, *Visages dans la tourmente, 1939–1945* (Paris: Albin Michel, 1946), 341.

16. Alain Navarro, *1945: Le retour des absents* (Paris: Stock, 2015), 20–24.

17. Pieter Lagrou, *The Legacy of Nazi Occupation: Patriotic Memory and National Recovery in Western Europe, 1945–1965* (Cambridge: Cambridge University Press, 2000), 118.

18. Ibid., 120.

19. Regula Ludi, *Reparations for Nazi Victims in Postwar Europe* (Cambridge: Cambridge University Press, 2012), 49.

20. Michel Reynaud, *L'Enfant de la rue et la dame du siècle: Entretiens inédits avec Germaine Tillion* (Paris: Tirésias, 2010), 163.

21. Louis le Bartz, "Le retour de nos martyrs," *Le Croix*, May 8, 1945; Bernard Lecache, "Sortis de l'ombre," *Les Lettres françaises* 55 (May 12, 1945); Emmanuel d'Astier, "L'autre retour," *Libération*, April 25, 1945; "Dante n'avait rien vu," *Libération*, April 20, 1945.

22. Charles Richet and Antonin Mans, *Pathologie de la déportation* (Paris: Plon, 1956). Richet should not be confused with his father Charles Richet (*père*), the Nobel Prize–winning physiologist.

23. On the experience of reentry see Patrick Coupechoux, ed., *Mémoires de déportés: Histoires singulières de la déportation* (Paris: La Découverte, 2003), esp. 385; Matard-Bonucci and Lynch, *La Libération des camps*, 111–127.

24. [Émile Copfermann], "Entretien avec Susie Rousset," F/Delta/1880/27/3, DR BDIC.

25. Cited in David Rousset and Émile Copfermann, *David Rousset: Une vie dans le siècle, fragments d'autobiographie* (Paris: Plon, 1991), 77.

26. Charles Richet, Alfred Gilbert-Dreyfus, Henri Uzan, and Louis Fichez, "Les séquelles des états de misère physiologique," *Bulletins de l'Académie nationale de médecine* 132 (1948): 649–653.

27. The phrase is Rémy Roure's, from his introduction of David Rousset, "Conférence du 17 novembre 1947, Théâtre Sarah Bernhardt," F/Delta/1880/45/2, DR BDIC.

28. See Maria Teresa Brancaccio, "From 'Deportation Pathology' to 'Traumatismes psychiques de guerre,'" in *The Politics of War Trauma: The Aftermath of World War II in Eleven European Countries*, ed. Jolande Withuis and Annet Mooij (Amsterdam: Aksant, 2010), 79–106; Christian Pross, *Paying for the Past: The Struggle over Reparations for Surviving Victims of the Nazi Terror* (Baltimore: Johns Hopkins University Press, 1998);

Michael Dorland, *Cadaverland: Inventing a Pathology of Catastrophe for Holocaust Survival* (Waltham, MA: Brandeis University Press, 2009).

29. Décret no. 53–438, *Journal officiel de la République française*, May 17, 1953, 4467–4468.

30. Charlotte Delbo, *Mesure de nos jours: Auschwitz et après*, vol. 3 (Paris: Éditions de Minuit, 1971), 54.

31. Reynaud, *L'Enfant de la rue*, 168, 158, 170.

32. Joanne Reilly, *Belsen: The Liberation of a Concentration Camp* (New York: Routledge, 1998), 155.

33. Born Agnès Franquinet in 1908 (and usually called Catherine, her Resistance nom de guerre), she had married Jacques Goetschel just months before his deportation.

34. Paul Arrighi, "Notes sur le système concentrationnaire," *Revue d'histoire de la Deuxième Guerre Mondiale* 2, no. 8 (October 1952): 35.

35. Jacqueline Fleury, "Paroles prononcées par l'auteur à la messe du 25 avril 1997 à Saint Jacques du Haut Pas," http://www.memoresist.org/resistant/helene-maspero/. See also François Maspero, *Les Abeilles et la guêpe* (Paris: Seuil, 2002), 11–12.

36. Jean Rabaud, "L'humour noir a sauvé David Rousset," *Lyon libre*, July 16, 1946.

37. Michelet, *Rue de la liberté*, 247.

38. Louis Martin-Chauffier, *L'Homme et la bête* (Paris: Gallimard, 1947), 243.

39. Wieviorka, *Déportation et génocide*, 188.

40. Louis Martin-Chauffier, *Chroniques d'un homme libre* (Paris: Éditions FNDIRP, 1989), 104.

41. Tzvetan Todorov, *Mémoire du mal, tentation du bien: Enquête sur le siècle* (Paris: Laffont, 2000), 167, 172.

42. Future CICRC members in the Assembly included Louis Martin-Chauffier, Paul Arrighi, Edmond Debeaumarché, Albert Forcinal, Henri Teitgen, and Rémy Roure.

43. See Olivier Lalieu, "La création des associations d'anciens déportés," in *La France de 1945: Résistances, retours, renaissances*, ed. Christiane Franck (Caen: Presses Universitaires de Caen, 1996), 193–203; Olivier Lalieu, *La Déportation fragmentée: Les anciens déportés parlent de politique, 1945–1980* (Paris: Boutique de l'histoire, 1994), 23–83; Wieviorka, *Déportation et génocide*, 132–135.

44. Wieviorka, *Déportation et génocide*, 126.

45. Martin-Chauffier, *L'Homme et la bête*, 195. See also Terence Des Pres, *The Survivor: An Anatomy of Life in the Death Camps* (Oxford: Oxford University Press, 1976).

46. Wieviorka, *Déportation et génocide*, 162 and 182.

47. Rémy Roure, "L'enfer de Buchenwald et d'Auschwitz-Birkenau," *Le Monde*, April 21, 1945; Albert Rohmer, "Aussenkommando H de Neuengamme: Helmstedt mine de sel," in *De l'université aux camps de concentration: Témoignages strasbourgeois* (Paris: Les Belles Lettres, 1947), 297–322.

48. Henri Frenay, in "Réunion de la Commission d'Histoire de l'Internement et de la Déportation," October 29, 1945, F/9/3225, AN. Participants included Tillion, Martin-Chauffier, Roure, and Henri Teitgen.

49. "150.000 Parisiens prient pour la paix du monde," *Témoignage chrétien* 59 (July 13, 1945).

50. The booklet is preserved in "Notes et articles relatifs au combat et à la déportation de A. Balachowsky," AB IP. See also Alfred-Serge Balachowsky, "'Block 46' de Buchenwald au procès de Nuremberg," *La République française* 3, no. 9 (September 1946).

51. See Wieviorka, *Déportation et génocide*, 446–75. See also David Cesarani and Eric J. Sundquist, eds., *After the Holocaust: Challenging the Myth of Silence* (New York: Routledge, 2012); Laura Jockusch, *Collect and Record! Jewish Holocaust Documentation in Early Post-*

*war Europe* (New York: Oxford University Press, 2012); Johannes Heuman, *The Holocaust and French Historical Culture, 1945–65* (Basingstoke, UK: Palgrave Macmillan, 2015).

52. See Henry Rousso, *The Vichy Syndrome: History and Memory in France since 1944*, trans. Arthur Goldhammer (Cambridge, MA: Harvard University Press, 1991), esp. 18–19; Olivier Wieviorka, *Divided Memory: French Recollections of World War II from the Liberation to the Present*, trans. George Holoch (Stanford, CA: Stanford University Press, 2012); Pierre Laborie, *Les Français des années troubles, de la guerre d'Espagne à la Libération*, rev. ed. (Paris: Seuil, 2003), 253–265; and, on intellectuals, Gisèle Sapiro, *La Guerre des écrivains, 1940–1953* (Paris: Fayard, 1999). For a recent account of the multiple wartime endeavors subsumed into the postwar imaginary of "the Resistance" see Robert Gildea, *Fighters in the Shadows: A New History of the French Resistance* (Cambridge, MA: Harvard University Press, 2015).

53. Megan Koreman, "A Hero's Homecoming: The Return of the Deportees to France, 1945," *Journal of Contemporary History* 32, no. 1 (1997): 9–22, at 10.

54. "Buchenwald, bagne maudit, mais page glorieuse de la Résistance française," *Le Patriote résistant*, numéro special, May 1946; Louise Alcan, "Retour à la vie," *Après Auschwitz* 1 (June 1945). On resistance in Buchenwald see Olivier Lalieu, *La Zone grise? La Résistance française à Buchenwald* (Paris: Tallendier, 2005); Sonia Combe, *Une vie contre une autre: Échange de victime et modalités de survie dans le camp de Buchenwald* (Paris: Fayard, 2014).

55. Frédéric Manhès, *Le Patriote résistant* 1 (January 1, 1946).

56. See Lagrou, *Legacy of Nazi Occupation*, 210–261; Ludi, *Reparations for Nazi Victims*, 32–75. On narratives available to Jewish survivors see Lawrence Langer, *Holocaust Testimonies: The Ruins of Memory* (New Haven, CT: Yale University Press, 1991), 162–205.

57. Bartz, "Le retour de nos martyrs."

58. Albert Camus, editorial, *Combat*, May 17, 1945.

59. Ludi, *Reparations for Nazi Victims*, 32–75.

60. Ibid., 58; Wieviorka, *Déportation et génocide*, 146.

61. Rémy Roure, "Nos déportés," *Le Monde*, July 29, 1945.

62. Martin-Chauffier, *L'Homme et la bête*, 159–160.

63. Charles Richet, Jacqueline Richet, and Olivier Richet, *Trois bagnes* (Paris: J. Ferenczi & fils, 1945), 7–15; Michelet, *Rue de la liberté*, 7 and 14.

64. Germaine Tillion et al., *Ravensbrück* (Neuchâtel: Cahiers du Rhône / Éditions de la Baconnière, 1946), 7; Martin-Chauffier, speech at 42 rue des Martyrs.

65. Germaine Tillion, "À la recherche de la vérité," in Tillion et al., *Ravensbrück*, 13; David Rousset, speech at Conférence européenne de la culture, Lausanne, [December 9, 1949], F/Delta/1880/4, DR BDIC.

66. Martin-Chauffier, *L'Homme et la bête*, 94.

67. David Rousset, *Les Jours de notre mort* (Paris: Fayard/Pluriel, 2012), 124; Rousset, "Conférence du 17 novembre 1947"; D'Astorg, "Réflexions d'un survivant," 693.

68. David Rousset, *L'Univers concentrationnaire* (Paris: Fayard/Pluriel, 2011), 187.

69. Ibid., 181.

70. Rohmer, "Aussenkommando H," 322; Arrighi, "Notes," 35 and 29. On the relationship between "the imperative to tell" and "the impossibility of telling" see Felman and Laub, *Testimony*, 78–79. The CICRC's future members framed the impossibility of witnessing in terms of a chasm between limit-case experience and language, not as a function of traumatized subjectivity nor as a result of the fact that the "complete witnesses"—those who "touched bottom"—did not return. Cf. Giorgio Agamben's *Remnants of Auschwitz*, trans. Daniel Heller-Roazen (New York: Zone Books, 1999), 34–39; Primo Levi, *The Drowned and the Saved*, trans. Raymond Rosenthal (New York: Random House, 1989), 83.

71. Arrighi, "Notes," 30.

72. Émile-Louis Lambert in 1948, cited in Wieviorka, *Déportation et génocide*, 151.

73. Other survivors flatly rejected *bildung* narratives—e.g., Charlotte Delbo, *Une connaissance inutile: Auschwitz et après*, vol. 2 (Paris: Éditions de Minuit, 1970); Jean Améry, *At the Mind's Limits: Contemplations by a Survivor on Auschwitz and Its Realities*, trans. Sidney Rosenfeld and Stella P. Rosenfeld (Bloomington: Indiana University Press, 1980), 19–20.

74. For further detail on Rousset's early years see Rousset and Copfermann, *David Rousset*.

75. Rabaud, "L'humour noir a sauvé David Rousset."

76. Rousset and Copfermann, *David Rousset*, 61.

77. Rousset, *L'Univers concentrationnaire*, 36 and 50. See also Philippe Mesnard, *Témoignage en résistance* (Paris: Stock, 2007), 55–58.

78. Rousset, *L'Univers concentrationnaire*, 115. On nakedness in *Les Jours* see Alain Brossat, "Le peuple nu," *Lignes* (May 2000): 13–25.

79. Rousset, *L'Univers concentrationnaire*, 116 and 114.

80. Ibid., 114; Rousset, *Les Jours*, 153.

81. Rousset, *L'Univers concentrationnaire*, 108.

82. Ibid., 161.

83. See Alfred-Serge Balachowsky, "J'ai vécu les dernières minutes de Buchenwald," in "Mémoires," AB IP; see also his Nuremberg testimony in *Trial of the Major War Criminals before the International Military Tribunal, Nuremberg, 14 November 1945–1 October 1946*, vol. 6 (Nuremberg, 1947–1949), 319. Rousset further addressed this problem in "La signification de l'affaire Dotkins-Hessel," *Les Temps modernes* 6 (March 1946): 1084–1088.

84. For a sympathetic underlining of this point see François Azouvi, *Le Mythe du grand silence: Auschwitz, les Français, la mémoire* (Paris: Fayard 2012), 134. For a reading more focused on the distortions of Rousset's optic see Samuel Moyn, *A Holocaust Controversy: The Treblinka Affair in Postwar France* (Waltham, MA: Brandeis University Press, 2005), 166.

85. Rousset, *Les Jours*, 84.

86. David Rousset, *Le Pitre ne rit pas* (Paris: Pavois, 1948); David Rousset, preface to François-Jean Armorin, *Des Juifs quittent l'Europe* (Paris: La Jeune Parque, 1948), 10.

87. Rousset, *L'Univers concentrationnaire*, 56–57.

88. David Rousset, "Réflexions de David Rousset," *Voix et Visages* 191 (July–August 1984), emphasis in original. On Rousset's defense of this view in the 1960s see Moyn, *Holocaust Controversy*.

89. Rousset, *L'Univers concentrationnaire*, 23.

90. Ibid., 184.

91. Antelme, "Témoignage du camp"; Rousset, *L'Univers concentrationnaire*, 186.

92. Yves Gandon, "La critique des livres," *Minerve*, July 5, 1946; Paul Moelle, "L'univers concentrationnaire et la condition humaine," *Franc-Tireur*, June 30, 1946.

93. Armand Hoog, *Carrefour*, June 20, 1946, cited in N[adeau?], "'L'Univers concentrationnaire' devant la critique," *La Revue internationale*, November 1946, 367.

94. Rousset, *L'Univers concentrationnaire*, 186–187.

95. Ibid., 181.

96. David Rousset, "Où en sommes-nous?," *Le Patriote résistant* 50 (March 23, 1948).

97. Rousset, *L'Univers concentrationnaire*, 187.

98. Ibid., 182.

99. Ibid., 181.

100. Ibid., 182.

101. Rousset, "Conférence du 17 novembre 1947."

102. Rousset, "Où en sommes-nous?"

103. Paul Guth, "L'interview de Paul Guth," *La Gazette des lettres*, July 6, 1946.

104. Fragments of *Les Jours* appeared in *Les Temps modernes* in March and April 1946. Several other pieces by Rousset were subsequently published in the journal. For Sartre's literary appreciation of Rousset see Jean-Paul Sartre, *Qu'est-ce que la littérature?* (Paris: Gallimard, 1948), 305. For Georges Bataille's praise see "Réflexions sur le bourreau et la victime: S.S. et déportés," *Critique* no. 17 (October 1947): 337–342.

105. E.g., see Jean Cayrol, "D'un romanesque concentrationnaire," *Esprit* 159 (September 1949): 340–357; Jean Cayrol, "Témoignage et littérature," *Esprit* 201 (April 1953): 575–578.

106. Thierry Maulnier, *Concorde*, July 4, 1946, cited in N[adeau?], "'L'Univers concentrationnaire,'" 367.

107. Michèle Goldschmidt, review of *Ravensbrück*, *Esprit* 133 (May 1947): 871–874, at 871.

108. On Tillion as an "ethnologist in the concentration camp" see Anise Postel-Vinay, "Une ethnologue en camp de concentration," *Esprit* 261 (February 2000): 125–134; on her fieldwork see Alice Conklin, *In the Museum of Man: Race, Anthropology, and Empire in France, 1850–1950* (Ithaca, NY: Cornell University Press, 2013), esp. 258–260.

109. Reynaud, *L'Enfant de la rue*, 166.

110. Tillion, "À la recherche," 49–50.

111. Commission de l'Historique de l'Internement et de la Déportation, "Compte rendu de la séance plénière," November 12, 1945, 9. F/9/3225, AN. She did, however, later regret not employing still more "personal" language. Germaine Tillion and Alison Rice, "'Dechiffrer le silence': A Conversation with Germaine Tillion," *Research in African Literatures* 35, no. 1 (Spring 2004): 162–179, at 169. See also Nancy Wood, *Germaine Tillion, une femme-mémoire: D'un Algérie à l'autre* (Paris: Autrement, 2003), 126.

112. Commission d'Histoire, "Compte rendu," 9.

113. Tillion, "À la recherche," 39.

114. Ibid., 41.

115. Rousset, *L'Univers concentrationnaire*, 116.

116. Tillion, "À la recherche," 24–25.

117. Ibid., 25.

118. Ibid., 44.

119. Ibid., 24–26.

120. One defendant died during the trial. Two of those sentenced to death managed to commit suicide. See Ulf Schmidt, "'The Scars of Ravensbrück': Medical Experiments and British War Crimes Policy, 1945–1950," in *Atrocities on Trial: Historical Perspectives on the Politics of Prosecuting War Crimes*, ed. Patricia Heberer and Jürgen Matthäus (Lincoln: University of Nebraska Press, 2008), 123–157; Michael J. Bazyler and Frank M. Tuerkheimer, *Forgotten Trials of the Holocaust* (New York: NYU Press, 2014), 129–158.

121. Robert Jackson, cited in Donald Bloxham, "Jewish Witnesses in War Crimes Trials of the Postwar Era," in *Holocaust Historiography in Context: Emergence, Challenges, Polemics and Achievements*, ed. David Bankier and Dan Michman (Jerusalem: Yad Vashem / Berghahn Books, 2008), 539–553, at 541.

122. Germaine Tillion, "Le procès des assassins de Ravensbrück," *Voix et Visages* 7 (March 1947).

123. Ibid.

124. Germaine Tillion, "Le procès de Ravensbrück," *Voix et Visages* 6 (February 1947).

125. Ibid.

126. Tillion, "À la recherche," 13.

127. Tillion, "Le procès des assassins."

128. Ibid.

129. Martin-Chauffier, *L'Homme et la bête*, 125, 20.

130. Ibid., 126.

131. Ibid., 79.

132. Ibid., 198.

133. Louis Martin-Chauffier, "Et s'il n'en reste qu'un ce sera trop!," *Le Patriote résistant* 15 (October 1, 1946).

134. Martin-Chauffier, *L'Homme et la bête*, 128. Mazeaud made the same point in *Visages dans la tourmente*, 327–328.

135. Martin-Chauffier, *L'Homme et la bête*, 144.

136. Ibid., 202.

137. Ibid., 126.

138. Ibid., 197 and 119.

139. Ibid., 197.

140. Ibid., 196 and 202.

141. Martin-Chauffier, speech at 42 rue des Martyrs.

142. Ibid.

143. Martin-Chauffier, *L'Homme et la bête*, 202; Martin-Chauffier, speech at 42 rue des Martyrs.

144. Martin-Chauffier, speech at 42 rue des Martyrs.

145. Armand Pierhal, *Temps présent*, cited in N[adeau?], "'L'Univers concentrationnaire,'" 366.

146. See Agamben, *Remnants of Auschwitz*, 26; Samuel Moyn, "Bearing Witness: The Theological Roots of a Secular Morality," in *The Holocaust and Historical Methodology*, ed. Dan Stone (New York: Berghahn Books, 2012), 127–142.

147. On the Holocaust as the "wrong atrocity" for the Cold War see Peter Novick, *The Holocaust in American Life* (Boston: Houghton Mifflin, 1999), 87 and 101.

148. Frédéric (Henri) Manhès, letter to David Rousset, July 1, 1946, F/Delta/1880/1/1, DR BDIC.

149. Louis Parrot, "Un monde sans liberté," *Les Lettres françaises*, July 12, 1946. However, the journal was less enthusiastic about *Les Jours*: André Ulmann, "Les morts et les vivants," *Les Lettres françaises*, June 20, 1947.

150. Pierre Fauchery, *Action*, July 5, 1946, cited in N[adeau?], "'L'Univers concentrationnaire,'" 368.

151. See Azouvi, *Le Mythe du grand silence*, 134. Jewish resisters were, in fact, present in *Les Jours* (notably Benjamin Crémieux).

152. Bernard Lecache, "C'était trop bien pour le Goncourt," *Le Clou*, July 1946, 21.

153. Pierre-Henri Simon, "L'age concentrationnaire," *L'Aube*, July 8, 1946.

154. Questioned about Soviet camps at an October 1947 event, Rousset dodged with a vague answer about "the extreme decomposition of the capitalist world": D'Astorg, "Réflexions d'un survivant," 695.

## 2. DAVID ROUSSET'S COLD WAR CALL TO ARMS

1. David Rousset, "Notre programme," *La Gauche* 1 (May 15–30, 1948).

2. Albert Béguin, "Le choix des victimes," *Esprit* 139 (November 1947): 696–705, at 698.

3. E. A. Runacres, circular note, May 25, 1949, FO/1110/172, BNA.

4. Pierre Daix, "Pierre Daix, matricule 59.807 à Mauthausen, répond à David Rousset," *Les Lettres françaises*, November 17, 1949.

5. David Rousset, "Au secours des déportés dans les camps soviétiques. Un appel de David Rousset aux anciens déportés des camps nazis," *Le Figaro littéraire*, November 12, 1949.

6. Theodor Adorno, "Cultural Criticism and Society," in *Prisms*, trans. Samuel and Shierry Weber (Cambridge, MA: MIT Press, 1981), 17–34, at 34.

7. The PCI disavowed the "Appeal," reminding the public that "the relations of David Rousset with the PCI have only been those of an adversary of Trotskyism" since 1946. *La Vérité*, December 1950, cited in David Rousset, Théo Bernard, and Gérard Rosenthal, *Pour la vérité sur les camps concentrationnaires (Un procès antistalinien à Paris)* (Paris: Ramsey, 1990), vii.

8. "LeBlanc" [David Rousset], "Propositions pour une nouvelle appréciation de la situation internationale," October 1945, F/Delta/1880/111/2/1, DR BDIC.

9. "LeBlanc" [David Rousset], "Lettre ouverte au comité central et aux membres du parti," n.d. [1946]; Rudolphe Praeger, letter to David Rousset, February 4, 1980, F/Delta/1880/111/ 2/1, DR BDIC.

10. David Rousset, response to *Confluences*, 1947, quoted in David Rousset and Émile Copfermann, *David Rousset: Une vie dans le siècle, fragments d'autobiographie* (Paris: Plon, 1991), 86.

11. Jean-Paul Sartre, David Rousset, and Gérard Rosenthal, *Entretiens sur la politique* (Paris: Gallimard, 1949), 18.

12. Editorial, *Franc-Tireur*, February 27, 1948.

13. Ian H. Birchall, "Neither Washington nor Moscow? The Rise and Fall of the Rassemblement Démocratique Révolutionnaire," *Journal of European Studies* 29 (1999): 365–404, at 372.

14. "Au rendez-vous 'démocratique et révolutionnaire,'" *Le Monde*, March 21–22, 1948.

15. David Rousset, "D'abord, gagner la bataille," *La Gauche* 7 (October 1948); Sartre, Rousset, and Rosenthal, *Entretiens sur la politique*, 191.

16. Rousset, "Notre programme."

17. Sartre, Rousset, and Rosenthal, *Entretiens sur la politique*, 206.

18. David Rousset, "Non! La Résistance n'avait pas voulu ça!," *La Gauche* 5 (August 1948).

19. The classic articulations are Tony Judt, *Past Imperfect: French Intellectuals, 1944–1956* (Berkeley: University of California Press, 1992), and François Furet, *Le Passé d'une illusion: Essai sur l'idée communiste au XXᵉ siècle* (Paris: Laffont/Calmann-Lévy, 1995). See also Pierre Rigoulot, *Les Paupières lourdes, les Français face au goulag: Aveuglements et indignations* (Paris: Éditions Universitaires, 1991).

20. Michael Scott Christofferson, *French Intellectuals against the Left: The Antitotalitarian Moment of the 1970s* (New York: Berghahn Books, 2004), provides an important exception and corrective.

21. Albert Camus, "Réponses à Emmanuel d'Astier de la Vigerie," *Actuelles: Écrits politiques* (Paris: Gallimard, 1950); Michel Riquet, "À quelques inquiets," *La Croix*, September 21, 1948; Claude Lefort, "Kravchenko et le problème de l'URSS," *Les Temps modernes* 29 (February 1948): 1490–1516.

22. Victor Kravchenko, *I Chose Freedom: The Personal and Political Life of a Soviet Official* (New York: Scribner, 1946), 295, in French as *J'ai choisi la liberté! La vie publique et privée d'un haut-fonctionnaire soviétique*, trans. Jean de Kerdéland (Paris: Éditions Self, 1947).

23. Simone de Beauvoir, *Lettres à Sartre, 1940–1963* (Paris: Gallimard, 1990), 337 (March 30, 1947).

24. See Quenby Olmsted Hughes, *"In the Interest of Democracy": The Rise and Fall of the Early Cold War Alliance between the American Federation of Labor and the Central Intelligence Agency* (Oxford: Peter Lang, 2011), 102.

25. Hugh Wilford, *The Mighty Wurlitzer: How the CIA Played America* (Cambridge, MA: Harvard University Press, 2008), 5.

26. David Dubinksy, quoted in Quenby Olmsted Hughes, "The American Federation of Labor's Cold War Campaign against 'Slave Labor' at the United Nations," in *American Labor's Global Ambassadors: The International History of the AFL-CIO during the Cold War*,

ed. Robert Anthony Waters Jr. and Geert Van Goethem (New York: Palgrave Macmillan, 2013), 23–38, at 25.

27. John Jenks, *British Propaganda and News Media in the Cold War* (Edinburgh: Edinburgh University Press, 2006), 138–140. See also Lowell H. Schwartz, *Political Warfare against the Kremlin: US and British Propaganda Policy at the Beginning of the Cold War* (New York: Palgrave Macmillan, 2009).

28. Foreign Office, Circular no. 065, June 19, 1950, FO/959/78, BNA.

29. Willard Thorp's and Toni Sender's statements to the UN Economic and Social Council on February 14, 1949, are representative; see also Susan L. Carruthers, *Cold War Captives: Imprisonment, Escape, and Brainwashing* (Berkeley: University of California Press, 2009), 123–124; Ralph Gilbert Ross, "Commission of Inquiry into Slave Labor," *Industrial and Labor Relations Review* 2, no. 4 (July 1949): 619–620; Albert Konrad Herling, *The Soviet Slave Empire* (New York: Wilfred Funk, 1951).

30. J. Brooke, letter to Information Research Department, March 2, 1949, FO/1110/171, BNA.

31. David J. Dallin and Boris I. Nicolaevsky, *Forced Labor in Soviet Russia* (New Haven, CT: Yale University Press, 1947), 98 and ix.

32. Irwin M. Wall, *The United States and the Making of Postwar France, 1945–1954* (New York: Cambridge University Press, 1991), 151.

33. For a reading of the case focused on its significance for the history of witnessing see Carolyn J. Dean, *The Moral Witness: Trials and Testimony after Genocide* (Ithaca, NY: Cornell University Press, forthcoming), chap. 2. For general treatments see Gary Kern, *The Kravchenko Case: One Man's War on Stalin* (New York: Enigma Books, 2007); Guillaume Malaurie, *L'Affaire Kravchenko* (Paris: Éditions Laffont, 1982); Jean-Pierre Rioux, "Le procès Kravchenko," in *Staline à Paris*, ed. Natacha Dioujeva and François George (Paris: Ramsay, 1982), 148–169.

34. *Le Procès Kravchenko contre Les Lettres françaises: Compte rendu des audiences d'après la sténographie* (Paris: La Jeune Parque, 1949), 12. Kravchenko's opening speech did invoke Hitler's camps, but only as a generic example of past evil; he did not suggest the USSR possessed similar ones.

35. Albert Béguin, "La bonne affaire Kravchenko," *Esprit* 155 (May 1949): 699.

36. See Nina Berberova, *L'Affaire Kravtchenko*, trans. Irène and André Markowicz (Arles: Actes Sud, 1990), 148; Carruthers, *Cold War Captives*, 112–115; Joë Nordmann, *Aux vents de l'histoire: Mémoires* (Arles: Actes Sud, 1996), 184.

37. David Rousset, letter to David Dallin, January 20, 1950, F/Delta/1880/61/2/1.

38. Birchall, "Neither Washington nor Moscow?," 389.

39. David Rousset, "La révolution doit se réaliser dans la pratique démocratique des travailleurs manuels et intellectuels," *La Gauche* 10 (December 1948).

40. Irving Brown, letter to Jay Lovestone, May 5, 1949, box 698, folder 1, JL HIA.

41. On Sartre's short-lived high hopes for the RDR see Annie Cohen-Solal, *Sartre* (Paris: Gallimard, 1985), 390–407.

42. Albert Camus, letter to David Rousset, April 26, 1949, F/Delta/1880/111/4/5, DR BDIC. Richard Wright sent a similar note.

43. Pierre Naville, "La politique américaine et le R.D.R.," *La Bataille socialiste*, May 13, 1949.

44. Sidney Hook, "Report on the International Day against Dictatorship and War," *Partisan Review* 16, no. 7 (July 1949): 722–732, at 726. Hook admired Rousset, however: "Politically, he is a man of quite a different kidney from Sartre" (729).

45. David Rousset, letter to Norris Chipman, August 8, 1949, F/Delta/1880/46/5/1, DR BDIC.

46. See Claire Blandin, "Les interventions des intellectuels de droite dans *Le Figaro littéraire*: L'invention du contre-engagement," *Vingtième siècle* 96, no. 4 (2007): 179–194; Ian H. Birchall, *Sartre against Stalinism* (New York: Berghahn Books, 2004), 110.

47. The phrase "*déportés politiques*" may appear ambiguous vis-à-vis "racial" victims, given its uses in French law, but Rousset eliminated any doubt about his meaning in subsequent articles: see chapter 3.

48. Rousset, "Au secours des déportés."

49. Ibid., emphasis in original. On the discourse of "duty" among survivors see Olivier Lalieu, "L'invention du 'devoir de mémoire,'" *Vingtième siècle* 69 (2001): 83–94. In referring to "le GOULAG," Rousset was introducing a still unfamiliar word into the French lexicon.

50. Rousset, "Au secours des déportés."

51. Ibid.

52. Ibid.

53. Ibid.

54. Ibid.

55. See Dora Apfel, *The Holocaust and the Art of Secondary Witnessing* (New Brunswick, NJ: Rutgers University Press, 2002).

56. Ibid.

57. Additional examples abound. President Truman, for instance, labeled the gulag the "most extreme violation of human rights on the face of the earth today": "Truman Commends Slave Labor Book," *New York Times*, September 19, 1952.

58. See Marco Duranti, *The Conservative Human Rights Revolution: European Identity, Transnational Politics, and the Origins of the European Convention* (Oxford: Oxford University Press, 2017); Samuel Moyn, *Christian Human Rights* (Philadelphia: University of Pennsylvania Press, 2015).

59. Rousset, "Au secours des déportés."

60. United Nations, "Universal Declaration of Human Rights," December 10, 1948, http://www.un.org/en/universal-declaration-human-rights/.

61. Rousset, "Au secours des déportés." On the non-linkage of "crimes against humanity" to human rights discourse in the postwar period see Samuel Moyn, *The Last Utopia: Human Rights in History* (Cambridge, MA: Harvard University Press, 2010), 82.

62. United Nations, "Universal Declaration."

63. Steven A. Barnes, *Between Death and Redemption: The Gulag and the Shaping of Soviet Society* (Princeton, NJ: Princeton University Press, 2011), 160.

64. Alexander Dolgun, quoted ibid., 167.

65. Golfo Alexopoulos, *Illness and Inhumanity in Stalin's Gulag* (New Haven, CT: Yale University Press, 2017), 243–244.

66. Barnes, *Between Death and Redemption*, 2.

67. Rousset, "Au secours des déportés."

68. To observe that the gulag was not geared toward racialized "final solutions" is not to suggest that the USSR's leaders refrained from various efforts to reshape the population. See Peter Holquist, "State Violence as Technique: The Logic of Violence in Soviet Totalitarianism," in *Landscaping the Human Garden: 20th Century Population Management in a Comparative Framework*, ed. Amir Weiner (Stanford, CA: Stanford University Press, 2003), 19–45.

69. Rousset, "Au secours des déportés." The text also referred in passing to Jewish political prisoners.

70. Ibid.

71. Hannah Arendt, "The Concentration Camps," *Partisan Review* 15, no. 7 (July 1948): 742–763, at 742. See also Raymond Aron, "Une enquête: L'Allemagne dans la Communauté Européenne," *Évidences* 19 (May–June 1951): 19–21.

72. Arendt, "Concentration Camps," 754, 750, 762.

73. On the Sartrean conception of writerly responsibility see Gisèle Sapiro, *La Responsabilité de l'écrivain: Littérature, droit, et morale en France (XIXᵉ–XXIᵉ siècle)* (Paris: Seuil, 2011), 667–688; Jonathan Judaken, *Jean-Paul Sartre and the Jewish Ques-*

*tion: Anti-antisemitism and the Politics of the French Intellectual* (Lincoln: University of Nebraska Press, 2006), 147–183.

74. David Rousset, "Réponse à ceux qui ne veulent pas de l'ouverture d'une enquête," *Le Figaro littéraire*, January 14, 1950.

75. David Rousset, "Les camps de concentration seront mis hors la loi," *Le Figaro littéraire*, March 4, 1950.

76. On the schism see Olivier Lalieu, *La Déportation fragmentée: Les anciens déportés parlent de politique, 1945–1980* (Paris: Boutique de l'histoire, 1994); Pieter Lagrou, *The Legacy of Nazi Occupation: Patriotic Memory and National Recovery in Western Europe, 1945–1965* (Cambridge: Cambridge University Press, 2000), 233–234, 270–272.

77. Henri Teitgen, letter to David Rousset, November 15, 1949, F/Delta/1880/46/5/1, DR BDIC.

78. Robert Maddelena, "Les déportés de 'Témoignage chrétien' répondent," *Témoignage chrétien*, November 18, 1949.

79. Le R. P. Riquet, "Quelque part en Europe ou en Asie Mauthausen continue . . . ," *Le Figaro littéraire*, December 3, 1949.

80. "Les anciens déportés répondent à l'appel de David Rousset," *Le Figaro littéraire*, November 19, 1949.

81. Statement of Léon Mazeaud, transcript, "Conférence de presse donnée par M. David Rousset mardi 15 novembre 1949," F/Delta/1880/53/2, DR BDIC.

82. Rémy Roure, "Les morts vivants," *Le Monde*, November 11, 1949.

83. Rémy Roure, transcript, "Conférence de presse"; "Assemblée générale," *Voix et Visages* 24 (February–March 1950), 2.

84. Léon Blum, "Quand les staliniens plaident coupable," *Le Populaire*, March 7, 1950.

85. Émile-Louis Lambert, Assemblée Nationale, *Compte rendu analytique officiel*, 2ᵉ séance du mardi 12 décembre 1950.

86. Jean Cayrol, letter to David Rousset, n.d. [November 1949], F/Delta/1880/46/5/1, DR BDIC, emphasis in original.

87. "Des déportés répondent à David Rousset," *Le Patriote résistant*, December 12, 1949; Marcel Prenant, "Des déportés répondent à David Rousset (II)," *Le Patriote résistant*, December 31, 1949.

88. Robert Antelme, letter to David Rousset, n.d. [November 1949], and attached copy of response to be published in *Le Figaro littéraire* on November 19 as "J'accepte sous conditions," F/Delta/1880/53/4, DR BDIC.

89. "Ce qu'on propose," *Le Patriote résistant*, February 6, 1950.

90. Julien Unger, "Réponse à David Rousset," *Le Patriote résistant*, December 12, 1949.

91. Marcel Paul, "L'histoire jugera David Rousset," *Le Patriote résistant*, February 27, 1950.

92. These included Georges Wellers (Auschwitz), Jean-Jacques Bernard (Drancy), and Suzanne Birnbaum (Auschwitz). See also Lalieu, *La Déportation fragmentée*, 90–95; Rebecca Clifford, *Commemorating the Holocaust: The Dilemmas of Remembrance in France and Italy* (Oxford: Oxford University Press, 2013), 39–40.

93. Fédération Nationale des Déportés et Internés Résistants et Patriotes, communiqué to *Le Figaro littéraire*, January 19, 1950, F/Delta/1880/53/6, DR BDIC; Henri Manhès, letter to David Rousset, February 15, 1950, F/Delta/1880/53/6, DR BDIC.

94. FNDIRP, communiqué.

95. Manhès, letter to Rousset.

96. Daix, "Pierre Daix."

97. "Réplique à la campagne D. Rousset," *Ce soir*, November 29, 1949.

98. Marcel Prenant, Président de l'Amicale de Neuengamme, letter to M. le Secrétaire Générale de l'UNADIF, December 27, 1950, F/Delta/1880/56/1/2, DR BDIC. This was the same Marcel Prenant who had saved Louis Martin-Chauffier's life in Neuengamme.

99. F.-H. Manhès, "Lettre ouverte du président de la FNDIRP à David Rousset," *Le Patriote résistant*, February 27, 1950.

100. "Sur un air américain," *Action*, November 24, 1949.

101. André Leroy, "Trois points marqués contre les diviseurs," *Le Patriote résistant*, March 26, 1950; Paul, "L'histoire jugera David Rousset."

102. Association des Déportés, Internés et Familles des Disparus du Département de la Seine, open letter, n.d. [1950], F/Delta/1880/53/6, DR BDIC.

103. Leroy, "Trois points marqués," emphasis in original.

104. David Rousset, "Notre silence ne serait pas seulement un reniement, mais une défaite," *Le Figaro littéraire*, November 19, 1949; [Rousset], "Tâches réalisées."

105. Daix, "Pierre Daix."

106. David Rousset, letter to Danenberg, January 28, 1950, F/Delta/1880/61/2/1, DR BDIC.

107. Claude Bourdet, "Balayer devant notre porte," *Combat*, November 14, 1949.

108. David Rousset, "Oui ou non, les camps de concentration existent-ils en URSS?," *Franc-Tireur*, November 14, 1949.

109. Claude Bourdet, "Pour tous ou pour un seul?," *Combat*, November 16, 1949.

110. Marcel Cerbu, in "Les anciens déportés répondent à l'appel de David Rousset."

111. Cayrol, letter to Rousset, n.d. [December 1949], emphasis in original.

112. Louis Martin-Chauffier, letter to David Rousset, November 13, 1949, F/Delta/1880/54/3, DR BDIC.

113. Jean Paulhan, quoted in Judt, *Past Imperfect*, 90. See also David Caute, *The Fellow-Travellers: Intellectual Friends of Communism*, rev. ed. (New Haven, CT: Yale University Press, 1988), 256.

114. David Rousset, letter to Louis Martin-Chauffier, December 1, 1949, F/Delta/1880/46/5/2, DR BDIC.

115. M. Merleau-Ponty and J.-P. Sartre, "Les jours de notre vie," *Les Temps modernes* 51 (January 1950): 1153–1168, at 1165.

116. Ibid. On widespread overestimations of the gulag population see Carruthers, *Cold War Captives*, 102.

117. Merleau-Ponty and Sartre, "Les jours de notre vie," 1163. See Maurice Merleau-Ponty, *Humanisme et terreur* (Paris: Gallimard, 1947).

118. Merleau-Ponty and Sartre, "Les jours de notre vie," 1162–1163.

119. Ibid., 1161.

120. On Sartre's approach to Jewish suffering in his 1946 *Réflexions sur la question juive* see Judaken, *Jean-Paul Sartre and the Jewish Question*.

121. Merleau-Ponty and Sartre, "Les jours de notre vie," 1168.

122. Albert Camus, *Carnets*, vol. 2 (Paris, Gallimard, 1964), 235.

123. Groupe de Liaison Internationale, in "Après l'appel de David Rousset," *Le Figaro littéraire*, December 31, 1949.

124. Pierre Emmanuel, letter to David Rousset, November 11, 1949, F/Delta/1880/46/5/1, DR BDIC.

125. Jean-Marie Domenach, "David Rousset accuse," *Esprit* 162 (December 1949): 983–986, at 984.

126. *Humanisme et terreur* made no substantive reference, however, to the gulag. Its subject was the execution of party elites.

127. T.M. [Jean-Paul Sartre and Maurice Merleau-Ponty], "L'Adversaire est complice," *Les Temps modernes* 57 (July 1950): 1–11, at 5–6, emphasis in original.

128. Sartre, "Réponse à Albert Camus," *Situations*, vol. 4 (Paris: Gallimard, 1964), 105, originally published in *Les Temps modernes* 82 (August 1952): 334–353.

129. Ibid., 107. Sartre would revisit the Rousset Affair yet again in 1961, in seemingly aporetic terms, in his remembrance essay for Merleau-Ponty, "Merleau-Ponty vivant," *Les Temps modernes* 184–185 (October 1961): 304–376.

130. David Rousset, "Jean-Paul Sartre en Chine ou les cynismes d'un mandarin," *Demain*, January 5–11, 1956.

131. Rousset, "Les camps de concentration seront mis hors la loi."

132. David Rousset, letter to Saul Padover, December 31, 1949, F/Delta/1880/61/2/2, DR BDIC.

133. E. A. Runacres, Minutes, November 24, 1949, FO/1110/179, BNA.

134. Ralph Murray, "Report on the Work of Information Research Department," 1950, FO/1110/359, BNA.

135. P. F. D. Tennant, letter to Ralph Murray, December 3, 1949, FO/1110/179, BNA.

136. Jay Lovestone, letter to Irving Brown, November 7, 1950, box 11, folder 12, JL MMA.

137. David Rousset, letter to an "ami," September 20, 1950, F/Delta/1880/47/9, DR BDIC; David Rousset, letter to Jay Lovestone, November 29, 1950, F/Delta/1880/69/1, DR BDIC.

138. David K. E. Bruce, telegram to Secretary of State, January 9, 1950, RG 59, box 3646, NARA.

139. Jay Lovestone, letter to Norris Chipman, January 26, 1950, box 35, folder 11, JL MMA. The British situation was different. But as the *Economist* put it in "Conference of the Unforgetting," May 26, 1951, "There is perhaps no respect in which British insularity and detachment from continental European thinking is so marked as in the happy lack of the experience which has left its indelible mark on countries formerly occupied by the Nazis" (1225).

140. Display advertisement, *New York Times*, February 28, 1950; David Rousset, "An Appeal to the Conscience of the World," *New Leader* 33, no. 10 (March 1950).

141. "Coupures de presse concernant le procès David Rousset c/ 'Les Lettres Françaises.'" F/Delta/1880/56/1/3, DR BDIC. On the trial's unfolding see Dean, *Moral Witness*; John V. Fleming, *The Anti-Communist Manifestos: Four Books That Shaped the Cold War* (New York: Norton, 2009), 244–262.

142. R. A. S. Breene, letter to P. A. Wilkinson, January 13, 1950, FO/1110/378, BNA.

143. "Damages in Paris Libel Action," *Times*, January 13, 1950.

144. Arthur Koestler et al., letter to the editor, *New York Times*, February 15, 1951.

145. Rousset, Bernard, and Rosenthal, *Pour la vérité*, 37–38.

146. Sténotypie, "Audience Vendredi 1 décembre 1950," 31 and 73. (These statements are summarized rather than reproduced in full in Rousset, Bernard, and Rosenthal, *Pour la vérité*, 27 and 35.)

147. Rousset, Bernard, and Rosenthal, *Pour la vérité*, 245 and 99.

148. Sténotypie, "Audience Vendredi 1 décembre 1950," 95; Sténotypie, "Audience Vendredi 8 décembre 1950," 148; Sténotypie, "Audience Samedi 25 novembre 1950," 2. (These statements are summarized or rephrased in Rousset, Bernard, and Rosenthal, *Pour la vérité*, 45, 62, 15).

149. André Fontaine, "Les défenseurs des 'Lettres françaises' multiplient les astuces de procédure," *Le Monde*, December 3–4, 1950.

150. Simone de Beauvoir, *La Force des choses* (Paris: Gallimard, 1963), 189.

151. Sténotypie, "Audience Vendredi 8 décembre 1950," 146; "La défense multiplie les incidents de procédure," *Le Monde*, December 2, 1950; "Premiers incidents à la 17ᵉ chambre correctionnelle," *Le Monde*, November 26–27, 1950.

152. Georges Altman, "Audience mouvementée et décisive au procès Rousset," *Franc-Tireur*, December 11, 1950; Georges Altman, "C'est d'abord le procès de l'inhumanité," *Franc-Tireur*, November 26, 1950.

153. Pierre Daix, *J'ai cru au matin* (Paris: Laffont, 1976), 257. See Joë Nordmann's recollections in "David Rousset contre *Les Lettres françaises*. Après coup (Entretien)," *Lignes* 2 (May 2000): 110–114.

154. Rousset, Bernard, and Rosenthal, *Pour la vérité*, 17.

155. Ibid., 38 and 98.

156. For example, "David Rousset demandait 10 millions aux 'Lettres françaises.' Il obtient 100.000 francs," *Libération*, January 13, 1951.

157. Rousset, Bernard, and Rosenthal, *Pour la vérité*, 251.

158. "Justice est rendue à David Rousset," *Le Figaro*, January 13–14, 1951; "M. David Rousset sort vainqueur des 'Lettres françaises,'" *Le Parisien libéré*, January 13, 1951; "Claude Morgan et Pierre Daix sont des diffamateurs," *Le Populaire*, January 13, 1951; "Claude Morgan et Pierre Daix paieront," *L'Aurore*, January 13, 1951; "David Rousset avait raison, estime le tribunal," *Franc-Tireur*, January 13–14, 1950.

159. Rousset, Bernard, and Rosenthal, *Pour la vérité*, 244.

## 3. FORGING THE INTERNATIONAL COMMISSION

1. On post-1914 "modern" NGOs see Bruno Cabanes, *The Great War and the Origins of Humanitarianism, 1918–1924* (New York: Cambridge University Press, 2014). For a longer-term perspective see Thomas Richard Davies, *NGOs: A New History of Transnational Civil Society* (New York: Oxford University Press, 2014). Lyman Cromwell White, *International Non-Governmental Organizations: Their Purposes, Methods, and Accomplishments* (New Brunswick, NJ: Rutgers University Press, 1951), provides a survey of the roughly one thousand international NGOs in existence when the CICRC was founded.

2. "Procès-verbal de la séance," February 20, 1950, F/Delta/1880/54/3, DR BDIC.

3. La Commission Française d'Enquête, "Lettre ouverte aux organisations de déportés à l'étranger," reproduced in Commission Internationale contre le Régime Concentrationnaire, *Livre blanc sur les camps de concentration soviétiques* (Paris: Pavois, 1951), 230–234, at 233.

4. Alfred-Serge Balachowsky, in CICRC, *Livre blanc sur les camps de concentration soviétiques*, 9.

5. Akira Iriye, *Global Community: The Role of International Organizations in the Making of the Contemporary World* (Berkeley: University of California Press, 2002), 65. Pieter Lagrou provides a useful summary and critique of the myth of wartime "Europe" in "La Résistance et les conceptions de l'Europe, 1945–1965," in *Le Rôle des guerres dans la mémoire des européens: Leur effet sur la conscience d'être européen*, ed. Antoine Fleury and Robert Frank (Berne: Peter Lang, 1997), 137–181.

6. Iriye, *Global Community*, 53.

7. Mark Mazower, *Governing the World: The History of an Idea, 1815 to the Present* (New York: Penguin, 2012), 323.

8. See Lagrou, "La Résistance," 154.

9. Louis Martin-Chauffier, "Fragments de conférences aux USA," dated May 20, 1946, and March–May 1947, dossier: Conférences sur Gide 2/2, MCH13, LMC IMEC.

10. Statement of Léon Mazeaud, transcript, "Conférence de presse donnée par M. David Rousset mardi 15 novembre 1949," F/Delta/1880/53/2, DR BDIC.

11. David Rousset, "Au secours des déportés dans les camps soviétiques. Un appel de David Rousset aux anciens déportés des camps nazis," *Le Figaro littéraire*, November 12, 1949.

12. Kogon declined to participate despite repeated entreaties over the years. On the political lessons he took from the camps see James Chappel, *Catholic Modern: The Challenge of Totalitarianism and the Remaking of the Church* (Cambridge, MA: Harvard University Press, 2018), chap. 5.

13. Louis Martin-Chauffier, *L'Homme et la bête* (Paris: Gallimard, 1947), 143.

14. Albert Rohmer, "Aussenkommando H de Neuengamme: Helmstedt mine de sel," in *De l'université aux camps de concentration: Témoignages strasbourgeois* (Paris: Les Belles Lettres, 1947), 297–322, at 319.

15. For the original text along with Tillion's comments on her "shame" see Germaine Tillion, *Ravensbrück* (Paris: Seuil, 1973), 54. The 1988 edition purged both.

16. Michel Riquet, "L'Europe à Mauthausen," *Études* (June 1945): 289–304, quoted in Émile Poulat, *Naissance des prêtres-ouvriers* (Paris: Casterman, 1965), 230. Thanks to Philip Nord for sharing forthcoming work on this theme.

17. This was the title of a 1953 speech by Paul-Henri Spaak to the Fédération Internationale Libre des Déportés et Internés de la Résistance, founded in 1952 by "Europeanist" survivors, including several CICRC participants: see Lagrou, "La Résistance," 167.

18. David Rousset, letter to David Dallin, January 20, 1950, F/Delta/1880/61/2/1.

19. David Rousset, "The Pact Is Obsolete," *Nation*, April 9, 1949.

20. David Rousset, letter to Norris Chipman, August 8, 1949, F/Delta/1880/46/5/1, DR BDIC.

21. "David Rousset renié par les anciens déportés allemands qui lui sauvèrent la vie et auxquels il avait dédié son ouvrage," *Les Lettres françaises*, March 23, 1950.

22. Rousset, letter to Chipman.

23. E. A. Runacres, "Minutes," November 24, 1950, FO/1110/179, BNA.

24. Handwritten note on Lockhart, report to F. R. H. Murray, November 25, 1949, FO/1110/179, BNA.

25. David Rousset, letter to Michel Riquet, January 13, 1950, F/Delta/1880/47/1, DR BDIC; "Notes sur la commission allemande," May 25, 1950, F/Delta/1880/58/1/1, DR BDIC. Schumacher's response was reported back through Margarete Buber-Neumann. The internal Socialist survivor group was born after the SPD splintered the umbrella antifascist federation that initially united Nazi victims in all four occupation zones.

26. Harold Marcuse, *Legacies of Dachau: The Uses and Abuses of a Concentration Camp, 1933–2001* (Cambridge: Cambridge University Press, 2001), 155.

27. "Bund der Verfolgten des Naziregimes," F/Delta/1880/55/3, DR BDIC.

28. See Pieter Lagrou, *The Legacy of Nazi Occupation: Patriotic Memory and National Recovery in Western Europe, 1945–1965* (Cambridge: Cambridge University Press, 2000), 219–225; Sonja van 't Hof, "A Kaleidoscope of Victimhood: Belgian Experiences of World War II," in *The Politics of War Trauma: The Aftermath of World War II in Eleven European Countries*, ed. Jolande Withuis and Annet Mooij (Amsterdam: Aksant, 2010), 49–78, at 58–60.

29. The directives Somerhausen received from the Fédération Internationale des Prisonniers Politiques throughout the Rousset Affair are documented in CEGES/AA/849/217, LS CEGESOMA.

30. M. Verhaegen, in Confédération Nationale des Prisonniers Politiques et Ayants Droit, "Procès-verbal de la réunion du Conseil National," February 19, 1950, CEGES/AA/849/211, LS CEGESOMA.

31. Luc Somerhausen, ibid.

32. Ibid.

33. "L'Union Belge des Prisonniers Politiques et Ayants Droit mesure ses forces et précise le sens de son action," n.d. [1952], 601/1/1, AA CEGESOMA; "U.B.P.P.A.," n.d., 601/1/1, AA CEGESOMA. The schism was also related to the "royal question"; it persisted

until 1957, when Union Belge members reintegrated into the CNPPA. See Lagrou, *Legacy of Nazi Occupation*, 225; Lagrou, "La Résistance," 169.

34. Reumont was not a member of the famous "Comet Line," though after his arrest his group integrated into that network.

35. Poulat, *Naissance des prêtres-ouvriers*, 485. See also Oscar Cole-Arnal, *Prêtres en bleu de chauffe: Histoire des prêtres-ouvriers, 1943–1954* (Paris: Éditions Ouvrières, 1992); Jean-Louis Jadoulle, "Les visages de l'Église de Belgique à la vieille du concile Vatican II," in *Vatican II et la Belgique*, ed. Claude Soetens (Louvain: Presses Universitaires de Louvain, 2012), 11–70.

36. Jean-Louis Jadoulle, "The Milieu of Left Wing Catholics in Belgium (1940s–1950s)," in *Left Catholicism, 1943–1955: Catholics and Society in Western Europe at the Point of Liberation*, ed. Gerd-Rainer Horn and Emmanuel Gerard (Leuven: Leuven University Press, 2001), 102–117, at 105 and 112; see also Jean-Louis Jadoulle, *Chrétiens modernes? L'engagement des intellectuels catholiques 'progressistes' belges de 1945 à 1958 à travers La revue nouvelle, La relève et l'édition belge de Témoignage chrétien* (Louvain-la-Neuve: Academia Bruylant, 2003); Véronique Riez, mémoire de licence, 1986–1987, Université de Liège, Faculté de Philosophie et Lettres, Section d'histoire, "Pour une église en marche: *Témoignage chrétien belge, 1948–1958*," esp. 39–40.

37. Damien Reumont, "Réponse à David Rousset," *Témoignage chrétien belge*, December 1949, 4; Damien Reumont, letter to David Rousset, December 29, 1949, F/Delta/1880/54/5, DR BDIC.

38. Poulat, *Naissance des prêtres-ouvriers*, 486. See also Damien Reumont, introduction in *Problèmes de l'Église en marche*, vol. 1, by Étienne Carton de Wiart et al. (Brussels: Éditions de Témoignage chrétien, 1948), 5–9.

39. Reumont, "Réponse à David Rousset."

40. Damien Reumont, letter to David Rousset, December 10, 1950, F/Delta/1880/58/1/4, DR BDIC.

41. On the ExPoGe see Lagrou, *Legacy of Nazi Occupation*, 248–250; Jolande Withuis and Annet Mooij, "From Totalitarianism to Trauma: A Paradigm Shift in the Netherlands," in *The Politics of War Trauma*, ed. Withuis and Mooij, 193–215, at 196–197.

42. Karel van Staal, letter to David Rousset, December 15, 1950 F/Delta/1880/54/2, DR BDIC.

43. N.a. [David Rousset?], "Note sur la discussion de l'affaire hongroise à la session plénière de la C.I.C.R.C. du 17 novembre 1956," F/Delta/1880/59/2/7, DR BDIC.

44. Karel van Staal, "Note," November 1951, GT BNF; Karel van Staal, letter to David Rousset, March 25, 1952, F/Delta/1880/64/2/1, DR BDIC.

45. Reumont, "Réponse à David Rousset."

46. The Dutch were not present for this Brussels meeting. However, they took part in a preliminary planning meeting at The Hague in July.

47. "Procès-verbal de la conférence," October 20–21, 1950, F/Delta/1880/58/1/2, DR BDIC.

48. David Rousset, letter to Georges André, October 11, 1950, F/Delta/1880/58/1/2, DR BDIC.

49. David Rousset, letter to Jay Lovestone, November 15, 1950, F/Delta/1880/48/1, DR BDIC.

50. Oral history of Harold Kaplan conducted by G. Lewis Schmidt, Association for Diplomatic Studies and Training Foreign Affairs Oral History Project, Information Series, October 10, 1999. On Kaplan's work see Brian Angus McKenzie, *Remaking France: Americanization, Public Diplomacy, and the Marshall Plan* (New York: Berghahn Books, 2005).

51. David Rousset, letter to Ignazio Silone, November 29, 1949, F/Delta/1880/46/5/2, DR BDIC. Silone's secret history as an informer to the Fascist police in the 1920s, uncovered in the 1990s, was not known to Rousset.

52. See Hugh Wilford, *The New York Intellectuals: From Vanguard to Institution* (Manchester: Manchester University Press, 1995).

53. David Dallin, letter to David Rousset, January 14, 1950, F/Delta/1880/61/2/1, DR BDIC.

54. David Rousset, letter to Danenberg, January 28, 1950, F/Delta/1880/61/2/1, DR BDIC.

55. Rousset, letter to Dallin, January 20, 1950.

56. David Rousset, letter to James Burnham, January 16, 1950, F/Delta/1880/61/2/1, DR BDIC.

57. Hugh Wilford, *The Mighty Wurlitzer: How the CIA Played America* (Cambridge, MA: Harvard University Press, 2008), 74.

58. National Security Council Directive on Office of Special Projects (NSC 10/2), June 18, 1948, reproduced in *CIA Cold War Records: The CIA under Harry Truman* (Washington, DC: Central Intelligence Agency, 1994), 213–216.

59. See Quenby Olmsted Hughes, *"In the Interest of Democracy": The Rise and Fall of the Early Cold War Alliance between the American Federation of Labor and the Central Intelligence Agency* (Oxford: Peter Lang, 2011); Anthony Carew, "The American Labor Movement in Fizzland: The Free Trade Union Committee and the CIA," *Journal of Labor History* 39 (1998): 25–42, esp. 26–27 and 38–40; Julia Angster, "'The Finest Labour Network in Europe': American Labour and the Cold War," in *The US Government, Citizen Groups and the Cold War: The State-Private Network*, ed. Helen Laville and Hugh Wilford (New York: Routledge, 2006), 100–115.

60. Ben Rathbun, *The Point Man: Irving Brown and the Deadly Post-1945 Struggle for Europe and Africa* (Washington, DC: Minerva, 1996).

61. Director's Log, Central Intelligence Agency, September 4, 1951, http://www.foia.cia.gov/sites/default/files/document_conversions/1700319/1951-09-01.pdf.

62. "The Most Dangerous Man," *Time*, March 17, 1952, 25.

63. Irving Brown, letter to Jay Lovestone, May 5, 1949, box 698, folder 1, JL HIA.

64. Irving Brown, letter to Jay Lovestone, January 25, 1950, box 11, folder 13, JL MMA.

65. Jay Lovestone, letter to Norris Chipman, January 26, 1950, box 35, folder 11, JL MMA.

66. On Rousset's involvement with the Congress see Frances Stonor Saunders, *Who Paid the Piper? The CIA and the Cultural Cold War* (London: Granta, 1999), 68–69, 88; Peter Coleman, *The Liberal Conspiracy: The Congress for Cultural Freedom and the Struggle for the Mind of Postwar Europe* (New York: Free Press, 1989), 6–7, 37, 49; Giles Scott Smith, *The Politics of Apolitical Culture: The Congress for Cultural Freedom, the CIA, and Post-War American Hegemony* (New York: Routledge, 2002); 96–97, 106. For contextualization of CCF activities in France see Alessandro Brogi, *Confronting America: The Cold War between the United States and the Communists in France and Italy* (Chapel Hill: University of North Carolina Press, 2011).

67. David Rousset, letter to Irving Brown, August 9, 1950, F/Delta/1880/47/8, DR BDIC.

68. Ibid.

69. Irving Brown, letter to David Rousset, August 18, 1950, F/Delta/1880/47/8, DR BDIC.

70. See Anthony Carew, "Towards a Free Trade Union Centre: The International Confederation of Free Trade Unions (1949–1972)," in *The International Confederation of Free Trade Unions*, ed. Anthony Carew et al. (Bern: Peter Lang, 2000), 187–340, at 236–242.

71. "Procès-verbal de la conférence," October 20–21, 1950. The ban on financing from parties, presented as a self-evidently "fundamental" precept, was actually acceptable to

Rousset only because he failed to secure funding from the Socialist International. "Pré-liminaires de la création de la CICRC, Notes sur les rapports avec le COMISCO," February 1950, F/Delta/1880/55/1, DR BDIC; "Notes sur les rapports avec COMISCO," n.d., F/Delta/1880/54/1, DR BDIC.

72. Rousset, letter to Lovestone, November 15, 1950.

73. Damien Reumont, letter to David Rousset, February 7, 1951, F/Delta/1880/58/1/7, DR BDIC.

74. Jay Lovestone, letter to Irving Brown, December 19, 1950, box 11, folder 12, JL MMA.

75. Irving Brown, letter to Jay Lovestone, March 7, 1951, box 29, folder 11, IB MMA; Lovestone, letter to Brown, December 19, 1950.

76. Damien Reumont, letter to David Rousset, March 13, 1951, F/Delta/1880/58/1/8, DR BDIC.

77. Damien Reumont, letter to David Rousset, March 28, 1951, F/Delta/1880/58/1/8, DR BDIC.

78. See Carew, "American Labor in Fizzland," 33 and 38–39.

79. Chief, International Organizations Division, memorandum to Director of Central Intelligence on "Report of the Ad Hoc UN Committee on Forced Labor and Exploitation Thereof," June 23, 1953, General CIA Records, CREST, NARA, https://www.cia.gov/library/readingroom/docs/CIA-RDP80R01731R003300310006-0.pdf. See also Harold Kaplan's 1999 discussion of how the CIA "must have helped" Rousset with his "enormous expenses" in Schmidt, oral history, 27.

80. David Rousset, letter to Michael Josselson, December 13, 1954, F/Delta/1880/61/6/1, DR BDIC. This was likely a result of diminishing CIA support for the FTUC: see Carew, "American Labor in Fizzland," 39; Jay Lovestone, letter to Irving Brown, November 30, 1953, box 29, folder 16, IB MMA.

81. John J. M. O'Shea, letter to David Rousset, August 25, 1955, F/Delta/1880/61/6/1, DR BDIC. These figures derive from accounting spreadsheets and bank credit statements in F/Delta/1880/62/3 (for 1956) and 1880/62/4 (for 1957). The deposits were cabled in US dollars to an account held by a Mr. Philip Godfrey, Madrid, at the Banque Privée in Geneva, from the Chemical Corn Exchange Bank in New York, "by order of John O'Shea." It appears likely that large portions of the money were passed on to third parties engaged in propaganda work technically under the aegis of the Centre International d'Édition et de Documentation but unrelated to the CICRC's own projects.

82. Rousset, letter to Josselson, December 13, 1954.

83. "Liberté de la culture et 'poing intellectuel,'" *Esprit* 171 (September 1950): 371–374, at 373.

84. David Dallin, letter to David Rousset, March 27, 1950, F/Delta/1880/61/2/2, DR BDIC.

85. "Les conditions de travail de la Commission d'Enquête Internationale," F/Delta/1880/58/1/2, DR BDIC.

86. Damien Reumont, letter to David Rousset, November 13, 1952, F/Delta/1880/58/2/5, DR BDIC.

87. "Procès-verbal de la conférence," May 21, 1955, F/Delta/1880/59/1/11, DR BDIC.

88. "Procès-verbal de la conférence," May 2–3, 1953, F/Delta/1880/58/2/9 DR BDIC; Théo Bernard, "Compte rendu du séjour à New York de Théo Bernard, 2 au 21 avril 1953," n.d., F/Delta/1880/67/1, DR BDIC.

89. Merle Curti, *American Philanthropy Abroad* (New Brunswick, NJ: Transaction Books, 1988 [1963]), 399.

90. "Declaration solonnelle faite à l'unanimité par le Conseil d'Administration de l'Association Nationale des Anciennes Déportées et Internées de la Résistance," *Voix et Visages* 29 (May–June 1951): 2.

91. "Procès-verbal de la conférence," May 21, 1955.

92. Rousset, letter to Burnham, January 16, 1950; Rousset, letter to Dallin, January 20, 1950.

93. Rousset, letter to Dallin, January 20, 1950; David Rousset, letter to Sol Levitas, January 27, 1950, F/Delta/1880/61/2/1, DR BDIC.

94. H. S. Marchant, letter to F. R. H. Murray, March 6, 1951, FO/1110/378, BNA.

95. David Rousset, "Une lettre," *Synthèse* 7 (1949): 66–70, at 69.

96. Rousset, letter to Josselson, December 13, 1954.

97. Tony Judt, *Postwar: A History of Europe since 1945* (New York: Penguin, 2005), 223.

98. 1951 correspondence in box 12, folder 17, IB MMA; David Rousset, letter to Irving Brown, February 13, 1953, F/Delta/1880/48/3/1, DR BDIC; David Rousset, letter to Jay Lovestone, February 22, 1955, box 12, folder 16, IB MMA.

99. Irving Brown, letter to Jay Lovestone, December 12, 1950, box 11, folder 12, JL MMA.

100. Rousset, letter to Lovestone, November 15, 1950.

101. Thomas Dodd, quoted in Ulrike Weckel, "The Power of Images: Real and Fictional Roles of Atrocity Film Footage at Nuremberg," in *Reassessing the Nuremberg Military Tribunals: Transitional Justice, Trial Narratives, and Historiography*, ed. Kim C. Priemel and Alexa Stiller (New York: Berghahn Books, 2012), 221–248, at 225.

102. Léon Mazeaud, Président de la Fédération Nationale des Déportés et Internés de la Résistance, "La Proposition David Rousset," F/Delta/1880/54/3, DR BDIC.

103. Commission Française, "Lettre ouverte," 232.

104. Commission Internationale contre le Régime Concentrationnaire, "Déclaration Fondamentale," October 21, 1950, reproduced in CICRC, *Livre blanc sur les camps de concentration soviétiques*, 229–230, at 229.

105. "3ᵉ Session: Bruxelles 17/18 décembre 1950, Projet de Mlle Tillion: Critères du régime concentrationnaire," GT BNF, emphasis in original.

106. Damien Reumont, "Note sur le régime concentrationnaire," February 23, 1951, F/Delta/1880/58/1/6, DR BDIC, emphasis in original.

107. Commission Française, "Lettre ouverte."

108. "Procès-verbal de la séance," February 20, 1950, emphasis in original.

109. Germaine Tillion and Alison Rice, "'Déchiffrer le silence': A Conversation with Germaine Tillion," *Research in African Literatures* 35, no. 1 (Spring 2004): 162–179, at 169.

110. "Rapport sur les travaux de la deuxième session de la Commission Internationale contre le Régime Concentrationnaire," November 12–13, 1950, F/Delta/1880/58/3, DR BDIC.

111. Ibid.

112. Ibid, emphasis in original.

113. Ibid.

114. Charles Germain, "Postwar Prison Reform in France," *Annals of the American Academy of Political and Social Science* 293 (May 1954): 140; Fondation Internationale Pénale et Pénitentiaire, *Méthodes modernes de traitement pénitentiaire* (Berne: n.p., n.d. [1951]), 127. See also Jacques-Guy Petit et al., *Histoire des galères, bagnes et prisons, XIIIᵉ–XXᵉ siècles* (Paris: Bibliothèque Historique Privat, 1991), which argues that in postwar France "there could be no controversy over the principle of penal labor, only over its modalities" (305). Western postwar prison reformers rarely mentioned the Nazi camps, appearing to view such nightmarish facilities as unrelated to the problems of penal modernization. *Méthodes modernes* did not reference any wartime forms of detention in its potted narrative of scientific "progress" in detainee management.

115. "Rapport sur les travaux de la deuxième session."

116. "3ᵉ Session: Bruxelles, 17/18 décembre 1950."

117. Ibid.

118. Reumont, "Note sur le régime concentrationnaire." He was quoting from "The Concentration Camps," which he had read in translation.

119. Ibid., emphasis in original.

120. Ibid., 6. Note Reumont's substitution of "freedoms" for "rights" even when discussing the Human Rights Commission.

121. "CICRC 5ᵉ Session," April 1–2, 1951, GT BNF.

122. "Réunion de la Commission Internationale contre le Régime Concentrationnaire," January 20–21, 1952, F/Delta/1963, CF BDIC.

123. CICRC, *Livre blanc sur les camps de concentration soviétiques*, 10.

124. "CICRC 5ᵉ Session," April 1–2, 1951, 3.

125. Jan Eckel, "The International League for the Rights of Man, Amnesty International, and the Changing Fate of Human Rights Activism from the 1940s through the 1970s," *Humanity* 4, no. 2 (Summer 2013): 183–214, at 197.

126. Commission Belge Contre le Régime Concentrationnaire, "Compte rendu," November 9, 1950, GT BNF. For related reasons, Gabrielle Ferrières-Cavaillès, never deported outside France, resigned from the CICRC in 1951.

127. Fédération Nationale des Déportés du Travail, letter to David Rousset, December 11, 1949, F/Delta/1880/46/5/2, DR BDIC; Rémy Roure, *Le Monde*, August 20, 1946, quoted in Lagrou, *Legacy of Nazi Occupation*, 188.

128. Transcript, "Conférence de presse."

129. David Rousset, "Réponse à ceux qui ne veulent pas de l'ouverture d'une enquête," *Le Figaro littéraire*, January 14, 1950.

130. David Rousset, letter to Julius Margolin, June 20, 1950, F/Delta/1880/47/6, DR BDIC. See also David Rousset, letter to Dr. M. Dvorjetski, March 4, 1950, F/Delta/1880/47/3, DR BDIC.

131. David Rousset, letter to Julius Margolin, July 17, 1950, F/Delta/1880/56/1/2, DR BDIC.

132. Ibid.

133. "Assemblée générale," *Voix et Visages* 24 (February–March 1950): 2.

134. Damien Reumont, letter to Jules Jaspar, October 22, 1951, F/Delta/1880/60/2/1, DR BDIC, emphasis in original. On Belgian Catholics' general opposition to the "criterion of suffering" see Lagrou, *Legacy of Nazi Occupation*, 222–223.

135. "Constitution" of the CICRC as an *association sans but lucrative*, published in *Le Moniteur belge* on April 14, 1951, GT BNF.

136. Balachowsky in CICRC, *Livre blanc sur les camps de concentration soviétiques*, 10.

137. Léon Poliakov, *Mémoires* (Paris: Grancher, 1999), 189 and 191; Jonathan Judaken, "Léon Poliakov, the Origins of Holocaust Studies, and Theories of Antisemitism: Rereading *Bréviaire de la haine*," in *Post-Holocaust France and the Jews, 1945–1955*, ed. Seán Hand and Steven T. Katz (New York: NYU Press, 2015), 169–192. See also Laura Jockusch, *Collect and Record! Jewish Holocaust Documentation in Early Postwar Europe* (New York: Oxford University Press, 2012), 63–65.

138. Poliakov, *Mémoires*, 203–204. Poliakov notes that this work provided his only income aside from royalties at one point.

139. Rémy Roure was an exception: "De l'euthanasie au génocide," *Évidences* 19 (May–June 1951): 2–12.

140. See chapter 6. She also later conducted similar work in Austria.

141. David Rousset, letter to Catherine Goetschel, February 8, 1954, F/Delta/1880/70/8, DR BDIC.

142. Untitled report, n.d., F/Delta/1880/70/8, DR BDIC.

143. Pierre Grappin, review of *La Bréviaire de la haine: Le IIIᵉ Reich et les Juifs*, by Léon Poliakov (Paris: Calmann-Lévy, 1951), in *Politique étrangère* 16, nos. 4–5 (1951): 430–431;

Jean-Henri Roy, review of *La Bréviaire de la haine* in *Les Temps modernes* 71 (September 1951): 574.

144. Hannah Arendt, "The History of a Great Crime," review of *La Bréviaire de la haine* in *Commentary* 13 (March 1952): 300–304.

145. Léon Poliakov, letter to David Rousset, March 25, 1954, F/Delta/1880/70/8, DR BDIC.

146. Léon Poliakov, *La Bréviaire de la haine: Le III<sup>e</sup> Reich et les Juifs* (Paris: Calmann-Lévy, 1951), 248–249.

147. David Rousset, letter to Théo Bernard, September 15, 1952, F/Delta/1880/67/6, DR BDIC.

148. On the "Jewish lawyers" roundup see Robert Badinter, *Un antisémitisme ordinaire: Vichy et les avocats juifs (1940–1944)* (Paris: Fayard, 1997); Julie Fette, *Exclusions: Practicing Prejudice in French Law and Medicine, 1920–1945* (Ithaca, NY: Cornell University Press, 2012), chap. 6. Especially significant works on Drancy include Annette Wieviorka and Michel Lafitte, *À l'interieur du camp de Drancy* (Paris: Perrin, 2012); Maurice Rajsfus, *Drancy: Un camp de concentration très ordinaire*, rev. ed. (Paris: Cherche Midi, 2012); Denis Peschanski, *La France des camps: L'internement, 1938–1946* (Paris: Gallimard, 2002).

149. Office de Radiodiffusion Télévision Française, unedited transcript of "Le monde concentrationnaire, écoute du jeudi 25 mars 1965," 28 and 23, F/Delta/1880/43/1, DR BDIC, 24.

150. Rajsfus, *Drancy*, 71 and 83; interview with Yves Jouffa, DCCCXLVI-10, CDJC.

151. Rajsfus, *Drancy*, 224, 266–267, and 278; Chef de Service Kanzlei-Effectifs, Note de Service no. 2 to M. Théo Bernard, Bureau des Effectifs, M. le Lt-Colonel Blum, Cdt. de Camp, September 3, 1943, CCLXXVI-8d, CDJC. This document "confirmed" Bernard in his role as *chef de service adjoint*, but the date of his appointment is unclear: "État du Personnel (Categorie C1)," August 5, 1943, CCCLXXVI-12, CDJC, already listed him as occupying the job. See also Wieviorka and Lafitte, *À l'interieur du camp*, 234 and 237.

152. Rajsfus, *Drancy*, 276.

153. Adam Rayski, *Le Choix des Juifs sous Vichy: Entre soumission et résistance* (Paris: La Découverte, 1992), 143; see also Wieviorka and Lafitte, *À l'interieur du camp*, 227.

154. Wieviorka and Lafitte, *À l'interieur du camp*, 237–238. On Effectifs' responsibility for roll call after Brunner's takeover see Rajsfus, *Drancy*, 191. From this point forward, however, Effectifs did *not* play a part in selecting deportees: see Georges Wellers, *L'Étoile jaune à l'heure de Vichy: De Drancy à Auschwitz* (Paris: Fayard, 1973), 251.

155. Emmanuel Langberg, "Note de Service," August 1, 1944, DLXIII-46, CDJC. Many accounts relate the deportation of children from Drancy; see especially André Rosenberg, *Les enfants dans la Shoah: La déportation des enfants juifs et tsiganes de France* (Paris: Éditions de Paris, 2013).

156. Théo Bernard, "Judenlager Drancy," *La Revue internationale* 5 (May 1946): 417–429, at 417.

157. Office de Radiodiffusion-Télévision Française, "Le Monde Concentrationnaire," 21–22.

158. Ibid., 17. See also Georges Wellers, "Birkenau, qu'est-ce que c'est?," *Le Monde juif* 68 (October–November 1986).

159. Bernard, "Judenlager Drancy," 417.

160. Damien Reumont, letter to Nicolas Plastiras, January 20, 1952, reproduced in Commission Internationale contre le Régime Concentrationnaire, *Livre blanc sur les camps d'internement en Grèce* (Paris: Pavois, 1953), 73.

161. Bernard, "Judenlager Drancy," 423.

162. Ibid.

163. Ibid., 418 and 417.

164. Rajsfus categorically labels Drancy a "camp de concentration." Wieviorka and Lafitte define it as such from the time of Brunner's arrival.

165. "Plaidorie de M. Théo Bernard, Audience du 10 June 1953, Cour d'Appel de Paris, 11ème chambre, Sténotypie par Cabinet Bluet, Fascicule 3," F/Delta/1880/56/3/2, DR BDIC.

166. Samuel Moyn, *The Last Utopia: Human Rights in History* (Cambridge, MA: Harvard University Press, 2010), 7.

167. Henry Damien Reumont, "The International Commission against Concentration Camp Practices," *Associations: The Review of International Associations and Meetings* 9 (September 1954): 405–407.

168. Ibid., 406.

169. "Procès-verbal de la conférence," October 20–21, 1950, F/Delta/1880/58/1/2, DR BDIC.

170. Ibid.; Alfred-Serge Balachowsky, in "Les anciens déportés répondent à l'appel de David Rousset," *Le Figaro littéraire*, November 19, 1949.

## 4. NUREMBERG RESTAGED

1. David Rousset, "Au secours des déportés dans les camps soviétiques. Un appel de David Rousset aux anciens déportés des camps nazis," *Le Figaro littéraire*, November 12, 1949.

2. Transcript, "Conférence de presse donnée par M. David Rousset mardi 15 novembre 1949," F/Delta/1880/53/2, DR BDIC.

3. Rousset, "Au secours des déportés."

4. Samuel Moyn, *The Last Utopia: Human Rights in History* (Cambridge, MA: Harvard University Press, 2010), 69.

5. On the European human rights regime see Marco Duranti, *The Conservative Human Rights Revolution: European Identity, Transnational Politics, and the Origins of the European Convention* (Oxford: Oxford University Press, 2017); A. W. Brian Simpson, *Human Rights and the End of Empire: Britain and the Genesis of the European Convention* (Oxford: Oxford University Press, 2001).

6. Henri Monneray, "La justice internationale," *La Nef* 60/61 (December 1949–January 1950): 63–68, at 65.

7. "Note sur la Commission Internationale contre le Régime Concentrationnaire, décembre 1950," December 28, 1950, F/Delta/1880/58/1/5, DR BDIC.

8. Commission Internationale contre le Régime Concentrationnaire, *Livre blanc sur les camps de concentration soviétiques* (Paris: Pavois, 1951), 174.

9. J. H. Peck, draft memorandum on "Anti-Communist Propaganda Operation," July 27, 1951, FO 1110–460, BNA.

10. Devin O. Pendas, "Seeking Justice, Finding Law: Nazi Trials in Postwar Europe," *Journal of Modern History* 81, no. 2 (June 2009): 347–368, at 353. On Nuremberg as "one of the Cold War's first major battles" see Francine Hirsch, "The Soviets at Nuremberg: International Law, Propaganda, and the Making of the Postwar Order," *American Historical Review* 113, no. 3 (June 2008): 701–730, at 703. On the political nature of international criminal law see Judith N. Shklar, *Legalism: Law, Morals, and Political Trials* (Cambridge, MA: Harvard University Press, 1964; 1986), esp. 151–179; Mark Osiel, *Mass Atrocity, Collective Memory, and the Law* (New Brunswick, NJ: Transaction, 1997); Gary Bass, *Stay the Hand of Vengeance: The Politics of War Crimes Tribunals* (Princeton, NJ: Princeton University Press, 2000); Gerry Simpson, *Law, War and Crime: War Crimes Trials and the Reinvention of International Law* (Cambridge: Polity, 2007), 11–29. On the politics of the post–World War II trials see Donald Bloxham, "Prosecuting the Past in the Postwar Decade: Political Strategy and National Myth-Making," in *The Holocaust and Justice: Rep-*

*resentation and Historiography of the Holocaust in Postwar Trials*, ed. David Bankier and Dan Michman (Jerusalem: Yad Vashem / Berghahn Books, 2010), 23–43.

11. Otto Kirchheimer, *Political Justice: The Use of Legal Procedure for Political Ends* (Princeton, NJ: Princeton University Press, 1961), 1.

12. On the sometimes unstable boundary between "real" and "show" trials see Simpson, *Law, War and Crime*, 105–131.

13. Lawrence Douglas, "From IMT to NMT: The Emergence of a Jurisprudence of Atrocity," in *Reassessing the Nuremberg Military Tribunals: Transitional Justice, Trial Narratives, and Historiography*, ed. Kim C. Priemel and Alexa Stiller (New York: Berghahn Books, 2012), 276–295, at 287.

14. Samuel Moyn, "From Aggression to Atrocity: Rethinking the History of International Criminal Law," forthcoming in *The Oxford Handbook of International Criminal Law*, ed. Kevin Jon Heller et al.

15. Annette Wieviorka, *The Era of the Witness*, trans. Jared Stark (Ithaca, NY: Cornell University Press, 2006), 56.

16. David Rousset, letter to Danenberg, January 28, 1950, F/Delta/1880/61/2/1, DR BDIC.

17. See Arthur Jay Klinghoffer and Judith Apter Klinghoffer, *International Citizens' Tribunals: Mobilizing Public Opinion to Advance Human Rights* (New York: Palgrave, 2002).

18. Martin-Chauffier had also hoped to testify at the Lüneburg Belsen Trial in 1945 and was indignant that he was not called upon to do so.

19. Jonathan Friedman, "The Sachsenhausen Trials: War Crimes Prosecutions in the Soviet Occupation Zone and in West and East Germany," in *Atrocities on Trial: Historical Perspectives on the Politics of Prosecuting War Crimes*, ed. Patricia Heberer and Jürgen Matthäus (Lincoln: University of Nebraska, 2008), 159–184, at 168.

20. David Rousset and Émile Copfermann, *David Rousset: Une vie dans le siècle, fragments d'autobiographie* (Paris: Plon, 1991), 98.

21. "Les conditions de travail de la Commission d'enquête internationale," n.d. [1950], F/Delta/1880/58/1/2.

22. Germaine Tillion, "Le procès des assassins de Ravensbrück," *Voix et Visages* 7 (March 1947).

23. Louis Martin-Chauffier, "Et s'il n'en reste qu'un ce sera trop!," *Le Patriote résistant* 15 (October 1, 1946); Louis Martin-Chauffier, "Le crime appelle le châtiment," *Le Patriote résistant* 16 (October 15, 1946).

24. David Rousset, *Les Jours de notre mort* (Paris: Fayard/Pluriel, 2012), 9.

25. *Sondages* 30 (November 15, 1946): 454.

26. Rémy Roure, "L'ineffaçable crime," *Évidences* 4 (October 1949): 27–30, at 30. See also Rémy Roure, "Il faut veiller," *Évidences* 18 (April 1951): 3. Roure was a staunch anticommunist, but it never occurred to him (or to anyone involved in the CICRC) to question Nuremberg's legacy because of the presence of Soviet judges, as later critics of the gulag sometimes do—e.g., Anne Applebaum, *Gulag: A History of the Soviet Camps* (New York: Doubleday, 2003), 568. Roure, alongside Martin-Chauffier, was also a major defender of France's domestic postwar trials.

27. André Boissarie, "La répression," *La Nef* 60/61 (December 1949–January 1950): 53–62, at 62.

28. Hannah Arendt, *Eichmann in Jerusalem: A Report on the Banality of Evil*, rev. ed. (New York: Penguin, 1994), 269; François de Menthon in *Trial of the Major War Criminals before the International Military Tribunal, Nuremberg, 14 November 1945–1 October 1946*, vol. 5 (Nuremberg, 1947–1949), 408 (January 17, 1946). See also Lawrence Douglas, *The Memory of Judgment: Making Law and History in the Trials of the Holocaust* (New Haven, CT: Yale University Press, 2001), 80–81.

29. "Rapport sur les travaux de la deuxième session de la Commission Internationale contre le Régime Concentrationnaire," November 12–13, 1950, 9–10, F/Delta/1880/58/3, DR BDIC.

30. "Les conditions de travail." The term "crimes against humanity" had nineteenth-century origins; its first formal use in relation to war crimes was an international 1915 declaration condemning Ottoman atrocities. But it was the post–World War II trials that brought the term firmly into international legal doctrine and common parlance. See Roger S. Clark, "History of Efforts to Codify Crimes against Humanity," in *Forging a Convention for Crimes against Humanity*, ed. Leila Nadya Sadat (New York: Cambridge University Press, 2011), 8–27, at 10; M. Cherif Bassiouni, *Crimes against Humanity in International Criminal Law*, 2nd rev. ed. (The Hague: Kluwer Law International, 1999); Michele Tusan, "'Crimes against Humanity': Human Rights, the British Empire, and the Origins of the Response to the Armenian Genocide," *American Historical Review* 119, no. 1 (February 2014): 47–77.

31. "Charter of the International Military Tribunal," http://avalon.law.yale.edu/imt/imtconst.asp.

32. United Nations War Crimes Commission, *History of the United Nations War Crimes Commission and the Development of the Laws of War* (London: HMSO, 1948), 179.

33. "Charter of the International Military Tribunal." Two defendants were ultimately convicted on this count alone, but the judgment justified the sentence through explicit discussion of the required nexus to armed conflict.

34. Cited in Bassiouni, *Crimes against Humanity*, 30. On failed World Jewish Congress efforts to encourage a more "victim-centered" justice at Nuremberg see Mark Lewis, *The Birth of the New Justice: The Internationalization of Crime and Punishment, 1919–1950* (Oxford: Oxford University Press, 2014), 150–180, at 165.

35. Cited in Douglas, *Memory of Judgment*, 50.

36. Devin O. Pendas, "The Fate of Nuremberg: The Legacy and Impact of the Nuremberg Trials in Postwar Germany," in Priemel and Stiller, *Reassessing the Nuremberg Military Tribunals*, 249–275, at 258. See also Steven R. Ratner, Jason S. Abrams, and James L. Bischoff, *Accountability for Human Rights Atrocities in International Law: Beyond the Nuremberg Legacy*, 3rd ed. (New York: Oxford University Press, 2009), 54; Kevin Jon Heller, *The Nuremberg Military Tribunals and the Origins of International Criminal Law* (New York: Oxford University Press, 2011), 250. Matters are further complicated by the fact that German courts did try Germans for pre-1939 "crimes against humanity" against other Germans until prohibited from doing so in 1951.

37. "Rapport sur les travaux de la deuxième session."

38. Legal historians tend to view the nexus requirement as fading gradually over time. The Nuremberg Principles drafted by the UN's International Law Commission in 1950 did remove the requirement with regard to "murder, enslavement, deportation and other inhuman acts done against any civilian population." Its 1951 and 1954 Draft Code did likewise. However, the initiative was subsequently shelved until the 1980s.

39. Henri de Linge, "Dernière audience au procès de Bruxelles," *Le Figaro*, May 26–27, 1951.

40. Robert Tréno [Ernest Reynaud], "Un crime contre l'humanité et le socialisme," *Franc-Tireur*, November 23, 1950.

41. "Notre carnet," *Preuves* 7 (September 1951): 32.

42. David Rousset, letter to Jay Lovestone, November 15, 1950, F/Delta/1880/48/1, DR BDIC.

43. CICRC, *Livre blanc sur les camps de concentration soviétiques*, 230.

44. See Frédéric Pottecher, *Le Procès Pétain* (Paris: Éditions Jean-Claude Lattès, 1980), 207–208.

45. Paul Arrighi and Léon Mazeaud, "Pièce no. 3," reproduced in CICRC, *Livre blanc sur les camps de concentration soviétiques*, 234–236.

46. Paul Arrighi, letter to David Rousset, November 7, 1950, F/Delta/1880/58/1/3, DR BDIC.

47. Arrighi and Mazeaud, "Pièce no. 3," 236.

48. "Rapport sur les travaux de la deuxième session"; David Rousset, letter to Paul Arrighi, November 29, 1950, F/Delta/1880/58/1/3, DR BDIC.

49. Georges André and Benjamin Stomps served as "*assesseurs*" and signed the final judgment, as did Balachowsky.

50. Damien Reumont, letter to David Rousset, March 22, 1951, F/Delta/1880/58/1/8, DR BDIC.

51. "Rapport sur les travaux de la deuxième session."

52. Jean Cayrol, letter to David Rousset, n.d. [December 1949], F/Delta/1880/46/ 5/1, DR BDIC.

53. David Rousset, letter to Damien Reumont, March 13, 1951, F/Delta/1880/58/1/8, DR BDIC.

54. "Rapport sur les travaux de la deuxième session."

55. As Simpson writes, "the failure of official criminal law to punish may not be fatal to efforts at stigmatizing those guilty of international crimes": *Law, War, and Crime*, 75. For a broader argument that assignment of moral stigma (and not, e.g., retaliation) is in any case the fundamental reason to prosecute "crimes against humanity" see Reinhard Merkel, "The Law of the Nuremberg Trial: Valid, Dubious, Outdated," in *Perspectives on the Nuremberg Trial*, ed. Guénaël Mettraux (New York: Oxford University Press, 2008), 555–576, at 575–576.

56. "Un fonctionnaire du NKVD et 7 juges anciens déportés sont les vedettes d'un procès sans accusé," *France-Soir*, May 22, 1951.

57. "Slave Labor on Trial," editorial, *New York Times*, May 21, 1951.

58. "Commission Internationale contre le Régime Concentrationnaire, V$^e$ session," April 1–2, 1951, GT BNF.

59. "Note de M. Rousset sur les décisions prises concernant le procès des camps soviétiques," April 7, 1951, GT BNF.

60. Albert Camus, editorial, *Combat*, September 27, 1944.

61. François de Menthon, in *Trial of the Major War Criminals*, vol. 5, 368 (January 17, 1946).

62. "Note de M. Rousset."

63. Telford Taylor, *The Anatomy of the Nuremberg Trials: A Personal Memoir* (New York: Knopf, 1992), 148–149.

64. See Douglas, *Memory of Judgment*, 95–182; Wieviorka, *Era of the Witness*; Shoshana Felman, *The Juridical Unconscious: Trials and Traumas in the Twentieth Century* (Cambridge, MA: Harvard University Press, 2002).

65. Karl Jaspers, quoted in Arendt, *Eichmann in Jerusalem*, 269.

66. Henri de Linge, "Dernière audience au procès de Bruxelles," *Le Figaro*, May 26–27, 1951.

67. "Le procès du régime concentrationnaire," *Le Soir* (Belgium), May 23, 1951.

68. CICRC, *Livre blanc sur les camps de concentration soviétiques*, 19.

69. However, for challenges to the notion that "victim-centered" jurisprudence necessarily provides victims with "closure" or other therapeutic benefits see Eric Stover, *The Witnesses: War Crimes and the Promise of Justice in The Hague* (Philadelphia: University of Pennsylvania Press, 2005); Marie-Bénédicte Dembour and Emily Haslam, "Silencing Hearings? Victim-Witnesses at War Crimes Trials," *European Journal of International Law* 15, no. 1 (2004): 151–177. For an influential defense of non-juridical "truth and reconciliation"

procedures as conducive to victim healing (in part through the "restorative power" of testimony) see Martha Minow, *Between Vengeance and Forgiveness: Facing History after Genocide and Mass Violence* (Boston: Beacon, 1999), 66.

70. Taylor, *Anatomy of the Nuremberg Trials*, 148–149.

71. Quoted in Ulrike Weckel, "The Power of Images: Real and Fictional Roles of Atrocity Film Footage at Nuremberg," in Priemel and Stiller, *Reassessing the Nuremberg Military Tribunals*, 221–248, at 223. On similar anxieties following the Armenian genocide and Ukrainian pogroms see Alexandra Garbarini, "Document Volumes and the Status of Victim Testimony in the Era of the First World War and Its Aftermath," *Études arméniennes contemporaines* 5 (2015): 113–138.

72. Douglas, "From IMT to NMT," 288. See also Heller, *Nuremberg Military Tribunals*, 141–146.

73. "Slave Camp 'Trial' Due to Open Today," *New York Times*, May 20, 1951.

74. David Rousset, letter to Anna Bourguina, March 22, 1950, F/Delta/1880/69/1, DR BDIC.

75. [Damien Reumont], "Conférence de Bruxelles des 25 et 26 février 1951," F/Delta/1880/58/1/7, DR BDIC.

76. Pierre Scize, "Les survivants des camps ont commencé d'instruire le procès de l'univers concentrationnaire soviétique," *Le Figaro*, May 22, 1951.

77. Elisabeth Ingrand, letter to David Rousset, February 20, 1951, F/Delta/1880/58/1/7, DR BDIC.

78. David Rousset, letter to Damien Reumont, February 17, 1951, F/Delta/1880/58/1/7, DR BDIC.

79. David Dallin, memorandum to the IRD, "Outline of the Conditions Required for the Investigation of Slave Labor," n.d. [November 1949], FO/371/78978, BNA.

80. Rousset, letter to Damien Reumont, February 17, 1951.

81. "CICRC, Commission d'Instruction, Interrogatoire des témoins, Questionnaire pour le cas de la Russie Soviétique," January 31, 1951, GT BNF.

82. "Conférence de Bruxelles des 25 et 26 février 1951," F/Delta/1880/58/1/7, DR BDIC.

83. Irving Brown, letter to David Rousset, March 10, 1951, box 12, folder 17, IB MMA.

84. Robert Daniel Murphy, Telegram 1782 to Secretary of State, May 9, 1951, RG 59, box 4361, NARA.

85. Dean Acheson, Telegram 1535 to American Embassy Brussels, May 17, 1951, RG 59, box 4361, NARA.

86. Dean Acheson, Telegram 1569 to American Embassy Brussels, May 22–23, 1951, RG 59, box 4361, NARA.

87. See Klinghoffer and Klinghoffer, *International Citizens' Tribunals*, 27, on the British government's resort to this tactic during the Reichstag "countertrial."

88. Damien Reumont, letter to Paul van Zeeland, March 10, 1951 (circulated to members May 10, 1951), GT BNF, emphasis in original.

89. Paul van Zeeland, letter to Damien Reumont, April 4, 1951 (circulated to members May 10, 1951), GT BNF.

90. On this third affair see Direction générale P 1ère Direction Section 3, "Note pour M. le Ministre, no. 452/1–411/12496," October 5, 1951, dossier no. 12.585 (Belgique-Russie), ADB.

91. "Procès-verbal de la conférence," May 8–9, 1951, GT BNF.

92. Ibid.

93. Damien Reumont, letter to CICRC members, May 12, 1951, GT BNF.

94. CICRC, *Livre blanc sur les camps de concentration soviétiques*, 11.

95. Ibid., 10–11.

96. Ibid., 16–17.

97. Ibid., 25.

98. Ibid., 160.

99. Several of the non-Soviet nationals had been living in the USSR prior to their arrest; only three Germans, two Poles, and the Czechoslovakian were deported from territory taken over by the wartime Red Army. One additional German was transferred from a POW camp.

100. Kostiuk testified at Brussels under the name Boris Podalak, Brońska-Pampuch as Jadwiga Kowalska, and Leonhard under her own name.

101. CICRC, *Livre blanc sur les camps de concentration soviétiques*, 128.

102. Donald Bloxham, *Genocide on Trial: War Crimes Trials and the Formation of Holocaust History and Memory* (Oxford: Oxford University Press, 2001), 219.

103. CICRC, *Livre blanc sur les camps de concentration soviétiques*, 158.

104. "Un fonctionnaire du NKVD," *France-Soir*, May 22, 1951.

105. CICRC, *Livre blanc sur les camps de concentration soviétiques*, 144. See Nick Baron, *Soviet Karelia: Politics, Planning, and Terror in Stalin's Russia, 1920–1939* (New York: Routledge, 2007), 133–134.

106. CICRC, *Livre blanc sur les camps de concentration soviétiques*, 160.

107. David Rousset, Théo Bernard, and Gérard Rosenthal, *Pour la vérité sur les camps concentrationnaires (Un procès antistalinien à Paris)* (Paris: Ramsey, 1990), 109.

108. CICRC, *Livre blanc sur les camps de concentration soviétiques*, 156.

109. Ibid., 160.

110. Ibid., 156.

111. This phrase was used by IRD operatives in relation to the earlier *Lettres françaises* case: L. Sheridan, "Minutes," January 9, 1951, FO/1110/378, BNA.

112. CICRC, *Livre blanc sur les camps de concentration soviétiques*, 46 and 33.

113. Ibid., 127 and 139.

114. Ibid., 76.

115. Ibid., 27, 33, 153, 154.

116. See especially Anthea Vogl, "Telling Stories from Start to Finish: Exploring the Demand for Narrative in Refugee Testimony," *Griffith Law Review* 22, no. 1 (2013): 63–86.

117. Stover, *Witnesses*, 129.

118. Robert Daniel Murphy, telegram 1893 to Secretary of State, May 29, 1951, RG 59, box 4361, NARA.

119. CICRC, *Livre blanc sur les camps de concentration soviétiques*, 33.

120. Ibid., 129.

121. "Le procès du régime concentrationnaire," *Le Soir* (Belgium), May 23, 1951.

122. Pierre Scize, "Pathétique confrontation entre deux enfers," *Le Figaro*, May 24, 1951.

123. Henri Laurent, "Les témoins de Rousset avouent qu'ils furent des mercenaires de Hitler!," *Le Drapeau rouge*, May 25, 1951.

124. "Le procès de Bruxelles," *Le Monde*, May 25, 1951; Henri de Linge, "Il y a en Russe 12 à 17 millions de détenus," *Le Figaro*, 25 May, 1951.

125. CICRC, *Livre blanc sur les camps de concentration soviétiques*, 105.

126. Ibid., 157.

127. Ibid.

128. "Le défilé des anciens détenus," *Le Monde*, May 26, 1951.

129. Rémy Roure, "Les silences de l'URSS," *Le Monde*, May 29, 1951.

130. Rousset, Bernard, and Rosenthal, *Pour la vérité*, 194.

131. On the Russell Tribunal's relationship to the Nuremberg legacy see Eleanor Davey, *Idealism beyond Borders: The French Revolutionary Left and the Rise of Humanitarianism, 1954–1988* (Cambridge: Cambridge University Press, 2015), 83–94.

132. Damien Reumont, "Concerne: Déclaration des témoins à décharge invités au procès de Bruxelles, mai 1951," June 1, 1951, GT BNF.

133. CICRC, *Livre blanc sur les camps de concentration soviétiques*, 11.

134. P.P., "Les camps soviétiques ont été jugés à Bruxelles," *Preuves* 4 (June 1951): 23.

135. "Trial Is Mock, but Not Punch in Reds' Noses," *Chicago Daily Tribune*, June 2, 1951. See also Luc Somerhausen, "Un ancien accusateur de David Rousset lui écrit," *Le Figaro littéraire*, January 26, 1963.

136. CICRC, *Livre blanc sur les camps de concentration soviétiques*, 161.

137. Ibid., 167–168.

138. Ibid., 173–174.

139. Ibid., 174.

140. Moyn, "From Aggression to Atrocity."

141. Germaine Tillion, letter to Adelaide Hautval, December 21, 1951, dossier "Publications de la Commission Internationale," folder "Germaine Tillion, lettres à divers, Envoi du compte-rendu de la Commission spéciale d'Enquête, 21 décembre 1951," GT BNF.

142. M. Cherif Bassiouni, "The 'Nuremberg Legacy,'" in Mettraux, *Perspectives on the Nuremberg Trial*, 577–598, at 595.

143. "Pour combattre 'l'univers concentrationnaire' partout où il s'installe: Les victimes deviennent juges," *Le Peuple* (Belgium), November 15, 1950.

## 5. INTO THE LABYRINTH OF FRANCO'S PRISONS

1. Elisabeth Ingrand, letter to David Rousset, February 20, 1951, F/Delta/1880/58/1/7, DR BDIC.

2. Ricard Vinyes, *Irredentas: La presas políticas y sus hijos en las cárceles de Franco* (Madrid: Temas de Hoy, 2002), 46. See also Ricard Vinyes, "Territoris de càstig (les presons franquistes, 1939–1959)," in *Notícia de la negra nit: Vides i veus a les presons franquistes (1939–1959)*, ed. Associació Catalana d'Expresos Polítics (Barcelona: Diputació de Barcelona, 2001), 43–61; Ricard Vinyes, "El universo penitenciario durante el franquismo," in *Una Inmensa prisión: Los campos de concentración y las prisiones durante la guerra civil y el franquismo*, ed. Carme Molinero, Margarita Tintó Sala, and Jaume Sobrequés i Callicó (Barcelona: Crítica, 2003), 155–175, at 160–162.

3. Vinyes, *Irredentas*, 32.

4. Commission Internationale contre le Régime Concentrationnaire, *Livre blanc sur le système pénitentiaire espagnol* (Paris: Pavois, 1953), 23.

5. Paul Preston, *The Spanish Holocaust: Inquisition and Extermination in Twentieth-Century Spain* (New York: Norton, 2012), provides a synthesis of the enormous literature on the Francoist repression. On prisons and camps, in addition to works cited elsewhere in this chapter, see Francisco Espinosa Maestre, ed., *Violencia roja y azul: España, 1936–1950* (Barcelona: Crítica, 2010); Gutmaro Gómez Bravo, *El exilio interior: Cárcel y represión en la España franquista (1939–1950)* (Madrid: Taurus, 2009).

6. See Javier Rodrigo, *Cautivos: Campos de concentración en la España franquista, 1936–1947* (Barcelona: Crítica, 2005); Javier Rodrigo, "Exploitation, Fascist Violence, and Social Cleansing: A Study of Franco's Concentration Camps from a Comparative Perspective," *European Review of History* 19 (2012): 553–573.

7. The CICRC's 1953 conclusions have played a role in scholars' debates over these numbers. See Domingo Rodríguez Teijeiro, *Las cárceles de Franco: Configuración, evolución y función del sistema penitenciario franquista (1936–1945)* (Madrid: Catarata, 2011), 85–94.

8. Preston, *Spanish Holocaust*, 509.

9. Julius Ruiz, "A Spanish Genocide? Reflections on the Francoist Repression after the Civil War," *Contemporary European History* 14, no. 2 (May 2005): 171–191, at 189; Rodríguez, *Las cárceles de Franco*, 90. On the 1940s as an era of "pacification," not "peace," see Javier Rodrigo, "'Our Fatherland Was Full of Weeds': Violence during the Spanish Civil War and the Franco Dictatorship," in *"If You Tolerate This . . .": The Spanish Civil War in*

*the Age of Total War*, ed. Martin Baumeister and Stefanie Schüler-Springorum (Frankfurt: Campus Verlag, 2008), 135–153, at 152. On the 1950s see Michael Richards, *After the Civil War: Making Memory and Re-Making Spain since 1936* (Cambridge: Cambridge University Press, 2013), 128–155.

10. Stanley Payne, *Fascism in Spain, 1923–1977* (Madison: University of Wisconsin Press, 1999), 401 and 477.

11. Ruiz, "Spanish Genocide?," 189.

12. Denis Peschanski, *La France des camps: L'internement, 1938–1946* (Paris: Gallimard, 2002), 36–41.

13. Ibid., 41–44. See also Geneviève Dreyfus-Armand, *Les Camps sur la plage: Un exil espagnol* (Paris: Autrement, 1995); Scott Soo, *The Routes to Exile: France and the Spanish Civil War Refugees, 1939–2009* (Manchester: Manchester University Press, 2013).

14. See Andrea Pitzer's account of Gurs's evolution over time in *One Long Night: A Global History of Concentration Camps* (New York: Little, Brown, 2017), 225–231 and 246–247.

15. David Wingeate Pike, *Spaniards in the Holocaust: Mauthausen, the Terror on the Danube* (London: Routledge, 2000), 11.

16. "Calmarza Vallejo, José," n.d., F/Delta/1880/55/5, DR BDIC.

17. "Condemnations de communistes à Montauban," *La Dépêche* (Toulouse), November 27, 1941, reproduced in Wilebaldo Solano, "De la lutte contre le fascisme à la centrale d'Eysses," in *Républicains espagnols en Midi-Pyrénées: Exil, histoire et mémoire*, ed. José Jornet (Toulouse: Presses Universitaires du Mirail, 2005), 189–195, at 194.

18. Pike, *Spaniards in the Holocaust*, 157. The committee included communists.

19. It also welcomed surviving spouses and children of Spaniards who had died in the deportation, for a total membership of roughly twenty-five hundred. "Fédération espagnole des déportés et internés politiques (F.E.D.I.P.)," F/Delta/1880/55/ 3.

20. Geneviève Dreyfus-Armand, *L'Exil des républicains espagnols en France: De la guerre civile à la mort de Franco* (Paris: Albin Michel, 1999), 196.

21. José Calmarza and José Domenech, letter to Trygve Lie, November 2, 1950, box 158, folder 1950, JE IISH; José Ester Borrás, letter to Damien Reumont, December 5, 1950, box 157, JE IISH.

22. Harry Truman, quoted in Robert Beisner, *Dean Acheson: A Life in the Cold War* (New York: Oxford, 2009), 384.

23. Fédération espagnole des déportés et internés politiques, *Dossier sur l'affaire espagnole: Plainte contre le régime du Général Franco* (Paris: FEDIP, n.d. [November 1950]).

24. Calmarza and Domenech, letter to Lie, November 2, 1950.

25. José Ester, letter to David Rousset, October 29, 1952, F/Delta/1880/48/2, DR BDIC.

26. Ester, letter to Reumont, December 5, 1950.

27. Arthur Koestler, *Scum of the Earth* (London: Hutchinson, 1968), 103. On Spanish memory of French internment see Francie Cate-Arries, *Spanish Culture behind Barbed Wire: Memory and Representation of the French Concentration Camps, 1939–1945* (Lewisburg, PA: Bucknell University Press, 2004). There is no indication that Spanish members contested the CICRC's definition of a "concentrationary regime," though José Ester, "Apuntes de la Réunion de la CICRC," December 17–18, 1950, box 157, JE IISH, is suggestive.

28. For instance, Albert Camus, "Pourquoi l'Espagne: Réponse à Gabriel Marcel," *Combat*, November 25, 1948.

29. On the Spanish Civil War as an event "integrated into the internal struggles of [French] national politics" see Pierre Laborie, *L'Opinion française sous Vichy* (Paris: Seuil, 1990), 132–133 and 164; David Wingeate Pike, *Les Français et la guerre d'Espagne* (Paris: Publications de la Sorbonne, 1975).

30. Quoted in Émile Temime, *1936, La guerre d'Espagne commence* (Brussels: Éditions Complèxe, 2006), 121. See also Maryse Bertrande de Muñoz, *La Guerre civile espagnole et la littérature française* (Ottawa: Didier, 1972), 93–95.

31. Louis Martin-Chauffier, "Message adressé au meeting organisé le 23 novembre 1950 par la Défense des Immigrés," 1CH2, LMC IMEC.

32. David Rousset, "Barcelone 1936" (speech), n.d. [1950], F/Delta/1880/31/2 DR BDIC; "Meeting contre Franco avec David Rousset, Georges Altman," *Le Populaire,* April 5, 1950. For Rousset's own account of his activities in Barcelona see "David Rousset's Testimony," in Miguel Romero, *The Spanish Civil War in Euzkadi and Catalonia, Notebooks for Study and Research 13* (Amsterdam: International Institute for Research and Education, 1991), 41–43. The narrative of antifascist combat woven into *Les Jours de notre mort* also begins in Spain.

33. Rousset, "Barcelone 1936."

34. David Rousset, letter to Peter Lutsches, July 12, 1952, F/Delta/1880/60/4, DR BDIC.

35. Rousset, "Barcelone 1936."

36. This should be contrasted with American antitotalitarian discourse: e.g., Hannah Arendt's *The Origins of Totalitarianism* (Cleveland: Meridian, 1958) categorized Spain among "nontotalitarian dictatorships" (309).

37. Camus, "Pourquoi l'Espagne."

38. Robert Tréno [Ernest Reynaud], "Le Munich espagnol est consommé," *Franc-Tireur,* January 11, 1951; Robert Tréno [Ernest Reynaud], "Du pareil au même," *Franc-Tireur,* January 13–14, 1951.

39. "Les condamnés à mort d'Espagne," *Preuves,* March 13, 1952.

40. Rousset, "Barcelone 1936."

41. Emmanuel Mounier, letter to David Rousset, February 7, 1950, F/Delta/1880/46/5/2, DR BDIC.

42. Richard S. Winslow, letter to Walter Kotschnig, February 27, 1950, RG 84, box 50, NARA.

43. Gerard Corley-Smith, letter to Basil Boothby, December 16, 1949, FO/371/78978, BNA.

44. R. A. S. Breene, letter to P. A. Wilkinson, January 13, 1950, FO/1110/378, BNA.

45. Irving Brown, letter to Jay Lovestone, January 14, 1953, box 355, folder 28, JL HIA; Irving Brown, letter to Jay Lovestone, March 7, 1951, box 29, folder 11, IB MMA.

46. Aguirre de Cárcer, Embajada de España en Paris, letter E-6, no. 52, to Sr. Ministro de Asuntos Exteriores, January 17, 1950, AGA.

47. D. Luis Lojendio, letter to Georges Albertini, January 24, 1950, AGA.

48. Conde de Morales, "Informes sobre el movimiento anticoncentralista," no. 613, n.d. [November 1950], AGA; Martín Artajo, telegram no. 326 to P. Exterior Europa Pasaportes, Embajador de España en Paris, November 8, 1950, AGA.

49. Conde de Morales, telegram no. 148 to Enc. Neg. de España, al Ministro de Asuntos Exteriores, November 29, 1950, AGA. Joaquín Ruiz-Giménez, El Embajador de España, Cerca de la Santa Sede, Rome, letter to Excmo. Señor Don José S. de Erice, Director General de Política Exterior, December 30, 1950, AGA; CICRC, *Livre blanc sur le système pénitentiaire espagnol,* 9; Damien Reumont, letter to David Rousset, November 1, 1952, F/Delta/1880/60/2/2 DR BDIC.

50. Casa Miranda, note no. 315 to Excmo. Señor Ministro de Asuntos Exteriores, June 5, 1951, AGA.

51. CICRC, *Livre blanc sur le système pénitentiaire espagnol,* 13.

52. "Procès-verbal de la conférence," January 20–21, 1952, F/Delta/1880/58/2/1, DR BDIC.

53. CICRC, *Livre blanc sur le système pénitentiaire espagnol,* 13.

54. Fédération espagnole des déportés et internés politiques, "Note concernant la réunion qui a eu lieu le 29 mars 1952," F/Delta/1880/97/1, DR BDIC.

55. José Domenech, "Convocatoria," January 9, 1951, box 158, folder 1951, JE IISH; "Cuestionario," n.d., box 158, folder 1950, JE IISH.

56. "Norsk Samband av Politiske Fanger," F/Delta/1880/55/3, DR BDIC.

57. Børsum was born September 18, 1908. Her writings on Ravensbrück include *Fange i Ravensbrück* (Oslo: Gyldendal, 1946) and *Speilbilder* (Oslo: Tiden, 1947). Her book on the gulag was titled *Fjerndomstol Moskva: Fra dagens Berlin og Sovjets fangeleirer* (Oslo: Gyldendal, 1951).

58. David Rousset, letter to Lise Børsum, March 18, 1952, F/Delta/1880/58/2/2, DR BDIC; "Procès-verbal de la conférence," March 16–17, 1952, GT BNF.

59. CICRC, *Livre blanc sur le système pénitentiaire espagnol*, 16–17.

60. David Rousset, letter to Damien Reumont, May 22, 1952, F/Delta/1880/60/2/2, DR BDIC.

61. CICRC, *Livre blanc sur le système pénitentiaire espagnol*, 16–17.

62. Ibid.

63. She had visited most of these men at San Miguel de los Reyes, but more were incarcerated at Burgos and Santander. Elisabeth Ingrand, letter to Léon Mazeaud, June 18, 1952, box 159, JE IISH.

64. Elisabeth Ingrand and Lise Børsum, letter to David Rousset, May 26, 1952, F/Delta/1880/97/1, DR BDIC.

65. Lise Børsum, "Les contrastes et l'arbitraire des prisons espagnols," F/Delta/1880/97/3, DR BDIC. This was a French translation of an article by Børsum in *Dagbladet*, November 18, 1952, the fourth in a series of essays on the CICRC voyage that she contributed to the paper.

66. Lise Børsum, "L'Espagne actuelle," F/Delta/1880/97/3, DR BDIC. This was a French translation of the second article in Børsum's *Dagbladet* series (November 15, 1952).

67. Lise Børsum, "Conditions de travail dans les prisons et dans les détachements de travail espagnols," F/Delta/1880/97/3, DR BDIC. This was a French translation of the fifth article in Børsum's *Dagbladet* series (November 19, 1952).

68. El C[omité] I[interior] de San Miguel de los Reyes, "Informe del Comité Interior del Penal de San Miguel de los Reyes sobre la visita de la Comisión contra el régimen concentracionario," May 30, 1952, box 159, JE IISH; Lise Børsum, "Les contrastes et l'arbitraire"; Lise Børsum, "Prisonniers politiques et prisonniers ordinaires en Espagne," F/Delta/1880/97/3, DR BDIC. This was a French translation of the seventh article in Børsum's *Dagbladet* series (November 21, 1952).

69. Børsum, "Les contrastes et l'arbitraire."

70. Børsum, "Prisonniers politiques et prisonniers ordinaires."

71. Lise Børsum, "Entre sept et huit mille prisonniers politiques dans les prisons et camps de travail espagnoles [*sic*]," F/Delta/1880/97/3, DR BDIC. This was a French translation of the first article in Børsum's *Dagbladet* series (November 13, 1952).

72. Børsum, "L'Espagne actuelle."

73. Lise Børsum, "Les prisonniers dans les prisons d'Espagne," F/Delta/1880/97/3, DR BDIC. This was a French translation of the third article in Børsum's *Dagbladet* series (November 17, 1952).

74. Agadia, letter to Lise Børsum and Elisabeth Ingrand, June 7, 1952, box 159, JE IISH.

75. Børsum, "Les prisonniers dans les prisons d'Espagne."

76. CICRC, *Livre blanc sur le système pénitentiaire espagnol*, 59 and 44; see also Børsum, "Prisonniers politiques et prisonniers ordinaires."

77. Børsum, "L'Espagne actuelle."

78. Damien Reumont, "Résumé de la lettre de M. Van Staal adressée le 10 juillet 1952 à M. David Rousset," July 12, 1952, F/Delta/1880/60/5/2, DR BDIC.

79. J. de Swart, letter to Damien Reumont, September 16, 1952, read aloud in "Compte rendu de la conférence," October 9, 1952, F/Delta/1880/58/2/4, DR BDIC.

80. Quoted in Damien Reumont, letter to David Rousset, October 20, 1952, F/Delta/1880/60/2/2, DR BDIC; "Compte rendu de la conférence," October 9, 1952.

81. David Rousset, letter to the Dutch Commission, October 6, 1952, F/Delta/1880/60/5/1, DR BDIC.

82. David Rousset, letter to Damien Reumont, July 12, 1952, F/Delta/1880/60/2/2, DR BDIC.

83. "Compte rendu de la conférence," October 9, 1952, F/Delta/1880/58/2/4, DR BDIC.

84. David Rousset, letter to Damien Reumont, June 4, 1952, F/Delta/1880/60/2/2, DR BDIC.

85. David Rousset, letter to Damien Reumont, June 18, 1952, F/Delta/1880/60/2/2, DR BDIC.

86. Commission Française contre le Régime Concentrationnaire, "Procès-verbal de la conférence," April 12, 1950, dossier "Commission Française," GT BNF.

87. Commission Internationale contre le Régime Concentrationnaire, *Livre blanc sur les camps d'internement en Grèce* (Paris: Pavois, 1953), 65. On political detention in Greece see Polymeris Voglis, *Becoming a Subject: Political Prisoners during the Greek Civil War* (New York: Berghahn Books, 2002).

88. CICRC, *Livre blanc sur le système pénitentiaire espagnol*, 65–67.

89. Børsum, "Entre sept et huit mille prisonniers politiques."

90. CICRC, *Livre blanc sur le système pénitentiaire espagnol*, 23.

91. Børsum, "Entre sept et huit mille prisonniers politiques."

92. A new version was approved in 1955.

93. CICRC, *Livre blanc sur le système pénitentiaire espagnol*, 66.

94. Ibid., 67; Børsum, "Entre sept et huit mille prisonniers politiques."

95. Børsum, "Conditions de travail"; Børsum, "Entre sept et huit mille prisonniers politiques."

96. David Rousset, "Le dossier de l'Europe occidentale est ouvert," *Le Figaro littéraire* March 7, 1953.

97. Ibid.

98. CICRC, *Livre blanc sur le système pénitentiaire espagnol*, 23.

99. Rousset, "Le dossier de l'Europe occidentale est ouvert."

100. "Compte rendu de la conférence," October 9, 1952.

101. Lise Børsum, letter to André Alers, October 29, 1952, 601/1, 4a, AA CEGESOMA.

102. "Extraits du P.V. de la réunion, convoquée par la FEDIP," November 11, 1952, F/Delta/1880/58/2/8, DR BDIC.

103. "M. David Rousset présente les conclusions de l'enquête sur le régime concentrationnaire," *La Dépêche du Midi*, March 3, 1953.

104. "Extraits du P.V. de la réunion, convoquée par la FEDIP," November 11, 1952.

105. Ester, letter to Rousset, October 29, 1952.

106. N. B. J. Huijsman of the Colonial Office, letter to D. S. Cape of the Foreign Office, December 20, 1949, FO/371/78978, BNA; United Nations, Economic and Social Council, Survey of Forced Labour and Measure for Its Abolition, Resolution 350, UN Doc. E/1730, 19 March 1951, para. 1 (a).

107. David Rousset, letter to Damien Reumont, March 20, 1951, F/Delta/1880/58/1/8, DR BDIC.

108. Forrest D. Murden Jr., Memorandum of Conversation, "NGO and United States Government Cooperation on Collection and Presentation of Forced Labor Materials,"

November 14, 1951, RG 84, box 50, folder: Labor, Compulsory, 1949–1953, NARA. Kotschnig met with Rousset on October 4, 1951: see Irving J. Fasteau, Social Welfare Attaché, Paris Embassy, memorandum to Department of State, January 21, 1952, no. 1918, RG 59, box 5158, NARA.

109. See Peter Willetts, "Consultative Status for NGOs at the United Nations," in *"The Conscience of the World": The Influence of Non-Governmental Organizations in the UN System*, ed. Peter Willetts (London: Hurst, 1996), 31–62.

110. Damien Reumont, "Conférence du 17 janvier [1952] devant les délégations de l'ONU," F/Delta/1880/67/5, DR BDIC.

111. "Procès-verbal de la conférence," July 6, 1952, F/Delta/1880/58/2/3, DR BDIC.

112. Damien Reumont, "Communiqué sur la déposition de la CICR[C] le 17 octobre 1952, à Genève, devant le Comité Spécial du Travail Forcé," F/Delta/1880/67/6, DR BDIC.

113. [Théo Bernard], "Rapport sur les relations avec les Nations-Unies (1952–1953)," F/Delta/1880/58/2/13, DR BDIC.

114. David Rousset, letter to Théo Bernard, September 15, 1952, F/Delta/1880/67/6, DR BDIC.

115. Théo Bernard, letter to David Rousset, September 19, 1952, F/Delta/1880/67/6, DR BDIC.

116. Reumont, "Communiqué sur la déposition de la CICR[C] le 17 octobre 1952."

117. Sandrine Kott, "The Forced Labor Issue between Human and Social Rights, 1947–1957," trans. Joel Golb, *Humanity* 3, no. 3 (Winter 2012): 321–335, at 327.

118. United Nations–International Labour Office, "Press Release no. ECOSOC/542: UN/ILO Forced Labour Committee Hears Anti-Concentration Camp Society," October 17, 1952.

119. United Nations–International Labour Office, *Report of the Ad Hoc Committee on Forced Labour* (Geneva, 1953), 348.

120. UN–ILO, "Press Release no. ECOSOC/542."

121. David Rousset, letter to Damien Reumont, October 18, 1952, F/Delta/1880/60/2/2, DR BDIC.

122. "Compte rendu de la conférence," November 9, 1952, F/Delta/1880/58/2/5, DR BDIC.

123. See Daniel Maul, *Human Rights, Development, and Decolonization: The International Labour Organization, 1940–1970* (New York: Palgrave Macmillan, 2012), 205; Kott, "Forced Labor Issue," 329–330. Ironically, Kott attributes this development to the NGOs that testified before the committee, the CICRC "above all."

124. F. C. Mason of the Foreign Office, letter to A. Greenough of the Ministry of Labour, July 17, 1952, FO/371/101454, BNA.

125. "Forced Labour in Africa: Meeting Held in Mr. Diack's Room, Foreign Office, Friday, 8th August, 1952," FO/371/101454, BNA; "Brief for Discussion with Sir Gledwyn Jebb: Pre-General Assembly Talks with the US Authorities. Brief on Forced Labour," n.d. [August 1952], FO/371/101454, BNA.

126. Georges Albertini, letter to D. Luis Lojendio, January 20, [1950], AGA.

127. Manuel María de Barandica, note to Sr. Lojendio, "La 'Conclusiones' del Grupo Rousset," November 8, 1952, AGA.

128. El Marqués de Santa Cruz, El Ministro de España en les Paises Bajes, letter to Alberto Martín Arajo, February 2, 1953, AGA.

129. Ibid.; see also Jean de Swart, letter to Le Ministre d'Espagne à la Haye, March 7, 1953, AGA.

130. El Marqués de Santa Cruz, letter to Luis Carrero Blanco, Ministro Subsecretario de la Presidencia del Gobierno, Encargado del Ministro de Asuntos Exteriores, March 10, 1953, AGA. The underlining was done by the recipient.

131. Manuel María de Barandica, "Nota para el Sr. Cortina, Asunto: Un dato más de la mala fe del Sr. David Rousset con respecto a España," March 26, 1953, AGA.

132. Alberto Martín Artajo, letter to the Ad Hoc Committee on Forced Labour, February 17, 1953, reproduced in UN-ILO, *Report of the Ad Hoc Committee*, 362.

133. Ibid., 363.

134. Ibid.

135. Ibid., 76, 225.

136. Letter from Elisabeth Ingrand, Lise Børsum, and André Alers to Georges André (to be communicated to the Spanish Embassy in Brussels), December 12, 1953, F/Delta/1880/67/4, DR BDIC.

137. Ibid.

138. Ibid.

139. "Procès-verbal de la conférence," January 9, 1954, F/Delta/1880/59/1/1, DR BDIC.

140. Ministerio de Asuntos Exteriores, Organismos Internacionales, "Informe," March 25, 1953, AGA.

141. Chief, International Organizations Division, memorandum to Director of Central Intelligence on "Report of the Ad Hoc UN Committee on Forced Labor and Exploitation Thereof," June 23, 1953, General CIA Records, CREST, NARA, https://www.cia.gov/library/readingroom/docs/CIA-RDP80R01731R003300310006-0.pdf.

142. Théo Bernard, "Le travail forcé devant l'ONU," *Preuves* 34 (December 1953): 67–70, at 69.

143. See N. D. Watson of the Colonial Office, letter to J. S. Somers Cocks of the Foreign Office, August 23, 1952, FO/371/101454, BNA, and "Brief for Discussion with Sir Gledwyn Jebb" on British determination to disallow debate on the issue. A milquetoast declaration of support from the General Assembly did not arrive until late 1954.

144. "Résolution de la CICRC au sujet du rapport sur le travail forcé (Travail intérieur)," November 7, 1953, F/Delta/1880/58/2/13, DR BDIC.

145. Germaine Tillion, letter to Elisabeth Ingrand, February 22, 1954, folder "CICRC, Correspondance, 1952–53–54," GT BNF.

146. José Calmarza, "Arrestations arbitraires et négations des droits de la défense en Espagne," *Bulletin d'information de la Commission Internationale contre le Régime Concentrationnaire* 1 (December 1954): 36–38, at 38. See also Miguel Sanchez-Mazas, "La crise espagnole et les nouvelles générations," *Saturne* 17 (January–March 1958): 62–81.

147. Rodrigo, *Cautivos*, xxi.

148. Vinyes, *Irredentas*, 39. For example, Rodríguez, *Las cárceles de Franco*, 85–89; Preston, *The Spanish Holocaust*, 509; Rodrigo, *Cautivos*; Helen Graham, *The War and Its Shadow: Spain's Civil War in Europe's Long Twentieth Century* (Brighton: Sussex Academic, 2012), 111–112; Julio Prada Rodríguez, *La España Masacrada: La represión franquista de guerra y posguerra* (Madrid: Alianza, 2010), 257–258.

149. Vinyes, *Irredentas*, 45.

150. Børsum, "Les contrastes et l'arbitraire."

## 6. TRIUMPHS AND TENSIONS ON THE GLOBAL STAGE

1. Léon Poliakov, review of *La Tragédie de la déportation, 1940–1945: Témoignages de survivants des camps de concentration allemands*, edited by Olga Wormser and Henri Michel, *Évidences* 6, no. 42 (August–September 1954): 48.

2. David Rousset, letter to Damien Reumont, December 28, 1954, F/Delta/1880/59/1/7, DR BDIC. The CICRC's difficulties over this issue provide an interesting antecedent to 1990s-era debates over the universality of human rights, likewise centered on East Asia.

3. "Compte-rendu de la conférence du 9 novembre 1952," F/Delta/1880/50/2/5, DR BDIC.

4. David Rousset, letter to Gerard Corley-Smith, November 12, 1953, F/Delta/1880/67/4, DR BDIC.

5. M. Messadi, letter to Damien Reumont, February 27, 1952, in Commission Internationale contre le Régime Concentrationnaire, *Livre blanc sur la détention politique en Tunisie* (Paris: Pavois, 1953), 7–8.

6. On the UGTT and Néo-Destour see Kenneth Perkins, *A History of Modern Tunisia* (New York: Cambridge University Press, 2004), 110–134; Abdesselem Ben Hamida, *Le Syndicalisme tunisien de la deuxième guerre mondiale à l'autonomie interne* (Tunis: Université de Tunis I, 1989). On Hauteclocque's "unprecedented wave of repression" see Mary Lewis, *Divided Rule: Sovereignty and Empire in French Tunisia, 1881–1938* (Berkeley: University of California Press, 2014), 174.

7. David Rousset, letter to M. Messadi, February 26, 1952, F/Delta/1880/98/2, DR BDIC.

8. Damien Reumont, letter to Farhat Hached, November 20, 1952, F/Delta/1880/98/1, DR BDIC.

9. Jean-Marie François de Hauteclocque, letter to Damien Reumont, April 2, 1952, F/Delta/1880/98/1, DR BDIC; Damien Reumont, letter to Jean-Marie François de Hauteclocque, April 12, 1952, F/Delta/1880/98/1, DR BDIC.

10. Damien Reumont, letter to Jean-Marie François de Hauteclocque, October 15, 1952, F/Delta/1880/98/1, DR BDIC.

11. "Compte-rendu de la conférence du 9 novembre 1952."

12. Farhat Hached, letter to Damien Reumont, November 26, 1952, F/Delta/1880/98/1, DR BDIC.

13. Anthony Carew, "Towards a Free Trade Union Centre: The International Confederation of Free Trade Unions (1949–1972)," in *The International Confederation of Free Trade Unions*, ed. Anthony Carew et al. (Bern: Peter Lang, 2000), 187–340, at 227.

14. Irving Brown, "Projet d'article," n.d., F/Delta/1880/98/5, DR BDIC.

15. Quoted in "Arbitraires policiers et tortures en Tunisie, Voici ce qu'a reconnu la Commission Internationale contre le Régime Concentrationnaire," *Franc-Tireur*, March 3, 1953.

16. David Rousset, letter to Damien Reumont, December 19, 1952, F/Delta/1880/98/2, DR BDIC. On Auriol's hostility to Hauteclocque see Martin Thomas, "French North Africa before the United Nations, 1932–1962," *Contemporary European History* 10, no. 1 (March 2001): 91–121, at 101.

17. David Rousset, letter to Damien Reumont, January 30, 1953, F/Delta/1880/98/3, DR BDIC.

18. Damien Reumont, letter to David Rousset, January 31, 1953, F/Delta/1880/98/3, DR BDIC.

19. He also left the embarrassing correspondence in question out of the Tunisian *Livre blanc*.

20. CICRC, *Livre blanc sur la détention politique en Tunisie*, 72.

21. G. Lewis Jones, American Consul General in Tunis, telegram no. 22 to Secretary of State, January 22, 1953, RG 59, box 4361, NARA.

22. CICRC, *Livre blanc sur la détention politique en Tunisie*, 85.

23. Ibid.

24. Ibid., 48.

25. "'Pas d'univers concentrationnaire en Tunisie,' déclare David Rousset," *Combat*, March 3, 1953; "Seule, l'U.R.S.S. connaît encore le système du travail forcé," *L'Aurore*, March 3, 1953.

26. Reproduced in CICRC, *Livre blanc sur la détention politique en Tunisie*, 31.

27. Rousset's interest was profound and persistent: after the CICRC's collapse, he composed hundreds of pages of an envisioned three-volume sociological study of China, never published.

28. Richard Wolin, *The Wind from the East: French Intellectuals, the Cultural Revolution, and the Legacy of the 1960s* (Princeton, NJ: Princeton University Press, 2010), 3. See also Kristin Ross, *May '68 and Its Afterlives* (Chicago: University of Chicago Press, 2002), 97.

29. David Rousset, letter to Charles de Gaulle, June 4, 1959, F/Delta/1880/61/7/1, DR BDIC.

30. On political detention and corrective labor in China in the early 1950s see, among others, Jean-Luc Domenach, *Chine, l'archipel oublié* (Paris: Fayard, 1992); Philip F. Williams and Yenna Wu, *Great Wall of Confinement: The Chinese Prison Camp through Contemporary Fiction and Reportage* (Berkeley: University of California Press, 2004); Jan Kiely, *The Compelling Ideal: Thought Reform and the Prison in China, 1901–1956* (New Haven, CT: Yale University Press, 2014). For comparison to Soviet detention see Klaus Mühlhahn, "'Repaying Blood Debt': The Chinese Labor Camp System during the 1950s," in *The Soviet Gulag: Evidence, Interpretation, and Comparison*, ed. Michael David-Fox (Pittsburgh: University of Pittsburgh Press, 2016), 250–267.

31. "Compte-rendu de la conférence du 9 novembre 1952."

32. Maurice Merleau-Ponty, *Les Aventures de la dialectique* (Paris: Gallimard, 1955), 312 and 314.

33. Pierre Naville, letter to David Rousset, May 9, 1953, F/Delta/1880/48/3/2, DR BDIC.

34. Claude Bourdet, letter to David Rousset, February 9, 1955, F/Delta/1880/48/5, DR BDIC.

35. Jean-Paul Sartre, "D'une Chine à l'autre," reproduced in *Situations*, vol. 5 (Paris: Gallimard, 1964), 7–24.

36. Jean-Paul Sartre, "La Chine que j'ai vue," *France-Observateur*, December 1, 1955.

37. David Rousset, "Jean-Paul Sartre en Chine ou les cynismes d'un mandarin," *Demain*, January 5–11, 1956; David Rousset, "Des mains sales aux mains fortes: Le complot gouvernemental dans la République Populaire de Chine et ses racines sociales," *Bulletin d'information de la Commission internationale contre le régime concentrationnaire* 5 (December 1955): 36.

38. Sartre, "Réponse à Pierre Naville," reproduced in *Situations*, vol. 7 (Paris: Gallimard, 1965), 135.

39. Open letter from the Section de Norvège de la CICRC (signed Lise Børsum), December 11, 1952, F/Delta/1880/58/2/6, DR BDIC, emphasis in original.

40. "Procès-verbal de la conférence," March 1–2, 1953, F/Delta/1880/58/2/8, DR BDIC.

41. Irving Brown, letter to Jay Lovestone, November 26, 1953, box 29, folder 13, IB MMA.

42. Department of State (signed Dulles), telegram no. 1645 to American Embassy Bangkok, December 29, 1954, RG 59, box 5639, NARA.

43. Section de Norvège, open letter, December 13, 1954, dossier "Bruxelles novembre 1954," GT BNF.

44. Section de Norvège (signed Gudny Høegh-Omdal, H. Cappelen, A. Middelthon, Ragnar Andersen, and Lise Børsum), open letter, October 30, 1954, F/Delta/1880/59/1/5, DR BDIC. See also the supporting letter from the Danish Section, November 3, 1954, F/Delta/1880/59/1/5, DR BDIC.

45. Børsum quoted Rousset speaking these words at the November 6, 1954, meeting in an open letter on November 25, 1954, F/Delta/1880/59/1/5, DR BDIC. She denied the charge as "absurd."

46. Rousset, letter to Reumont, December 28, 1954.

47. "Procès-verbal de la conférence," January 8, 1955, F/Delta/1880/59/1/7.

48. They were Zouhaier Chelli (Tunisia), Ignacio P. Lacsina (Philippines), Meliton Salazar (Philippines), Pajed Sivadut (Thailand), and M. Nishimaki (Japan). Nishimaki proved unable to attend.

49. Commission Internationale contre le Régime Concentrationnaire, *Livre blanc sur le travail forcé et les institutions concentrationnaires dans la République Populaire de Chine,* vol. 1 (Paris: Centre International d'Édition et de Documentation, 1957), 25.

50. A. Meyer, letter to John Rennie, May 17, 1955, FO/1110/726, BNA.

51. "Minutes. Summary of Discussions Held in IRD on the 21st October 1955, with M. David Rousset," October 24, 1955, FO/1110/726, BNA.

52. "Réunion du Bureau, Bruxelles, 29 octobre 1955," F/Delta/1880/59/1/13, DR BDIC.

53. K. R. Oakeshott, letter to John Rennie, July 25, 1955, FO/1110/726, BNA.

54. J. H. Oldenbroek, letter to David Rousset, December 2, 1955, F/Delta/1880/61/5, DR BDIC.

55. Philip B. Sprouse, chargé d'affaires, Brussels Embassy, letter no. 1203 to Department of State, May 4, 1956, RG 59, box 5074, NARA.

56. Lise Børsum, letter to the CICRC Secretariat, November 16, 1955, reproduced in "Rectification au procès-verbal de la 26ᵉ Conférence," dossier "Enquêtes CICRC," GT BNF.

57. See "Procès-verbal de la conférence," November 6, 1955, F/Delta/1880/59/1/13, DR BDIC.

58. Ibid.

59. CICRC, *Livre blanc sur le travail forcé et les institutions concentrationnaires dans la République Populaire de Chine,* vol. 1, 24.

60. "Procès-verbal de la conférence," November 6, 1955.

61. Agnès Goetschel, "Les travaux de la CICRC. 16 millions de concentrationnaires en Chine," *Voix et Visages* 51 (May–June 1956): 3.

62. CICRC, *Livre blanc sur le travail forcé et les institutions concentrationnaires dans la République Populaire de Chine,* vol. 1, 314.

63. "Réunion du Bureau, Paris, lundi 9 juillet, 1956," F/Delta/1880/59/2/4, DR BDIC.

64. Simone de Beauvoir, *La Longue marche: Essai sur la Chine* (Paris: Gallimard, 1957), 353–403, at 364 and 367.

65. Ibid., 365.

66. Gérard Rosenthal, "Le sang des autres," *Saturne* 16 (December 1957): 35–43, at 41 and 43.

67. CICRC, *Livre blanc sur le travail forcé et les institutions concentrationnaires dans la République Populaire de Chine,* vol. 1, 25–26.

68. "Réunion du Bureau, le vendredi 22 mars 1957, Paris," F/Delta/1880/59/2/8, DR BDIC.

69. On the French case see François Azouvi, *Le Mythe du grand silence: Auschwitz, les Français, la mémoire* (Paris: Fayard 2012), esp. 157.

70. Quoted in Tony Judt, *Postwar: A History of Europe since 1945* (New York: Penguin, 2005), 186.

71. Gennadi Kostyrchenko, "The Genesis of Establishment Antisemitism in the USSR: The Black Years, 1948–1953," in *Revolution, Repression, and Revival: The Soviet Jewish Experience,* ed. Zvi Gitelman and Yaacov Ro'i (Lanham, MD: Rowman & Littlefield, 2007), 179–192, at 182.

72. Pierre Daix, interview with Catherine Nay and Patrice de Néritens, "Pierre Daix, de l'autobiographie à l'autocritique," *Le Figaro magazine,* February 24, 2001. Cf. Dominique Desanti, *Les Clés d'Elsa* (Paris: Ramsay, 1983), 360–361; Pierre Daix, *Aragon, une vie à changer* (Paris: Seuil, 1975), 370.

73. Quoted in Marianne R. Sanua, *Let Us Prove Strong: The American Jewish Committee, 1945–2006* (Waltham, MA: Brandeis University Press, 2007), 72.

74. "Après les exécutions de Prague: Un appel du Congrès pour la liberté de la culture aux Nations Unies," *Preuves* 22 (December 1952), insert. See also Jewish and non-Jewish intellectuals' affirmative responses to the query posed in *Évidences* 4, no. 30 (January–February 1953): 1–17: "Must we judge that the life of Jewish populations in the countries of the East is in danger?"

75. [Léon Poliakov], untitled memorandum, n.d. [1953], box 12, folder 16, IB MMA. The phrase "l'étroite parenté" was handwritten over the typed words "certaines analogies étonnantes."

76. David Rousset, letter to Irving Brown, February 13, 1953, box 12, folder 16, IB MMA.

77. "Procès-verbal de la conférence," May 2–3, 1953, F/Delta/1880/58/2/9, DR BDIC.

78. David Rousset, letter to Georges André, December 2, 1952, F/Delta/1880/60/1, DR BDIC.

79. La Commission Internationale contre le Régime Concentrationnaire [Théo Bernard], "Les droits de la défense, moyens à mettre en oeuvre pour garantir judiciairement la liberté individuelle," December 10, 1952, F/Delta/1880/67/3, DR BDIC.

80. Bernard, "Compte rendu du séjour à New York de Théo Bernard"; "Procès-verbal de la conférence," May 2–3, 1953, F/Delta/1880/58/2/9, DR BDIC. The *mémoire* was distributed under code E/C 2/345, April 7, 1953. On UN rules see William Korey, *NGOs and the Universal Declaration of Human Rights: A Curious Grapevine* (New York: St. Martin's, 1998), 53.

81. "Reds Deny Forced Labor," *New York Times*, April 9, 1953.

82. "Communiqué de presse," n.d., reproduced in the "Procès-verbal de la réunion du bureau à Paris," December 9, 1952, F/Delta/1880/58/2/6, DR BDIC.

83. John Slawson, quoted in Sanua, *Let Us Prove Strong*, 72.

84. For overviews of the 1953 partial amnesty and bureaucratic reorganization see Jeffrey S. Hardy, *The Gulag after Stalin: Redefining Punishment in Khrushchev's Soviet Union, 1953–1964* (Ithaca, NY: Cornell University Press, 2016); Marc Elie, "Khrushchev's Gulag: The Soviet Penitentiary System after Stalin's Death, 1953–1964," in *The Thaw: Soviet Society and Culture during the 1950s and 1960s*, ed. Denis Kozlov and Eleonory Gilburd (Toronto: University of Toronto Press, 2013): 109–142.

85. David Rousset, "Rapport de M. David Rousset: Tâches réalisées par le secrétariat général et le Bureau d'édition et programme de travail," November 6–7, 1953, CICRC 1953, GT BNF. On the actual motivations behind post-Stalinist reforms see Hardy, *Gulag after Stalin*.

86. Rousset, "Nous avons arraché des milliers d'hommes à l'enfer des camps," *Saturne* 7 (March–May 1956): 3–8, at 3.

87. Although the CICRC would never have been included, other Western delegations *were* permitted controlled tours of certain Soviet penal facilities beginning in 1954: see Jeffrey S. Hardy, "Gulag Tourism: Khrushchev's 'Show Prisons' in the Cold War Context, 1954–1959," *Russian Review* 71 (January 2012): 49–78. On a 1956 visit to the Tula corrective labor colony by French SFIO representatives see Jean-Paul Brunet, "Socialisme et bolchevisme: L'image de la révolution d'Octobre et de l'Union Soviétique chez les socialistes français en 1956," *Revue française de science politique* 39, no. 5 (1989): 700–715.

88. "Procès-verbal de la conférence," July 9, 1954, F/Delta/1880/59/1/3, DR BDIC.

89. David Rousset, letter to Zachariah Shuster, August 5, 1954, F/Delta/1880/48/ 4, DR BDIC.

90. David Rousset, letter to Zachariah Shuster, September 23, 1954, F/Delta/1880/48/ 4, DR BDIC.

91. For an example of Rousset's treatment of Soviet antisemitism once no longer constrained by CICRC norms see "Retour à l'antisémitisme en U.R.S.S.," *Le Figaro*, April 7–8, 1962.

92. "Procès-verbal de la conférence," November 6–7, 1954, F/Delta/1880/59/1/5, DR BDIC.

93. [David Rousset], "Note sur la nécessité de trouver des locaux pour la CICRC," October 8, 1954, F/Delta/1880/55/1, DR BDIC.

94. "Procès-verbal de la conférence," November 6–7, 1954.

95. Ibid.

96. [Germaine Tillion], note, n.d., "CICRC 'Comptabilité,' divers, dont correspondance (dossier à reclasser)," GT BNF.

97. Germaine Tillion, letter to D. Berkhauer, February 24, 1954, "CICRC 'Comptabilité,' divers, dont correspondance (dossier à reclasser)," GT BNF.

98. Ibid.

99. Azouvi, *Mythe du grand silence*, 153.

100. Olga Wormser and Henri Michel, eds., *La Tragédie de la déportation, 1940–1945: Témoignages de survivants des camps de concentration allemands* (Paris: Hachette, 1954).

101. David Rousset, letter to D. Berkhauer, February 13, 1953, "CICRC 'Comptabilité,' divers, dont correspondance (dossier à reclasser)," GT BNF.

102. David Rousset, "La bataille du Ghetto de Varsovie," *La Revue internationale* 3, no. 15 (May 1947): 349–352; David Rousset, "La bataille du ghetto," *Le Patriote résistant* 52 (May 1948).

103. David Rousset, "À propos des changements qui auraient lieu dans la société soviétique (III)," *Saturne* 6 (January–February 1956): 6–33, at 14–15. Compare with Léon Poliakov, *La Bréviaire de la haine: Le III^e Reich et les Juifs* (Paris: Calmann-Lévy, 1951), 248–249.

104. "Procès-verbal de la conférence," April 6, 1957, F/Delta/1880/59/2/9, DR BDIC.

105. Ibid.

106. David Rousset, "Notre impuissance est devenue angoisse," *Le Figaro*, December 15, 1956.

107. Théo Bernard, "Les ouvriers de Poznan contre la prison et les camps," *Saturne* 8 (June–July 1956): 3–4.

108. "Dossier I," n.d., F/Delta/1880/101/2, DR BDIC.

109. David Rousset, "Le silence n'est plus tolérable," *Le Figaro*, October 30, 1956.

110. Ibid.

111. "Procès-verbal de la conférence," November 17, 1956, F/Delta/1880/59/2/7, DR BDIC.

112. N.a. [David Rousset?], "Note sur la discussion de l'affaire hongroise à la session plénière de la C.I.C.R.C. du 17 novembre 1956," F/Delta/1880/59/2/7, DR BDIC.

113. John O'Shea, letter to David Rousset, November 21, 1956, F/Delta/1880/61/6/1, DR BDIC.

114. "Nouvelle hommage des Parisiens à la Hongrie," *Le Figaro*, November 14, 1956.

115. The phrase is from Martin-Chauffier's speech, published as "Nous devons au peuple hongrois notre reconnaissance," *Saturne* 9 (August–November 1956): 18–21, at 20.

116. N.a., "Résolution," in "Compte-rendu du meeting du Vélodrome d'Hiver," in "Dossier VII," F/Delta/1880/101/2, DR BDIC.

117. "Résolution"; "Nous devons au peuple hongrois."

118. "Compte-rendu par la presse," in "Compte-rendu du meeting du Vélodrome d'Hiver," in "Dossier VII," F/Delta/1880/101/2, DR BDIC.

119. "Premières conclusions de la manifestation du Vélodrome d'Hiver," in "Dossier VIII," F/Delta/1880/101/2, DR BDIC.

120. David Rousset, telegram to Dag Hammarskjöld, published as "Pour que les déportations en Hongrie soient arrêtées," *Saturne* 10 (December 1956): 18.

121. Théo Bernard, letter to Germaine Tillion, January 14, 1957, dossier "CICRC Commission française, correspondance, 1950–1960," folder "CICRC, CF, correspondance, sans date," GT BNF; Damien Reumont, "Note sur l'activité de M. Théo Bernard aux NU concernant les événements de Hongrie," January 11, 1957, F/Delta/1880/67/7, DR BDIC.

122. Edmond Michelet, speech at the United Nations General Assembly, December 4, 1956, published as "Le peuple hongrois a héroïquement lutté pour le droit à la vérité," *Saturne* 10 (December 1956): 20–27, at 20.

123. Théo Bernard, "L'affaire hongroise aux Nations Unies," *Saturne* 10 (December 1956): 5.

124. Théo Bernard, letter to David Rousset, December 20, 1956, F/Delta/1880/67/7, DR BDIC.

125. United Nations Special Committee on the Problem of Hungary, *Report of the Special Committee on the Problem of Hungary, General Assembly Official Records: Eleventh Session Supplement*, no. 18 (A/3592) (New York: 1957), 223.

126. Bernard, letter to Rousset, December 20, 1956.

127. United Nations Resolution 1127 (XI) of November 21, 1956.

128. Bernard, "L'affaire hongroise," 5.

129. Martin-Chauffier, "Nous devons au peuple hongrois," 20.

130. Bernard, "L'affaire hongroise," 5.

131. Théo Bernard, "Que vive la Hongrie," *Saturne* 13 (May–July 1957): 3–7, at 7.

132. Rousset, "Notre impuissance est devenue angoisse," 3.

133. Ibid.

134. Ibid.

## 7. FROM AUSCHWITZ TO ALGERIA

1. "Réunion du Bureau, le vendredi 22 mars 1957, Paris," F/Delta/1880/59/2/8, DR BDIC.

2. David Rousset, letter to John O'Shea, n.d. [December 3, 1957], F/Delta/1880/61/6/2, DR BDIC.

3. Rémy Roure, letter to David Rousset, March 22, 1956, F/Delta/1880/99/2, DR BDIC.

4. Germaine Tillion, letter to Lise Børsum, December 15, 1960, folder "CICRC Commission française, correspondance, 1950–1960," GT BNF.

5. Michael Rothberg, *Multidirectional Memory: Remembering the Holocaust in the Age of Decolonization* (Stanford, CA: Stanford University Press, 2009), esp. 193. For additional approaches see Jim House, "Memory and the Creation of Solidarity during the Decolonization of Algeria," *Yale French Studies* 118/119 (2010): 15–38; Max Silverman, *Palimpsestic Memory: The Holocaust and Colonialism in French and Francophone Fiction and Film* (New York: Berghahn Books, 2013); Brian Cheyette, *Diasporas of the Mind: Jewish and Postcolonial Writing and the Nightmare of History* (New Haven, CT: Yale University Press, 2014); Debarati Sanyal, *Memory and Complicity: Migrations of Holocaust Remembrance* (New York: Fordham University Press, 2015).

6. See Martin Evans, *The Memory of Resistance: French Opposition to the Algerian War (1954–1962)* (Oxford: Berg, 1997); Eleanor Davey, *Idealism beyond Borders: The French Revolutionary Left and the Rise of Humanitarianism, 1954–1988* (Cambridge: Cambridge University Press, 2015), 74–76; Darcie Fontaine, *Decolonizing Christianity: Religion and the End of Empire in France and Algeria* (New York: Cambridge University Press, 2016), 123–124. However, the multivalent language of memory was also mobilized by militant supporters of *Algérie française*, among them many ex-resisters (e.g., Georges Bidault and Jacques Soustelle). See Marie-Pierre Ulloa, "Memory and Continuity: The Resistance, the

Algerian War, and the Jeanson Network," in *Memory, Empire, and Postcolonialism: Legacies of French Colonialism*, ed. Alec Hargreaves (Lanham, MD: Lexington Books, 2005), 112–124, at 122.

7. Sylvie Thénault, *Violence ordinaire dans l'Algérie coloniale: Camps, internements, assignations à residence* (Paris: Odile Jacob, 2012), 10. See also Sylvie Thénault, "Interner en République: Le cas de la France en guerre d'Algérie," *Amnis* 3 (2003), http://amnis. revues.org/513; Benjamin Stora, "La politique des camps d'internement," in *L'Algérie des Français*, ed. Charles-Robert Ageron (Paris: Seuil, 1999): 295–299; Fabian Klose, *Human Rights in the Shadow of Colonial Violence* (Philadelphia: University of Pennsylvania Press, 2013), 133–138.

8. On the modalities of torture in Algeria see Raphaëlle Branche, *La Torture et l'armée pendant la guerre d'Algérie: 1954–1962*, rev. ed. (Paris: Gallimard, 2016).

9. G. Ciosi, "Note à Monsieur le Gouverneur Général," June 18, 1955, folder "Rapport sur fonctionnement des camps," 12CAB/160, ANOM.

10. 10ᵉ Région militaire, État-majeur, Bureau Psychologique, "Note au sujet de l'Action Psychologique à mener dans les camps," March 15, 1957, folder "Action Psychologique," 12CAB/160, ANOM.

11. For further discussion of the law see Sylvie Thénault, "L'état d'urgence (1955–2005): De l'Algérie coloniale à la France contemporaine; destin d'une loi," *Le Mouvement social*, no. 218 (2007): 63–78.

12. *Journal officiel de la République Français—débats*, séance no. 1 du 31 mars 1955, 2162 and 2168.

13. On euphemisms employed under the Third Republic and Vichy see Denis Peschanski, *La France des camps: L'internement, 1938–1946* (Paris: Gallimard, 2002).

14. Ciosi, "Note à Monsieur le Gouverneur Général."

15. Décret no. 56–274 du 17 mars 1956, *Journal officiel de la République Français*, March 19, 1956, 2665.

16. "Réunion du 19 mars 1957," folder "Rapports sur fonctionnement des camps," 12CAB/160, ANOM.

17. Thénault, *Violence ordinaire*, 296.

18. Directeur du Service Central des Centres d'Hébergement, "Note pour M. Gorlin, Conseiller Technique au Cabinet du Ministre de l'Algérie," August 14, 1957, folder "CICRC," 12CAB/184, ANOM; Commandement Superieur Interarmées, 10ᵉᵐᵉ Région Militaire, État-Major—5ᵉᵐᵉ Bureau, "Situation des Centres de Triage et de Transit à la date du 9 septembre 1957," folder "Centres de Triage," 12CAB/160, ANOM. The taxonomy of internment facilities later became more complex with the creation of *centres militaires d'internement, centres de rééducation*, and metropolitan camps.

19. Assemblée Nationale, no. 4404, "Annexe au procès-verbal de la séance du 5 mars 1957. Rapport fait au nom de la Commission de l'Intérieur," folder "Centres d'hébergement," 12CAB/165, ANOM.

20. See folder "Voyages de délégations étrangères, voyages d'information, authorisations," 81F/64, ANOM.

21. See 12CAB/222, ANOM. Brown was personally banned from Algeria in May 1956.

22. Pour le Ministre de l'Intérieur et par délégation, Le Directeur Adjoint du Cabinet, letter to M. le Ministre des Affaires Étrangères, October 28, 1956, folder "Comité International de la Croix Rouge," 81F/142, ANOM.

23. On this history see Jennifer Johnson, *The Battle for Algeria: Sovereignty, Health Care, and Humanitarianism* (Philadelphia: University of Pennsylvania Press, 2016), 126–156; Raphaëlle Branche, "Entre droit humanitaire et intérêts politiques: Les missions algériennes du CICR," *Revue historique* 301, no. 1 (January–March 1999): 101–125. Several relevant ICRC documents are reproduced in Maurice Faivre, *La Croix-Rouge pendant*

*la guerre d'Algérie: Un éclairage nouveau sur les victimes et les internés* (Panazol: Charles Lavauzelle, 2007).

24. Its seventh report, however, was leaked to *Le Monde* in January 1960 by Edmond Michelet (or possibly Gaston Gosselin, a fellow Dachau survivor in Michelet's 1959–1961 Ministry of Justice).

25. Pour le Ministre de l'Intérieur et par autorisation, Le Directeur des Affaires d'Algérie, letter to M. le Gouverneur Général de l'Algérie, January 27, 1956, folder "Comité International de la Croix Rouge," 81F/142, ANOM.

26. Christian Pineau, address to United Nations General Assembly, February 4, 1957.

27. "Il existent des camps d'internement en Algérie," *Témoignage chrétien*, January 6, 1956.

28. "Un premier dossier sur la répression en Algérie," *Saturne* 6 (January–February 1956): 3–4.

29. Editorial, *Tunisie-France*, January 24, 1953.

30. "Après la conférence de presse de David Rousset, les milieux officiels de Tunis relèvent 'certaines inexactitudes,'" *Le Monde*, March 4, 1953.

31. "Un premier dossier sur la répression en Algérie," 3–4.

32. Charles Richet, letter to Georges André, March 18, 1956, F/Delta/1880/99/ 4, DR BDIC.

33. Rémy Roure, "Ne faites rien sans la France," *Preuves* 13 (March 1952): 5–6.

34. Roure, letter to Rousset, March 22, 1956.

35. Rémy Roure, letter to David Rousset, April 20, 1956, F/Delta/1880/99/2, DR BDIC.

36. David Rousset, letter to Rémy Roure, April 16, 1956, F/Delta/1880/99/2, DR BDIC.

37. On her activism during the 1954–1962 war see Donald Reid, *Germaine Tillion, Lucie Aubrac, and the Politics of Memories of the French Resistance* (Newcastle, UK: Cambridge Scholars, 2008); Fabien Sacriste, *Germaine Tillion, Jacques Berque, Jean Servier et Pierre Bourdieu: Des ethnologues dans la guerre d'indépendance algérienne* (Paris: L'Harmattan, 2011), 73–90; Nancy Wood, *Germaine Tillion, une femme-mémoire: D'une Algérie à l'autre* (Paris: Autrement, 2003).

38. Testimonials to the value of this work include Nelly Forget, "Le Service des centres sociaux en Algérie," *Matériaux pour l'histoire de notre temps* 26 (January 1992): 37–47; Pierre Vidal-Naquet and Jean Daniel, "La justice et la patrie: Une Française au secours de l'Algérie," *Esprit* 261 (February 2000): 140–147; Isabelle Raymonde Deblé, "Une exception éducative: Les centres sociaux en Algérie (1955–1959)," *Esprit* 308 (October 2004): 157–165.

39. Germaine Tillion, *L'Algérie en 1957*, in *L'Afrique bascule vers l'avenir* (Paris: Minuit, 1960), 56.

40. See James D. LeSueur, *Uncivil War: Intellectuals and Identity Politics during the Decolonization of Algeria* (Philadelphia: University of Pennsylvania Press, 2001), 168.

41. Tillion, *Les Ennemis complémentaires* (Paris: Minuit, 1960), 27. This text was written in November 1957.

42. E.g., Jean-Marie Domenach, "Démoralisation de la nation," *Esprit* 249 (April 1957): 577–579, at 577.

43. Tillion, *L'Algérie en 1957*, 56.

44. Jacques Soustelle, letter to M. Leprettre, Président de la Comité d'Action de la Résistance, April 26, 1956, F/Delta/1880/99/4, DR BDIC; Germaine Tillion, letter to G. Ciosi, n.d., folder "CICRC, Enquête sur les prisons d'Algérie; papiers liés au voyage, 18 juin 1957– juillet 57. Dossier de l'enquête," GT BNF.

45. G. Ciosi, letter to Germaine Tillion, May 22, 1956, F/Delta/1880/99/4, DR BDIC, emphasis in original.

46. David Rousset, letter to Germaine Tillion, May 15, 1956, F/Delta/1880/99/4, DR BDIC.

47. On the Comité d'Action see LeSueur, *Uncivil War*, 35–61.

48. Edgar Morin, *Autocritique* (Paris: Julliard, 1959), 190–92; "Que veut le comité d'action des intellectuels français?," *Saturne* 6 (January–February 1956): 101–103.

49. David Rousset, letter to Germaine Tillion, January 12, 1956, F/Delta/1880/99/2, DR BDIC.

50. David Rousset, letter to Georges André, June 17, 1957, F/Delta/1880/99/1, DR BDIC.

51. David Rousset, "Le préalable algérien," *Demain*, January 3–7, 1957; Raphaëlle Branche, "La commission de sauvegarde pendant la guerre d'Algérie: Chronique d'un échec annoncé," *Vingtième siècle* 61 (January–March 1999): 14–29, at 15.

52. Roure was also invited to serve but declined, explaining that his opposition to "defeatist attacks directed against the methods of the pacification" was too well known for him to pose as a neutral observer.

53. Guy Mollet, letter to Georges André, November 14, 1956, reproduced in "Le Crime est accompli," *Saturne* 9 (August–September 1956): 4.

54. "Designation imminente des membres de la Commission," *La Croix*, April 27, 1957.

55. Louis Martin-Chauffier, "Journal de voyage en marge d'une enquête," *Saturne* 15 (October–November 1957): 5–10, at 7.

56. Including André Boulloche, a Buchenwald and Flossenbürg survivor.

57. Irwin M. Wall, *France, the United States, and the Algerian War* (Berkeley: University of California Press, 2001), 24; see also Rhodri Jeffreys-Jones, *The CIA and American Democracy*, 3rd ed. (New Haven, CT: Yale University Press, 2003), 124.

58. John Foster Dulles, quoted in Wall, *France, the United States, and the Algerian War*, 89; see also Matthew Connelly, *A Diplomatic Revolution: Algeria's Fight for Independence and the Origins of the Post–Cold War Era* (Oxford: Oxford University Press, 2002).

59. Rousset, letter to O'Shea, n.d. [December 3, 1957].

60. This language appears in an unsigned, undated account of the CICRC's loss of funding in F/Delta/1880/50/1/1, DR BDIC and also in David Rousset, "Propos sur l'heur et le malheur des temps," *Saturne* 19 (January–March 1959): 6.

61. Rousset, letter to O'Shea, n.d. [December 3, 1957].

62. David Rousset, letter to Michael Josselson, December 13, 1954, F/Delta/1880/61/6/1, DR BDIC.

63. Germaine Tillion later misremembered the Dutch delegate as Benjamin Stomps, a mistake that has been reproduced in some secondary literature touching on the voyage.

64. "Conclusions de la délégation d'enquête en Algérie," July 25, 1957, F/Delta/1880/99/8, DR BDIC.

65. Teitgen was the son of Buchenwald survivor and early CICRC participant Henri Teitgen.

66. Louis Martin-Chauffier, letter to David Rousset, June 29, 1957, F/Delta/1880/99/4, DR BDIC.

67. "1957-CICRC," in "CICRC, carnet, 1957," GT BNF.

68. Michel Reynaud, *L'Enfant de la rue et la dame du siècle: Entretiens inédits avec Germaine Tillion* (Paris: Tirésias, 2010), 243.

69. Louis Martin-Chauffier, "Journal de voyage en marge d'une enquête (III)," *Saturne* 17 (January–March 1958): 8–23, at 11.

70. For example, Louis Martin-Chauffier, "Toute la vérité, rien que la vérité," *Saturne* 12 (March–April 1957): 3–13.

71. Martin-Chauffier, "Journal de voyage (III)," 14 and 16.

72. Louis Martin-Chauffier, "Journal de voyage en marge d'une enquête (II)," *Saturne* 16 (December 1957): 7–16, at 15.

73. For an example of Lacoste's propagandistic use of the slaughter see Ministère de l'Algérie, Cabinet du Ministre, *Aspects véritables de la rebellion algérienne* (Paris, 1957).

74. Georges André, letter to David Rousset, June 27, 1957, F/Delta/1880/99/4, DR BDIC.

75. Louis-Martin Chauffier, "Journal de voyage en marge d'une enquête (II)," *Saturne* 16 (December 1957): 9.

76. "Rapport de la Commission d'Enquête," F/Delta/1880/99/7, DR BDIC.

77. Martin-Chauffier, "Journal de voyage (II)," 11.

78. It remained in operation, however.

79. Robert Martin, Inspecteur Général de l'Administration, "Report pour M. le Ministre de l'Algérie," August 10, 1957, folder "Paul-Cazelles," 12CAB/160, ANOM.

80. "Rapport de la Commission d'Enquête."

81. Ibid.

82. "Conclusions de la Délégation d'enquête en Algérie"; Martin-Chauffier, "Journal de voyage (III)," 20.

83. "Motion Middelthon," May 15–16, 1954, F/Delta/1880/59/1/2, DR BDIC.

84. "Procès-verbal de la conférence," May 15–16, 1954, F/Delta/1880/59/1/2, DR BDIC.

85. David Rousset, "Le sens de notre combat," in Paul Barton [Jiří Veltruský], *L'Institution concentrationnaire en Russie (1930–1957)* (Paris: Plon, 1959), 21 and 27.

86. David Rousset, "Notre tâche permanente," *Saturne* 17 (January–March 1958): 3–7, at 3.

87. On this drama see Reid, *Germaine Tillion*. Tillion's own account is in *Ennemis complémentaires*, 31–67.

88. Martin-Chauffier, "Journal de voyage (III)," 11.

89. "Procès-verbal de la réunion de Bureau élargi," January 5, 1957, F/Delta/1880/59/2/8, DR BDIC.

90. Reynaud, *L'Enfant de la rue*, 244; Lise Børsum, letter to Germaine Tillion, July 11, 1957, folder "CICRC Commission française, correspondance, 1950–1960," GT BNF.

91. "Les délégués de la Commission contre le régime concentrationnaire publient leur rapport sur l'Algérie," *Le Monde*, July 27, 1957.

92. "Conclusions de la délégation d'enquête."

93. Ibid.

94. See also Théo Bernard, "Le pouvoir administratif en Algérie," *Saturne* 16 (December 1957): 44–54.

95. Børsum, letter to Tillion, July 11, 1957.

96. "Conclusions de la délégation d'enquête."

97. Ibid.

98. J. H. A. Watson, memorandum on "Imprisonment of Five Algerian Peace Workers," September 3, 1957, FO/371/125949, BNA.

99. Maurice Duverger, "Les Camps," *Le Monde*, July 20, 1957.

100. "Conclusions de la délégation d'enquête."

101. "2ème frappe," folder "CICRC, Enquête sur les prisons d'Algérie; papiers liés au voyage, 18 juin 1957–juillet 57. Dossier de l'enquête," box 124, GT BNF.

102. "Conclusions de la délégation d'enquête."

103. For example, "Une commission internationale d'enquête reconnaît: De véritables tortures (électricité, tuyau d'eau, baignoire, pendaison) ont été infligées en Algérie," *L'Humanité*, July 27, 1957; "Une commission internationale a constaté l'existence des tortures," *Libération*, July 27–28, 1957. Earlier, *L'Humanité* had dismissed the possibility that the commission would return critical conclusions: Georges Buvard, "Une commission David Rousset?," *L'Humanité*, April 26, 1957.

104. "Procès-verbal de la conférence," November 9, 1957, F/Delta/1880/59/2/11, DR BDIC.

105. "Algérie: 'Pas de régime concentrationnaire' constate la délégation des anciens déportés," *Le Populaire*, July 27–28, 1957.

106. François Musard, editorial, *L'Aurore*, July 27, 1957.

107. "L'enquête en Algérie," *Le Figaro*, July 27, 1957; "Il n'y a pas de régime concentrationnaire en Algérie," *Le Figaro*, August 9, 1957. Rousset blamed Pierre Brisson's absence during *les vacances* for this *"carence."*

108. Pierre Emmanuel, "À qui de droit," *Témoignage chrétien*, August 23, 1957.

109. "Compte rendu de l'A.F.P. de la Conférence de presse du Dr. André du 8 aout 1957," and "Compte rendu complet de l'Agence Belga sur les conférences de presse du Docteur André," both attached to Raymond Bousquet, Ambassadeur de France en Belgique, letter to Christian Pineau, Ministre des Affaires Étrangères, August 9, 1957, folder "CICRC," 12CAB/184, ANOM.

110. E.g., "Le président de la Commission contre le régime concentrationnaire: On ne saurait établir de comparaison entre la rebellion algérienne et la résistance," *L'Echo d'Alger*, August 9, 1957.

111. "Communication de Madame Lise Børsum," December 14, 1957, folder "CICRC Commission française, correspondance, 1950–1960," GT BNF.

112. "Jugement nuancé d'une norvégienne sur les excès de la guerre d'Algérie," *La Croix*, September 3, 1957. See also "Mes déclarations ont été mal interprétées," *Le Figaro*, September 2, 1957.

113. Françoise Giroud, "La lettre de *L'Express*," *L'Express*, August 16, 1957.

114. Directeur du Service Central des Centres d'Hébergement, "Note pour M. Gorlin," August 14, 1957.

115. *Journal officiel de la République Français—débats*, November 12, 1957, 4718. Børsum was indignant at this misrepresentation.

116. Ibid., 4720.

117. See Connelly, *Diplomatic Revolution*.

118. Christian Pineau, débats à l'Assemblée Nationale, July 28, 1955, quoted in Raphaëlle Branche, "Comment rétablir de la norme en temps d'exception: l'IGCI/CICDA pendant la guerre d'Algérie," in *Contrôler les agents du pouvoir*, ed. Laurent Feller (Limoges: Pulim, 2004), 299–310, at 300.

119. Christian Pineau, address to the United Nations General Assembly, November 30, 1957.

120. Rothberg, *Multidirectional Memory*, 193.

121. M. Merleau-Ponty and J.-P. Sartre, "Les jours de notre vie," *Les Temps modernes* 51 (January 1950): 1153–1168, at 1155.

122. "Procès-verbal de conférence," November 9, 1957.

123. Rousset, letter to O'Shea, n.d. [December 3, 1957].

124. Ibid. O'Shea's November 26 letter to Rousset is not in the archival dossier, but Rousset's December 3 response quotes it at length, specifying that the original was in French.

125. Ibid.

126. David Rousset, Georges André, Damien Reumont, and Charles Coppieters't Wallant, resolution, n.d. [March 8, 1958], F/Delta/1880/61/6/2, DR BDIC.

127. David Rousset, letter to Théo Bernard, May 23, 1958, F/Delta/1880/61/6/2, DR BDIC.

128. John O'Shea, letter to David Rousset, May 6, 1958, F/Delta/1880/61/6/2, DR BDIC.

129. Tillion was also close to Charles de Gaulle's niece Geneviève de Gaulle-Anthonioz, a Ravensbrück survivor and a member of André Malraux's Cultural Affairs cabinet. They would be "Panthéonized" together in 2015.

130. David Rousset, letter to G. Loubet, Directeur du cabinet de M. Malraux, July 25, 1958, F/Delta/1880/49/2/1, DR BDIC.

131. David Rousset, letter to Charles de Gaulle, June 4, 1959, F/Delta/1880/61/7/1, DR BDIC.

132. Charles de Gaulle, letter to David Rousset, April 30, 1959, F/Delta/1880/59/2/14, DR BDIC.

133. Tillion, letter to Børsum, December 15, 1960.

134. Ibid.

135. Germaine Tillion, introduction [1960], in *L'Afrique bascule vers l'avenir*, 23; Germaine Tillion, preface to Michel Cornaton, *Les Regroupements de la décolonisation en Algérie* (Paris: Économie et humanisme, 1967), 7–10. On regroupment see also Benjamin Claude Brower, "Partisans and Populations: The Place of Civilians in War, Algeria (1954–62)," *History & Theory* 56, no. 3 (September 2017): 389–397.

136. For example, in Germaine Tillion, *La Traversée du mal: Entretien avec Jean Lacouture* (Paris: Arléa, 1997), 109–110.

137. Germaine Tillion, "À propos du livre de Simone de Beauvoir," *Le Monde*, March 11, 1964.

138. Tillion, *Ennemis*, 152.

139. Tillion, letter to Børsum, December 15, 1960.

140. See Pierre Vidal-Naquet, *L'Affaire Audin, 1957–1958* (Paris: Minuit, 1989).

141. Martin-Chauffier, "Journal de voyage (III)," 23.

142. Louis Martin-Chauffier, draft of "Rapport d'instruction," n.d., F/Delta/1880/99/5, DR BDIC.

143. Louis Martin-Chauffier, "Ce que j'ai vu en Algérie," *Demain*, August 15–21, 1957.

144. François Mauriac, "Bloc-Notes," *L'Express*, August 23, 1957.

145. Martin-Chauffier, "Journal de voyage (II)," 9; Martin-Chauffier, "Journal de voyage (III)," 13.

146. Louis Martin-Chauffier, letter to David Rousset, July 5, 1958, F/Delta/1880/49/2/1, DR BDIC.

147. "Analyse des réponses au questionnaire adressé en fevrier 1958," June 1, 1958, F/Delta/1880/64/3/6.

148. Louis Martin-Chauffier, "Dialogue avec nos lecteurs," *Saturne* 19 (January 1959): 8–17, at 14 and 16–17.

149. See Louis Martin-Chauffier, *Algérie an VII: L'examen des consciences* (Paris: Julliard, 1961).

150. David Rousset, letter to Germaine Tillion, June 11, 1960, F/Delta/1880/49/4/3, DR BDIC.

151. Rousset, "Le préalable algérien."

152. David Rousset, letter to Rémy Roure, February 7, 1957, F/Delta/1880/99/2, DR BDIC.

153. See David Rousset, "La piège tendu par l'O.A.S.," *Le Monde*, January 8, 1962; David Rousset, letter to Ernest Cazelles, May 21, 1962, F/Delta/1880/50/2.

154. David Rousset, "Le sens de la négociation," *Le Monde*, March 22, 1961.

155. David Rousset, letter to Georges André, September 22, 1962, F/Delta/1880/50/2, DR BDIC.

## EPILOGUE

1. Hannah Arendt, *The Origins of Totalitarianism* (Cleveland: Meridian, 1958), 436, 441–442. A footnote specifically naming Rousset follows this last sentence.

2. David Rousset, letter to Edgar Morin, June 2, 1961, F/Delta/1880/50/1/1, DR BDIC.

3. David Rousset, "David Rousset lance un appel aux rescapés des camps de concentration staliniens," *Le Figaro littéraire*, January 5, 1963.

4. One point of evidence for how much had changed: Pierre Daix, Rousset's onetime courtroom foe, had just written an earnest preface to the French translation of Aleksandr Solzhenitsyn's *One Day in the Life of Ivan Denisovich*.

5. Henry Rousso, *The Vichy Syndrome: History and Memory in France since 1944*, trans. Arthur Goldhammer (Cambridge, MA: Harvard University Press, 1991), 91.

6. André Schwarz-Bart's novel *Le Dernier des justes* was published in 1959, and Anna Langfus's *Les Bagages de sable* in 1962; both won the Goncourt. In 1963 Rolf Hochhuth's play about the Catholic Church and the Holocaust, *Le Vicaire*, opened in Paris.

7. Samuel Moyn, *A Holocaust Controversy: The Treblinka Affair in Postwar France* (Waltham, MA: Brandeis University Press, 2005), is especially elucidating here.

8. Quoted in François Azouvi, *Le Mythe du grand silence: Auschwitz, les Français, la mémoire* (Paris: Fayard 2012), 189–190.

9. Annette Wieviorka, *The Era of the Witness*, trans. Jared Stark (Ithaca, NY: Cornell University Press, 2006), 88.

10. On the GIP see Perry Zurn and Andrew Dilts, eds., *Active Intolerance: Michel Foucault, the Prisons Information Group, and the Future of Abolition* (New York: Palgrave Macmillan, 2016); Philippe Artières, Laurent Quéro, and Michelle Zancarini-Fournel, eds., *Le Groupe d'information sur les prisons: Archives d'une lutte, 1970–1972* (Paris: IMEC, 2003). The group particularly emulated the CICRC in exalting victims' own testimony: "The single watchword of the GIP," wrote Foucault, "is to let the detainees speak." Michel Foucault, *Dits et écrits, 1954–1988*, vol. 2 (Paris: Gallimard, 1994), 304. However, see also Cecile Brich, "The Groupe d'Information sur les Prisons: The Voice of Prisoners? Or Foucault's?," *Foucault Studies* 5 (January 2008): 26–47.

11. Domenach dramatically reconciled with Rousset in 1959 after a long public feud over communism. He was also well acquainted with other CICRC members, including Michelet and Tillion. Interestingly his son, Jean-Luc Domenach, became an internationally leading scholar of the Chinese *laogai*.

12. Tzvetan Todorov, *Mémoire du mal, tentation du bien: Enquête sur le siècle* (Paris: Laffont, 2000), 164–165, makes the comparison. On Amnesty see Stephen Hopgood, *Keepers of the Flame: Understanding Amnesty International* (Ithaca, NY: Cornell University Press, 2006); Tom Buchanan, "'The Truth Will Set You Free': The Making of Amnesty International," *Journal of Contemporary History* 37, no. 4 (October 2002): 575–597; Anne Marie Clark, *Diplomacy of Conscience: Amnesty International and Changing Human Rights Norms* (Princeton, NJ: Princeton University Press, 2001).

13. Samuel Moyn, *The Last Utopia: Human Rights in History* (Cambridge, MA: Harvard University Press, 2010), 5.

14. "In Memoriam. T. R. P. Damien, de Mons (Henri Reumont), 1892–1965," CEGES/AA/1448/66/8, CEGESOMA.

15. See Jean-Pierre Said, "'Minute' sera-t-il enfin condamné?," *Droit et Liberté*, no. 269 (January 1968).

16. Louis Martin-Chauffier, *Chroniques d'un homme libre* (Paris: Éditions FNDIRP, 1989), 163, 71, and 104.

17. "Assemblée générale," *Voix et Visages* 24 (February–March 1950): 1–2.

18. Germaine Tillion, *À la recherche du vrai et du juste: À propos rompus avec le siècle* (Paris: Seuil, 2001), 395.

19. Ibid., 333, from her published response to Charles de Gaulle's notorious 1967 comments on the Jewish "*peuple d'élite*."

20. Germaine Tillion, letter to Pierre Vidal-Naquet, quoted in Pierre Vidal-Naquet, *Réflexions sur le génocide* (Paris: La Découverte, 1995), 242.

21. Interview, 1968, quoted in David Rousset and Émile Copfermann, *David Rousset: Une vie dans le siècle, fragments d'autobiographie* (Paris: Plon, 1991), 176.

22. Sanche de Gramont, "Two Who Bridge the Generation Gap," *New York Times Magazine*, September 29, 1968, 25.

23. David Rousset, "L'esprit et la lettre," *Notre république* 309 (May 10, 1968), emphasis in original.

24. David Rousset, *La Société éclatée: De la première à la séconde révolution mondiale* (Paris: Grasset, 1973); David Rousset, *Sur la guerre* (Paris: Ramsay, 1987).

25. David Rousset, "Le porte-voix des 'cancereux,'" *Le Figaro littéraire*, October 19–25, 1970. On the reasons behind the outsize response to Solzhenitsyn's publication see Michael Scott Christofferson, *French Intellectuals against the Left: The Antitotalitarian Moment of the 1970s* (New York: Berghahn Books, 2004).

26. André Glucksmann, *La Cuisinière et le mangeur d'hommes: Essai sur l'état, le marxisme, les camps de concentration* (Paris: Seuil, 1975), 35. For Rousset's critique see Julian Bourg, *From Revolution to Ethics: May 1968 and Contemporary French Thought* (Montreal: McGill–Queen's University Press, 2007), 250.

27. David Rousset, review of *Hommes et femmes d'Auschwitz* by Hermann Langbein (Paris: Fayard, 1975), in *La Quinzaine littéraire* 216 (September 1–15, 1975): 16.

28. See Moyn, *Holocaust Controversy*, 82–83. Vidal-Naquet assured Rousset that he personally continued to view *Les Jours de notre mort* as a "masterpiece": Pierre Vidal-Naquet, letter to David Rousset, November 1988, F/Delta/1880/4, DR BDIC.

29. Rousset's documentary history of German antisemitism, *Le Pitre ne rit pas*, was reissued in 1979 following the French airing of the *Holocaust* miniseries.

30. Moyn, *Holocaust Controversy*, 159.

31. The English translation of Todorov's *Mémoire du mal*, for example, is *Hope and Memory: Lessons from the Twentieth Century*, trans. David Bellos (Princeton, NJ: Princeton University Press, 2003). As Carolyn J. Dean underlines, the celebration of Rousset's "universalizing" project also feeds into French discourses on a supposed "excess" of particularizing "Jewish memory": *Aversion and Erasure: The Fate of the Victim after the Holocaust* (Ithaca, NY: Cornell University Press, 2010), 86.

32. Tzvetan Todorov, "Judging the Past," trans. John Anzalone, *Salmagundi* 96 (Fall 1992): 43–51, at 48.

33. François Hollande, Speech at the Panthéon, May 27, 2015.

34. Michel Crépu, "Décès," *La Croix*, December 16, 1997.

35. Jean-Michel Krivine, "La mort de David Rousset," *Inprecor*, January 1998.

36. Antoine de Gaudemar, "David Rousset," *Libération*, December 15, 1997.

37. "David Rousset: Mort d'un grand témoin," *L'Humanité*, December 15, 1997.

# Index